The Planner's Use of Information

Second Edition

Edited by
Hemalata C. Dandekar

PLANNERS PRESS
AMERICAN PLANNING ASSOCIATION
Chicago, Illinois
Washington, D.C.

Contents

List of Tables

List of Figures

Preface and Acknowledgements

Our experience with *The Planner's Use of Information* (first published as a hardbound edition in 1982 and reissued by the American Planning Association (APA) in paperback in 1988) has corroborated its usefulness for beginners and practitioners alike. The book presented material to help planners acquire essential skills (e.g., those related to collecting, organizing and communicating information) necessary for effective practice.

In our opinion, this approach to problem solving and the selection of methods and techniques continue to have value. This extensively revised edition has retained and adapted useful material from the first edition. However, after 20 years, the need to change and expand sections of the book was necessary to reflect the impact of forces that we more clearly recognize as affecting societal action, and the transformation in information technology that has dramatically affected the practice of planning in the intervening years. The diversity of resident populations—a result of increasingly global and integrated economies—and the proliferation of computerization, the Internet and telecommunications networks have revolutionized the way planners go about their business and ply their trade.

When we first wrote the book in 1980, we had nighttime access to a dedicated Xerox word processor in the administrative office, which used discs so large that one could eat dinner on them! Authors provided *handwritten notes* to Nancy Nishikawa (an assistant on the project and author of Chapter 2, "Survey Methods for Planners"). Nancy amazed us with her mastery of the new machine by making text additions and revisions in a seemingly effortless manner, liberating us from the tyranny of the office secretary. We started to write in more flexible ways. Appropriately for a book on communications, this book was—and, in this revised edition, continues to be—a product of group effort.

All of the authors of the first edition lived in Ann Arbor, Michigan and met often for animated discussions. The book's structure and central themes evolved through several meetings of the collective and informal one-on-one discussions at convivial places around the University of Michigan. For this revised edition, technology has enabled exchange over great distances. Authors were located on different continents in seven cities stretching from Honolulu, Hawaii to Cardiff in the United Kingdom.

We communicated with each other, and critiqued and discussed each other's work on a dedicated Web site using Work Tools (a proprietary software program developed at the University of Michigan). Electronic mail and digital files sped across space. The editor was able to communicate to the group with the click of a mouse on a home computer in the middle of the night. However, at critical moments, the telephone and face-to-face contact have been essential, underscoring one of the central premises of this book. Good use of planning techniques involves rational,

The diversity of resident populations —a result of increasingly global and integrated economies—and the proliferation of computerization, the Internet and telecommunications networks have revolutionized the way planners go about their business and ply their trade.

substantive analysis; use of technically sophisticated gadgets and tools; *and* an acute sense of the qualitative, subjective, emotional, political and economic elements of the moment.

In this revised edition, we underscore this message. A successful planning approach gives room to an emotive, qualitative and subjective understanding of the human relationships that we know influences the more rational approach to choices of methods. We have moved more purposefully to acknowledge that planning practitioners leaven their analysis, which may be grounded in technical rationality, with a communicative process that takes a pulse of the moment and the human social context.

I would like to acknowledge the efforts and contributions of my co-authors for this 21st century revision of *The Planner's Use of Information*, including Vivienne Armentrout, Peter Ash, Elaine Cogan, Richard Crepeau, Kristina Ford, Andrea Frank, Nancy Nishikawa, Alfred W. Storey, Maria Yen and Grace York. I would also like to thank Frank So and Sylvia Lewis of the APA for their encouragement in undertaking this revision and in surmounting the many hurdles along the way. I would like to thank Rebecca Price for timely assistance in identifying Internet sources for Chapter 3. In addition to authoring a chapter, Vivienne Armentrout provided invaluable help in her meticulous prepublication copyediting. She brought substantive insight to the material from her service as a county commissioner. Most especially, I am grateful to Allan Feldt, Mitchell Rycus and Katharine P. Warner who were authors of chap-

ters in the first edition. They gave their original work for our use—verbatim or with adaptations—generously and in the interests of the planning profession. The College of Architecture and Urban Planning at the University of Michigan was my academic home when this revised book was written. I am grateful to it and the university for the extensive support that enabled completion of this work.

WHAT HAS CHANGED IN THIS REVISED EDITION?

The original authors have significantly updated four of the ten chapters of the first edition. The remaining six chapters have been extensively revised and written by new authors with insight and comments from the original authors: Allan Feldt, Mitchell Rycus, Katharine P. Warner and Hemalata C. Dandekar.

We have added a new, final chapter revealing the political context in which a planner must be effective. This chapter underscores a point that was more indirectly addressed in the first edition: planning occurs in *politically charged contexts* and must be practiced with an acute awareness of that fact. Virtually all of the revised chapters reflect the capabilities, uses and impacts of *21st century technologies*. Equally significant—and reflected in various chapters—is the fact that direct *public input* as a source of information has become as central to a planner's functioning (particularly in the public sector) as the use of census information, secondary sources, inventory of physical context and structured surveys of attitudes and perceptions.

> *... planning practitioners leaven their analysis, which may be grounded in technical rationality, with a communicative process that takes a pulse of the moment and the human social context.*

In recognition of this, we have addressed the techniques of conducting focus groups, visioning, open houses, large public meetings and a variety of public input events in various chapters of this book. We have tried to reflect new sensitivities and approaches to imbue practice as it deals with an *increasingly diverse population* unprecedently differentiated by race, culture, ethnicity, sexual preference and the politics of gendered spaces. As in the first edition, effective communication, which is crucial to successful interactions with various public and client groups, remains a central theme.

We hope that this revised edition of *The Planner's Use of Information* is successful in identifying the emerging needs of the planning profession and will continue to be useful for many years.

—Hemalata C. Dandekar
Tempe, Arizona

As in the first edition, effective communication, which is crucial to successful interactions with various public and client groups, remains a central theme.

Introduction

Hemalata C. Dandekar

TWO SCENARIOS

On a warm Friday afternoon in May, Orville C. Lorch, mayor of Middlesville, Hiatonka telephoned the city's planning director to tell her that he had just met with a delegation from the chamber of commerce. They had come to complain about the amount of trash regularly blowing around on Main Street and had demanded that something be done about it. They added that customers are avoiding this trashy location and that the city's image as a prime shopping and business area was at stake.

"Kay," said the mayor helpfully, "see what you can do. Maybe you can look into getting some more whaddyacallems . . . not garbage cans . . . you know what I mean?"

"Some additional trash receptacles?" asked Kay, the planning director.

"Right. Trash receptacles."

"People aren't using the ones we've already got in the central business district," the planning director said.

"Well," the mayor answered, "maybe if we put up some posters with catchy phrases . . . you know, kinda cute pictures and slogans . . . the good folks of Middlesville will pitch in. See what you can do, Kay."

The mayor hung up, mopped his brow and went home early.

Scenario 1: Old Method

The city planning director called in Assistant Planner (a recent graduate of the Department of Urban Planning at Hiatonka State University) and directed him to examine catalogs of trash containers, select a suitable receptacle and come up with some "cute" poster ideas by Monday. On Wednesday, the planning director received a four-page report from Assistant Planner list-ing seven types of containers by cost, dimensions, materials and manufacturers, and 15 poster ideas. The planning director sent a copy to Mayor Lorch noting that, unless the mayor disagreed, she would present this information, along with her carefully considered recommendations, to the city planning board at its next Thursday evening meeting.

The planning director heard nothing further from the mayor. At the end of a long meeting involving a zoning variance request by a prominent city developer for prime property on Main Street, she presented Assistant Planner's report on trash receptacles and poster ideas to the planning board. The planning board referred both the information and the director's recommendations to a "Downtown Beautification" subcommittee that they created that night.

Members of the planning board who doubted the wisdom of creating this subcommittee did, however, succeed in having the board send a memo to the city comptroller asking for an assessment of the affordable range of costs. Once they received this information, the subcommittee submitted a six-page report to the planning board agreeing with the planning director's original recommendation. The planning board sent a memo, with copies to Mayor Lorch and the executive committee and officers of the chamber of commerce, to the comptroller recommending the purchase of a number of the desired trash receptacles.

Once the comptroller's request for authorization of an unscheduled capital outlay exceeding $500 had been favorably processed by the finance department, the receptacles were ordered, delivered after a few delays, inspected and installed just before the Labor Day weekend. Two weeks later, the mayor received a delegation from the chamber of commerce, complaining that the containers were ugly ("eyesores" was one of the gentler descriptions), no one was using them, the posters were being defaced and were accumulating graffiti, and they were blowing off and adding to the trash on Main Street.

The mayor mopped his brow and went home early.

Scenario 2: New Method

The city planning director asked Mayor Lorch the names of the men and women who had visited him on behalf of the chamber of commerce. The mayor's secretary was able to furnish a complete list. The planning director called in Assistant Planner (a recent graduate of the Department of Urban Planning at Hiatonka State University) and assigned him to spend some time on Main Street that day and over the weekend to get impressions of the problem. Furthermore, Assistant Planner was to contact the chamber members on Monday to see what solutions they would suggest, and to get some comparative data about downtown trash pickup from nearby cities of similar size.

By Wednesday, Assistant Planner was ready to meet with the chamber of commerce. In his discussions with them, he agreed that the trash on Main Street was disgraceful. He told them that he had heard how impressed the mayor had been by the delegation's visit and was careful to mention each member by name. He showed them catalog pictures of various kinds of trash containers, asked them to study the possibilities (keeping in mind cost and durability as well as aesthetics) and arranged to meet with them the following week to obtain their recommendations.

Following the planning director's instructions, Assistant Planner continued to observe the situation on Main Street, taking photographs at various times of the week on the office's digital camera and talking to store owners and their customers. He learned that, for two days after the regularly scheduled Tuesday

trash pickup, Main Street remained relatively free of trash. However, by Friday, the stores' dumpsters were full; by Saturday, they were overflowing; by Sunday, the trash had spread along back alleys and sidewalks on to Main Street; by Monday, the chamber of commerce delegation's description of the scene was fully justified.

Assistant Planner recommended to the planning director that the Board of Public Works (BPW) reschedule refuse collection in the downtown district for Friday or even Saturday morning to minimize weekend build-up and scattering (as he phrased it). With the approval of the planning director, he made a PowerPoint presentation to the chamber of commerce in which he combined his photographs, notes from his conversations on Main Street and a quick "back-of-the-envelope" calculation of trash receptacle acquisition and maintenance costs.

By doing this, he demonstrated that their concerns had been heard; solutions had been researched, taking into account the perspectives of the community doing business on Main Street; their choice of receptacles, in the amount they desired, would cost the city more than $15,000; and, the rescheduling of trash pickup was a fiscally prudent alternative. They agreed that this solution was worth trying. Two weeks later, at a meeting attended by the planning director, Assistant Planner and representatives from the chamber of commerce, the BPW agreed to change the refuse collection schedule.

Six weeks after the original complaint, the mayor, the planning director and Assistant Planner met with the chamber of commerce. All agreed that the situation had been much improved. The planning director and Assistant Planner returned to their offices.

The mayor mopped his brow and went home early.

WHY THIS BOOK?

We hope that the two scenarios presented in the sidebar entitled "Two Scenarios" will provide an amusing introduction to a serious and useful discussion of *effective communication* and *judicious selection of methods and techniques* in planning. Many of us may recognize certain elements of our own experience in the practice of urban and regional planning, and probably wish that reaching a solution—acceptable and affordable to everyone—was always amenable to clever strategy.

Most planning problems, particularly those affecting the everyday life-space of communities, generally involve a considerably longer process of working through problem assessment, data collection, analysis, community involvement, consensus building, budgeting, implementation and the monitoring of solutions. Each step requires planners to be skillful in listening to, and communicating with, a range of constituencies. It also requires them to bring information to the table (i.e., analyzed data collected as systematically as possible) as well as techniques to help constituencies understand this information and the spatial and economic consequences of alternative decisions.

To do this well, the planner draws on interpersonal, communicative and analytic skills, and uses an intuitive, qualitative process to take a large amount of disparate information and condense it into something relevant and useful to the formulation of plans and policies. With the proliferation of information made accessible by electronic communi-

Effective practice requires the planner to integrate theory and analysis, and synchronize it with a planning process externally governed, generally political and outside of their control.

cations, these judgment skills are becoming more important.

Where does the planner learn the skills to do this critical, integrative task? The ability to gather the kind and level of information needed to process it, and effectively communicate findings and recommendations, are highly valued in practice. In fact, that is where they are learned: *on the job.*

Planning schools have traditionally emphasized teaching a variety of substantive skills stressing theory or various sophisticated analytical tools. This tendency of teaching either concepts or methods/techniques characterizes the curriculum—not just of schools training researchers and granting doctoral degrees, but also those training planners for professional practice. Usually, planning problems are formulated in academia in the mode of the social sciences favoring positivistic hypothesis testing, empirical research and theory building. However, planning practice is often involved in process, consensus building, policy formulation and action utilizing cost-effective methods. To do this, planning practitioners select methods that range from highly quantitative to completely qualitative and observational.

Effective practice requires the planner to integrate theory and analysis, and synchronize it with a planning process externally governed, generally political and outside of their control. In this endeavor, the planner's ability to communicate views, analyses and ideas in a convincing and timely way is crucial to success. Sophisticated, conceptual models and complex analysis are insufficient—and at times counterproductive—if not interpreted and presented as accessible to the audience. Effective planners must extrapolate the essentials and communicate them convincingly to clients and interested constituents.

This book offers assistance to the planner who might have "zoned out in the methods class," but is now facing situations where they have to decide whether a survey, focus group, content analysis of local publications, site reconnaissance, judicious phone interviews of community power brokers or a large public meeting is going to most efficiently and effectively yield needed information or insight. Making good choices from the wide range of available tools, techniques and data sources can make a significant difference to outcomes. To assist in this, we provide the practitioner concise overviews of practical methods for researching, analyzing and presenting planning problems and possible solutions.

USE IN PLANNING PRACTICE

The professional planner often needs to formulate public policy based on information that is painfully inadequate for problem solving. Information about social and economic factors, pertinent to the current problem, comes in many forms: straightforward, disguised or hidden, often outdated and frequently not directly applicable. The planning practitioner has to obtain needed information as rigorously as possible and analyze it efficiently to arrive at policy conclusions in a defined (and generally short) time period, which is often determined by political considerations. In addition to policy formulation, the planner

is also called upon to design, program, budget, administer, manage and persuade, applying a variety of oral, graphic, writing and interpersonal skills using available information.

In the collection, analysis and dissemination of information, the planner usually works as a member of a team of specialists with diverse professional backgrounds and varied experiences. All practitioners eventually face the task of turning a group of independent individuals into a synergetic team of professionals that produce required planning products on schedule. They must work effectively and provide the leadership to enable such teams to work successfully.

Besides the interpersonal skills needed in a professional group, a planner has to communicate with clients and constituent groups who will be affected by planning decisions. These consist of individuals with significantly varying levels of planning sophistication. Although the audience or client group changes its composition (particularly in the public domain), the planner has to maintain a continuous channel of communication to the groups that will be affected.

The selection of appropriate media is important. The mode of communication used in planning varies, depending upon the actors involved in the planning process; the language, which must be common to, or at least understood by, all participants (increasingly important as our population becomes more ethnically and racially diverse); the channels of communication, their structure and points of contact; the scale and nature of the problem; and available finances. On-the-job lessons (e.g., knowing when,

Besides the interpersonal skills needed in a professional group, a planner has to communicate with clients and constituent groups who will be affected by planning decisions.

what and how to say something; deciding to write it and, when written, whether or not to send it and to whom) are all essential to effective practice.

Information is collected, analyzed and presented in planning in a combination of ways: written, mathematical, verbal and graphic forms, supplemented by subtle, nonverbal, nongraphic and nonwritten communication, based on interpersonal skills and psychological and political acuity. To become successful practitioners, planners must cultivate skills to ask the appropriate questions and select the right techniques to effectively communicate their findings. These skills, learned through thoughtful and sensitive practice, constitute planning's unwritten folklore.

This book seeks to help planners learn some of the judgment, thinking, weighting and intuition that go into making "inspired" and correct choices of technique and method.

This book seeks to help planners learn some of the judgment, thinking, weighting and intuition that go into making "inspired" and correct choices of technique and method. It has been organized to reflect three broad categories: *collecting, organizing* and *communicating information.*

The collecting, organizing and communicating phases of planning are usually *iterative* rather than *linear.* Planning decisions often result from negotiations in which a problem is perceived and needed information is collected from people, secondary sources and on-site observations. This information is then analyzed in a group process, usually between specialists. The findings (and later the conclusions) are tested on a group loosely defined as a client or recipient. On the basis of feedback or a second look at the context and additional information collection, another round of analysis occurs. During this iterative process, communication can flow one way or as an exchange between planners and clients.

Experience teaches a professional about relative weighting and the importance of considering various tacks in problem solving and communications. Initially, planners trained to execute particular aspects of a planning project tend to apply those skills in the belief that this will achieve success. Consequently, planners tend to overwrite, overdraw and overtalk a project because they rely on their best skill instead of learning complementary skills in other areas that may lead to more crucial and effective communication. Keeping a clear perspective of what is significant in decision making, assessing what counts, figuring out how to do it and acquiring the skills that are required to do it well are all important.

Before a planner decides which modes of presentation to use, they must identify the decision makers and assess what will make the most impact on them. For example, if public verbal presentations are the major sales mechanism for a project, the planning firm should hone its skills for effective oral presentation; if mass media releases are crucial, the planner should know how to write them. It is not very useful if a planning firm spends most of its energy compiling an elaborate report with in-depth, sophisticated analyses and complex graphics if the decision makers are not going to read it or will not be able to understand it.

When a project is completed, practitioners may find it useful to identify the most effective modes of communication in order to guide allocation of staff resources for future projects and contexts (e.g., a review of the importance of effective interpersonal lobbying versus mass media publicity versus substantive, technical analyses may result in reallocation of resources and more fruitful outcomes). This book highlights the need for such weighing of alternative modes of communication, and clarifies the organization and structure needed to successfully accomplish particular planning tasks.

This book also seeks to assist the planner in anticipating, supplementing and amplifying experience. Hypothetical and real case studies of typical planning situations illustrate the weighting process underlying the right choice in information collection, analysis and communication. The text provides overviews supplemented with annotated bibliographies on topics such as using computers in planning, matching appropriate techniques for tasks and budgets at hand, thoughtfully analyzing and playing a constructive role in the small-group dynamics of work groups and dealing with other decision points in planning practice. It amplifies experience by providing guidelines useful to consider when a planning problem arises, an important presentation is nearing, a team of consultants is to be formed, or a report or graphic document is to be compiled. Thus, this is a practical book designed to be fully read as well as used for reference.

In dealing with the need for collecting information to assist in decisions, planning practitioners choose from a spectrum of techniques that are used in the natural and social sciences—from research methods used to develop basic theories to those yielding immediate utility in applications. Their choice of methods is subject to a rough, almost intuitive, cost-benefit analysis of what is worth doing evaluated on the basis of what information and insights it might yield that may be useful in formulating policy, and the budget and time available.

RELATIONSHIP TO THE PLANNING PROBLEM

Planning often starts with a perceived problem or an opportunity to bring about change. There is often a constituency that forcefully articulates the need for such change. In response, planning in the public domain utilizes an information-gathering strategy that aims at obtaining a better identification and definition of the problem as well as a clarification that additional information is needed. In the effort to understand reality (given that systematic research for the practitioner is a compromise between the ideal and the possible), practitioners must gather information relatively quickly, assess if the right questions are being asked, define the problem as accurately as possible and move to ameliorative recommendations. The initial step of defining the problem is critical.

As you will note in the first scenario of the sidebar entitled "Two Scenarios," Assistant Planner learned (no doubt to his chagrin) that although planning, particularly in the public domain, may start with a perceived problem and someone's demand for change, an effective solution does not usually flow out of a direct response to the problem as it is

Planning often starts with a perceived problem or an opportunity to bring about change.

originally presented. An analysis of the factors contributing to the condition as it is perceived, and a reformulation of what constitutes a problem in a more contextual frame, are essential tasks of the professional planner.

In the first scenario, Assistant Planner plays the traditional role of planner as technical facilitator by accepting the mayor and chamber of commerce's definition of the problem (accumulation of trash on Main Street and their solution of more trash cans for its disposal) and making a rational, systematic assessment of the most efficient, useful and available trash containers. This culminates in the selection and installation of a container with embarrassing and wasteful consequences.

The premises on which particular groups of people identify a problem require careful investigation to identify the specific nature and content of their complaints. Problems are, by definition, "problems" because of the observer's particular viewpoint and framework of reality, which may differ—often quite substantially—from others of a different social, economic, religious or political persuasion, or according to sex, age, race or nationality. Also, the proverbial "squeaky wheel" usually attracts the most attention. A special interest group's formulation of a problem is predicated on the concept of reality shared by that group or held by individual members or the group's leaders. It may also be a matter of politics, greed or self-aggrandizement and not necessarily founded on reality.

Similarly, the information that a researcher first thinks of gathering about a project or problem reflects that person's internalized model of the problem and its potential solutions. This model helps to define those characteristics that make a problem a "problem," and identifies areas about which more information is needed and why. A planner needs to understand this and learn to ask the right questions about a situation described as "problematic." Once a problem is fully articulated and specifically defined, it contains the basic structure of the solution.

There is no universally right way to do research, fact finding, site visits or preliminary field investigations; there are only guidelines. Many different skills and methods can be brought to bear on an investigation—skills that are enhanced through practice, experience and learning by doing. A method is best learned by working in a context on an actual and specific problem and by assessing if the right questions are being addressed. These questions may emerge from speculative thinking, a good idea or theory; their premises have to be confirmed, modified or refuted by finding out (through empirical and/or other means) about reality.

A major benefit of doing a site reconnaissance or using other field methods (see Chapter 1, "Field Methods for Collecting Information") to collect information *in situ* (on location and in "the field") is that exposure to a variety of stimuli, received firsthand, can result in a re-examination of the premises, the arguments and diagnosis of the problem.

There is no universally right way to do research, fact finding, site visits or preliminary field investigations; there are only guidelines.

An impeccably scientific and rational sequence of inquiry is usually not possible in planning practice. The political, temporal and budgetary constraints and other pressures, including an atmosphere of crisis, are not conducive to this. More often than not, the planner tries to complete the best investigation possible in a tight time frame. This is usually accomplished by drawing on skills and experience with which the planning team is most comfortable.

Therefore, in the normal, headlong rush to meet deadlines, it is useful to jot down some basic parameters of the inquiry:

- What are you studying?
- Why is it a problem?
- What concepts and models are guiding your approach?
- What theories or assumptions underlie these concepts?
- What is the objective of this research? What do you think/hope this endeavor will yield?

Such a list can help a planner clarify objectives and rationale. The list can provide a useful reference point if the complexities of the findings and the vast amounts of information start to muddy the overall picture, and one is in danger of losing sight of key objectives. The list is also useful in selecting methods to achieve desired ends.

SEQUENCE OF INQUIRY

The methods planners use to research problems may at times appear sporadic and haphazard; however, they parallel the steps of inquiry in more theoretically driven fields of social science. Planners' methods in practice, related to the discrete steps that constitute the so-called scientific method, are described below.

Selecting a Research Topic

An investigation starts from a variety of questions or problems that have one common characteristic: they lend themselves to observation or experimentation that may provide needed information for some answers. A topic is suggested by theoretical interest or dictated—more typical in planning—by practical concerns.

The former is likely to involve a study of specific situations as illustrative examples of a general class of phenomena. In the energy planning case study in Hiatonka and East Victoria (see "Issue #3 (Regional Scale): Energy Planning for Hiatonka and East Victoria" within the chapter entitled "A Planning Case Study"), a laboratory test measures the efficiency of two different energy sources.

The latter is likely to involve study of a situation to obtain more information about it. For example, in the transportation case of City Opportune (see "Issue #2 (City/County Scale): Transportation Plan for Middlesville" also within the chapter entitled "A Planning Case Study"), topics of research include measurement of traffic flows and accidents to identify bottlenecks and safety hazards, or the surveys to assess the relative importance of alternative modes of transport for people in different socioeconomic strata.

An investigation starts from a variety of questions or problems that have one common characteristic: they lend themselves to observation or experimentation that may provide needed information for some answers.

Formulating the Problem

In academic research, problems are made concrete and specific, and the topic is narrowed to make the task manageable and amenable to completion. Although planning problems can generally appear to be quite concrete and specific, narrowing the topic can be particularly difficult as it usually involves the choice of the right level of openness and closure, and thus defines what elements of a system to study and in what detail.

There are conflicting urges: to ask the seemingly peripheral but potentially interesting questions about a problem, or to hone in, given existing pressures and emphasis on efficiency, on what will potentially result in products in a given budget and time frame. Scenarios 1 and 2 of the sidebar entitled "Two Scenarios" are illustrative.

Formulating the Hypotheses

In academic research, problems are made concrete and specific, and the topic is narrowed to make the task manageable and amenable to completion.

The role of hypotheses in research is to suggest preliminary, testable explanations of certain facts and to guide ensuing investigations. Hypotheses may be developed from various sources. A hypothesis may be based on a hunch or an intuition, which may ultimately make an important contribution to the discipline. However, when such a hypothesis is tested in only one study, there are two limitations to its usefulness.

First, there is no assurance that the relationship between two variables found in the study will be replicated in other studies. Second, there is no defined connection with a larger body of knowledge.

If the hypothesis arises from the findings of other studies, it is freed to some extent from the first of these limitations. A hypothesis stemming from findings of other studies and from a theory stated in more general terms is freed from both limitations. However, in many areas of social relations, including planning, significant hypotheses do not exist, and exploratory research and learning through trial and error are important, needed and useful in formulating policy and action.

Relating Findings to Other Knowledge

Planning research can be a communal enterprise in that each study can rest on earlier work and provide a basis for future study. There are two major ways of relating a given study to a larger body of knowledge:

1. Plan the study to relate it to existing work at as many points as possible.
2. Formulate the research problem more abstractly so that its findings can be related to others.

Researching planning problems can thus be conceptualized with two objectives in mind:

1. to resolve the immediate problem while drawing on past experience
2. to attempt to relate it to more generic problems, thus assisting in future problem solving

Designing the Research

Research activities can be placed into four general categories according to their major objectives:

1. formulative or exploratory studies
2. descriptive studies

3. studies to draw causal inference from experiments
4. studies to draw inferences from other completed studies

Formulative or *exploratory studies* have the objective of formulating the problem for more precise investigation or for developing hypotheses. The paucity of planning research makes it inevitable that much research will be of a pioneering character.

Certain methods are likely to be fruitful in the search for important variables and meaningful hypotheses:

- survey of the literature, particularly in related fields, for concepts and hypotheses that may serve as leads for further investigation in the planning field
- information collection from those experienced in the field by interviewing a selected sample of practitioners in the area, focusing the interview on what works and identifying the change-producing agents (an approach frequently taken in planning)
- analysis of insight-stimulating examples, in which the attitude and integrative powers of the investigator, coupled with the techniques of analysis as described in Chapter 4, "Analytical Methods in Planning," are major factors in success

Second are *descriptive studies*. These use a wide range of techniques but are not as flexible as exploratory studies. The aim is to obtain complete and accurate information. As a result, the recommended procedures need to be carefully planned and provi-sions must be made to guard against bias. The steps taken in a descriptive study are:

- formulating the objectives
- designing data collection methods so that they are as bias-free as possible
- selecting the sample
- collecting and checking the data
- analyzing the results (planned in detail before starting the actual work, including the statistics to be used and the coding method)

The remaining two categories are studies to *draw causal inference from experiments* and to *draw inferences from other completed studies*. Information gathering toward these objectives is rarely attempted in professional planning; therefore, these approaches are not discussed in detail here. However, drawing causal inferences from techniques such as population projections may move the techniques from mere curve-fitting exercises to something based on a more careful reading of local circumstances. Also, regression analysis in a causal inference undertaking may have a useful place in the professional planner's tool kit. (Other examples are noted in Chapter 4, "Analytical Methods in Planning.")

Once the nature of the necessary information has been systematically defined, the planner can determine how to go about obtaining it. Chapter 2, "Survey Methods for Planners," describes the steps needed to construct a quick survey and the ways one might go about developing and executing it. Chapter 3, "Information from Secondary Sources," describes where and how to go about getting the information

Once the nature of the necessary information has been systematically defined, the planner can determine how to go about obtaining it.

from secondary sources. Professional planners need to recognize that the techniques of gathering information used in the field in the required form (given time, budget and personnel and skill constraints) are legitimately rooted in the research tradition. Their pragmatic approach is justified and is detailed in the chapters that follow; however, that pragmatism does not diminish the worth of their findings.

Collecting Data

A planner's task devolves into three major categories:

1. collecting and synthesizing information about the problem at hand
2. analyzing the information to generate alternatives for action, and to define and formulate a strategy for intervention
3. communicating these observations and findings, in various forms, to different groups and constituencies

These three categories of activity are not mutually exclusive or sequential but are iterative and ongoing. When the developer in the Middlesville case study (see "Issue #1 (Neighborhood Scale): Urban Development in Middlesville" within the chapter entitled "A Planning Case Study") listens to the reaction of the citizen groups to his development proposal at city hall, he is both communicating his plan of action and collecting and synthesizing information about the problems standing in the way of its implementation.

When he returns to his consultant planning team, and urges them to react creatively to the opposition by generating a more acceptable alternative, and

directs them to find other opinion leaders and mobilize them behind his proposal, he is involved in analysis and strategy. Thus, various forms of information gathering are useful throughout the stages of a research endeavor.

BOOK CONTENT AND ORGANIZATION

The material covered in this book can be separated into two major categories:

1. *discussions of methods* emphasizing techniques of information gathering, organizing and delivering
2. *discussions of processes* such as public participation and small-group dynamics

Each chapter includes suggestions on problem definition and diagnosis, which is helpful in the selection of appropriate technique and method or in organization. The aim is to help planners choose the best way to set about a particular professional task. The techniques described are illustrative rather than all-embracing and the descriptions indicate the importance of careful choice among them.

The book is organized into three parts, addressing three kinds of questions:

PART 1: What kinds of information does a planner require, and where and how do they obtain it?

PART 2: How does the planner organize this information so that it is useful to decision making?

PART 3: In what ways can the planner communicate information and ideas in order to inform and guide decisions and outcomes?

Each chapter includes suggestions on problem definition and diagnosis, which is helpful in the selection of appropriate technique and method or in organization.

Three case studies of planning situations at the neighborhood, city and regional scales provide hypothetical contexts, which are expounded in various chapters to illustrate the tools planners can use to be effective practitioners. Each chapter begins with a discussion of why and how the covered material is important and relevant to the current and future practice of planning, and provides a "road map" to the chapter. The body provides concise overviews of useful methods with references to specialized and, at times, book-length treatments that may be useful for gaining further mastery. They conclude with some applications and an annotated bibliography to help the reader purposefully draw on literature specific to a topic or technique.

Consistent with the first edition, this reissue of *The Planner's Use of Information* emphasizes the importance—even urgency—of planners becoming more effective communicators. It will enable the planning practitioner to explore and develop new skills to achieve this effectiveness.

. . . The Planner's Use of Information *emphasizes the importance—even urgency— of planners becoming more effective communicators.*

A Planning Case Study

A hypothetical case study is presented in this chapter describing planning issues at three geographic scales (neighborhood, city/county and regional) and illustrating stereotypical positions that stakeholders might take in public forums. In engaging in discourse with such stakeholders, and interacting around such issues, a planner's organizational and communication skills may be critical in affecting decisions.

The case offers semirealistic contexts in which the techniques described in this book might be successfully applied. Unlike the story of Assistant Planner (see the sidebar "Two Scenarios" in the chapter entitled "Introduction"), this case provides no solutions or happy endings. There is no astute planning director, creative Assistant Planner or obvious sides to take on the issues. Planning heroes and villains are not the subject of this book; helping planners think clearly and communicate effectively are.

ISSUE #1 (Neighborhood Scale): Urban Development in Middlesville

A developer has bought several parcels of land in a transitional area on the fringes of the revitalizing central business district (CBD) of Middlesville, a university town of 100,000 in the Midwest. Existing structures in this transitional area, some of which are on properties belonging to the developer, include eight older houses rented to lower income families or students, two run-down commercial structures occupied by a tattoo shop and a massage parlor, a city-owned building that houses various social service agencies, a modest (and the oldest) church in the city

constructed during the early years of the town's settlement and a neighborhood park that is used daily by a nearby child-care center. This transitional area is located in one of the oldest parts of the city. There are other structures here that have significant historical importance.

The developer's consultants—a team of architects and planners—have completed a quick market assessment of the development potential for the site. Given the fact that it is within walking distance of the CBD and a prestigious university with diverse cultural offerings (which have become increasingly attractive for prosperous, retired alumni), the team recommends a high-density, luxury apartment complex as the most profitable development option. Schematics for 150 units consisting of five-story-and-garage apartment buildings have been completed. A zoning change from R-1, C-1 (single-family residential with convenience commercial) to R-4 multifamily housing has been submitted. It is being reviewed by city planning staff that is advisory to the planning commission.

Established city procedures require that the developer present and describe the project at a regular planning commission meeting, which is open to the public. The meeting's agenda has been announced in the local newspapers in the customary manner. Property owners in the immediate neighborhood of the site have been informed of the request and the presentation as required. Tenants living in the houses slated for demolition if the project is built have rallied the neighborhood with warnings of the gentrifi-

PC-1. Development site in Middlesville

cation process that will start if this zoning change is approved. On the other hand, local merchants in the CBD, delighted by the prospect of increased business and the influx of upper income residents, have mobilized to support the developer's application for the zoning change. They also back him on his request for a variance that would reduce the parking requirements for the project.

City officials are surprised by the large public turnout at the hearing. Reactions for and predominantly against the proposed apartments are vehemently expressed. This citizen uproar signals to the planning staff a need to re-examine the project. The planning department is in the midst of developing a comprehensive revitalization plan for the CBD and fringe neighborhoods. The staff recommends that the developer's request be held in abeyance until the plan is completed in the next six months, at which time the proposed project can be evaluated in the context of the master plan.

Upon this notice, the developer rushes back to his consultant team with instructions to revise the proposal, and create a development package with built-in strategies to convince and "appease" the neighbors. The six-month delay represents a financial cost to the developer and puts the whole project in jeopardy. The public hearing has served to mobilize the neighborhood residents against the proposed high-rise apartment. To strengthen their case, the residents team up with the historic district commission, which has been studying the area, and propose designation of two of the homes that would have been slated for demolition in the developer's proposal as architecturally significant examples of early "carpenter" Gothic structures from the 1890s.

Here are some representative but divergent points of view:

Public official: "This is great! It will bring more business downtown and more money into Middlesville's economy. We'll be known as a city that welcomes development and supports commercial enterprise."

Elderly renter: "I don't want to lose my home. I have no transportation to get to alternative housing suggested by the city."

Student activist: "I don't expect to live here, but I am going to raise hell. The university should not let the city push the poor students around."

Developer: "I own several of these properties and I have every right to develop them within the bounds of the law. The zoning change will benefit everyone. The project will bring more jobs and more money to the city. The environment will be made safe for senior citizens."

City residents: "The project will cause parking problems because the variance requests a lower parking ratio. Parking downtown is a problem even now, so why make it worse? Furthermore, services in the area will deteriorate because of overload."

Journalist: "Is the mayor's wife working for this developer? How is it that the city routinely turns down requests for zoning changes and this one gets a hearing?"

The public hearing has served to mobilize the neighborhood residents against the proposed high-rise apartment.

ISSUE #2 (City/County Scale): Transportation Plan for Middlesville

The urban lobby in Washington, D.C. was able to pressure Congress to appropriate funding for studies of transportation solutions for urban sprawl around medium-sized cities with populations of 100,000 to 500,000. They have argued that investment in public transit systems will be a critical issue in containing sprawl in the 21st century. On hearing this initiative, the mayor of Middlesville phoned the heads of the city's planning and transportation departments, and strongly urged them to submit a proposal to study Middlesville's traffic congestion and to assess the need for alternative transit modes.

Middlesville received a grant of $250,000 from the federal government for a preliminary transportation study. Highway department representatives contacted the planning department to advise them of a federal government program that would provide Middlesville with up to $60 million in subsidies if the transportation plan were to consist predominantly of an expansion of the highway network. In addition to garnering extensive federal funds, they argued, the city would be building upon existing infrastructure and a tested and proven system. The automobile industry lobby had explained how an expanded highway network would benefit the auto industry as well as many other county groups.

The city planners and transportation engineers, along with their consultants, had initially explored the feasibility of developing alternative forms of mass transport including fixed rail, subway, buses, bicycle paths and a dial-a-ride service. The highway lobby was persuasive, however, and a highway expansion plan was developed. The planners drafted a preliminary environmental impact statement (EIS) to go with the study. The plan was scheduled to be presented to the city planning committee at a public hearing.

A week before the hearing, the major local newspaper printed an article on the study. It inaccurately concluded that the highway extension, which the city advocated, would cut a swath through one of the city's poorest neighborhoods and serve to segregate the "problem areas" from the abutting downtown redevelopment project (currently underway). A public outcry ensued with protests centered on transportation issues. The themes ranged from "No more taxes!" to "We need more mass transit . . . now!"

Some representative interests included:

Inner-city resident: "I can't afford to keep a car, so I have no use for highways. We need more public transportation so I can get to upcoming jobs in the outskirts of the city."

Sierra Club: "Before anything is done, we want to get an assessment of the implications for air quality and wildlife in the area's only remaining wetlands through which the highway expansion has been routed."

Antitax and antigovernment residents: "I'm against this! Why change anything when we are doing fine without all these 'big-brother' interventions?"

Construction industry sales representative: "Highway construction will represent a number of jobs for our workers and help the local economy."

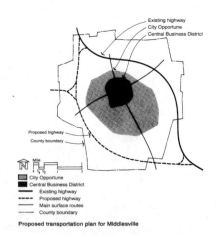

Existing highway
City Opportune
Central Business District

Proposed highway
County boundary

Mile

City Opportune
Central Business District
Existing highway
Proposed highway
Main surface routes
County boundary

Proposed transportation plan for Middlesville

PC-2. Proposed transportation plan for Middlesville

Senator from the surrounding rural constituency: "Middlesville usually gets the largest share of federal funds for this county. Let's get some transportation money for our rural areas in order to attract industry out here and create jobs."

Low-income neighborhood resident: "They can take their highways and shove them through their neighborhoods."

ISSUE #3 (Regional Scale): Energy Planning for Hiatonka and East Victoria

The State of Hiatonka, in which Middlesville is located, and the adjoining State of East Victoria import over 90% of their energy requirements. Fuel industry lobbies are actively trying to get deregulation of fuel prices. Studies indicate that deregulation of liquid fuel oil will result in a doubling of the cost of fuel oil to citizens in Hiatonka and East Victoria and a tripling of the cost of natural gas. Although availability of electricity will not be affected, its cost is expected to rise in proportion to fuel prices. It is rumored on Capitol Hill that federal oil pricing regulations could occur in the near future. The governors of Hiatonka and East Victoria, worried about the economic impact of impending price jumps, convince their state legislators to fund a study of alternative energy sources with a view to promoting self-reliance and use of local resources.

Planning Solutions (a private consulting firm specializing in energy strategy) is hired to investigate use of wind, water, coal, solar, nuclear and other

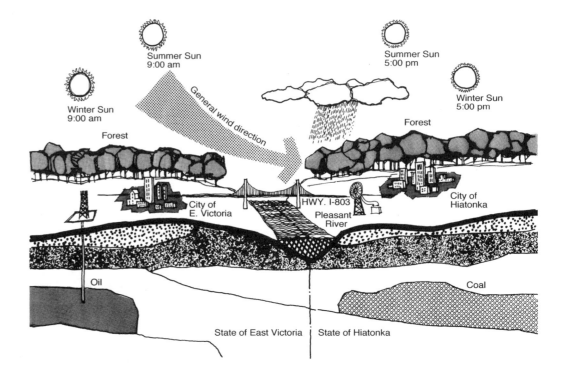

PC-3. Energy resources in Hiatonka and East Victoria

energy sources. The consultants complete their study, circulate their report containing recommendations and present their findings to a body of public officials from both states. The energy department staffs in the respective governors' offices are expected to use the team's findings to formulate state policies in anticipation of changes in national energy strategy.

Some representative interests include:

Utility company: "We supply a major proportion of power in this region. We certainly want to be involved to make sure those 'advocates' don't make far-fetched claims that cannot be implemented. We don't want to exclude coal or increased use of electricity as part of the alternatives."

Nuclear plant manufacturer: "We can provide plants on line that have served this nation for over a decade."

Environmental groups: "As soon as you put the bulldozer out, Mr. Nuclear, I'm going to be lying in front of it."

Construction unions: "We need more jobs. This project will employ 2,500 people for 10 years."

Public service commission: "Let's talk about differential rate costs."

Information Collection

from clients, the public, users,
secondary sources and observation

The articulation and elaboration of a perceived planning problem, as part of a search for appropriate policies and programs, require the collection of information:

- by observation of both human and animal behavior; and the examination of physical plant, both natural and man-made
- by administering questionnaires and carrying out and recording interviews
- by simple and complex projective techniques and creative examination of existing records

These different methods of gathering information, their strengths and limitations, are addressed in the three chapters in **Part 1**.

The questions addressed are:

- What kind of information does a planner need?
- How should they weigh and choose among the alternative forms in which it is available?
- What methods should be used to acquire such information?

Chapter 1 describes some of the direct, firsthand methods of gathering information in the field.

Chapter 2 presents the different forms of information to be obtained from various types of surveys.

Chapter 3 examines information available from secondary sources.

Field Methods
for Collecting Information

Hemalata C. Dandekar

COLLECTING INFORMATION FIRSTHAND IN THE FIELD

When Assistant Planner was given the assignment of the weekend trash litter on Middlesville's Main Street, the first thing he did was to execute a basic site reconnaissance. Before he left his office, he located and copied a promotional map of downtown showing the area in detail.

That afternoon, while strolling down Main Street with digital camera in hand, he photographed the pedestrian activity in the street, observed the levels of litter blowing around, and noted on his map where likely spots for further observation would be, including public trash receptacles. He made a list of receptacles at key locations and noted the level of trash in each.

On Friday afternoon, he noticed that the receptacles were not full and there was not much litter on the street. He paused to eat an ice cream cone at the street plaza on Liberty and Main Streets, and was eventually joined by numerous high school students who, he knew, had adopted this corner as their usual after-school hangout. He noticed that they and other people present were mostly careful to deposit their trash in receptacles. Office workers heavily used this particular plaza during lunchtime. A group of four homeless men were also using the plaza as their daytime hangout. He observed that the men were making good use of the trash receptacle near their bench. The plaza was relatively litter-free at that time of the afternoon. In addition to public trash receptacles, Assistant Planner noted that a number of businesses had dumpsters in alleys not too far from public view. Some of these were already full, though not overflowing.

The next morning, Assistant Planner revisited Main Street. He noted the level of trash in the chosen public receptacles, using a simple form he had prepared on his computer. Most were now full. Business dumpsters, especially those for restaurants, were full to overflowing. A cup of coffee at Central Café (a place popular with university students and staff) provided an opportunity to talk with the café owner, Joe, and his clients, and to observe the activity of people on that part of Main Street through the café's front window.

Joe told him that most of his suppliers made their largest material deliveries on Fridays in preparation for the weekend crowds. This meant that Joe needed to dispose of a number of bulky containers that evening or early Saturday morning, which filled his dumpsters to capacity and, at times, left them overflowing. He did not enjoy, he said a bit defensively, contributing to the trash littering the alley behind the café but, between the limited space in the alley where the dumpsters were kept and the high cost of additional dumpsters, he didn't have much choice but to continue to let the trash pile up.

By late Saturday afternoon, Assistant Planner's notes and camera recorded the fact that overflowing public receptacles had additional cups and other trash placed on and around them. Meanwhile, trash from the overloaded dumpsters was blowing around the alleyways and onto the street. The plaza had cups and fast-food containers left on benches near the overloaded receptacles.

He went back to his office, typed up his notes from interviews, added some observations, printed out his digital images on the office's color printer and summarized the data on levels of trash in receptacles over the twenty-four hours he had been recording them. He e-mailed all the files to himself so that he could access them from home.

INTRODUCTION

Although the story in the sidebar "Two Scenarios" in the chapter entitled "Introduction" is something of a caricature, problems can and do end up on a planner's desk in similarly circuitous ways: a mix of perception, rumor, anecdote and misinformation. A planner needs to get good information that provides insight into the problem, and enables changes in policy and action that can remedy or ameliorate the problem or turn it into an opportunity for change and development. Getting an intuitive sense of the situation and the problem context by collecting information firsthand, *in situ,* can often be a good investment of a planner's time. As the sidebar entitled "Collecting Information Firsthand in the Field" illustrates, field methods offer a way to research a problem, focus on the topic of interest and formulate the questions that need to be asked in the process of doing the research.

This chapter describes various methods (generically categorized as *field methods)* that planners use to investigate existing conditions on the site. These are used to gather data from primary sources of information on a particular place, issue or problem. They include direct observations, scrutiny of materials only available on the site and conversations with (and observations of) individuals who have some personal connection with or knowledge of the situation. The information is gleaned from sources generally unavailable except by actual visits to the specific locale.

Field methods are often categorized as *qualitative* rather than quantitative; in fact, field methods often *do* tend to assess a situation qualitatively. However, they can also be structured to provide systematic observations, over time, that yield quantitative indicators used in evaluation and policy formulation. The definition of what constitutes a qualitative versus a quantitative method (determining where a method is positioned in the range between qualitative and quantitative methods and the debate about which types of methods are most useful in planning) has periodically been addressed in academic planning literature. Although interesting, this discussion is not particularly useful here as it has little direct relevance to planning practice.

Selecting the right field method for a particular task is often a function of time, resources, person-power, skills, readily available technology, the political economy of the context in which the information is available and the anticipated outcome and use of the collected information. It is usually not a question of knowing which method is *best*, but rather of knowing which one is *adequate* and *do-able* given such constraints.

One important purpose of field methods—and the descriptive studies that can result from it—is to provide the planner and ultimately the client (a public or private entity) with an intuitive, integrative, conceptual framework for understanding the problem, and for placing in context other quantitative and technical information developed during additional stages of a project or inquiry.

A planner needs to get good information that provides insight into the problem, and enables changes in policy and action that can remedy or ameliorate the problem or turn it into an opportunity for change and development.

. . . the first concern in effective practice is a good and "grounded" definition of the problem. Field methods can often provide such valuable, grounded assessments. . . . They can yield a qualitative understanding of process, dynamics, relationships between actors and the political—in short, the economy of context.

In this chapter, general suggestions are offered about which field techniques might be particularly effective in certain situations, but the selection of a method and approach that make trade-offs between efficacy, utility and affordability will always need to be customized to a particular context and time.

In framing the steps involved in formulating a planning problem (see the chapter entitled "Introduction"), the first concern in effective practice is a good and "grounded" definition of the problem. Field methods can often provide such valuable, grounded assessments. They can also yield insight on the types of information needed for further analyses. The subject of whether or not field methods—particularly when designed to yield qualitative information—provide sufficiently and rigorously collected information for theoretical or policy formulation has been vigorously questioned since the 1980s. Books are now available on how to execute robust and rigorous qualitative, field-based research and analysis (see this chapter's "Bibliography").

At times, field methods are the *only* way that a planner can obtain a strategic view of issues needing attention. They can yield a qualitative understanding of process, dynamics, relationships between actors and the political—in short, the economy of context. This chapter highlights tried and tested field methods that planners have used in practice with good effect, and provides a brief overview noting their strengths and limitations.

In the story in the sidebar entitled "Collecting Information Firsthand in the Field," Assistant Plan-ner used some simple methods to gather initial impressions, make a few observations and collect some primary data. His choice of methods was related to the time frame in which he had to work, his contacts in and the information about the affected place, the technology available to him and the issues and people driving his inquiry. Field methods can usually be used quite flexibly and allow for such accommodation to the practical constraints on an information-gathering exercise.

Information gathered in the field is rich and at times overwhelming. To get some sense of what was learned, a planner may initially organize it under the following nonexclusive and overlapping categories: *spatial, social, economic, political* and *historic*. This categorization may enable a planner to understand a complex reality. However, the planner's task is not to disaggregate in-the-field findings into these separate compartments, but rather to integrate and establish the relationships and connections between them.

For example, the planner visiting the transitional area project under debate in Middlesville (see "Issue #1 (Neighborhood Scale): Urban Development in Middlesville" under the chapter entitled "A Planning Case Study") might record the age and condition of housing and its state of repair or disrepair. The field studies will be combined with other methods, such as use of secondary sources, to collect the necessary data and establish checks and balances in relating this information to the economic activity, racial mix and historic evolution of the area as well as the politics behind the allocation of public funds in the city.

SOURCES OF FIELD METHODS

Field methods used in planning are drawn and adapted from a number of disciplines. These methods often accommodate a specific interest in place, space and the physical characteristic of locale; they often yield information useful in application, policy formulation and in transforming physical and spatial realities. Unfortunately, planning consultants and practitioners rarely document their field methods in any detail. Mastery of the techniques and skills of field work often requires apprentice-like relationships with an experienced planner. Planners in the private sector can be guarded about revealing the nitty-gritty applications involved in their favorite methods, and consider them somewhat proprietary and the basis for future consulting contracts.

This lack of documentation of field conditions and coping mechanisms is not unique to the planning practice; it is generally encountered in academic, field-based research. Records and descriptions of field research usually screen out the methodological problems of execution in the interests of clarity and brevity and, perhaps, in an effort to convey a systematic, scientific and therefore unquestionable set of discoveries. A neat sequence of events and observation is described, which includes only those steps that were instrumental in getting the researcher from point A to point B, remaining mute on the explored paths that did not yield good—or worse, contradictory—information. In general, a robust literature on the specific methods and problems of executing field studies is lacking; expertise is acquired in apprenticeship and personal experience.

In the social sciences, researchers are concerned about justifying the relevancy of the topic of investigation. It is accepted that values and personal judgments, in addition to available information, play a great part in the selection of research topics and the types of data collected. The ethical and moral responsibilities of the researcher toward the subject group, informants and other researchers are also a concern that is addressed in most field method discussions. In planning, where one is potentially intervening in areas of great interest to a variety of constituent groups, such careful scrutiny of values and criteria that are brought to bear on the investigation of a problem is quite essential. The planner needs to recognize the ethical dilemmas encountered in the process of doing field work and resolve them as they would resolve the dilemmas in daily social life.

CHOOSING A FIELD METHOD

The choice of a method with which to gather information in the field about a specific site and problem is determined by various factors. A major consideration is the location of the site vis-à-vis the location of the planner and the scale and budget of the planned work. Local, neighborhood-scale projects obviously call for a different mix and sequence of methods than those of a regional, national or international scale. It is relatively easy for Assistant Planner

. . . planning consultants and practitioners rarely document their field methods in any detail. . . . Mastery of the techniques and skills of field work often requires apprentice-like relationships with an experienced planner.

to take a walk down to Main Street on Friday afternoon and make repeated visits to the area; to observe and record over time; to identify potential informants who can provide more, different and completely new perspectives on the problem; and to request and carry out in-depth interviews or participate in local activities to see how the system works.

It is somewhat more difficult and expensive for the energy commissioner or consulting energy planner of the newly formed bistate energy committee for Hiatonka and East Victoria (see "Issue #3 (Regional Scale): Energy Planning for Hiatonka and East Victoria" under the chapter entitled "A Planning Case Study") to take a quick look at timber production patterns and yields in the two states, and assess the impact of changes in the costs of alternative fuel sources on the energy consumption of people in various economic strata. It would also be more expensive to estimate citizen preferences for alternative transport means, or assess if anything needs to change in the transportation pattern in Middlesville and make conjectures about how to do it.

Although field visits and firsthand information may eventually be gathered, the first tack may be to examine existing information sources for the initial analysis of the problem in both situations. A planner's approach to selecting an appropriate method is weighed by practical concerns of *affordability* and *time frames* within which insight must be obtained.

When dealing with a small-scale planning problem, one may find that there is little secondary source documentation or statistics that are disaggregated

When dealing with a small-scale planning problem, one may find that there is little secondary source documentation or statistics that are disaggregated enough to be useful.

enough to be useful. For example, to preserve the anonymity of respondents, census studies judiciously suppress information at a microblock or neighborhood scale; therefore, minimal recourse exists to either make assumptions about the data or to do the necessary research. In either case, firsthand field investigation can be illuminating and informative.

Upon gathering information on a small, rural community of perhaps 1,000 people, a planner may be shocked to discover that there is not even a rudimentary map of the settlement. To begin a systematic survey, they may have to laboriously map the location of all the housing units, or update and interpret information from a satellite photograph. In the process, they might learn of greater complexity in social relations, which are embedded in the spatial layout, than had been imagined in the original community model.

Field investigations are valuable in this way. They serve to provide information where none exists and update it where it does. A town like Middlesville may have surprisingly little useful and/or current documentation of statistics, maps and qualitative descriptive material. This is particularly true when one is looking at a problem affecting an area of only one or two blocks within a city or town.

Besides *scale* and *location* of a project, *time* and *budget* are also interlinked elements in the decision to choose an appropriate field method. Critical factors in a project are the deadlines that need to be met for completing discrete components of the work, the personnel who can do it and whether or not the project budget is sufficient to afford their services.

The experience, strengths and pool of planning team members' skills have to be considered before the decision to gather information can proceed. The important questions in the cost-benefit weighting of this decision are what yields can be expected for a given expenditure of time and other resources, and the likely usefulness of the findings in problem analysis or policy formulation.

SOME FIELD METHODS

In his first attempt at getting a preliminary contextual and holistic understanding of the problem, Assistant Planner used a combination of methods that could loosely be categorized as:

- *site reconnaissance* (the walk or drive down Main Street while recording, photographing and noting)
- *participant observation* (eating an ice cream cone with the high school students and having coffee with the college crowd)
- *field interviews* (the chat with Joe about the state of garbage in his back alley)
- *physical accretion measures* (photographs of the level of trash in various areas, at different times of the day and over the week)
- *use of secondary sources* (review and analysis of computer-generated information regarding the trash pickup schedule for Middlesville)

In addition, he could have reinforced his case with an *economic analysis* (a comparison of the cost of installing, servicing and maintaining new trash receptacles versus increasing personnel to allow for weekend garbage pickups), or *quasi-experimental techniques* (the installation of temporary receptacles, perhaps borrowed from the parks and recreation department, and an observation of whether increasing the number of receptacles would result in less street trash).

In endeavoring to establish the facts of a particular situation or problem, the following field methods may be particularly useful to the practicing planner:

- *visual*, *observational* and *descriptive* data collection methods, such as site reconnaissance and windshield surveys
- *interaction* with, questioning and observation of, people and the dynamics among them, such as interviews and participant observation
- methods where the researcher's presence is understated, and data are construed from indirect extrapolations of *unobtrusive measures*, some of which may be generated by way of quasi-experimental techniques

The recording of information obtained in the field can be implemented in the following forms:

- handwritten notes
- questionnaires completed, including responses
- tape recordings
- observations the researcher makes in the field in note and/or sketch form or through interviews
- photographs (either digital or film, depending on how they are to be used)
- maps
- sketches
- annotations and overlays on existing graphics

The experience, strengths and pool of planning team members' skills have to be considered before the decision to gather information can proceed.

- videotapes and films of sights, images and sounds

Project budgets and the equipment available for editing and incorporating the data into final products will influence the choice of recording mode. Field data-recording methods increasingly involve use of visual evidence in the form of photographs and digitized video images that are becoming simple and inexpensive to use (see Chapter 10, "Graphic Communication"). Some of the widely used and long-standing methods are featured in this chapter.

Site Reconnaissance

A *site reconnaissance* is usually made to get an initial body of firsthand information (qualitative and quantitative) about a problem. The strength of this approach is the qualitative information collected because it calls for direct contact with people and the physical plant to be affected, and thus provides the opportunity for anecdotal or firsthand observational insight. The visit to Main Street allowed Assistant Planner to analyze, or at least question, the presuppositions about relationships in the area articulated by the mayor, the chamber of commerce and the planning director, permitting him to develop his own understanding of the problem.

Such direct, firsthand, experiential knowledge can be surprisingly powerful. Statements based on it have a persuasive quality far beyond their statistical representativeness. The information Assistant Planner acquired was largely nonquantitative and statistically insignificant, but it allowed him fresh insights into the relationships at play on Main Street and revealed different facets of the initially stated problem, which enabled him to translate and reformulate the problem.

A site reconnaissance can give the researcher a broader and more integrated picture of the terrain, vegetation, scale and quality of the built environment and infrastructure: the mix of people, their races, ages and sexes; and an indication of their economic position from observations of their dress, age and condition of automobiles and quality of housing. Most of all, a site visit provides an opportunity to experience the quality of life in the area. Does it feel safe and inviting or is it alienating? Is it well maintained and well served with amenities or run down and lacking in services?

Experienced investigators pick up hundreds of clues about the quality of a neighborhood: the kind of furniture and its condition that is being moved into a house in the area being reconnoitered; the number of "For Sale" and vacancy signs; the languages being spoken; the level of traffic; the types of cars; the numbers of people on the sidewalks or front porches and their activities; and the age and size of the housing (single family, multiple units, the mix of old and new)—all providing information on the history of the area's development.

Before the energy-alternatives teams for Hiatonka and East Victoria (see "Issue #3 (Regional Scale): Energy Planning for Hiatonka and East Victoria" under the chapter entitled "A Planning Case Study") go too far in their discussion and analysis of alternatives, they would be well advised to make a site visit to the areas under consideration. A project to construct a hydroelectric dam, and planning for an ancillary recreation and tourism industry, will succeed only if both the physical (land) and human (people) resources will allow it. A firsthand investigation can give some sense of this.

Windshield Surveys

Windshield surveys are quick site surveys, often made in a vehicle, to enable the surveyor to cover a large area to be reconnoitered and record initial impressions. If the area is small, reconnoitering by foot or on a bicycle may allow closer scrutiny and interaction with users of the area, assuming that is advisable.

A windshield survey allows a planner to record the general ambience of an area. The survey is generally repeated at different times of the day, during various days of the week, in different seasons and when there are various special occasions, such as the high school football game in Middlesville. The extent and content of the site surveys are determined and limited by the scale and location of the site and by the time, budget and personnel skills of the group or individual conducting the study.

Experienced planners begin to develop certain methods for particular contexts. For example, when visiting a new or familiar city, an initial drive through the area—early in the morning before business traffic starts—is an excellent preliminary survey technique. Even in a busy city, human and vehicular traffic is minimal at this time, and the observer can concentrate on the physical plant and its characteristics as well as cover wider areas. Understanding the context and site conditions over time was useful for Assistant Planner in Middlesville.

Windshield surveys can be used for various purposes. Often, a first objective is to inventory the current site conditions, and update the available information and ensure its accuracy. This initial inventory may include graphically mapping and recording information with photographs and sketch overlays. It should preferably be made with some awareness of available secondary sources of information that can be updated or clarified in light of these site observations.

Augmenting and checking secondary information sources by firsthand field observations can be the least expensive way of getting needed data. The synthesis of firsthand, visceral information and data from available secondary sources must be continuous and ongoing. New interconnections must be identified, and the problems and mechanisms at work must be reassessed so that new information builds upon and amplifies or corrects the old.

Ideally, a windshield survey (especially one using a vehicle) is made by two or three people: one person drives; another navigates, observes and comments; and a third records. Recordings can be of various types, such as oral descriptions or maps that are modified, sketched over and augmented. Selection of the right recording medium for the work at hand can minimize the costs of analyzing and integrating the information into planning products and/or make information collection more efficient.

On his visit to Main Street, Assistant Planner used a note pad and pencil, a digital camera and some time, patience and a receptive mind. The Middlesville developer's team visiting the project site or interviewing political representatives for their views on the proposed project might need to make a more detailed recording and documentation of their activity (see Figure 1-1) in order to reconstruct and model the physical fabric they have observed, and connect it to the anecdotal and observational information they have gathered.

Field Interviews

Interviews can be an effective and useful technique for gathering information in the field. The types of interviews can cover a wide spectrum—from very informal (a chat across the fence with a tenant in the threatened Middlesville neighborhood) to a formal, structured administration of a standardized questionnaire. The informal interview can be quite conversational in tone. The planner may have some ideas of what they think may be important areas of investigation, and can query the respondent in a loose and exploratory manner.

At the other end, a highly structured interview may consist of a list of carefully worded questions, in a thoughtfully planned sequence, that have been pretested and modified to allow comparisons of responses from a large number of people obtained by different investigators covering a wide geographic area. This latter form of field interview may differ only slightly from carefully structured, long

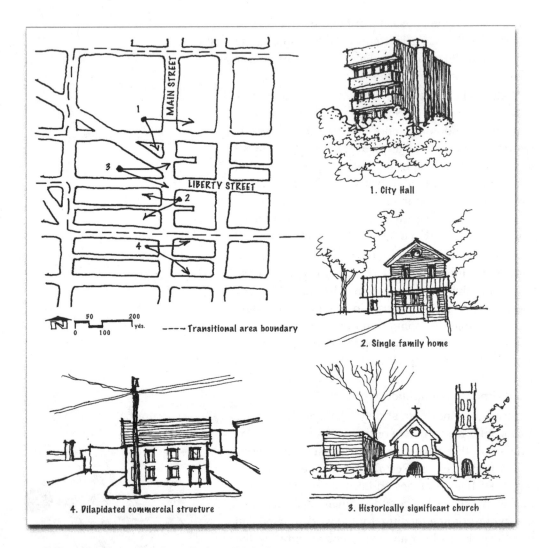

1. City Hall

2. Single family home

3. Historically significant church

4. Dilapidated commercial structure

---- Transitional area boundary

1-1. Thumbnail sketch of a walk down Main Street

interviews executed in the process of a systematic survey (see Chapter 2, "Survey Methods for Planners"). Generally, in field interviews, the investigator is not seeking to obtain a systematic sample of respondents. The goal is to find the best informants in the community in order to elicit the richest set of insights and observations.

Various combinations of formal and informal interview techniques exist between these extremes. Among them is the structured but open-ended questionnaire that allows the researcher to collect some standard information and include open-ended questions. This format provides freedom to pursue subjects that surface as important during the conversation itself or from observations of the person's environment, dress, speech and other considerations.

The interviewer's ability to establish *rapport* with the interviewee is essential—and often difficult—in the process of obtaining good information. Maintaining a pleasant and open demeanor, coupled with a genuine interest in both the respondent and the information they are communicating, is a useful start. It is helpful if the interviewer's style is nonargumentative, supportive, sympathetic and understanding. Contrary opinions can be elicited indirectly by general statements followed by a question, such as "There are people who say . . . but how do you feel about that?" Dressing and grooming in a similar manner as the interviewee is also useful because it reduces the psychological distraction of being sized up by the subject. Aiming to be just slightly cleaner and better groomed than the respondents may be a good choice.

Practice (i.e., by becoming familiar with the questions and thus avoiding stumbling over words or phrases) facilitates a good interview. So does being prepared to interpret questions that the respondent does not understand. By using certain leading phrases (e.g., "You mentioned . . ." and "Can you tell me more about . . .?"), the interviewer can probe and stimulate the respondent to answer the more problematic questions. Probing questions like these should be as neutral as possible in order to elicit unbiased responses. If several field investigators are being trained to administer a questionnaire, some common probes need to be suggested so that, if they do introduce a bias, the bias will at least be common across the whole survey.

An interviewer needs to be unafraid of silence, sit quietly and wait for more information. A simple query such as "Anything else?" may evoke the desired response. There are direct and indirect ways to ask questions; the interviewer, keeping the respondent in mind, has to choose the appropriate approach. The interviewer can introduce a broad topic and allow the respondent to talk on any aspect of it. Individuals may be questioned alone or in groups. Note that answers are affected by this choice: groups can inhibit as well as stimulate detailed responses.

The type of interviews to be conducted (structured or unstructured) is determined both by the nature of the information needed (from qualitative

The interviewer's ability to establish rapport with the interviewee is essential—and often difficult—in the process of obtaining good information.

If the respondent is not self-conscious and does not object, a taped record of an interview—particularly an open-ended one—can be extremely helpful.

and anecdotal, to precise and measurable units of information) and by the size and characteristics of the population to be studied. An appropriate choice of interviewers (in terms of age, sex, race and class), in order to be compatible with the population surveyed, also deserves attention. A good practitioner can elicit richer and more complete information, while a poor interviewer may fail to get any that is useful.

Recording: The interviewer might choose to commit the conversation to memory if the interview is extremely informal, generalized and fact-finding in nature. However, notes—from jotting down points raised to a complete documentation of what is said—are usually helpful. Even if the interview is unstructured, it is important to make an interview guide, which can be as simple as a checklist or inventory of subjects one wants to talk about.

Some leading questions, such as "What do you think about . . .?" can be written in this interview guide to help the interviewer overcome long silences. In open-ended interviews, the temptation to summarize, to paraphrase and to correct bad grammar while recording should be avoided in the interest of keeping the flavor of what is being said. Interviewers should try to record what is said exactly as it is given; marginal comments can elaborate on and interpret distinctive gestures or difficult-to-understand jargon.

Interviews should be transcribed as soon as possible. They will be an amalgam of summaries and notes of general points, verbatim transcripts and pieces of analysis or ideas. Software is now available that allows one to turn spoken material into a digital, written file. This can be very helpful in transcribing recorded field tapes or in turning oral field notes into written documents. To help in bookkeeping, a face sheet (i.e., the front page of the interview) can be created, which lists factual data about the interview such as name and/or number of persons interviewed, place, sex, age and education. Critical data vary from project to project. The face sheet may be completed at the start of an interview or filled in later, depending on what will set the best stage for the interview.

If the respondent is not self-conscious and does not object, a taped record of an interview—particularly an open-ended one—can be extremely helpful. Freed of the need to make written notes, the interviewer can observe the subject and make comments and notes about areas that require further investigation. However, too many hours of taped interviews, like too much statistical information, can be so intimidating in their volume that they are never used.

Another danger is that the interviewer, relying on the tape recording, may not listen carefully. To avoid this, they should jot down key points. The interviewer must choose the most appropriate recording method. If a tape recorder is used, it should be a small one that does not make distracting noises at critical junctures in the conversation. Interviewers should become familiar with its operation before taking it to the field. The sight of the interviewer wrestling with a tape recorder or other equipment will not inspire a respondent's confidence. A tape recorder should never be used without the respondent's knowledge and permission.

Whom, when and where to interview: It is important to consider who is to be interviewed and when and where. (For information on sampling designs, see Chapter 2, "Survey Methods for Planners.") Selecting interviewees in a preliminary site visit might be as random as stopping people in the street and starting a conversation. Restaurants, bars, bus stations, parks and stores can offer opportunities in which to strike up such conversations. Finding a place conducive to conversation is important. Planners need to use sensitivity as to when and where they will approach people and ask them questions. Generally, they will not receive an optimum response from a passerby on a noisy, windy street corner on a cold day.

There are many ways to identify potential informants. The local papers can provide references to people who have participated in discussions of the issue. Lists can be obtained from municipal or other governmental departments or chambers of commerce, which identify representatives of civic service organizations; cultural groups; neighborhood groups; local religious groups; existing committees and commissions; business, professional and trade groups; community institutions such as schools and colleges; and elected representatives of different governmental units. Chapter 6, "Public Participation," discusses identification of community leaders.

A researcher needs to be aware of the infighting that can, and often does, go on in communities. A planner can get drawn into these feuds by interviewing one opinion leader but not another. To maintain balance and the ability to re-enter the community for future planning research, it is wise to make sure that different sides, and their respective leaders, have a chance to tell their stories through interviews.

Interviews with such potential respondents can be arranged on the telephone. Before making the call, the planner needs to develop a convincing explanation of the kinds of information needed from the person and to have some persuasive reasons why the person should cooperate. A planner needs to be prepared to accept that some individuals are likely to reject a request for interviews or decline to participate in other forms of information collection (see Chapter 2, "Survey Methods for Planners").

Usually, when such opinions are sought, no payments are made for the information. At other times, in more comprehensive and systematic information-gathering attempts, incentives can range from taking someone out for lunch or coffee, to small gifts such as free passes to an event or gift certificates, to payment of an agreed-upon amount of money for a given amount of time. Every researcher has to reconcile the ethical and economic aspects of this issue for each situation.

Information obtained from interviews—particularly from informal conversations with random respondents—must be carefully contextualized in a larger framework. Individual defensiveness about a

Information obtained from interviews—particularly from informal conversations with random respondents—must be carefully contextualized in a larger framework.

subject can give rise to inadequate or distorted estimates and information. Particular rationalizations may be widely shared in a culture and the planner needs to be able to identify them. Asking similar questions of a number of individuals, the same question of many individuals and of the same individual over time, and then checking for consistency, are some ways to validate responses.

Secondary sources can also provide validation. For example, suppose that some older residents in a low-income neighborhood of Middlesville complain in field interviews that they are being discriminated against in the level of, and access to, public transportation. An evaluation of citywide budget allocations, disaggregated spatially, on public transport would validate or negate the substance of the statement. However, the fact that this perception exists is still a legitimate understanding gleaned from the interview. Going back to these older, low-income respondents with the data might provide the planner with additional insight from them concerning the delivery of the service as planned. Some on-site observations of delivery would also be revealing. Thus, an appropriate backup study has evolved that is successful in cross-checking anecdotal information and developing alternative explanations about cause and remedy.

Another example of useful cross-checking is comparing glowing descriptions that citizens might give of transport facilities as they were in previous (and better) years to the picture that emerges after doing archival work in the library or the city's hall of records. Anecdotal material can be a colorful and

welcome foil to the more systematically collected secondary sources of information with which it must be validated but which often make for dull reading. Interviews are a good way of obtaining useful anecdotes and stories.

Participant Observation

Participant observation techniques, patterned after pioneering ethnographies of Branislaw Malinowski (published starting in 1922), have been developed by cultural anthropologists as they sought to study people in social systems and cultures that were very different and "other" than their own. The method generally involved extended residence and immersion in these communities, and a systematic and what was initially termed "objective" recording of observations. Subsequently, the method was embraced and adapted by sociologists who examined subcultures within their own societies. It has also been adopted and adapted by researchers in professional fields, such as planning and other applied disciplines, where the technique was applied for a much more limited period of time in order to yield insights into social relationships and human dynamics within subset communities.

In a traditional participant observation study, a researcher becomes a member of a group or a participant in a social event under study to collect data about the other participants. In this process (involving the study of people who were sometimes from very different, "exotic" cultures), gaining entry to and acceptance by a group were the first hurdles

In a traditional participant observation study, a researcher becomes a member of a group or a participant in a social event under study to collect data about the other participants.

faced by the researcher/participant observer. This continues to be the case in the different forms in which the method is practiced today. Gaining entry can be an anxious and difficult period. Most investigators try to be introduced by a contact person who is accepted by the group. This can generally help shorten the initial testing period to which the researcher will be subjected and provide at least one opportunity to establish connections.

Outside researchers typically gain access through contacts they have already established through their friends, acquaintances, colleagues, professional connections or relatives. This "first person" often refers the researcher to others within the group, and a chain or snowball effect is used to build upon pre-existing relations of trust to remove barriers to entry.

Once accepted by the group and interaction with its members has begun, the researcher is likely to act as a change agent, despite their best efforts to be just another member. They can, sometimes unwittingly, provide the study group with the same exposure to new ideas and culture as they gain from interacting with them. The relationship with the group generally—and informants especially—is personal. Dependencies are established. In some studies, the researcher establishes a friendship and rapport that elicit needed confidences. There can be a moral conflict for the researcher in using this information. An ethical responsibility exists for the interviewer in being aware of the confidences offered and conducting work so that the group studied does not feel exploited. Evidence of having won the group's trust

is implied when the group offers that researcher, or others, the same opportunities and access to them over time.

There is a fundamental dilemma in using the participant observation method: how secretive or open should the researcher be in observing and recording the activities of other participants? The dilemma lies both in methodological and ethical considerations and in conflicts between these. A researcher too open about their objectives can affect the participants' actions and the dynamics of the group itself. For a professional planner, there are additional complications. Withholding the professional interest at the start may prove counterproductive if the group discovers that their observations have influenced policy decisions affecting them, especially if they do not support these policies.

It is well worth researchers' time to think out an explanation of what they are trying to do with the investigation so that the explanation seems plausible and appropriate in depth and coverage for the intended audience. If people are going to give a researcher access to their opinions, views, experiences and feelings, they are quite justified in wanting to know why they should reveal these and what purpose it will serve.

At the entry stage of the research, the right level of knowledge about the system may facilitate a fruitful exchange. In certain contexts—particularly for younger researchers—a strategy of presenting oneself as a learner, or someone slightly incompetent, may be effective in establishing an apprenticeship

Outside researchers typically gain access through contacts they have already established through their friends, acquaintances, colleagues, professional connections or relatives.

position in the group. However, in other more technical or elite contexts, the researcher may have to demonstrate more knowledge and competency as a way to gain access to the serious business and endeavors of the group.

The researcher also needs to maintain a courteous and respectful relationship with members of the group by:

- asking for a convenient time and obtaining their permission to phone or ask questions
- providing accounts to people who have been helpful and informing them of their progress
- asking permissions from dependent and subordinate groups such as the elderly or children, and not just their caretakers
- reducing the burden of time and effort on the respondents

In many cases, researchers attempt to maintain a degree of the respondents' confidentiality in reporting and using findings. Real names of people, places and organizations are not necessarily central to the argument. In other situations, assurances of confidentiality may have to be limited (e.g., if the context is specific and the research is related to the workings of a public agency). Assuring confidentiality might be appropriate at lower levels of the organization but not at the higher managerial levels where public accountability is mandated. Researcher assurances of confidentiality may therefore have to be limited, and the researcher must make judicious decisions about what levels can be promised and provided before they start field work.

The primary role of the researcher in a participant study can vary from observation of people's roles, relationships and their interactions, to participation in the tasks in which the group is involved.

One danger of participant observations is that a researcher can begin to empathize with the study group (or "go native," as it was traditionally termed in anthropology) and lose needed objectivity about the subject. Also, researcher biases and observations can change with increasing familiarity of the group and the phenomenon under scrutiny. Being a participant observer can also be emotionally stressful as a fear of disclosure may arise if one is "passing" as someone else. There is stress in empathizing, wanting to help and dealing with the situation at personal and professional levels. There can also be significant physical discomforts in being in the field over an extended period of time.

The primary role of the researcher in a participant study can vary from observation of people's roles, relationships and their interactions, to participation in the tasks in which the group is involved. In the latter case, the researcher has to remember that mastering the task is not the primary agenda; rather, it is observing how and what others do with the task. Getting involved in the work is merely the mechanism through which the group's condition can be better understood.

A field worker tries to fill as many roles as possible including a master role, which is constant and central, and as many subroles and relationships as possible, with the rationale that different facets of a system are revealed in multiple encounters. The field worker establishes a regular routine of observations, interviews and recordings on a number of topics—some of primary importance and others secondary.

In anthropological literature, participant observers are admonished to maintain frequent, brief visits to particular places, people or institutions in the primary study area, and to take regular walks through the larger area and rigorously observe particular times and routes. In planning practice, where there are multiple pressures and different projects vying for time, a planner/investigator might use time-lapse photography or conduct long interviews, or assign a local person to make documentary photos based on prearranged criteria or an established schedule to record activity.

Most group members are not familiar with all facets of the group life. It is therefore important to establish contacts with selected informants familiar with different aspects. It may be useful to compile a list of key positions and match it to members of the group who might be willing to act as informants. The researcher must establish the reliability of each informant and have this in mind when recording the data received from them. If there are language differences, and a long-term investigative activity is contemplated, the researcher might attempt to learn the language because interpreters tend to act as an extra interface. At the very least, the researcher might master enough of the language to monitor the work of needed interpreters.

A participant observer must find a good vantage point—both physically and socially—from which to observe. Assistant Planner's selection of a window seat proved to be an excellent choice in making observations for his limited study. Central Café was a strategic choice; the clientele was regular and large and was likely to be open and communicative. If more extensive work is anticipated, it is useful for the researcher to choose a location at the center of the activity, and to arrange living or working quarters that permit rapid and widespread observations. Covered outdoor workspaces and open porches are useful for these kinds of observations.

Locating oneself in more public realms renders the researcher more accessible to members of the study community. Anthropological literature also suggests that field researchers make their residences available for leisure activities with offers of food, games, music or other activities commensurate with the group's interests; and to avoid classifying observations in terms of their own cultural experience and instead try to understand the relationships and functions within the group under study. Practicing planners who work at the community level have noted that food, music, simulation games (which allow a group to explore consequences of actions in the threat-free context of play) and other ice-breaking, community-building activities are essential in contexts where they are in a participatory, observational and data-gathering community context.

Field notes or records are the product of field observations. Since their creation and maintenance are critical to the study's success, the necessary discipline and time should be part of the research design from the outset. The field notes should include factual observations, maps, descriptions, comments and photographs. Mental and observational notes of the

It is . . . important to establish contacts with selected informants familiar with different aspects (of the group life). It may be useful to compile a list of key positions and match it to members of the group who might be willing to act as informants.

field should be jotted down in a running log as soon as possible. In addition to factual and descriptive material, the impressions, ruminations and conjectures of the researcher should be recorded in a day-to-day fashion. This may take as long (or longer) than the time needed to make the observations or complete the interview in the first place. In writing notes, the researcher often sees integrating themes and concepts emerge. Field notes are the place to record these, however tentative and exploratory they may be; these initial conjectures may later help establish the conceptual framework that makes larger sense of the study.

Unobtrusive Measures

No matter how well integrated an observer is in an area or group, they are still a foreign element with the potential to bias the information collected. Innovative measures have been developed and introduced to obtain necessary information from primary sources without requiring an observer to be physically present and visible in a system. These *unobtrusive measures* include measuring physical traces of erosion and accretion; referring to data periodically produced for other-than-scholarly purposes such as occasional, episodic descriptions of events found in the media, local publication or private records; and making simple and contrived observations using hidden hardware to avoid human error.

Proponents of the approach claim that questionnaires and interviews depend upon the linguistic abilities of the subjects, and are costly and weaker in their capacity to reveal past behavior or change. Nonreactive measures, they claim, can gain more accurate and cheaper information. If a single method must be used for data collection, a verbal report from a respondent may be the best choice. However, it is often advisable to consider other complementary measures and to use various multiple methods to ensure checks and balances.

An example of unobtrusive measures that can be categorized as *simple observations* is recording car license plates in various national parks and noting their state of origin as a way to establish the "distance draw" of a particular recreational facility. Mechanical devices that measure the number of vehicles, or pedestrians who cross a particular location, are among other commonly used methods of obtaining simple observations. Photo documentation of current site conditions—from angles and vantage points that were used in available historic photographs or other delineations such as tin types, wood blocks or paintings—is a widely used method for comparing the changes and evolution in man-made, built form over time. The literature in visual anthropology, which utilizes such approaches for comparisons of both place and people over time, is useful in its detailing of methods.

Another potentially rich source of information too often ignored by planners are measures of *physical traces*. These are measures of physical evidence not specifically produced for comparison and inference, but which can be used for planning purposes by an imaginative researcher. Possible sources of such physical traces are measures of *erosion* and *accretion*.

An example of physical erosion are vinyl floor tiles in front of a particularly popular exhibit that are wearing out much more rapidly than in other areas. Physical accretion measures are defined as those using the build-up of residues and patinas on surfaces and forms as indicators. The unit of measurement is the amount and extent of material deposited (e.g., the thickness and extent of wall graffiti, the volume and subject material of posters on buses or subways, the wear of park benches and the density of fingerprints or nose prints on different store windows with differing displays).

In the design and planning of built form and space, measures of physical erosion or accretion can provide information on the activities and uses in the space under consideration, and can contribute to the observer's understanding and enhance design decisions. A well-recognized application is the designer who takes cues from worn-out paths on grassy public spaces that pedestrians have made as they take shortcuts. These are laid with paving stones, resulting in efficient walkways.

The literature also describes quasi-experimental techniques that can be imaginatively used in the field to gather information. Some involve deploying hidden hardware or control; others set up physical situations as a way to record human reactions and responses. For example, efforts to assess the level of social ownership and responsibility in a community study could involve leaving a car, unlocked and with the headlights on, in public spaces of different neighborhoods, and recording the time lapse before a passer-by intervenes along with the nature of the intervention. The desire to assess traffic behavior in different communities has provided many opportunities for such quasi-experimental techniques (e.g., placement of hardware to measure vehicles as they slow down in response to various traffic signs and physical barriers).

Another useful, unobtrusive source of information are documents such as meeting notes, journals, workbooks and project files that have been maintained on a continuing basis. For example, local real estate books documenting properties for sale and the asking price, the "event calendar" in local newspapers, and maps published in local magazines or newspapers showing incidence and type of crime can allow for historical comparisons with in-field observations of current realities and interactions.

Gaining a longer term frame from local documentation, which often can only be found through in-field investigation, can shed light on the observations made, the issues debated and the actions taken in the time period covered in the record. They provide insights when compared to current events and observations of social and physical factors. For example, attending a city planning meeting in Middlesville, and following up with a review of the minutes of these meetings for the preceding couple of years, could give a developer some idea of the types of projects they can anticipate being controversial in that town. An analysis of the voting pattern of the

The literature also describes quasi-experimental techniques . . . Some involve deploying hidden hardware or control; others set up physical situations as a way to record human reactions and responses.

planning board members could provide them with some understanding of the politics of the group and of the coalition to be expected.

Time-series photographs are another excellent technique that have been successfully used in planning and design. William H. Whyte's (1980) study of a New York public plaza using this technique has been widely read, and the film depiction (1988) of the research, findings and applications have been widely viewed. As illustrated in Whyte's work, photo recordings are analyzed to give usage patterns over a time period (e.g., a day, a month or a year). Whyte's film vividly documents the use of this method; it is enlightening and amusing as it depicts and comments on people and their use of physical, built-up space and outdoor furnishings. Primarily used in the study of social dynamics and the utilization of built form, this technique has great potential for the study of long-term interactions between people and place/space.

COMMUNITY PARTICIPATION IN FIELD RESEARCH

In traditional planning studies, communities are approached as the subject of investigation where an outside researcher studies a community as an "object." With the increased recognition, respect and importance given in democratic societies to the concept of citizen participation in various aspects of governance—and in the planning for, and intervening in, the public domain—techniques of participatory planning research have now emerged in which the community is approached as an active, empowered entity that is trained to study and document itself. In this approach, the community is provided with appropriate, professional assistance and guidance to organize itself, identify what should be investigated, determine how and collect information and documents needed from the field.

Some elements of this approach are mentioned in Chapter 2, "Survey Methods for Planners," with respect to community-run surveys that have emerged as a valuable tool for planners. Field methods to incorporate community participation have included techniques such as:

- online, Web-based data gathering
- documentation of oral histories
- mapping and surveying by community members of architecturally significant resources or sites of dilapidation
- photodocumentation, including the use of disposable cameras to record details of daily life

The use of the Internet and a Web-based approach—in informing the community about local, physical and economic conditions, and in building up a database of information with community involvement in collecting grounded observational data—has also gained popularity. In this effort, a considerable investment is required in training the local community to use the technology, and learn the processes and techniques of systematic data collecting and input, which also requires long-term funding and institutional commitment. Additionally, such Web-based interfaces require ongoing technical

The use of the Internet and a Web-based approach—in informing the community about local, physical and economic conditions, and in building up a database of information with community involvement in collecting grounded observational data—has also gained popularity.

support for maintaining and managing the Web site, troubleshooting and problem solving when difficulties are encountered by community participants, and maintaining the hardware and providing ongoing technical support where access and input by the community occurs.

In impacted and subject communities where incomes are low, special sites (where computers, hardware and technical support are dedicated to the project) must often be established within the geographic locus of that community. University involvement in such efforts is often beneficial. There are several examples of such in-field observation approaches supported by universities and incorporating the energies of the community (e.g., The East St. Louis Action Research Project sponsored by the University of Illinois at Urbana-Champaign and Neighborhood Knowledge Los Angeles (NKLA) supported by the University of California at Los Angeles). (See the "Bibliography.")

CONCLUSION

Field methods are information-gathering techniques that are particularly useful to planners. They can quickly and inexpensively update existing secondary source information, allow for a firsthand sense of the problem and provide colorful and interesting insights. To validate findings, multiple information-gathering techniques should be used so that the data collected from one source can be cross-checked, confirmed and reinforced by the findings from another.

Information collected in the field can make a unique contribution by allowing a holistic first cut of the problem. The internalization and firsthand identification thus evoked helps to break down presuppositions about relationships and can result in a reformulation of the problem itself. It can also be designed to yield information on an ongoing, longer time frame; provide snapshot information at selected time intervals; build up a robust and reliable source of information for basing social policy; influence the design of built elements; and inform action and theory. Collecting information in the field is fun, and allows for immediate and direct contact with people.

APPLICATIONS

1. Imagine you are a prospective developer visiting Middlesville for a long weekend. You are interested in, and are debating between, developing a housing and/or a commercial property.
   a. What field methods might you use to collect information to acquaint yourself with the town and enable you to select areas for further investigation?
   b. How would you develop a list of people you would like to interview to give you additional information or insights?
   c. What units of observation of neighborhoods might you use to categorize "declining" or "improving" areas?
2. Think of a planning issue that concerns you in your neighborhood (e.g., lack of play equipment for young children in the public park).

a. What questions might you ask, and of whom, to get a representative sample of residents' views on this issue?

b. What observations might you make to substantiate a need for such equipment?

3. You are the mayor of Middlesville. You want to get some intuitive sense of who uses public transport in Middlesville and for what reasons. How might you go about getting this information?

4. You are the planning director of Middlesville. You need a rough idea of current public transport usage in the city. The department budget does not allocate money for a formal survey. Think of some unobtrusive measures that might provide you with useful information. How might the nature and form of information you collect differ from the kind of information you collect for Application #3, above?

BIBLIOGRAPHY

**Designing the Field Work
and Choosing Appropriate Methods**

Robson, Colin. *Real World Research: A Resource for Social Scientists and Practitioner-Researchers.* Cambridge, MA and Oxford UK: Blackwell, 1993.

This is a practical guide to designing policy-oriented research plans, offering a bridge between academic and practice research. It also discusses field methods such as experiments, case studies, evaluation, data collection and analysis.

Whyte, William Foote. *Learning from the Field: A Guide from Experience.* Beverly Hills, CA: Sage Publications, 1984.

The author discusses the experience of 50 years of field research in a wide variety of settings around the world. He makes a distinction between scientific research versus research for social change and action and the need to integrate survey information and anthropological research. He avoids the arguments about what constitutes "theory" and states that his effort has been to seek a conceptual framework, which strengthens the observer's power of understanding and interpreting behavior and organizations. Participant observation, other observational methods and interviewing are addressed in Chapters 2, 5 and 6, respectively.

Site Reconnaissance/Windshield Surveys

Clay, Grady. *Close-up: How to Read the American City.* New York: Praeger, 1973.

Clay develops a strategy for looking at the city at the microcosm, and argues for the descriptive case built on observations of the material characteristics of the city fabric.

____. *Right Before Your Eyes: Penetrating the Urban Environment.* Washington, DC: American Planning Association, 1987.

This is a journalist's articulation of what the author calls the "grammar of landscape." Clay demonstrates, with case examples, ways to describe and extrapolate from a close observation of the landscape what is recognized by ordinary viewers and users as being orderly, coherent and responding to natural and human processes.

____. *Real Places: An Unconventional Guide to America's Generic Landscape*. Chicago: The University of Chicago Press, 1994.

The author explores places on the American landscape, and argues for a method to integrate the understandings attained from looking at maps and documents as well as histories, interviews, photography and careful observation. He describes and gives labels to classes of place, and provides interpretations of places that are organized spatially as a trip through a cross-section of the area under observation.

Jacobs, Allan B. *Looking at Cities*. Cambridge, MA: Harvard University Press, 1985.

This book leads the reader through the process of looking at the fabric of cities, using visual clues and observations, to interpret both the physical elements of the cityscape and the movements and interactions of people in these spaces. It makes a case for site observation as a primary method of inquiry and analysis and as a basis for serious action. In the first chapter, the author demonstrates how to start to look at the city, and argues that walking is the best way as it allows the "observer to be in the environment with all its sensual experience—noises, smells, even the feel of things."

Lynch, Kevin. *The Image of the City*. Cambridge, MA: MIT Press, 1960.

Lynch offers a seminal work that introduces planners and urban designers to the concept of city image, its elements—paths, edges, districts, nodes, landmarks and their interrelations—and the shifting nature of this image.

____. *A Theory of Good City Form*. Cambridge, MA: MIT Press, 1981.

This is a classic text that provides physical planners and designers theories and ways to deconstruct and understand the spatial components of a city. It demonstrates how the physical fabric of a city can be categorized and analyzed.

Interviewing and Participant Observation

Bastin, Ron. *Applied Qualitative Research.* "Participant Observation in Social Analysis," pp. 92-100, edited by Robert Walker. Brookfield, VT: Gower Publishing Company Limited, 1985.

Bastin traces the research method from its start in the pioneering ethnographies of Branislaw Malinowski (1922, 1927, 1929, 1935) and the subsequent use of the method in anthropology, pointing out that its potential contribution to policy planning has been greatly underutilized. He argues for using the approach for shorter field work periods in policy-oriented research, and demonstrates it by adapting the classical methods to a hypothetical urban, industrialized setting. For example, he suggests accessing secondary sources of documentation to define the population and context, and reducing—with the policy formulation objectives in mind—the number of events and elements that are examined and documented.

Burawoy, Michael, et al. *Ethnography Unbound: Power and Resistance in the Modern Metropolis.* Introduction, pp.1-7; Chapter 13, "The Extended Case Method," pp. 271-290. Berkeley, CA: University of California Press, 1991.

Through case examples, Burawoy demonstrates how the technique of participant observation is used to examine the way in which "power and resistance play themselves out in social situations that are invaded by economic and political systems . . . and explore resistance to it." He discusses the extended case method (and places it in the context of ethnomethodology), the interpretive case and grounded theory, and adapts the classical methods to a hypothetical urban, industrialized setting.

Gans, Herbert Julius. *The Urban Villagers: Group and Class in the Life of Italian-Americans.* New York: Free Press, 1962.

> This is a classic case study illustrating the applications of participation-observation techniques in an American, urban, inner-city context.

Jorgensen, Danny L. *Participant Observation: A Methodology for Human Studies.* Beverly Hills, CA: Sage Publications, 1989.

> Jorgensen describes participant observation in terms of seven basic characteristics, and notes that the data from this technique generally take the form of fairly detailed, qualitative definitions and descriptions. The author notes that basic concepts are defined phenomenologically (i.e., in terms of what these ideas and actions mean to people in particular situations), and adds that it is a technique very concerned with attaining dependable and trustworthy findings. Questions of validity revolve around whether or not the researcher has gained access to the insider's world of meaning and action.

Lofland, John and Lyn H. Lofland. *Analyzing Social Setting: A Guide to Qualitative Observation and Analysis.* 3rd ed. Belmont, CA: Wadsworth Publishing Company, 1995.

> This is an essential reference for any planner designing a large-scale, data-gathering effort using interviews and observation. It is an excellent guide for social science field studies (also called ethnography), qualitative studies, case studies or qualitative field studies. It provides details on the two central techniques used in such studies: participant observation and intensive interviewing. This book guides the researcher in gathering data in the field, focusing it and analyzing it with the audience in mind.

McCall, George J. and J. L. Simmons, editors. *Issues in Participant Observation: A Text and Reader.* Reading, MA: Addison-Wesley Publishing Company, 1969.

> This collection of articles deals with issues and solutions from the literature on participant observation. Particularly useful are Chapter 2, "Field Relations" (including a piece by Raymond L. Gold entitled "Roles in Sociological Field Observations") and Chapter 3, "Data Collection, Recording and Retrieval."

Walker, Robert, editor. *Applied Qualitative Research.* Sue Jones, "Depth Interviewing," pp. 45-55 and "The Analysis of Depth Interviews," pp. 56-70; Alan Hedges, "Group Interviewing," pp. 57-71. Brookfield, VT: Gower Publishing Company Limited, 1985.

> Jones builds a case for the depth interview as one way to understand why people act they way they do, and the meaning and significance they give to their actions. She discusses the issue of how structured or nondirective the interview should be; the need to pay attention to nonverbal data regarding posture, gesture, voice, facial expression, eye contact, etc.; and methods such as cognitive mapping to represent beliefs. Hedges discusses the rationale for group interviews and where they are useful, as well as a number of factors and methods involved in these interviews. He also discusses the role of scientific rigor and its proper limit in sociological investigation. In his opinion, one of the aims of qualitative research is to take us into fields that are important but not easily measurable.

Whyte, William Foote. *Street Corner Society: The Social Structure of an Italian Slum.* 2nd ed. Chicago: University of Chicago Press, 1961.

> This is a case study that illustrates the use of participant observation in an American, urban, inner-city context.

Williams, Thomas Rhys. *Field Methods in the Study of Culture.* New York: Holt, Rinehart and Winston, 1967.

> The author's experiences as a cultural anthropologist in North Borneo are drawn on to detail preparation for field work: selecting and moving into a site; managing the first month of study; setting up a routine of research; interviewing and setting up methods to verify data so obtained; choosing informants; and coping with departure from the community and ethical responsibility. He notes that conclusions based on findings from more than one source will have more credibility for all concerned: the researcher, the policy maker and the affected population groups.

Yin, Robert K. *Case Study Research: Design and Methods.* Thousand Oaks, CA: Sage Publications, 1984.

> Yin provides a useful reference for the case study method, and describes the operative paradigms in this approach while distinguishing between quantitative and qualitative techniques.

Unobtrusive Measures

Campbell, Donald T. and Julian C. Stanley. *Experimental and Quasi-Experimental Designs for Research.* Chicago: Rand McNally, 1966.

> This small, readable book examines the validity of sixteen experimental designs, in which variables are manipulated and their effects on other variables are observed against common threats to valid inference.

The descriptions of various experimental structures suggest application possibilities in planning contexts.

Collier, John. *Visual Anthropology: Photography as a Research Method.* Albuquerque: University of New Mexico Press, 1986.

Hales, Peter. *Silver Cities: The Photography of American Urbanization 1839-1915.* Philadelphia: Temple University Press, 1984.

Webb, Eugene, Donald T. Campbell, Richard D. Schwartz and Lee Sechrest. *Unobtrusive Measures: Nonreactive Research in the Social Sciences.* Chicago: Rand McNally, 1966.

> Webb, Campbell, Schwartz and Sechrest direct attention to social science research data obtained by methods other than the interview or questionnaire. The goal is not to replace the interview, but to supplement and cross-validate it with measures that do not require the cooperation of a respondent and that do not themselves contaminate the response. The authors illustrate through examples that unorthodox approaches to measurement problems are often significantly helpful in determining attitudes.

Whyte, William H. *The Social Life of Small Urban Spaces.* Washington, DC: The Conservation Foundation, 1980.

____. *The Social Life of Small Urban Spaces.* 16 mm film and 1/2-inch VHT videotape. Color. Direct Cinema Limited, distributors, 1988, ©1979.

> This film provides entertaining documentation of people and their movements with time-series photography to illustrate and develop some principles of human behavior in public spaces in the city. It demonstrates charting and mapping techniques to analyze thick visual, spatial and photographic information gathered in the field.

General Background

Babbie, Earl. *Survey Research Methods.* Belmont, CA: Wadsworth Publishing Company, 1973.

> Babbie provides classical text on research methods. Sections that are relevant to field methods are Chapter 9, "Data Collection II: Interviewing" and Chapter 2, "Science and Social Science."

Denzin, Norman K. and Yvonna S. Lincoln, editor. *Handbook of Qualitative Research.* Thousand Oaks, CA: Sage Publications, 1994.

Guba, Eson G., editor. *The Paradigm Dialog.* Newbury Park, CA: Sage Publications, 1990.

**Examples of Web Sites
Involving Community Participation**

nkla.sppsr.ucla.edu

> Neighborhood Knowledge Los Angeles (NKLA) has its origins within the applied community-based research program at the University of California at Los Angeles Department of Urban Planning. "NKLA provides tools for accessing property and neighborhood data and works with neighborhood residents, community organizations, and policy makers to mobilize support for community improvement in the Los Angeles area."

www.eslarp.uiuc.edu

> The East St. Louis Action Research Project is sponsored by the University of Illinois at Urbana-Champaign. "Many planned solutions fail when they are imposed on a community by outsiders . . . because local individuals and neighborhood organizations participate in goal setting, program development, and plan implementation, these projects are more likely to become self-sustaining."

www.jcci.org/index.htm

> The Jacksonville, Florida initiative: "JCCI [Jacksonville Community Council Inc.] . . . seeks to improve the quality of life in Northeast Florida by positive change resulting from the informed participation of citizens in community life, through open dialogue, impartial research, and consensus building."

Survey Methods
for Planners

Nancy Nishikawa

It is a truism that an urban planner must understand *what is* before they can develop and communicate a program of *what should be*. The more information available about people's actual needs and preferences, the better planners can try to satisfy them. However, few analyses of planning issues can be completely researched on the basis of available information. Chapter 3, "Information from Secondary Sources," provides a long list of information available from secondary sources; however, such datasets may not cover the desired geographical scale or may omit critical variables. Moreover, secondary source data are often obsolete. Plans and policies are formulated amid constantly evolving circumstances. Planners need information about a changing client population, yet depending on data from other agencies such as the U.S. Census Bureau means that information availability is beyond the local planner's control.

The survey is a way of creating an area-specific, customized database. Even a hurriedly put-together survey can fill a critical information gap. The particular advantage of a sample survey is that it allows planners to generalize findings from a relatively small number of respondents to a larger population. With increasing emphasis on *representative* citizen participation, surveys offer a useful method for gathering input from people who typically are not consulted on planning issues. Designed properly, the survey is both efficient and rigorous. Nevertheless, because it requires resources—time, money and skills—that may be limited, most planning offices do not carry out their own surveys.

Survey work is often perceived as a research tool for academicians or policy institutes that are backed by large budgets and include banks of trained phone interviewers. This chapter aims to make surveys more accessible. Attention is given to the concerns of professionals for whom the survey is more likely a short-term project rather than an elaborate piece of scholarly research. Whether the survey is conducted in house or contracted to a professional consultant, it remains an important means of obtaining primary data, and planners need to be familiar with the major components of the survey process.

Several techniques can be classified under the broader heading of survey methodology, including personal and telephone interviews and mail-in and Web-based questionnaires. Each of these major survey tools is examined in this chapter.

It is appropriate to start with an important caveat. Questionnaires, interviews and observations by a so-called objective outsider are intrusive measures. The appearance of a researcher and/or survey introduces an extraneous element in the normal course of social and physical interactions. Therefore, measurements taken in the field reflect the situation a survey was designed to measure as well as the particular interactions between respondents and the survey instrument.

Sometimes, a survey may be undertaken, in part, to change social dynamics. For example, a downtown business association may use a survey and attendant publicity to recruit new members or to educate and mobilize existing members. While information-

WHY SURVEY?

The merchants in downtown Middlesville were pleased with city hall's handling of the trash problem, so when they heard that a big-box discount retailer was opening in the next town, they asked Mayor Lorch for help. Anxious to prevent the loss of Main Street businesses, the mayor turned to the planning director—and Assistant Planner—to investigate the competitiveness of the downtown commercial district.

Assistant Planner spent a day putting together an inventory of existing businesses. He then looked through old phone directories, tax records and maps to document the commercial evolution of downtown.

The Downtown Merchants Association provided a report based on a downtown users' survey. The results looked interesting, but they were 10 years old and significant changes had occurred during the intervening years. Assistant Planner pondered the usefulness of updating the survey, finding out where current downtown users come from and what attracts them to the area.

His next task: writing a proposal to the planning director.

gathering methods can have such secondary objectives, it is also possible that distortions caused by such effects can become a source of error in the survey.

Another source of error results from the fact that a survey instrument cannot always be designed to operationalize theoretically complex social issues. A workable survey instrument is developed in three steps, each a progression of a researcher's logic. As a researcher, Assistant Planner would first define one or more concepts central to the study (e.g., "competitiveness" as in the case of downtown Middlesville). The second step is to choose indicators to assess these phenomena.

Continuing our example, Assistant Planner may decide that "adequate parking" or "specialty retailers" are important—and more concrete—elements of competitiveness. (The appropriateness of this determination will vary depending on cultural factors associated with the population being studied.) The third step involves constructing questions where the response will better describe, evaluate or provide understanding of each element. The responses are usually translated or coded into some measurable form, such as frequencies, rankings or percentages. There are numerous possibilities:

- How often do you use a car to travel to the downtown area?
- On a graded scale from A to F, how would you rate the availability of parking in downtown?
- Is "adequate parking" a major or minor consideration in your decision to visit downtown?

What if the respondent is more concerned about other aspects of parking, such as proximity to the final destination or costs? As you can see, with each succeeding step, the planner-researcher faces the challenge of establishing a connection between broad concepts and specific questions—all without losing important information through error or by pursuing unproductive tangents.

Given the types of errors found in any single data-gathering process, planners must be diligent in cross-validating survey results against measurements and findings from other sources, including common-sense explanations. One of the factors that accounted for the success of Middlesville's planning department in resolving its downtown trash crisis was implementation of this kind of strategy. Assistant Planner's information-gathering effort used several direct approaches: he consulted with the chamber of commerce, performed a site reconnaissance and talked with people working in the area. In this way, he was able to get a comprehensive picture of the actual conditions producing the trash.

SURVEY RESEARCH OBJECTIVES

The survey research process begins with the planner asking questions rather than identifying specific data to be obtained. The broader question, "What do I want to learn from the study?" precedes the more directed question, "What data am I looking for?" The answers form an initial statement of objectives. Delineating the purpose and objectives of the project

Another source of error results from the fact that a survey instrument cannot always be designed to operationalize theoretically complex social issues.

enable one to decide whether a survey is an appropriate information-gathering device.

Preliminary discussions about the survey should involve all members of the research and planning staff. Potential ambiguities need to be clarified by defining the terms used in the survey framework. For example, Middlesville's survey "to assess the *competitiveness* of the CBD" may hold different connotations for different groups. Residents may see a survey on competitiveness as a mechanism for improving the attractiveness of the CBD. Some merchants may see the survey as making the CBD a more profitable location for their business. Others may see efforts as stimulating gentrification—in effect, increasing the cost of doing business. Someone is sure to ask, "Competitive relative to what?"

The question of *whose* views are being measured must be clarified. Do residents alone constitute the public? What about visitors or workers who live outside? Surveys typically include the adult population, but fail to include children whose living space is even more confined within the territorial boundaries of the neighborhood.

The group responsible for designing and conducting the survey should write down an initial statement that explains the specific purpose of the survey, the kinds of results expected and the specific areas to be covered by the survey to meet those objectives. If the survey is part of a larger planning effort, the group should consider the subsequent action program (e.g., whether or not the data will serve as a baseline with follow-up surveys used to measure progress or change).

One way to avoid later revisions is to encourage all interested parties to participate in the task of preparing a list of practical and/or theoretical questions to be covered in the survey. Potential data users should be encouraged to create mock-up tables they would like to see generated from the survey data. While this takes a little extra time at the beginning, it is useful to check that cross-tabulations can be produced or if the data can be aggregated or disaggregated as desired.

A written list will begin to sharpen the focus of the study and also define the categories of data needed. Once a project is actually underway, there is a tendency to widen the survey's scope to obtain the greatest amount of information possible, since the marginal cost of adding one more item to the questionnaire or interview schedule is far less than the cost of going back to the field to retrieve information missed the first time around.

Any widening of the scope (for example, if the planning department then wanted to inquire about residents' reactions to more intensive or mixed land use in their neighborhood) should be permitted only if the main purposes of the survey are not adversely affected by spreading resources more thinly.

Trade-offs inevitably must be made between a longer, comprehensive survey and one that respondents perceive as an imposition on their time or of dubious validity because the questions seem less relevant. If changes are deemed acceptable, they should be

KEY QUESTIONS TO ASK BEFORE YOU START A SURVEY

- Why should a survey be conducted?
- What kind of information am I looking for?
- What types of information are particularly important?
- How will this information be used?
- How accurate does the information need to be?
- Who will use the information?

accommodated as soon as possible so that new or revised questionnaire items also pass through the normal round of pretesting.

TYPES OF
SURVEY INFORMATION

. . . it is prudent to determine if there is a good fit between the types of information a survey can provide and the types of information planners need for analysis.

Before undertaking a survey, it is prudent to determine if there is a good fit between the types of information a survey can provide and the types of information planners need for analysis. One typology, described below, distinguishes four categories of survey data.

Profile Data

Profile data describe characteristics of the survey population. Data are commonly collected on six characteristics: age, sex, marital status, race and/or ethnicity, family or household income and occupation. The relevancy of these characteristics will depend on the focus of the problem. These six variables serve to organize the information collected and allow the investigator to see patterns of relationships within the findings.

Collecting such standard profile information can help indicate when comparisons between survey results and other datasets, such as U.S. Census tabulations, are appropriate. (For a summary of U.S. Census Bureau surveys and publications, see Chapter 3, "Information from Secondary Sources.") Profile data are also an important part of many sampling procedures as this information is used to check the representativeness of the chosen sample vis-à-vis the study population as a whole.

Environmental Data

Questions dealing with the environment describe the circumstances in which the respondents live. Examples include the character of the immediate neighborhood, type of housing, or spatial characteristics such as the proximity of friends or relatives, or the boundaries that delimit routine social interactions. Similarly, environmental data can be used to suggest measures that will allow the planner to identify concepts such as neighborhood cohesion or neighborhood identity. Such information is useful, for example, in identifying project areas for Community Development Block Grant funding or evaluating the outcome of specific programs.

Behavioral Data

A gamut of relevant social behavior can be surveyed successfully. In transportation planning, journey-to-work surveys are now widely used; this information is also available from recent censuses. More extensive questions could also be included on a survey schedule, such as distinguishing between use of public and private modes of transportation and different types of trips (commute, shopping and recreational travel). Most surveys pertaining to behavior either ask about past experiences or cover relatively major forms of habitual behavior for which generally reliable information can be obtained.

Psychological Data

Data in this category cover a broad area of psychological information including opinions, preferences, attitudes, awareness, motives and expectations. For a planner, it is the area in which there are least likely to be secondary sources of data. Through opinion polls, planners can get a glimpse of the qualitative dimension of behavior. Determining attitudes and the reasons for holding them is another important survey objective:

- What is the level of support for an existing or proposed policy or action?
- What kinds of people tend to approve or disapprove of a particular policy position and why?
- Taking it a step further, what kinds of corrective measures or changes would members of the community like to see?

Opinions are often influenced by people's level of information about the circumstances surrounding the issue. One cannot assume that issues and events are understood equally by everyone, and it is difficult to assess people's positions unless their understanding of the issue is also known. The survey can help to gauge whether the community is responding from an informed base and thereby help to design or modify a strategy to improve awareness.

Motive refers to an individual's reasons for behavior and, more generally, to the forces impelling some action. Expectations represent a person's future orientation (i.e., opinions and attitudes about what will happen or plans for future behavior).

WHEN TO CONSIDER AN ALTERNATE METHOD OF INFORMATION COLLECTION

Investigators often use surveys to unearth sentiments generally unknown to planners working back in their offices. The exploratory aspect of survey research should not be ignored, but overusing surveys can tax the goodwill of potential respondents. Rather than use surveys solely to "beat the bushes," when there is insufficient background knowledge to construct a well-conceived instrument, the investigator needs to ask if there are other ways of getting this information (perhaps by carrying out field investigations, or visiting deliberately chosen, representative areas of a designated place and talking with residents there). These techniques are discussed in Chapter 1, "Field Methods for Collecting Information."

Some categories of human behavior are less appropriate for measurement by surveys:

- Surveys are not appropriate to obtain accurate information about a sequence of historical events. Instead of relying on the memories and impressions of many people whose involvements in those situations are varied, archival research or selective, in-depth interviews with key actors may be a more economical means of procuring this information.
- Surveys provide discrete statistical measures and are not good for tapping the flow of activities at individual or group levels. An account that calls for measurement of continuous behavioral activities, such as the shopping patterns of

One cannot assume that issues and events are understood equally by everyone, and it is difficult to assess people's positions unless their understanding of the issue is also known.

downtown patrons, might be better obtained from a participant-observation study.

- Surveys are not the most effective tool to assess involvement in illicit activities. Without clear assurances of confidentiality—or even with them—respondents may not be forthcoming about their participation in illegal activities, though the type of survey technique used can be critical to success or failure.

FACTORS DIFFICULT
TO CONTROL IN SURVEYS

To a large extent, a survey's success depends on the cooperation of the respondents. Investigators can execute a survey more or less effectively depending on factors internal to the study, such as the quality of the questionnaire, training of interviewers and good administrative capability. Other dynamics are also at work in the population to be surveyed over which the research staff has minimal control:

- The level of interest already present in the community about the survey's subject matter must be evaluated. All other things being equal, a higher level of interest can be expected to generate a higher response rate, except in the case of very controversial issues or illegal activities where respondents may fear indiscretion. Surveys that stretch out over a length of time with attendant publicity can increase interest in the survey. In such cases, however, the disparity in interest between earlier and later respondents can introduce error in the survey findings.

To a large extent, a survey's success depends on the cooperation of the respondents.

- Participation is affected by prior surveys that in all likelihood have no relation to the study at hand. This includes the number and frequency of previously conducted surveys, and the impression they made, as well as lengthy surveying periods. This are known as *contamination effects*.

- The relationship between the respondents and the investigators or the conditions under which the survey is undertaken is another factor. Students and military personnel have a consistently higher response rate because they constitute something of a captive audience. In surveys conducted using the general population, the perceived authority factor is considerably reduced and often nonexistent.

- The respondent group's sense of security and privacy must be considered. While once confined to inner-city areas, today there is a generally high level of stress and fear operating within a wider range of potential respondent groups, and many people are quickly put on guard when approached. Investigators can alleviate some of the anticipated effects of suspicion by affiliating with a recognized and respected institution such as a nearby university.

THE ADMINISTRATIVE FACTOR

The administrative details of survey research are as important as the theoretical aspects and should not be underestimated if a project is to be completed successfully. Whether the survey project is large or small, inadequate resources and ill-planned execution can throw a carefully designed survey out of kilter. High priority is readily given to the scientific aspects of surveying, such as sampling and measurement, yet sloppy organization can introduce unnecessary error into the study just as easily. For example, lack of sufficient funds to pay interviewers could mean that some portions of the sample must be dropped or fewer callbacks made, leaving only responses from more readily accessible people.

The administrative plan should identify all components of the project. Individual tasks can then be delegated along with instructions about how they should be accomplished. The survey organizers should have a clear idea of how the various tasks are related to each other. Organizational information should not be confined to a select few. All team members like to be aware of what is going on (e.g., how one person's tasks fit in with those of another; how much leeway is allowed for decision making at one rank and when decisions should be referred upward; and how individual performance contributes to the successful completion of the entire project).

Travel and personnel costs usually account for the bulk of the sample survey budget. The project will likely need administrative staff, clerical staff, field staff, in-house professional staff (such as a statistician, economist or health specialist) and outside consultants.

Estimates of travel costs and living expenses in the field should cover the time spent for sampling, testing the questionnaire, training the interviewers and performing actual field work. Interview costs are usually the largest item in the budget. However, on average, only one-third of an interviewer's time is directly attributable to interviewing; the other two-thirds are spent on less critical tasks such as travel, research, editing questionnaires and other routine clerical tasks. For in-person interviews, large survey organizations have budget allocations of $50 to $120 per respondent, depending on the geographical scope of the survey.

Costs drop dramatically for telephone surveys (ranging from $15 to $40 per completed interview) depending on the length of the average call and toll charges. Basic mail surveys can cost even less since they do not require trained interviewers. The major expenses are for stationery, printing, postage (outgoing and return) and clerical assistance to address and assemble the survey packages and postcard reminders.

The administrative plan should state the order in which tasks must be accomplished and the amount of time necessary for each. Like cost budgets, time budgets are often underestimated. Allocating contingency time beyond the normal time budget can mitigate the later occurrence of unforeseen obstacles and delays. Another way of building in contingency time is to work with core procedures while allowing the option of adjusting different tasks when expected outcomes do not result.

SURVEY DESIGN

The specific procedures and methods to be used in a survey are established in the project design phase.

The administrative plan should identify all components of the project. Individual tasks can then be delegated along with instructions about how they should be accomplished.

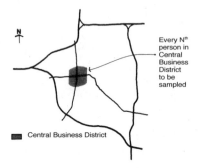

2-1. Unweighted cross-section

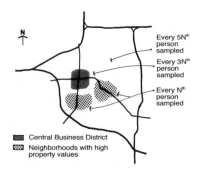

2-2. Weighted cross-section

These include selecting the sample population, sample size and method of administering the questionnaire and constructing the questionnaire itself. Planners have numerous alternatives from which to put together the final survey project. The major options are briefly discussed here as a starting point for relative comparisons. More detailed information can be obtained from the several excellent books listed at the end of this chapter (see the "Bibliography").

It is easy for novices to get caught up in the pros and cons of various techniques and strategies. Nevertheless, one of the best ways to learn how to complete effective surveys is to do it! With successive iterations, researchers will be able to devise a survey methodology that fits the requirements of the working environment and capitalizes on the skills and talents of the survey team.

BASIC TYPES OF SURVEY DESIGNS

There are many ways of classifying the different types of survey designs. For an introductory review, a useful typology is the distinction between the simple cross-sectional survey and the longitudinal survey.

Cross-sectional Surveys

Unweighted cross-section: The one-time, unweighted survey is probably the design most familiar to planners. It produces a "snapshot" for measuring the characteristics of a population at a given point in time. For example, as part of the CBD revitalization plan in Middlesville, the local planners may want to measure public opinion concerning the attractiveness of the CBD as a shopping district. By polling a random sample of persons, the planners will be able to assess public sentiments representing the targeted population (Figure 2-1).

Weighted cross-section: Another version deliberately oversamples a certain subgroup of the population. Usually, this group has special significance for the survey but is known to constitute a minority within the total population. In such cases, an unweighted cross-sectional survey would not yield enough cases to complete a meaningful analysis. A planning department interested in developing facilities for the annual ethnic fairs as part of the CBD plan may want to survey the subpopulation that would use these facilities most extensively.

One way of reaching a large number of fair participants is to double or triple the sampling rate in census blocks having high concentrations of people in ethnic groups that sponsor fairs (Figure 2-2). This assumes that people living in these areas have a greater interest in and a tendency to use the facilities. (If some groups are oversampled, it is important to readjust those cases to their proper contribution of the total sample for data analysis.)

Contrasting samples: Sometimes it is useful to draw samples from groups that are already known to show substantial differences with regard to an important study variable. For example, if the planners were interested in the issue of employee mobility, they may interview employees of firms that had moved (e.g., from the CBD to an exurban location). The purpose of such a survey would be to discover differences in the attitudes and characteristics of employees who remained in the original locale compared to those who relocated and continued working for the firm (Figure 2-3). These kinds of data could provide useful input into transportation planning, labor development and training programs, and business retention or recruitment efforts.

Longitudinal Surveys

In longitudinal surveys, the objective is to study the degree and direction of change in a situation rather than its static state. It is therefore necessary to obtain measurements at more than one time for comparison. Before-and-after studies and trend analyses make use of longitudinal surveys.

Before-and-after study: The design is used to measure the effect of some stimulus on a target population. Accurate assessment of the effect—whether there has been improvement, decline or no change—requires measurement before and after the event has taken place (Figure 2-4). The difficulty usually lies in obtaining the "before" or "baseline" data because researchers often begin their work after the stimulus has occurred. Nevertheless, with some ingenuity, it may be possible to find ways of estimating or reconstructing the "before" situation, for example, through respondents' recall of that information, other data sources and/or related survey material.

Trend analysis: The study of trends depends on more extensive monitoring and measurements over a longer period of time than just before and after a particular event. Periodic collection of data on attitudes toward transportation systems, education, housing or revision of the zoning ordinance could serve as continuing social inputs in the planning process. The availability of computers has increased the attractiveness of extensive databases by providing easy storage, access and manipulation capability.

One variation of trend analysis calls for the data to be collected predominantly from the same sample of respondents, called a *panel*. The advantage of repetitive contact with respondents is that it allows the researcher to build up comprehensive datasets on individuals that almost amount to case histories. There is usually some mechanism through which individuals can enter or leave the study. For example, if the panel is based on a sampling of addresses, a family that moves to another location is out of the study and the new occupants take their place as respondents.

SELECTING THE POPULATION TO BE SURVEYED

Probability Sampling

The findings of a sample survey accurately relate only to the population from which the sample is selected. Therefore, it is critical to arrive at a clear definition of the *target population*—the body about which conclusions will be drawn. Determination of the target population consists of two elements. The first is specifying the spatial area to be covered by the study, such as a city or a neighborhood. Alternatively, it could be a physical unit, such as a factory, school or dwelling.

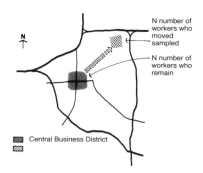

2-3. Contrasting sample

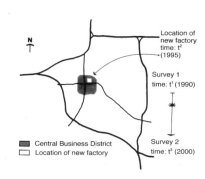

2-4. Before-and-after study

The second is selecting the actual person to be interviewed. This selection depends on the type of information desired and practical considerations of convenience and access. When accurate information about a person can come only from that person (as is often the case in attitude surveys), it is essential to have a predetermined plan for randomly selecting people within the household. On the other hand, if the survey deals mainly with information about the household and its occupants that any adult can provide, careful prior selection is less important.

This section on sampling design should not be confused with the earlier discussion on survey design. Here we discuss methods of selecting the sample to be used in the survey, while the earlier discussion dealt with formulation of the overall survey design to achieve specified objectives.

Unlike a census, which collects data from every member of a given population, a sample takes a much smaller portion of the population as the basis for making (estimated) assertions about the original population. A key advantage of this method is economics. A scientific survey design is based on the theory of *probability sampling* in which there is a known probability or chance that any individual person will be included in the sample. The ability to calculate the representativeness of a sample is what allows the investigator to make generalized conclusions from sample findings. Probability theory depends on mathematical calculations to determine how many respondents are needed to achieve a certain level of accuracy in the survey results.

When properly executed, sampling can enhance the accuracy of data gathering even more than a full-count census. From a practical standpoint, it is apparent that handling smaller numbers permits the collection of more detailed information. In many cases, much more can be learned from an interview of 30 minutes than six meetings of five minutes each. Furthermore, because smaller numbers are handled throughout the survey, greater attention can be paid at all stages, from data gathering through processing and analysis. Additionally, the cost of the investigation in time, staff and inconvenience to the public are all substantially reduced.

A central concern of probability sampling is to avoid bias in selecting the sample. Bias, or *sampling error*, refers to a discrepancy between the distribution of characteristics in the sample population and the population as a whole. In the first case study, a large university is located adjacent to Middlesville's CBD. If Middlesville's planning department wanted to poll people's opinion on downtown parking, they could have someone interview every 10th person who passed by a particularly busy street corner, or mail a questionnaire to every 10th person on the city's list of property owners.

More than likely, the street interviewer would conclude that there was enough parking downtown (though not enough bike routes), having talked to quite a few university students who did not have cars. One could expect opposite sentiments from property owners, the majority of whom live farther away from the CBD and normally drive to town.

Either view is skewed and probably would not be an accurate reflection of how Middlesville residents (students, homeowners and others) felt overall.

Sampling Frame

The sample is selected from some form of *sampling frame*. Those used most frequently are lists, registers and maps—either singly or combined. The essential requirements are that the frame must cover the entire population, must be complete (exclude no one), avoid duplication (include no one twice), be accurate and up to date, and be accessible and available for use by the investigator. In the Middlesville parking example, the city tax assessor's list would not qualify by itself because it does not include residents who rent property. If any of these factors is lacking, the situation should be remedied before sampling begins.

Given the constraints of fixed schedules and budgets, it may be more feasible to alter the survey design to compensate for inadequacies in the sampling frame. In the Middlesville case study, planners may believe that the revitalization plan requires mapping the location and obtaining characteristics of families with school-aged children living in the study area. They may already have decided to use an unweighted cross-section survey design.

A sample can then be obtained by selecting every *n*th family from the files of the school board—the sampling frame. Realizing that planning educational facilities requires a lead time of several years, the planning department also has decided to supplement the school board files with the birth registration lists of the past five years to account for families with children not yet in school. The sampling design in which every *n*th family on a list was chosen is known as *systematic sampling* (Figure 2-5). To guard against any human bias in using this method, the first unit is selected randomly.

Another—and more elementary—form of probability sampling is the *simple random sample*. The most

First unit selected at random

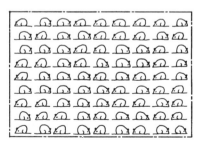

GIVEN POPULATION

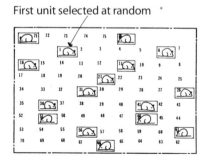

SAMPLE

Every Nth (5th) unit selected, first unit at random

2-5. Systematic sample

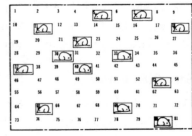

GIVEN POPULATION   **SAMPLE**

2-6. Simple random sample

a) Predetermined number
(13) taken at random

b) Predetermined number
(13) taken using random numbers

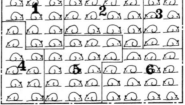

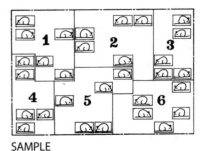

Stratified by census tracts, income,
age or other category

N (5) individuals sampled in each
stratum

GIVEN POPULATION   **SAMPLE**

2-7. Stratified sampling

important criterion in selecting a sample by simple random sampling is that each unit has an equal chance of selection. This can be achieved by two basic methods, which are variants of each other. In the first case, each unit is assigned a number, which is well mixed. Numbers are drawn from the pool one by one until the sample reaches a previously determined size. In the second case, units are again assigned numbers; however, the selected numbers correspond to the numbers on a table of random numbers. Tables of random numbers are usually generated by a computer and often can be found as an appendix in statistics textbooks (Figure 2-6).

Both the simple random sample and the systematic sample use a single stage; however, most surveys (especially area surveys) make use of multistage sampling. Two common forms of multistage sampling are stratified sampling and cluster sampling.

In *stratified sampling*, the total population is first divided into subpopulations called *strata*. Each unit is then placed in one (and only one) stratum. The first stage of the sample includes all strata.

For example, if a survey is to be conducted in a neighborhood, each housing unit could be categorized in a particular census block (the stratum). All census blocks would be included in the first-stage

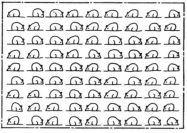

GIVEN POPULATION

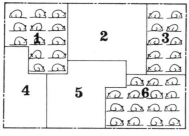

SAMPLE

Survey all units in selected categories
(census tracts 1, 3 and 6)

2-8. Cluster sampling

listing. In the second stage, a sample of individual units would be selected randomly from each census block (Figure 2-7).

The process is inverted in *cluster sampling*. In this case, the researcher chooses a sampling of census blocks in the first stage. Subsequent data would be collected from all units within a census block. Thus, there is a denser sample within selected sample blocks (Figure 2-8).

Sample Size

The size of the sample is another matter of choice and is based upon several factors. Sample size depends heavily on the homogeneity of the population being studied. *Homogeneity* is the degree to which units are alike with respect to the characteristics being measured. A population that has a greater degree of similarity can be represented with a smaller sized sample. Thus, it is necessary to have some estimate of the degree of homogeneity (or heterogeneity) when establishing the sample size. When such data are already available (perhaps through a pilot survey, census material or other secondary source), one need not have as large a sample as when little is known about the population.

Sample size is also related to the sampling method chosen. In general, stratified sampling calls for the fewest number of cases; however, this presumes sufficient information to stratify effectively. With less descriptive data, the simple random survey is recommended even though it requires more cases. Cluster sampling calls for at least as many cases as, or more cases than, the simple random survey.

The way in which collected data will be used in the analysis phase also affects sample size. The more categories by which the data are to be analyzed, the larger the sample needed. Information output will be eroded if a complex analysis yields categories that contain few or no cases. One rule of thumb is to have no fewer than 20 cases per cell, but even this may be insufficient when there is a lot of variability among units in the sample and when the total number of cases is small. As an exercise during the survey planning phase, the survey administrators—together

TYPES OF ERRORS

While sampling errors are perhaps the foremost concern of researchers, other types of nonsampling errors are equally significant. Lavrakas (1993), Salant and Dillman (1994) and Dillman (2000) refer to four sources of error that, together, constitute total survey error:

• *Sampling Error:* This results from surveying only some, and not all, elements of the survey population. In this case, the findings might not be representative of the larger survey population.

• *Coverage Error:* This results from not allowing all members of the survey population to have an equal chance of being in the sample (e.g., if a mail survey is based on an incomplete address list, or a Web-based survey is conducted when a significant proportion of the survey population lacks computers and Internet access).

• *Measurement Error:* This results from vague or misleading question wording, or illogical ordering of questions or interviewer actions that may bias responses, whether intentional or not. In other cases, the respondents may be unwilling or unable to provide an accurate response.

• *Nonresponse Error:* This results from systematic differences between people who responded to a survey versus those who did not.

NONPROBABILITY SAMPLE DESIGNS

Henry (1990) offers several additional types of nonprobability sampling, selecting cases based on subjective judgment and predetermined criteria. For planners, these practical approaches may satisfy the research objectives at hand.

• *Matching or Contrasting Cases:* Select cases that represent very similar conditions or, conversely, very different conditions (e.g., surveying two communities with similar socioeconomic characteristics or surveying two communities at opposite ends of a region's income range).

• *Typical Cases:* Select cases that are expected to represent mainstream positions.

• *Critical Cases:* Select cases strategically for being key to overall acceptance or credibility (e.g., those who may have been adversarial in the past, but whose support is seen as essential).

• *Snowball:* Early cases identify subsequent cases to be included in the sample (e.g., an initial set of interviewees is asked to suggest others whom the investigators should interview).

with the report writers and other data users—should attempt to construct the data tables to verify that information about the desired cases indeed can be collected.

Finally, cost considerations and the time and personnel available for survey work have direct consequences for sample size. The task of juggling these factors will be even more complicated when the survey represents only one component of an organization's overall activities and allocation of resources.

Sample Error and Confidence Levels

Quantity is not a substitute for quality. Sample size does not eliminate error; a sample does not gain in accuracy when the numbers are increased if the selection procedure is itself biased or faulty. Sampling error built into any sample design affects the reliability of all subsequent estimates and thus impairs the generalizability of survey conclusions to the total population. By employing probability sampling at all stages, the researcher has greater control over the quality of results. Statistical theory in effect identifies the level of error attached to a given sample design. The researcher is responsible for deciding how tolerable that error is.

An investigator often uses another statistical tool to establish scientific rigor—the *confidence level*—that specifies the degree to which they are confident that the estimate obtained from the sample is correct. At a 95% confidence level, the researcher is willing to accept the probability of being wrong five times out of a hundred.

Nonprobability Sampling

Although probability sampling is regarded as a superior method, the planner should not rule out surveys based on nonprobability methods. When the cost of probability sampling is prohibitive or if representativeness is not necessary, nonprobability sampling may be an efficient course of action and pursued as assiduously as one would a scientifically rigorous methodology. Four commonly used types of nonprobability sampling methods are availability sampling, purposive or judgmental sampling, quota sampling and volunteer sampling.

One of the least expensive sampling methods to employ—*availability sampling*—is to stop people passing a certain location. The emphasis here is on subject availability and convenience for the interviewer. Survey respondents may be chosen haphazardly, or it may be desirable to stop the first x number of people (sometimes called *chunk sampling*). These techniques would probably be only slightly more sophisticated than field interviews conducted as part of site reconnaissance. While they can yield some interesting insights and colorful quotations to perk up the report, such survey findings should not be used to make general statements relating to the population as a whole.

Another type of *convenience sampling* is to survey people already assembled as a group. With the growing emphasis on public participation, it is not uncommon for a survey to be folded into an interactive group exercise. For example, participants at a regional transportation workshop may be asked to prioritize transportation projects. This input later helps the policy committee winnow the list of projects submitted for federal funding.

In *purposive* or *judgmental sampling*, the researcher relies on their own familiarity with the population and its characteristics. One use of this sampling technique is to select the widest variety of respondents possible to identify inadequacies in the survey instrument, such as questions subject to different interpretations by different subgroups in the sample. This is more accurately a pretest rather than a survey. Nevertheless, it illustrates the more limited purposes for which such data would be used.

Quota sampling begins with a matrix in which the rows and columns are categories of descriptive characteristics relevant to the target population. Each cell is assigned a sample size in proportion to the number of persons in the total population possessing those characteristics. The researcher then surveys persons having all the characteristics of a given cell until the quota is filled. Quotas may be loosely defined. For example, interviewers may simply be instructed to find and interview 15 (each) men and women 18 to 64 years old, and 10 (each) men and women 65 years or older. As a further check, the information can be assigned a weight coinciding with its portion of the total population when analyzed. On the other hand, the matrix may be constructed more carefully by using profile information to determine cell distributions. The effectiveness of quota sampling lies in the accuracy of the initial matrix and minimizes any biases in the selection of persons sampled within a cell. Stratifying variables should be chosen carefully because certain characteristics (such as sex, age and race) are more readily apparent than others (such as income, occupation and level of educational attainment).

Volunteer sampling involves a self-selected group of survey participants, such as in surveys of radio audiences, magazine readership polls and "quick votes" using touch-tone telephones that are popular with local news programs or found at news Web sites. People who respond tend to have high levels of interest in the survey subject. The planner may find it beneficial to use this sampling method to get a sense of strong public reactions, whether positive or negative.

DATA-GATHERING METHODS

Prior to constructing the questionnaire, another decision must be made regarding the research strategy: the mode by which the survey is conducted. Three traditional methods are the face-to-face personal interview, the telephone interview and the mail-in questionnaire. Surveys conducted via the Internet (Web-based questionnaires) are increasingly popular.

Face-to-face Personal Interview

The interviewer-administered questionnaire method is supported by several strong advantages:

- An interviewer can better arouse the respondent's interest in the study and thereby increase the chance that an individual will participate.
- By creating an atmosphere conducive to discussion, an interviewer can often motivate the

SELECTING A SURVEY METHOD

The following matrix compares four major survey methods under varying conditions of resource constraints, survey needs and respondent characteristics.

	Interviewer-administered		Self-administered	
	Face-to-face	Telephone	Mail	Web-based
Resource Constraints				
Inadequate sampling frame (e.g., incomplete mailing list or directory)	++	++	--	--
Quick turnaround to complete survey	--	++	--	++
Limited skilled staff	--	--	++	++
Limited budget	--	+	++	++
Special Needs				
Multiple languages	-	-	+	++
Maps or other visual materials	++	--	++	++
Complex instructions or need to follow precise order	++	++	--	-
Need to probe, explain unclear questions	++	++	--	--
Some items require additional research	-	--	++	++
Anonymity needed for sensitive responses	--	++	+	++
Respondent Characteristics				
Large sample size	--	-	++	++
Geographically dispersed	--	+	++	++
Survey must be conducted at specific location	++	--	--	--
Target population is difficult to contact	++	-	-	--

Symbols arrayed on a spectrum, where "++" indicates more suitable, "-" indicates neutral and "--" indicates less suitable.

respondent to provide complete and accurate answers.

- An interviewer can avoid circumstances under which the respondent would have decided to skip a question. A skilled interviewer can clarify vague responses, repeat questions and make questions or words more intelligible to the individual (without influencing the response given).

  An on-the-spot interviewer can probe for more detail when a response seems irrelevant or incomplete. Furthermore, an interviewer can note characteristics, such as the respondent's appearance, living area and reaction toward the study. The opportunity for interviewers to observe a respondent's nonverbal behavior should not be overlooked.

- An interviewer has greater control over sequencing questions, often a critical aspect of the survey instrument.

- Employing interviewers can often increase accessibility to members of the population who are relatively isolated or physically less mobile.

- Responses can be enhanced through the use of such visual aids as maps, diagrams and photographs. As is often said, a picture sometimes can communicate an idea more quickly and precisely than word descriptions, which require the respondent to construct a mental image.

The high costs of time and travel expenses, need for skilled interviewers and the possibility that an interviewer will distort a response or inadvertently inject their own opinion into the phrasing or emphasis of a question or the recording of an answer need to be weighed against these advantages.

Telephone Interview

This method has many of the advantages of the face-to-face interview with the additional advantage of greater economy. Results from telephone surveys can usually be obtained in a shorter time frame than personal interviews and mail surveys, and the marginal cost of covering a larger geographical area is not much greater. There is some control over who actually responds to the questions, since interviewers can screen for desired characteristics (e.g., head of household, voter in last general election, household with bicycles or residents within certain geographical boundaries). Telephone interviews can avoid some of the physical risks to interviewers of working in high crime areas, which is exacerbated by a need to work after dusk when a majority of the sample population is likely to be at home. Respondents who are fearful of opening their door for a stranger may be willing to talk at length to the same person on the telephone.

Computer-assisted telephone interviewing (CATI) has increased the sophistication of telephone surveys. Skip patterns can be programmed so that a particular response automatically triggers a preset series of follow-up questions. Another handy feature is the ability of CATI technology to randomly shuffle the order in which choices are read to avoid potential biases (i.e., whether or not there is a tendency to favor the first choice or last choice a respondent

hears). CATI also allows the data collection and data entry tasks to be compressed. Responses typed directly into the computer during the interview are automatically compiled in a database. In the traditional pen-and-paper method, interviewers fill out call sheets during the interview and the appropriate, coded responses are keyed in after the fact.

The advent of random-digit dialing has helped to get around a major sampling problem—namely, incomplete sampling frames. Nevertheless, telephone interviews have their own disadvantages. One of the most significant limitations of the telephone interview is the difficulty of establishing the same degree of social rapport and interaction between interviewer and respondent that is possible in face-to-face situations. The respondent can end the interview simply by hanging up. As a result, questionnaires used are usually shorter and less demanding than those used in other data-gathering methods. In some areas, residents may be biased against telephone surveys if they have been widely used as lead-ins to a sales pitch or other types of solicitation by phone.

Mail-in Questionnaire

Dillman (2000) has made the mail survey a more manageable process by providing step-by-step instructions, collectively called the "tailored design method." To maximize the response rate, Dillman advises the following sequence:

- Send a pre-notice (warm-up) letter to the respondent several days before the questionnaire.

The advent of random-digit dialing has helped to get around a major sampling problem—namely, incomplete sampling frames.

- Mail out the questionnaire accompanied by a detailed and persuasive cover letter (the "sales pitch") and a stamped return envelope. The questionnaire should be clearly worded and visually distinctive.
- Send a thank-you postcard (also a reminder) a few days to a week after the questionnaire.
- Mail out a replacement questionnaire to nonrespondents two to four weeks after the initial survey package.
- Make a final contact to nonrespondents via phone or special delivery (e.g., priority U.S. mail or Federal Express) about a week later.

By far, the greatest advantage to this strategy is its low cost. Unlike the previous two methods, there is no need for trained interviewers since the respondents themselves completed the questionnaires. For this reason, mail surveys are suitable for organizations with limited human resources. Most of the tasks involved—mailing out questionnaire packets, sending out follow-up postcards or replacement questionnaires and keying responses into a database—are essentially clerical in nature.

Mail-in questionnaires also benefit from the fact that they allow participants to complete the forms at their leisure. Under some circumstances, it may be desirable to give respondents an opportunity to check their responses against other records before writing them down or to confer with others. Like the face-to-face method, mailed questionnaires can include maps and other graphics. On the other hand, the researcher cannot control the respondent's sur-

Clearly, the more work required of the respondent—whether in the form of a long questionnaire or the need to look for an envelope and attach postage—the lower the response rate.

vey experience. For example, respondents can skip ahead in the questionnaire; previewing items may affect the way questions are answered.

One criticism of mail surveys is the notoriously low response rate, although Dillman contends that response rates are comparable to other methods. Clearly, the more work required of the respondent—whether in the form of a long questionnaire or the need to look for an envelope and attach postage—the lower the response rate. Some type of personal touch may be advantageous, such as using unusual stamps, colored stationery or a personally addressed introductory letter (not too difficult with the help of mail merge, which is common in most word processing programs). Other devices have also been used successfully, such as the promise of a state lottery ticket, restaurant gift certificate or cash in exchange for a completed questionnaire (check state and local laws regarding the legality of give-aways). Finally, the greater the intrinsic interest of the subject matter to respondents or the greater links between the researchers and respondents, the larger the response rate.

Web-based Questionnaire

Electronic surveys offer further efficiencies by dispensing with paper, postage and data-entry costs. At present, surveys can take two different electronic forms: the questionnaire, which is attached to or incorporated within an e-mail message; and the survey, which is posted on a Web site. Of these two, the latter offers greater potential for becoming a mainstream survey technique.

Like mail surveys, the Web-based questionnaire is self-administered. However, the computer software can give the researcher more control over the survey experience (e.g., by restricting display of the questionnaire to one or more questions at a time). The respondent would be prompted to provide an answer before a new set of questions appears on a new screen. Depending on the response given, the questionnaire can be programmed to skip ahead to the appropriate screen.

Maps, photos and plans can be scanned and incorporated into the questionnaire. Color can be used to highlight and emphasize. Indeed, survey designers have more flexibility than ever before with continuous software improvements that now include drop-down boxes, split screens, embedded programs (applets), animation and video and sound tracks. With such powerful options at hand, researchers must keep in mind that respondents will have different computer hardware and have different screen configurations, browsers and transmission speeds. A respondent is less likely to participate in a survey if it takes several minutes to download, no matter how spiffy the display.

The most serious considerations in Web-based surveys relate to the representativeness of the responses—a two-sided issue. First, is the Internet amenable to a scientific sample? A large number of respondents do not correct the problem of self-selection. No scientific generalizations can be made if the respondents do not represent the larger population. (The results would, however, reflect the views and experience of survey participants, and sometimes this narrower objective is acceptable.)

An ongoing concern is the uneven distribution of computing resources in society. This problem has diminished over time, and a recent study by the Pew Internet & American Life Project (see the "Bibliography") found that the online population is looking more and more like the general population, with Internet usage increasing especially among women, minorities and families with modest incomes. Nevertheless, coverage error (the inability to include segments of the population in the sampling frame) remains a significant issue; a prudent recourse is to combine Internet surveys with other, more traditional means.

A second issue is indiscriminate access, where questionnaires are completed by persons who are not in the sample and could therefore skew the representativeness of the results. This situation can arise if the questionnaire is posted on a public Web site. The most common solution is to provide prospective respondents with a personal identification number or password (see Chapter 7, "Computers and Planning").

Finally, creating and posting surveys on the Internet require competence that may or may not be readily available within a planning office. A basic Web-based survey is not significantly more difficult than Web page design and Hypertext Markup Language (HTML). Someone with prior experience in this area is likely to find it a relatively easy extension to add a survey to a Web site. Nesbary's book (2000) provides a step-by-step guide. Others may find it more efficient and economical to hire an outside consultant.

The most serious considerations in Web-based surveys relate to the representativeness of the responses —a two-sided issue.

Two basic categories of questions are the open- versus the close-ended inquiries.

Mixed Modes

Any of the four survey techniques can be used in combination. One of the most successful uses of telephone interviews has been in follow-ups of face-to-face interviews. Similarly, a telephone call can be made to remind potential respondents to return their mail-in questionnaire, or researchers can personally deliver the mail-in questionnaire (and explain its purpose) and/or pick up completed questionnaires. Another option is to fax, rather than mail, the questionnaire. Applied Development Economics (a Berkeley, California planning firm) has successfully increased response rates by calling businesses to get their participation in a survey, then faxing out the questionnaire while the request is still fresh.

Even if people cannot be persuaded to participate in the study, it may be possible to at least obtain some profile characteristics so they may be compared with the characteristics of people who did respond to check for nonresponse bias.

DESIGNING THE QUESTIONNAIRE

The common element in the data-gathering methods discussed above is their use of a questionnaire. Researchers have several options in designing the exact format of the questionnaire, primarily in constructing and sequencing questionnaire items.

Constructing Questionnaire Items

Two basic categories of questions are the open- versus the close-ended inquiries. In *open-ended questions*, the respondent comes up with their own answer and therefore has considerable freedom in relating to the question. With *close-ended questions*, the respondent is asked to select a single answer from a list provided by the researcher (one which "best fits") or multiple answers ("all those that apply"). Researchers should note, however, that multiple answers can pose a coding nightmare and open-ended questions usually end up being post-coded.

Close-ended questions are useful when the respondent is asked to make distinctions of degree. The *rating scale* is one technique and provides an ordinal measurement of degree. A common method is the semantic differential that presents a set of opposite word pairs and asks the respondent to indicate a position between them: "How would you usually describe the street activity outside your house or apartment?" (Answers would range from "Noisy" to "Quiet.")

Another popular scale, the *Likert scale*, calls for the respondent to indicate the extent to which they agree with a statement: "There are enough adequate parking facilities in the major business district on Main Street between Second and Fifth Streets." (Answers are selected from "Strongly Agree," "Agree," "Disagree," "Strongly Disagree" or "Undecided.")

In a *numerical scale*, the respondent correlates their position to a numerical rank: "Please rank the following city services on a scale of 1 to 5, with '1' being least satisfactory and '5' being most satisfactory." The scale is often constructed to mimic the familiar task of assigning grades. Make sure there is consistency in the rating scheme. It does not matter if a favorable rating is at the low or high end of the scale, but it should be that way throughout the questionnaire to avoid confusing the respondent and your analysis.

Choices do not have to be indicated by words. In one case, an urban vest-pocket park was designed successfully with help from citizens who completed picture ratings of preferable park layouts. The pictures (photographs of simple models) were a highly suitable communication medium. Not only were the pictures engaging, thereby inviting people to participate in the survey, but they also provided sufficient imagery so that people untrained in design could work on the problem.

Ranking Preferences

The responses prompted by open-ended questions are usually more difficult to code and analyze because they do not fall neatly into predetermined categories. However, lack of structure, an opportunity for self-expression and spontaneity can bring important new insights to a study if researchers are willing to put up with human idiosyncrasies.

General Guidelines

The choice of questions used will ultimately depend on the aims of the study, the type of respondents (and their competence to reliably answer particular questions) and the purpose of the specific questions. Some general guidelines apply to all questionnaire items:

- Questions should be straightforward and unambiguous.

- The investigator should not expect respondents to give a single answer to what is actually a combination of questions. Keeping items short can avoid double-barreled questions. In any case, it is safe to assume that many respondents will read items quickly or will pay less than full attention to the interviewers and want to provide quick answers. Under these conditions, clear and short items can lessen the possibility of misinterpretation.

- Questions should be relevant to most respondents. When attitudes are queried on topics that few respondents have thought about, the results are not likely to be useful unless information about the level of interest is purposefully requested. Similarly, researchers must be careful to avoid *expert error* (the error of attributing to the respondent a degree of expertise that they do not possess in the field in question).

- Care should be exercised in the choice of words. Avoid slang and jargon. Each respondent will be able to understand and interpret the questionnaire items according to their own experiences. Therefore, the investigator formulating the items should constantly ask, "What do the questions mean to me?" and "What do they mean to the respondent?" In the latter case, profile data (such as age, education, sex and ethnicity) can aid the estimation of the respondents' frame of reference.

The investigator should not expect respondents to give a single answer to what is actually a combination of questions.

Many of the specific details regarding design of the survey strategy and instrument will be worked out satisfactorily only after a great deal of discussion, revision and reorganization.

Ordering Questionnaire Items

With careful planning, the survey researcher can often work out a questionnaire design that combines a variety of response forms and uses each advantageously. This then becomes largely a matter of patterning questionnaire items. The most basic patterns are the funnel sequence and the inverted funnel. The *funnel sequence* refers to a procedure in which the interviewer first asks the most general, open and unrestricted questions. In contrast, the *inverted funnel* starts with specific questions and then moves to more general issues.

When sequencing questions, the researcher should be sensitive to the logic respondents follow, thereby helping them to provide accurate information. It is especially important that the relationship of a question and the overall purposes of the study make sense to the respondent. Use of transitional questions, brief explanations or headings should be inserted to signal a change of topic or to show how the new topic relates to what had been previously asked.

Special attention should also be given to skip patterns where questions are directed to a subset of respondents. Instructions and graphic cues (such as arrows) should enhance movement through the questionnaire so that respondents answer all pertinent questions—and skip over the irrelevant ones.

EVALUATING THE SURVEY INSTRUMENT

Many of the specific details regarding design of the survey strategy and instrument will be worked out satisfactorily only after a great deal of discussion, revision and reorganization. By putting the study into operation and seeing how it works, the researcher can evaluate issues ranging from where to locate sensitive items within the interview schedule to what questionnaire layout is appealing yet functional. Making use of such tools as the pilot study, pretest and trial run can most efficiently accomplish a preliminary evaluation.

In the *pilot study,* the researcher can anticipate situations they will face under full-scale operating conditions so that contingency procedures for dealing with potential problems can be mapped out in advance. The pilot study can be either for the purpose of exploration (what happens if we do this?) or estimation (e.g., checking various characteristics of the population and/or environment to confirm sample group selection and availability).

The *pretest* is essentially evaluative and is used to help decide which alternative procedures should be used:

- Did respondents react to the questionnaire in the way investigators expected?
- Were they able to follow instructions?
- Did respondents complete the questionnaire in the time expected?
- Was the list of choices in close-ended questions adequate? Should additional choices be added based on write-in responses?

A key element of the pretest is debriefing respondents and using their experience as feedback to adjust the survey instrument or script (in the case of telephone interviews).

The *trial run* is used for a final check of whether all possible alternatives have been considered and the most efficient procedures have been chosen. It is intended to evaluate the operational plan as a whole before the final run. The trial run is also important as a training tool for all personnel who will take part in the actual survey. In addition to making sure that all materials are available when necessary, those who will use them can familiarize themselves with the materials under realistic conditions.

As a result, the trial run gives the research and planning staff preliminary information about the adequacy of personnel and operations. They can learn where more or different personnel may be needed, how communications can be improved and how long it will take from initial contact with respondents until data are ready for analysis. On the basis of concrete information from the trial run, many procedural problems can be ironed out and last-minute adjustments made to the financial and/or time budgets.

ALTERNATIVES TO THE SURVEY

Observations

One of the investigator's greatest fears is that their work will meet with resistance from the population being surveyed. In such an eventuality, *observation* provides an alternative data-gathering tool. For example, retail outlets in the CBD may refuse to be surveyed because they suspect competitors will learn about their business conditions. However, the investigator can still observe the activity of delivery vehicles or the number of employees and customers arriving and departing at various times. Like the survey methods, an observation schedule must be carefully designed to minimize inaccuracy and bias. The observation and recording of data can be aided with a list of required information that was devised before the field survey begins. In this way, the observer knows where to concentrate their attention when confronted with a barrage of sensual stimuli.

Every item must be fully recorded; reliance should never be placed on memory. Moreover, recorded information should distinguish between observations of actual occurrences and interpretations. To resolve the problems of recording events simultaneously with their spontaneous occurrence, note-taking can be supplemented by use of a portable tape recorder.

Key-informant Technique

Anthropologists studying the structure and behavior of cultures have used the *key-informant technique* most extensively. It refers to an information-gathering method that taps the knowledge of a few people, usually through unstructured personal interviews. These people occupy positions or roles that allow them to communicate a broad, synthesized picture about a certain subject and/or a specialized picture of that topic. Use of key informants is appropriate when the objective is to obtain comprehensive or in-

One of the investigator's greatest fears is that their work will meet with resistance from the population being surveyed.

depth information not expected from a sampling of the population. The low costs are also appealing.

Before using this method, the investigator must consider the qualifications of proposed key informants to decide whether each possesses the relevant information. Consideration should also be given to the sources of any biases the informant may have, possibly as a result of that unique role. This problem may be controlled somewhat by using multiple informants. In any case, the key-informant technique is not meant to take the place of survey data with its emphasis on unbiased estimates that can be projected to a more general population.

Key informants are especially valuable where there is a communication gap between the target study population and the researcher. Individuals are selected for their ability to bridge the gap by speaking the language of both sides. The interviews will often be held as a preliminary phase of a research project to see that the right problem, relevant issues and critical variables have been identified—similar to a pilot study.

Focus-group Interviews

Much of the work on focus-group interviews has been in the area of market research. It involves a nondirective interview process that allows participants to comment, explain and share experiences and opinions. In part because of its popularity, the term "focus groups" has been attributed to different types of group interviews. However, the technique is actually quite distinctive. Krueger (1994) describes it as follows:

Focus-group discussions . . . are conducted without pressure or expectations of reaching a particular end point.

Focus groups have a rather narrow purpose for which they work particularly well—that is to determine the perceptions, feelings, and manner of thinking of consumers regarding products, services, or opportunities. Focus groups are not intended to develop consensus, to arrive at an agreeable plan, or to make decisions about which course of action to take. (p. 19)

In particular, focus groups resemble brainstorming techniques that are similarly open and spontaneous; however, brainstorming sessions, as well as nominal groups and Delphic processes, are often used to solve particular problems. Focus-group discussions, on the other hand, are conducted without pressure or expectations of reaching a particular end point.

Focus groups typically involve six to 12 persons and are best conducted with participants who are similar to each other. A moderator or facilitator typically begins by pointing out the commonality shared by group members. They then stimulate discussion by posing a series of open-ended questions.

With several participants, a single person is not responsible for coming up with an answer or opinion. The group structure reduces the level of anxiety sometimes found in personal interview situations. It seeks to emulate a more real-life environment in which people interact, and listen to and mutually influence each other. The group format makes it possible for people to explore more thoroughly and reflectively the similarities and differences in their experiences. One person's comments may spark new ideas in another person, thus setting off a chain reaction and causing viewpoints to evolve.

At the same time, it is possible for the group dynamics to deteriorate. The facilitator must be skilled in handling dominant personalities, loud-mouths and bullies who may intimidate or harass other participants. To balance out unevenness in individual sessions, the researcher should conduct interviews with several groups. Repetition also helps to identify trends and patterns by the frequency and consistency of comments.

On the whole, this method is relatively inexpensive and focus groups are fairly easy to organize. However, there are potential hurdles (e.g., in recruiting participants, particularly if the subject matter is not compelling, or finding a skilled moderator). Analyzing the results of the sessions may also present a challenge if the researcher is not familiar with qualitative data:

- How do you judge one person's comments against another's?
- What effect did the group's environment have on the statements made?
- Is it valid to take statements out of their context?

Focus-group research can provide useful information about human experiences not found in numbers and it is, therefore, an effective complement to quantitative studies. Focus groups held before a survey allow researchers to learn a target population's vocabulary and how it reasons. This is especially helpful in questionnaire development to avoid using unfamiliar terms, omitting important response choices, presenting questions in a seemingly illogical sequence or failing to ask critical questions. Focus groups held after a survey can help researchers interpret the results or formulate follow-up actions.

CONCLUSIONS

Despite the plethora of data stored in computer banks or in hard-copy files, planners will still rely on surveys as one of the basic methods for collecting information pertinent to their activities. This chapter has outlined the major components of survey research, some available options and factors to consider in putting together a project. It has been emphasized that the specific nature of a survey project will depend on the objectives being sought and the resources available for such an endeavor. Successful completion of a survey calls for adequate strategic planning, general attention to tactics and the ability to maneuver in midstream. The survey is a tool that will continue to serve diligent and creative planners well.

APPLICATIONS

1. The planning department in Middlesville is in the midst of revising a comprehensive revitalization plan for the CBD and surrounding neighborhoods. The city planners believe that adequate information is available on public needs and preferences. Assistant Planner, realizing that the planning process would benefit greatly from direct citizen participation, proposes that a survey be conducted. He even suggests a title for the study: "Middlesville Tomorrow: Toward the Year 2050."

a. Draw up a list of objectives for such a survey. Begin by asking questions you would like the survey findings to answer. For example, you may want to investigate the relationship between a vital, high-density CBD and a high-quality urban lifestyle. Compare your list with that of one or two other persons and try to resolve any differences in survey objectives.

b. Draw up a list of objectives that a neighborhood group called Citizens Against Towers (CAT) would adopt if it were to conduct a separate survey.

2. After consulting a sampling expert and weighing administrative costs, the city's planning committee for the survey decides on a mail-in questionnaire as most appropriate.

a. Prepare a cover letter to send with each questionnaire. The primary objective of the letter is to encourage participation and thus minimize the nonresponse rate.

b. CAT, an organization comprised of volunteers, feels that telephone interviewing is a more effective strategy. Write out an introduction—concise, yet engaging—that can be presented verbally.

3. At one point, the possibility of distributing the city's questionnaire as an insert in the only local paper was considered. What are the pros and cons of this approach? How would your assessment differ if newspaper officials informed you that the Sunday edition was delivered to 85% of the households in Middlesville? How would it differ if an address list were also supplied?

4. One alternative to surveys discussed in the chapter is the focus-group interview. To practice this technique, set up groups of six to eight people with one person as the moderator and another as the recorder. In half of the groups, members should read the same news account of a prominent local planning issue. In the other half, members should read an editorial or letters to the editor on the same issue. The moderator's role is to find out the range and intensity of opinions from group members and elicit suggestions about ways to address the issue. Spend about 15 minutes for this discussion. Follow with results of each groups' discussion by the recorders, then compare.

BIBLIOGRAPHY

Dillman, Don A. *Mail and Internet Surveys: The Tailored Design Method*. 2d ed. New York: John Wiley & Sons, Inc., 2000.

The author, a noted authority and advocate of self-administered surveys, is credited with raising the status of mail surveys. Frequently plagued by low response rates, Dillman has developed a system of notification, contact and follow-up to maximize the data yield. Backed by more than 20 years of experience in the field, he discusses elements of his "tailored design method" in fine detail. This latest volume also includes a chapter on self-administered surveys using newer technologies, such as the Internet and interactive voice response.

Fowler, Jr., Floyd J. *Improving Survey Questions: Design and Evaluation.* Applied Social Research Methods Series, Vol. 38. Thousand Oaks, CA: Sage Publications, 1995.

Questionnaire design lies at the heart of collecting the type of information needed. This book focuses on how to write good survey questions through choice of words and format. It is a detailed yet practical how-to book, replete with examples for a wide range of situations.

Henry, Gary T. *Practical Sampling.* Applied Social Research Methods Series, Vol. 21. Thousand Oaks, CA: Sage Publications, 1990.

Figuring out the sample size is still perceived as a major hurdle (or stumbling block) in many survey projects. This book helps to demystify the sampling issue. While statistical formulas and distribution curves are unavoidable, the author does not make them a focal point of the text. Explanations, supplemented by tables and flow charts, are clear and targeted to specific sampling questions. There is an excellent presentation of different sampling strategies and options.

Krueger, Richard A. *Focus Groups: A Practical Guide for Applied Research.* 2d ed. Thousand Oaks, CA: Sage Publications, 1994.

In this compact and comprehensive textbook, equal attention is given to all aspects of the process of conducting focus groups—from logistics and recruiting participants, to moderating the sessions, to analyzing and reporting the results. Read Chapter 7, "Principles of Analyzing Focus Groups Results" first, because it highlights the qualitative and interpretive elements of this research method, as distinct from the surveys.

Lavrakas, Paul J. *Telephone Survey Methods: Sampling, Selection, and Supervision.* 2d ed. Applied Social Research Methods Series, Vol. 7. Thousand Oaks, CA: Sage Publications, 1993.

This is an indispensable guide for anyone undertaking a telephone survey and the next best thing to on-the-job training. It is especially useful in helping to anticipate problems that might arise when the survey is executed and recommending ways of responding to problems that do.

Nesbary, Dale K. *Survey Research and the World Wide Web.* Boston: Allyn and Bacon, 2000.

An early book on online survey research that is readily available and worth a quick look by readers who need a basic orientation. The author has conducted two interesting experiments pitting the Web-based survey against one administered by regular mail—with mixed results. Unfortunately, the definitive book on online survey and polling research is still to be written. The most productive tips are likely to come from the private sector where online market research continues to develop in creative ways.

Rainie, Lee and Dan Packel. Pew Internet & American Life Project. "More Online, Doing More." Washington, DC: The Pew Internet & American Life Project, 2001 (www.pewinternet.org)

Rea, Louis M. and Richard A. Parker. *Designing and Conducting Survey Research: A Comprehensive Guide.* 2d ed. San Francisco: Jossey-Bass Publishers, 1997.

Although the title of this book refers to designing and conducting surveys, a significant portion is devoted to analyzing and presenting the results. Where most texts on survey research end with data collection or construction of the database, this one extends into the data analysis phase, covering topics such as tests of significance and measures of association. There is also a brief, but useful, chapter on writing up the survey findings.

Salant, Priscilla and Don A. Dillman. *How To Conduct Your Own Survey.* New York: John Wiley & Sons, Inc., 1994.

This book has become a classic for novice survey researchers. It is the user-friendly version of Dillman's more academic textbook. A self-proclaimed nuts-and-bolts guide, the authors break down the survey process into discrete, do-able tasks, and provide illustrations and examples for virtually every step along the way. After reading this book, it's hard not to feel that anybody can do a survey.

Information from Secondary Sources

Maria Yen and Grace York

It is a brave new world for planners, community groups and private citizens searching for reliable information that will lead to effective plans. While public sector agencies remain the primary gatherers and repositories of secondary source information, they are joined in the 21st century by private companies that can tailor a data search to a client's specific planning needs, and by not-for-profit groups that collect information for communities and populations previously overlooked by government agencies.

The expansion of the sources that collect planning data goes hand in hand with the democratization of access to this data. A private citizen can as easily gather information on a neighborhood from the U.S. Census Bureau as can the experienced planning professional, if they both have access to a computer and an Internet connection.

In this new world, secondary source information can be combined with new technologies for visual presentations that make data easier to grasp and applicable to real planning problems. Geographic Information System (GIS) mapping and analysis, computer animation and virtual reality programs are some of the tools planners can use to breathe life into dry statistics. These technologies, along with guidance on searching for and using secondary source materials, can be made available to community groups, empowering them to understand the challenges and potentials facing their neighborhoods. In this way, the high-tech world of the Internet, and the tools to analyze and display data, serve to further the core mission of planners: *to help improve the communities they serve.*

Thanks to the expanding number of organizations collecting planning data, coupled with the Internet as an entry point to search for data, people and organizations at the smallest geographic level are gaining access to valuable information that they can use to plan for their communities. At the same time, local challenges often have global implications. Revitalizing a downtown business district dependent on garment manufacturing requires access to information on the links of this industry to overseas manufacturers, and on its dependence on international migrant workers, many of whom are women. Searching for low-cost and efficient alternatives to subways will lead transportation planners to seek information from cities across the globe that are designing their own creative mass-transit solutions.

This chapter focuses on the substantial amount of information directly relevant to local planning that has already been collected by local and state governments, federal agencies, professional organizations, private businesses, international organizations and nonprofit groups. This information can often be found in published form or on computer databases at public or university libraries, in the files and records of private businesses and public agencies, or on Web pages identified through Internet search engines. Finding and using secondary sources of information enable a planner to quickly develop relatively inexpensive background information and analyses on particular planning issues and sections of the city.

The expansion of the sources that collect planning data goes hand in hand with the democratization of access to this data.

INCREASING RANGE AND AVAILABILITY OF SECONDARY SOURCES OF INFORMATION

Geographic Information System mapping and analysis programs, virtual reality software and other technologies for generating, storing, analyzing and displaying spatial data have become accessible to trained planners as well as community members. Combining these tools with access to information can democratize the planning process by bringing on board those who will be affected by land use, economic development and other decisions that affect the local quality of life.

There is a growing movement among community-based nonprofit organizations, local governments and educational institutions around the world to develop electronic community networks that provide the public with access to useful information across a range of topics. Some of these networks also provide the technologies to visualize and analyze communities using programs for mapping and computer animation.

Community groups and individuals can use the tools and data made available on community networks in many ways to improve the local quality of life. For example, residents in the City of Los Angeles, concerned about a saturation of abandoned and neglected structures in their neighborhood, can access data on property tax delinquencies from the Neighborhood Knowledge Los Angeles (NKLA) Web site. Here, residents can create maps that depict the spatial distribution of these properties and link these to census data, showing a disproportionate number of abandoned structures in low-income or minority communities.

In another case, a group of entrepreneurs in Jefferson County, Missouri can use the Jefferson County Online Information Network (JOIN-N) to get information on business licenses, economic development plans and delays due to road construction that might affect the opening of a new enterprise. The fol-lowing selected Web sites illustrate this movement to democratize data and put the tools to analyze local information in the hands of communities.

Boulder Community Network
bcn.boulder.co.us

> Users can click on several resource "centers" to get access to information such as a sample lease agreement for landlords and renters, the latest minutes from city council meetings and an extensive list of community groups serving the Boulder County area.

InfoResources West Philadelphia
westphillydata.library.upenn.edu

> Residents of West Philadelphia can find useful information about their local quality of life, including data on public health issues, housing and total population in their neighborhoods, zip codes or census tracts. They can visualize the spatial distribution of this data through maps. The University of Pennsylvania's Department of City and Regional Planning developed this site.

Jefferson County, Missouri Online Information Network (JOIN-N)
www.join-n.org

> JOIN-N is a community network that strives to provide access to a vast array of community-oriented groups, both governmental and nongovernmental, and the information they possess. Users can find tax forms, voter information, business license forms and instructions, information on local road construction plans, links to human service organizations and many other useful links.

Neighborhood Knowledge Los Angeles (NKLA)
nkla.ucla.edu

> Proclaiming on its home page that "Neighborhood Improvement and Recovery is Not Just for the Experts," NKLA's Web site (developed at the University of California at

Los Angeles) provides access to information on conditions such as tax delinquencies, nuisance properties, code violations and other indicators that can serve as early warnings of neighborhood decline. Users can create maps with this information, along with demographic data from the U.S. Census Bureau, to visualize the needs and potential of their neighborhoods.

Shaping Dane Project
www.lic.wisc.edu/shapingdane

The "Shaping Dane" pilot project, run by Dane County, Wisconsin, seeks to involve citizens in evaluating the land use choices facing their area. The challenge of accommodating growth while preserving the area's character and quality of life provides the background for this project, which is centered in the town of Verona. Residents can use the site to create maps depicting how much land is being used in Dane County and for what purposes, and to consider alternative plans for their communities.

Woodberry Down Regeneration Team (WDRT)
of Hackney Council, United Kingdom
www.casa.ucl.ac.uk/woodberry

WDRT's Web site was developed by the Centre for Advanced Spatial Analysis, University College London, to communicate the redevelopment of some 2,500 housing units in Woodberry Down, London to its local residents. Residents who visit the site can take a virtual tour of the plans for their housing estate, "stepping inside" certain parts of the neighborhood for a closer look. This tour allows them to visualize alternative scenarios, on which they can comment and vote over the Web.

While more organizations form to provide planning information, and while planners and the public can access this information more easily today, challenges do exist in finding and using secondary sources. First, information has usually been collected for some purpose other than the needs of the local planning office. For example, a city transportation planner may be excited to learn that the Federal Highway Administration (FHA) publishes data on fatal accidents, including information on the vehicle, type of crash, persons involved and other key variables down to the place level of census geography.

However, the excitement may fade when the planner realizes the data have been collected only for highway fatalities, and cannot help in designating those city intersections that have been the scenes of repeated deadly accidents. While the city's police department may not yet have data for fatal accidents on the Internet, it may be the most reliable source in finding information about this problem. In addition, an organization that in the past has collected information useful for planners may simply cease collecting and publishing the information, making plans based on trend analysis far more challenging. This happens frequently in government agencies where funding priorities may shift under different political administrations.

A second challenge is created by the enormous diversity in types and sources of information that exist. A small-town planner wants to determine how much local retail business is being lost to a neighboring large city. Should he or she turn to sales tax

. . . while planners and the public can access this information more easily today, challenges do exist in finding and using secondary sources.

THE PLANNER FINDS INFORMATION

While dealing with the problem of the Main Street trash receptacles in Middlesville, Assistant Planner is asked to get background information on another issue that had been brewing for a while in another neighborhood of Middlesville: the need to develop a plan to revitalize Walnut Hill Park.

A few miles east of Main Street is the Walnut Hill neighborhood. Once a district of fine homes for the city's elite, the past decade has seen the flight of wealthier residents to the suburbs. While no longer a high-income enclave, Walnut Hill is a lively and bustling community whose population has grown due to a surge of immigration from Latin America. Houses that once held single families have been converted to apartments; schools that once were threatened with closure are now bursting with pupils.

Walnut Hill Park, however, is one city amenity that is not keeping up with this surge in growth and activity. Planned in the 1950s, the park contains playground equipment, a few deteriorating picnic tables and a large baseball diamond. In such a busy community, the parks and recreation department is surprised to find minimal park usage. The baseball field—once the center of neighborhood life in the summer evenings—is mainly deserted. The picnic tables and playground equipment are in dire need of replacement. It is obvious that few families spend time in Walnut Hill Park.

Assistant Planner knows that observations using field methods, interviews and surveys will provide valuable primary, first-hand information on the community's recreation needs. However, he also knows that basic background information might be available from secondary sources. Finding this information could put the issue of the park's low usage in context and help to identify the kind of additional information needed to remedy the situation.

Assistant Planner devises a quick strategy to guide his search:

- *Problem:* Walnut Hill Park has become run down and underutilized.
- *Approach:* Compile information on the area and write a recreation needs assessment to see how the park can better fit neighborhood needs.
- *Information:* Demographic, recreation and education information is required.

Assistant Planner's first stop is the U.S. Census Bureau's Web site at www.census.gov, where he can gather basic background data on the people of Walnut Hill. He is initially overwhelmed by the amount of available information in the American Community Survey on this neighborhood, but decides to focus solely on race, place of birth, year of migration, age and sex.

From this data, he does a quick analysis and discovers that 85% of the neighborhood population consists of people who are Latinos of various races, and 60% have migrated to Walnut Hill directly from various Latin American countries within the past five years. He works up an age/sex pyramid and notes that the population has a large group of children who are under five years old. Projecting 10 years ahead, he realizes that this group will be a major presence in the local primary and middle schools in the near future.

This leads Assistant Planner to call the Middlesville school board. His contact there confirms his assessment, provides more recent data on the school population in Walnut Hill and suggests he talk to the neighborhood elementary school principal. The principal expresses concern that the park, while bordering the school grounds, is run down and barely used. At the same time, the school's own recreation spaces are insufficient. "The children are forced to play soccer in the streets or in narrow spaces between houses," she tells Assistant Planner. "Soccer has really become the primary sport in this neighborhood; few are interested in baseball."

Assistant Planner realizes that the 1950's design of the park does not reflect or respond to the culture and preferences of the new residents in Walnut Hill. On the advice of the city's parks and recreation department head, Assistant Planner visits the National Recreation and Park Association Web site, where he orders a handbook on designing parks in urban areas. A

search on the Internet also reveals a nonprofit organization, the Hiatonka Outdoor Enthusiasts, which is accepting proposals for park improvement schemes. Worthy groups will be granted $10,000 to improve neighborhood parks.

Before writing his background analysis and coming up with a proposal, Assistant Planner must carry out more field research and perhaps a survey of neighborhood children. However, this first hunt for secondary source material has already given him a preliminary understanding of the changing recreation needs in Walnut Hill.

---

receipts from his or her town or the big city, U.S. Census data on the town's total size, a study undertaken by a university's extension program or some other source? An overview of major types of information, along with some planning scenarios, are presented here to assist planners facing these types of choices.

The third challenge arises in assessing the quality of information found on the Internet. The Internet makes available information from sources at all geographic levels and across a stunning array of topics relevant to planning. For example, planners interested in data on crimes can use the World Wide Web to find information from local sources such as neighborhood watch groups, national sources such as the Federal Bureau of Investigation (FBI), and global sources such as the International Criminal Police Organization (INTERPOL).

Careful searches allow access to records once only available from numerous treks to city clerks' offices and local libraries. However, while the World Wide Web offers the potential for quicker and more com-

prehensive searches of secondary source information, access to greater quantities of information does not necessarily translate into higher quality data for planning purposes. Not all data presented on the Web are accurate, updated and thorough. Given the time and effort needed to keep updated records on the Internet, some organizations simply allow their Web sites to languish, leading to stale information that should not be used in constructing fresh planning initiatives.

If planners seek to compare local information from different geographic areas or over different time periods, they may run into trouble with Web-based sources since the quality and currency of organizations' data can vary so drastically. It is a good idea to review the quality of information from any source before relying on it (see the sidebar entitled "Evaluating the Quality of the Data"). This is especially true for Internet sources.

The best technique for finding planning information may remain old-fashioned, human contact. Knowledgeable employees of local organizations can point planners in the right direction; sometimes a simple phone call will do the trick. At other times, a trip to the library is a good way to begin a secondary source information search. Most libraries have a password to the Online Computer Library Center World Catalog, so they can identify the location of material they may not own and borrow it for you.

The Internet can serve as a sort of high-tech "Yellow Pages" for enterprising planners—a place where they can search out human contacts in local agencies and libraries, who can then direct them to

The best technique for finding planning information may remain old-fashioned, human contact.

EVALUATING THE QUALITY OF THE DATA

Whether a planner finds secondary source information from the library, from a trip to a governmental office, or online through an Internet search, he or she should carefully evaluate the quality of the information to avoid the "garbage in, garbage out" dilemma of analyzing poor data and then producing poorly conceived plans. This checklist is a good starting point in evaluating the usefulness of secondary source information:

Data Quality Checklist

WHO paid for collecting the data?
- private corporation
- governmental organization
- nongovernmental organization

WHO collected the data?
- trained/untrained personnel
- experienced/inexperienced personnel
- high-level/low-level staff

continued on page 87

both hard-copy and computer-based secondary sources. Using the Internet can also help planners network across agencies. (A sample of Internet Web sites useful to planners is listed in the "Bibliography.") It is likely that some will change their address or their Uniform Resource Locator (URL). You can often identify the new URL by shortening the address or by using an Internet search engine. Some Web sites will change their information content or fade away over time while newer, improved versions may be developed.

This chapter begins by introducing the granddaddy of all planning-related secondary sources in the United States: the Censuses of Population and Housing. The U.S. Census provides comprehensive and reliable information for planners interested in creating a demographic portrait of their local areas. The sections that follow are organized by planning issue:

- population and demographics
- housing and construction
- economics
- transportation
- health and welfare
- education
- environment, natural resources and recreation
- crime
- governmental activities
- laws, legislation and regulations

Two final sections deal specifically with resources at the federal, state and local levels. Wherever possible, the sections list public agency, private business and nonprofit sources of planning information across geographical levels (local, regional, state, national and, where relevant, international). Not all planning issues are covered by all types of organizations (public, private and nonprofit) and not all planning issues lend themselves to analysis at every geographic level. Moreover, it is inevitable that the reader will come across useful sources that are not mentioned in this chapter.

Since considerable variability exists among the types of information gathered and published by agencies at the local, state and national levels, the reader should check with the relevant agency to see if the information described in this chapter is, in fact, available in their locality of interest. The reader will note that some sources make appearances in several sections (e.g., local school boards are mentioned both in the section on education and on demographics). Since school boards sometimes provide updated counts of neighborhood school-aged children, planners can use this information to describe general community demographics when U.S. Census data are unavailable or old.

U.S. CENSUSES OF POPULATION AND HOUSING

The most comprehensive source of data on people and their communities is the United States Census. The U.S. Census Bureau conducts three major counts: the Censuses of Population and Housing, the Economic Census and the American Community Survey.

- The Census of Population and Housing collects data every 10 years, in the years ending with a zero, on population and housing characteristics from the national to the county, city and neighborhood levels.

- The Economic Census collects data every five years on every business establishment in the U.S. (see also the section in this chapter entitled "Local Information Sources").

- The American Community Survey collects policy-relevant population and housing data on selected communities every three or five years, depending on the size of the community. When fully implemented in 2003, it is expected to provide neighborhood (or census tract) data similar to the Decennial Census. It may replace the long (sample) census form in 2010.

The Censuses of Population and Housing that are collected every 10 years gather information on a limited number of questions asked of every person and housing unit existing in the U.S. These questions make up the short form—or "100% characteristics"—since they cover 100% of all respondents. (Of course, not 100% of all people in America respond to the census.)

In addition, a more detailed set of questions is asked of a sample of people (generally one in six) and housing units. This more detailed questionnaire makes up the long form—or "sample characteristics." (See the sidebar entitled "The Censuses of Population and Housing.") Actual questions that are contained on the short- or long-form questionnaires can vary from census to census, making comparability across time challenging. For example, the 2000 census was the first that permitted people to identify

themselves as multiracial. As a result, racial data in 2000 is not entirely comparable with earlier years.

Census geography is not necessarily intuitive, as Figure 3-1 (a diagram constructed by the Census Bureau to represent census geographic entities in the year 2000) illustrates. Census geography contains confusingly similar entities such as urban areas (cities defined by total population and density of settlement) and places (cities defined as political entities).

For the local area planner, the most useful approach to understanding U.S. Census geography, beyond reading the many online guides available on the Census Bureau's Web site and from the sources listed in the annotated bibliography, is to see it from the neighborhood level on up. As Figure 3-2 (a diagram produced by the Census Bureau) shows, the smallest geographic unit for which the Census Bureau tabulates data is the *block* (lower left-hand corner of the diagram).

Blocks are generally bounded by streets or other distinguishing features and contain about 85 people—similar to the neighborhood concept in city planning. Up from the block is the *block group* (a collection of census blocks sharing identifying numerical codes and containing an average of 1,000 people). Block groups together make up *census tracts* (averaging about 4,000 people). They tend to have stable boundaries, although there is variation over time, especially in fast-growing cities.

Up from census tracts are *places* (incorporated geographic entities with concentrations of people and legally prescribed boundaries, powers and functions).

continued from page 86

- highly regarded/not highly regarded staff
- organized/unorganized director
- skilled/unskilled communicator
- culturally aware/unaware staff
- less interested third party/ stakeholder

WHAT data were collected?
- relevant/irrelevant to planning issue
- consistent/inconsistent over time

WHY were the data collected?
- ongoing monitoring/response to a crisis
- response to an internal need/fulfill an external requirement

HOW were the data collected?
- systematically/haphazardly
- random/nonrandom sample

WHEN were the data collected?
- after planning/during a crisis
- recently/in the past

Adapted from So, Frank S. and Judith Getzel, editors. *The Practice of Local Government Planning.* 2d ed. Washington, DC: International City/County Management Association, 1988, p. 475.

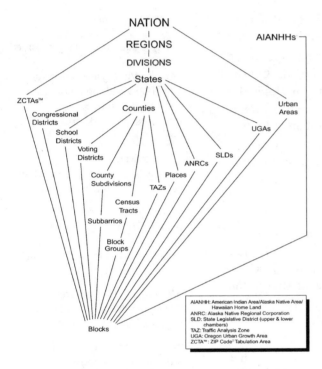

```
                NATION
                  |
                REGIONS                          AIANHHs ─┐
                  |                                        │
               DIVISIONS                                   │
                  |                                         │
                States                                      │
                                                            │
ZCTAs™                    Counties              Urban        │
                                                Areas        │
Congressional                                                │
Districts                                       UGAs         │
  School                                                     │
  Districts                                                  │
     Voting                              SLDs                │
     Districts              ANRCs                            │
       County              Places                            │
       Subdivisions    TAZs                                  │
           Census                                            │
           Tracts                                            │
   Subbarrios                                                │
         Block                                               │
         Groups                                              │
                                                             │
     Blocks ──────────────────────────────────────────────┘
```

AIANHH: American Indian Area/Alaska Native Area/
          Hawaiian Home Land
ANRC: Alaska Native Regional Corporation
SLD: State Legislative District (upper & lower
          chambers)
TAZ: Traffic Analysis Zone
UGA: Oregon Urban Growth Area
ZCTA™: ZIP Code® Tabulation Area

3-1. Standard hierarchy of census geographic entities

THE CENSUSES OF POPULATION AND HOUSING

Short-form Questions (100% characteristics) from Census 2000

- household relationship
- sex
- age
- Hispanic or Latino origin
- race
- tenure (whether home is owned or rented)
- vacancy characteristics

Long-form Questions (sample characteristics) from Census 2000

Population

- marital status
- place of birth, citizenship and year of entry
- school enrollment and educational attainment
- ancestry
- migration (residence in 1995)
- language spoken at home and ability to speak English
- veteran status
- disability
- grandparents as caregivers
- labor force status
- place of work and journey to work
- occupation, industry and class of worker
- work status in 1999
- income in 1999

Housing

- value of home or monthly rent paid
- units in structure
- year structure built
- number of rooms and number of bedrooms
- year moved into residence
- plumbing and kitchen facilities
- telephone service
- vehicles available
- heating fuel
- farm residence
- utilities, mortgage, taxes, insurance and fuel costs

These are closest to what planners and the public consider "cities." Places exist in Minor Civil Divisions or Census County Divisions (legally defined divisions of counties and often referred to as townships). The final level of local census geographies, before reaching the states, is *counties* (primary divisions of most states). See also the discussion of census geography in Chapter 4, "Analytical Methods in Planning."

Just as the questions from the long and short forms may change from census to census, geographic boundaries can also change over time. This makes drawing conclusions about the evolution of a local area tricky. However, census tracts tend to remain relatively stable; when their boundaries do change, the Census Bureau provides conversion tables that reflect these changes. The conversion tables appear at the beginning of the printed census tract volumes through 1990 and are available on the Web beginning with the 2000 census.

Census data are released in two different formats: *summary tabulations* and *microdata*. Summary tabulations are tables that present counts and basic cross-tabulations of information collected from both the 100% (short-form questions) and sample (long-form questions) population and housing characteristics. They are available in *summary files* and are numbered from 1 through 4.

Summary File 1 provides 100% data and Summary File 3 provides sample data. The tables can provide detailed information on household structure such as the number of single-mother families. There are census tract data for single years of age to 99 with

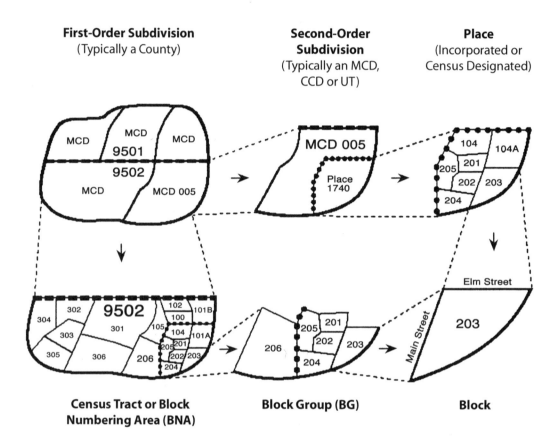

3-2. Census small-area geography

What is the best way for planners to approach the Censuses of Population and Housing?

three additional age groups over 100. You will find school enrollment, income and poverty data by race, means of transportation to work (walk, bicycle, bus and car), commuting time to work and occupation. Summary Files 2 and 4 are reiterations of 1 and 3 by detailed race (e.g., one could identify the census tracts in Washington, D. C. that have a concentration of Salvadoran households by household size in Summary File 2).

The tables constructed from these summary files are accessible through the Census Bureau's American Factfinder Web site (see the "Bibliography" for all Web site addresses) and on Compact Disk–Read-Only Memory (CD-ROM) or digital video disc (DVD). American Factfinder provides detailed data, reference maps and thematic maps to the block level for the entire nation. While the data for 1990 are limited to Summary Files 1 and 3, the 2000 data include all of the files. Maps for 2000 identify individual city block numbers and all street names. The CD-ROMs and DVDs lack maps but offer greater flexibility in tailoring the tables, extracting large numbers of geographic units and establishing tailored radii. The printed census reports prevalent through the 1990 census have been all but eliminated in 2000. However, most major public and academic libraries maintain the historic printed collection along with the current CD-ROMs or DVDs. American Factfinder can be accessed from the office, from home or at the library.

In addition to raw and summarized numbers conveying population and housing characteristics, the Census Bureau publishes a number of reports after each major census. Many contain potentially useful information for local planners including the *School District Data Book* and the *Census Transportation Planning Package*. The Equal Employment Opportunity Special File issued after the 1990 census provided employment data by race and sex in 514 occupations for all places of 50,000 or more, as well as educational attainment by age, race and sex.

The second format for census data is the Public Use Microdata Samples (PUMS). These files are the actual responses to census questionnaires, with the names and addresses removed and the geography sufficiently broad to protect confidentiality. Since PUMS bear close resemblance to the raw data gleaned from the long-form (sample) questionnaires, they allow a user to make their own custom tabulations and cross-tabulations, not relying solely on the tables constructed by the Census Bureau.

PUMS data are available through CD-ROM and on the Census Bureau's Web site via the American Factfinder. Historic PUMS data through 1990 are available via free registration from the University of Minnesota's IPUMS/USA project and from the Public Data Queries (see the "Bibliography"). In order to protect confidentiality, the data are only available for geographic areas of 100,000 people or more.

What is the best way for planners to approach the Censuses of Population and Housing? The Census 2000 Gateway is an excellent starting point for copies of the questionnaires, brief facts, publication schedules, and explanations of the subject and geographic concepts. It features downloadable PowerPoint slides that highlight census results as well as technical information.

When you need pre-1990 data or a live person, start a census data search with assistance from a research librarian at a university library or State Data Center (SDC). The SDC Program was developed by the Census Bureau to assist local governments and the public in using census materials. A complete list of the centers and their local affiliates, including university libraries and local planning agencies, is available on the Census Bureau Web site. Trained specifically to assist in querying the census, these professionals provide the type of advice rarely available on line or through written materials.

Let's say a planner needs current and past population totals for a city. American Factfinder only dates back to 1990. The *1990 Census of Population and Housing CPH-2* reports have been digitized and are linked through the main 1990 census Web page. This is a set of publications that contains tables showing place populations from 1970, 1980 and 1990. Comparable publications are unavailable on the Web but exist in libraries for 1960 and earlier.

A powerful way to use census data is by linking it to a GIS mapping program, thereby producing maps that spatially analyze demographic data and not just present it in tabular form. Once a planner retrieves population data for a city over the past 30 years, he or she can link that to a computer-mapping program and visually compare it to, for example, the growth of housing in that city. Many states maintain reposi-

tories for GIS data, and these may be more comprehensive than the data available on the Census Bureau's Web site. See the "Bibliography" for a list of sources for geographic data that can be linked to mapping programs.

Two of the most useful census publications are the *County and City Data Book* and the *Statistical Abstract of the United States*. The *County and City Data Book* is published every four years. It provides current information for cities of 25,000 people or more, for all counties and for all states. While most data are based on the recent Economic and Decennial Censuses, it incorporates additional sources on building permits, birth and death rates, government finances, physicians, hospitals and crime rates. This book is the most generally useful census reference for providing basic data on most cities and is worthwhile to have on hand in the office. Recent editions of the *County and City Data Book* can also be found on the Census Bureau's Web site and at the University of Virginia.

The *Statistical Abstract of the United States*, published annually, provides social, economic and political information on the nation, states and large cities. Most useful to local planners is this publication's listing of hundreds of other sources of information, including sources with data on smaller geographic areas. The paper edition can be purchased from the Government Printing Office (GPO) or accessed in Adobe Portable Document Format (PDF) from the Census Bureau's Web site.

A powerful way to use census data is by linking it to a GIS mapping program, thereby producing maps that spatially analyze demographic data and not just present it in tabular form.

POPULATION AND DEMOGRAPHICS

Demography is defined as the statistical study of human populations, especially with reference to size and density, distribution and vital statistics. While the U.S. Census Bureau is an excellent starting point for demographic information, it cannot answer all planners' questions. The Census Bureau publishes annual population estimates for states, counties, metropolitan areas and places on its Web site. Most states provide annual or five-year counts of population based either on actual, complete counts (censuses) or on estimates of local populations in between the Decennial Censuses. The resulting publications can be found through creative searching of the Census Bureau's SDC Web site. State departments of transportation produce population counts as well. Population estimates can be subject to considerable error, however, and caution needs to be taken in evaluating the methods used in coming up with figures.

Nationally, the *Vital Statistics of the United States* (published annually by the National Center for Health Statistics until 1993) was the most comprehensive summary of demographic information such as births, deaths, marriages and divorces. The natality and mortality components have been virtually replaced by the Centers for Disease Control (CDC) on their Wonder Web site, which provides data for every state and county. Natality data can be searched by sex, weight and plurality of the birth; the education, race, age and prenatal care of the mother; and time period. Mortality data can be searched by age, race, sex, detailed cause of death and time period.

The U.S. Census and other sources of demographic information may overlook populations of interest to planners.

Local planners should be aware, however, that these data are only a compilation provided by local county health departments to their state agencies. Thus, a valuable source for local demographic information is the local county health office. The organization and access to this data for the public varies considerably from county to county. State health departments may limit access to some data to protect the confidentiality of individuals.

The U.S. Census and other sources of demographic information may overlook populations of interest to planners. It can then be useful to turn to national and community-based organizations that target special populations and their characteristics. For example, the Office of Refugee Resettlement, based in the U.S. Department of Health and Human Services, can provide local-level information on refugees from Southeast Asia, Russia, Sudan and other areas. The U.S. Bureau of Citizenship and Immigration Services (BCIS) is another national governmental agency that can provide data on immigrants.

In communities where diverse ethnic and racial groups live, or in communities where diversity has led to conflict, human relations commissions affiliated with city and country governments are sometimes formed to investigate complaints of racial injustice, and promote greater awareness and harmony among groups. These commissions often publish reports about the different demographic sectors represented in local areas.

Nonprofit groups, such as community-based neighborhood and faith-based organizations, sometimes conduct their own censuses of certain communities in order to assess social service needs. If a particular population is missed by the census, planners can creatively search for other ways to understand its characteristics.

At times, local planners need access to international demographic data. For planners working for national and international organizations, such data are essential. Sources of information on international populations include:

- the U.S. Census Bureau's International Population Data Base
- the United Nations Demographic Yearbook
- the United Nations Population Fund
- the United Nations Population Information Network
- the World Health Organization (WHO)

Most international sources only provide country-level data. However, City Population and the United Nations Demographic Yearbook display data for the world's largest cities. Earthlights illustrates population density through nighttime photographs from a National Aeronautics and Space Administration satellite. Foreign government statistical agencies often include population data for their respective regions and cities with an accompanying text in English.

What are some quick methods to estimate population size in a small local area if formal counts are unavailable? Water usage is surprisingly stable and can be a good indicator of the population of an area for which usage figures are known. Local water and sewer departments can be queried for this data.

However, it is important to make allowances for differences in water usage due to rate hikes, drought or neighborhood norms (e.g., suburbs where perfectly green lawns are enforced by peer pressure may disproportionately use more water).

Another quick method of generating a rough estimate of population size is through sales tax information for localities that collect sales taxes. Information on receipts is frequently reported by local political jurisdiction. Receipts for basic necessities such as food or clothing are generally more reliable indicators, but these commodities are often exempted from sales taxes to minimize the impact on lower income families. Again, as with water usage, it is important to recognize the limits on using this indicator to estimate population size; it is useful only to get a very rough estimate.

Local school boards usually maintain some form of a school census that provides a basis for anticipating future demands for educational facilities by determining the number of young children living in individual school districts. These can be accurate counts of children for small neighborhood areas. These data provide another way to estimate total population, keeping in mind that childless couples are ignored by this method.

Numerous private for-profit and nonprofit agencies also provide international, national, state and local demographic data. These include the Population Reference Bureau, the Social Science Research Council, the Metropolitan Life Insurance Company, other major life insurance companies, and a number

HOUSING INFORMATION FOR POLITICAL CONTEXTS

Assistant Planner is puzzling over how to respond to a flood of e-mails received at the Office of Planning and Community Development, all protesting a local nonprofit group's proposal to build a transitional shelter for homeless women in a Middlesville neighborhood. An effort is apparently underway in the neighborhood to block the shelter.

What is the best way to balance the fears of the neighbors against the needs of the homeless? Where can Assistant Planner turn to find information that will clarify the direction the city should take? Complicating the issue is the fact that the mayor wants a quick resolution before the campaign for re-election begins.

Uncertain where to start, Assistant Planner conducts an Internet search using the key words "conflict resolution" and "homeless." He is directed to www.bettercommunities.org and discovers a link for a private consulting company in Middlesville with experience in mediating community disputes.

After an initial meeting with the consultant, the planning director agrees to hire the mediator. In the meantime,

continued on page 95

of private publishing companies such as R. L. Polk, Rand McNally, the F. W. Dodge Division of the McGraw-Hill Publishing Company and Claritas. Many have extensive online information available.

HOUSING AND CONSTRUCTION

In addition to the Decennial Censuses of Population and Housing, the Census Bureau's American Housing Survey offers a major source of information on housing characteristics published for 47 of the larger metropolitan areas on a rotating, four-year basis. It is conducted for the Census Bureau by the U.S. Department of Housing and Urban Development (HUD). The survey includes traditional census variables (such as the year the unit was built), tenure (whether the unit is owner- or renter-occupied), vacancy and equipment. However, it adds information about the building height and condition, building and lot size, neighborhood quality and why residents moved there.

The American Community Survey, available through American Factfinder, documents housing units and tenure between the censuses for smaller geographic areas. The Census Bureau tracks new residential building permits by county, as well as the value of new construction and household repairs at larger geographic levels in its Construction Reports series. HUD provides maps on the Internet that display public housing projects, community development projects, hazardous waste sites, brown fields, incentive areas, census tracts and recreational areas.

The maps can be searched by state, zip code and street address.

Many communities participate in HUD's Consolidated Plan for affordable housing. Many of the previous executive summaries are archived on HUD's Web site. Other useful HUD publications include its *Annual Report* and monthly *Housing Statistics* report. The U.S. Bureau of Labor Statistics occasionally publishes bulletins and reports on new housing starts, cost of housing and trends in building permit activity.

Nonprofit organizations at various geographic levels publish reports on housing issues in the U.S. and across the globe. Information relevant to planners can be found in reports from the United Nations Human Settlements Programme (UN-HABITAT), the global trade association called The International Union for Housing Finance, the Social Science Research Council, the Urban League, the Ford Foundation and the National Association of Home Builders. The National Housing Institute (a nonprofit organization addressing U.S. affordable housing and community development issues) publishes *Shelter-Force, The Journal of Affordable Housing and Community Building* (also available on line).

Private sector firms provide information on the costs and volume of construction. These include the F. W. Dodge division of the McGraw Hill Publishing Company, which publishes the monthly *Dodge Construction Contract Statistics* and the weekly *Engineering News-Record* by the same publisher.

Finally, cities' comprehensive plans usually contain housing needs assessments—a good starting point for planners interested in finding data on their communities' housing situations. In states that have metropolitan area governments, Regional Housing Needs Assessments (RHNAs) are another valuable source of information for planners. RHNAs include data on community affordable housing requirements, and a variety of demographic and economic indicators and projections used to assess regional housing needs.

ECONOMICS

In addition to the residence-based employment data available from the Decennial Censuses of Population and Housing, planners can find workplace-based employment data from the Census Bureau's Economic Census. The Economic Census presents a detailed portrait of the nation's economy from the national to the local level, every five years. Reports from this census are published industry by industry and area by area, and cover nearly all sectors of the U.S. economy.

Economic sectors are classified into like groups. In 1997, the Census Bureau replaced the Standard Industrial Classification with the North American Industry Classification System. Although the Census Bureau published bridge tables between the two systems at a national level, it is difficult to create a time series incorporating both systems at the local level. Data are available through American Factfinder and separately in PDF reports on the Census Bureau's Web site.

The Census Bureau also publishes more current data on establishments and employment by detailed industry for the nation, states, counties, metropolitan areas and larger cities in its annual report, *County Business Patterns*. The Census Bureau's *County and City Data Book* contains economic data for counties and cities along with population data.

The federal government's Bureau of Labor Statistics is a good source for current and historic information on the American employment scene. Its Local Area Unemployment Statistics allows users to extract monthly employment and unemployment data for states, metropolitan areas and cities over 25,000 since 1992. Salary data by detailed industry is accessible through its State and County Employment and Wages, while wages by detailed occupation are listed for states and metropolitan areas in Wages by Area and Occupation.

The Bureau of Economic Analysis (BEA), part of the U.S. Department of Commerce, publishes Bureau of Economic Analysis Regional Facts (BEARFACTS). These are narratives describing current and projected personal income statistics for states, counties and metropolitan statistical areas. It also maintains the Regional Economic Information System (REIS) database, which provides local area economic data back to the year 1969—a good source for trend analysis. These data are issued on CD-ROM but are also available through the BEA Web site and through the University of Virginia.

continued from page 94

she asks Assistant Planner to gather information relevant to the case. Not sure where to begin, the planning director suggests that he first gather information that addresses the community's fears.

Example

- Neighbors express the fear that the transitional shelter will increase criminal activities in their community.

Information in Response

- Locate list of transitional shelters for homeless women across the state by contacting the state's Department of Social Services.
- Get crime data for the neighborhoods from local police departments where these shelters exist.
- Search the nonprofit National Housing Institute's journal, *ShelterForce*, for articles from communities that have successfully sited transitional shelters for ideas on how they addressed community opposition.

This secondary source information, along with the professional assistance of the mediator, provides Assistant Planner with a swift entry into a politically volatile planning challenge.

ECONOMIC INFORMATION FOR POLITICAL CONTEXTS

Another planning controversy crosses Assistant Planner's desk: neighbors are up in arms over the congregation of day laborers near the parking lot of a home improvement shopping center. Largely male and Latino, these informal sector workers await short-term employment opportunities from construction contractors. Neighbors complain that they loiter aimlessly, causing overcrowded sidewalks and blocking entrances to nearby businesses. A thinly veiled subtext in their complaints is the suspicion that the day laborers are, or might become, involved in criminal activities.

Assistant Planner has been asked to write a brief background report for the planning director on the day laborers, focusing on who they are, the work they seek, community concerns and possible solutions. He will need to do primary research, but first he scours secondary source materials in order to better understand the phenomenon.

Assistant Planner's first stop are two venerable government sources of employment data--the Census Bureau's Economic Census and the Bureau of Labor Statistic's Wages by Area and Occupation. He tries to use these sources to discover the extent of day

continued on page 97

The Consumer Price Index (CPI) measures the rate of change in the cost of living for the U.S., regions and 26 metropolitan areas. The "market basket" that comprises the base for measurement includes food products, gasoline, health care, housing costs and utilities. Both the index and average price data are available for local areas since 1992 on the U.S. Bureau of Labor Statistics' Web site.

The American Chamber of Commerce Researchers' Association publishes a quarterly Cost of Living Index, which provides selected price data and comparative living costs for over 300 cities. Several real estate firms offer free Web sites with comparative living costs, including Yahoo Real Estate, HomeFair and Virtual Relocation.

In order to obtain a clearer picture of current economic conditions and possible future conditions, it is important to supplement these reports with statistics gathered at the local level. State departments of economic development provide useful information on local economies. For example, some states have the Labor Market Information Division within their Employment Development Departments. This organization collects data on employment by industry, occupational staffing patterns by industry and industry and occupational projections.

Other national organizations that publish information on local economies include the Urban Institute, the Real Estate Research Corporation, the Urban Land Institute and HUD. Regional organizations, such as economic development districts and councils of government, also collect data and write analyses

on local economic issues. Academic and public policy institutes that conduct research on economic development planning, such as the Council for Urban Economic Development, are also valuable sources for local economic information.

Sales tax receipts, collected at different levels of local government, can give a planner a rough picture of the economic condition of a local population, including its purchasing power. The business firm, Sales and Marketing Management, issues an annual *Survey of Buying Power and Media Markets*, which gives effective buying income and retail sales by type of business for states, metropolitan areas, counties and cities.

Local advertisements in Web directories and the Yellow Pages, while covering only a portion of local businesses, are a good place to start in assessing the type of retail and other economic activities underway in a local area. Social service providers, both governmental and private, can give valuable details about how a locality's population is doing economically. Perusing local want ads can give a planner an impression of what types of jobs appear to be in demand.

Local chambers of commerce are good sources for data on the number, types and health of area businesses. Economic development districts and other agencies, whose missions include revitalizing the business opportunities in local areas, often contain useful data on economic indicators. Finally, when looking for indications of local economic health, planners should not overlook contacts in the private sector, and in areas such as housing construction, retail development and tourism.

TRANSPORTATION

State departments of transportation are a good place to start in seeking transportation data. The Association of State Highway and Transportation Officials identifies the Web sites of its members. States submit regional transportation plans built from data at the local level, which provide good secondary source material for planners. Many local communities are part of Regional Transit Districts (RTDs) that plan for the mass transit and disabled transit needs of a regional area. These RTDs are also good sources of information on local transportation data.

At the national level, the FHA publishes national and state data on road miles and vehicle miles traveled, as well as state and local highway finance. The Fatality Analysis Reporting System allows users to extract data on highway fatalities by a combination of data on the vehicle, person, type of crash, road conditions and time of death for states, counties and places. The Bureau of Transportation Statistics annually publishes National Transportation Statistics, a compendium of U.S. data on types of roads, age of urban transit vehicles, new car sales, airport delays and railroad crossing fatalities.

Traffic flow data on the volume of commodities shipped are collected from a sample of industries during the Economic Census and released as state-level reports in the Census Bureau's Commodity Flow Survey. The data are organized by means of transport, size, origin and destination of shipments.

Access to safe and affordable mass transit is a growing planning concern—from isolated rural areas to mega-cities. Bus riders' unions and other non-profit advocacy groups can provide background information on the mass transit challenges in planners' communities.

HEALTH AND WELFARE

A broad range of agencies within the U.S. Department of Health and Human Services provides information on the well being of the U.S. population. The CDC issues guidance on handling public health emergencies. It also provides surveillance statistics on contagious diseases (e.g., Human Immunodeficiency Virus (HIV) and tuberculosis) for various levels of geography.

The National Center for Health Statistics is the primary publisher of health data in the U.S. Among its programs are the National Health Interview Survey, the National Health Care Survey the National Health and Nutrition Examination Survey, and the National Immunization Survey. Its Data Warehouse provides tabulated and microdata at the national and state levels on natality, morbidity and mortality, as well as state health targets.

The Administration for Children and Families publishes national data on adoption, child abuse and recipients of the Temporary Assistance to Needy Families.

continued from page 96

laboring as an employment niche in Middlesville and its wage range. However, he quickly realizes that these data sources are not useful since they do not track informal economy sector employment—jobs and wages for those who are often paid under the table.

Assistant Planner discovers that the Coalition for Humane Immigrant Rights in Los Angeles (CHIRLA) has conducted a number of studies about day laborers in the Los Angeles area. CHIRLA's findings are useful as a starting point for Assistant Planner.

He realizes he can partially explain the rise of day laboring in Middlesville by showing a concurrent rise in the construction trades and housing starts—data he obtains from *Dodge Construction Contract Statistics*, the Census Bureau's Economic Census and a local private developer.

Using the Web site www.grass-roots.org, Assistant Planner approaches a Middlesville nonprofit group advocating for immigrant worker rights about collaborating on a survey of the day laborer population. A library search of academic journals reveals that many cities with day laborers have devised one-stop community centers where they can look for work and receive job training. His background report is well on its way.

Formerly known as Health Care Financing Administration (HCFA), the Centers for Medicare and Medicaid Services issue state- and county-level data on Medicare enrollment, some state data on Medicaid eligibility and performance plans for the State Children's Health Insurance Program. The federal government's official Medicare Web site allows users to identify and compare local nursing home and dialysis facilities.

Summary File 3 (sample data) from the Decennial Census identifies persons with sensory, physical, mental, self-care, go-outside-home and employment disabilities as well as public assistance income to the block and group levels.

State health and social service agencies often provide state and county data on natality, mortality, marriage, divorce and public assistance. The agencies can be identified by subject in the StateSearch Web site.

County health offices are good sources for planners interested in health and welfare in their local areas. As discussed in the section entitled "Economics," local governmental and nongovernmental social service agencies can provide rich front-line data on the health and welfare of a city's population.

The Agency for Healthcare Research and Quality offers training and workshops for local planners.

International sources for health data include the WHO and the International Red Cross. Additional useful sources may be found in the *Annual Report of the American National Red Cross* and the *Annual Directory of the United Community Funds and Councils of*

America. Directories, journals and annual reports of many other concerned groups, such as the National Association of Social Workers and the Public Welfare Association, may also be useful sources of information, although not usually for local areas.

The American Hospital Directory provides free access to summary data on individual hospitals with more detailed information available for a charge. The Joint Commission on Accreditation of Healthcare Organizations provides a searchable directory of accreditation reports for hospitals, nursing homes and behavioral care facilities. Private firms, such as Solucient, as well as *U.S. News and World Report*, rate the top hospitals by the type of care given.

HealthWeb is a searchable database of the best Web sites on medical topics and health care administration. PubMed indexes and abstracts journal articles on medical and health administration issues. The National Library of Medicine makes it available free of charge to the public.

EDUCATION

The U.S. Department of Education sponsors and publishes extensive research on preschool through post-graduate education. The ERIC Database is a freely accessible index to both reports and journal articles since 1966. The National Center for Education Statistics (NCES) issues numerous compendiums of federal- and state-level statistics on schools, school staffing, educational finance and outcomes of education. NCES also conducts numerous surveys, including the National Assessment of Educational

The American Hospital Directory provides free access to summary data on individual hospitals with more detailed information available for a charge.

Progress, Schools and Staffing Survey, Household Education Survey and the Common Core of Data. By-products of the Common Core are the Public School, Public School District and Private School Locators. Each directory is searchable by name, geography and available grades. Available data include pupil-teacher ratios, percentages of pupils eligible for a free or reduced lunch and enrollment by race.

State departments of education may be a better source of information for test scores and educational finance at the school district or school level. For example, the *Michigan Schools Report* publishes test results for statewide-administered tests by individual school buildings.

Local school districts can provide interesting information to planners on more than enrollment figures and test scores. Schools are important community institutions and their students reflect the population living in a neighborhood. Sometimes the first indication of how a neighborhood may be undergoing change in its racial and ethnic makeup comes from a change in the student population. Teachers and school administrators may have their fingers on the economic and public health pulses of their communities. In short, local school districts can provide information on the schools as well as on the communities these schools serve.

The R. R. Bowker Company, the Council of State Governments and the National Catholic Welfare Conference publish other sources of information. For international data, the primary source is the United Nations Educational, Scientific and Cultural Organization.

ENVIRONMENT, NATURAL RESOURCES AND RECREATION

The U.S. Environmental Protection Agency (EPA) issues extensive research reports on environmental management, air quality, ecosystems, pollutants, toxic wastes, watersheds and water treatment. Some are available directly from the main EPA Web page; others are indexed through the *EPA Online Library System*, EPA Publications Search and *National Environmental Publications Internet Site*.

The EPA provides a useful *National Hydrography Dataset* for natural resource planners on its Web site. Envirofacts features several databases. The *Toxic Release Inventory* is a searchable directory of individual business establishments by type of pollutant. There are similar databases on hazardous wastes and Superfund cleanup sites. The Enviromapper permits users to create their own maps displaying watersheds and various polluting facilities.

The Bureau of National Affairs publishes the *Environmental Reporter* that contains the section "Current Developments" (a weekly review of pollution control and related environmental management problems). Current environmental issues, legislation and related topics can be found in *Environmental Quality* (the annual report of the Council on Environmental Quality) and the *Environmental Planning Quarterly* (a publication of the Environmental Division of the APA).

Schools are important community institutions and their students reflect the population living in a neighborhood.

The United Nations Environmental Programme is the leading international organization concerned with the protection of the environment.

The National Climatic Data Center issues daily weather information on its Web site. Its most detailed product, Local Climatological Data, provides daily temperature and precipitation data for individual weather stations. It requires a password, which should be available at many federal depository libraries. The EPA's Global Warming section projects the effects of global warming on areas within each state, and lists federal and state grants to combat it.

The United States Geological Survey (USGS) publishes topographic maps for every quadrangle in the nation. The printed maps are available at many federal depository libraries and can be purchased through the vendors listed on the USGS Web site. Themes in its *National Atlas of the United States* range from butterfly cover, to volcanoes, to cases of the West Nile virus. The main site links to numerous other mapping products and fact sheets on minerals, earthquakes and water supplies.

Various agencies within the Department of Energy issue annual reports on nuclear energy sources and activities, electrical energy generation, natural gas production and consumption and on a number of other energy resources. The Tennessee Valley Authority, the American Gas Association, the Edison Electric Institute, the National Coal Association and the National LP-Gas Association provide similar reports by private and semipublic agencies.

Information on public lands and park resources can be found in publications issued by the Bureau of Land Management, the Department of Agriculture, the Department of Interior and the National Park Service. A number of city governments and regional governing bodies will have on file EISs on certain proposed developments. These can provide a wealth of background data for planners interested in the local environmental issues they cover.

The 1997 Census of Agriculture was the first census conducted by the U.S. Department of Agriculture and National Agriculture Statistical Services (NASS)—instead of the Census Bureau—and is available on the NASS Web site.

Nongovernmental environmental advocacy organizations, such as the Sierra Club and the World Wildlife Fund, also publish reports, some of which concern local-level issues.

Information on recreation and leisure activities and facilities may be found in publications such as the *Recreation and Park Yearbook* of the National Recreation and Park Association and the *Monthly Public Use of National Parks* by the National Park Service. Many states have offices of outdoor recreation with Web sites that carry recreation data and reports. Some allow users to order a state park pass, renew a license or reserve an overnight camper space. The National Recreation and Park Association carries a number of publications that can be ordered from their Web site, including guides to designing and managing parks and creating parks in high-risk neighborhoods.

The United Nations Environmental Programme is the leading international organization concerned with the protection of the environment. Its *Global Environmental Outlook* relates environmental problems to social, demographic and economic factors, and describes environmental initiatives in various regions of the world. The World Resources Institute publishes national-level data on endangered species, water and pollution, and some city-level data on pollution and waste management. United Nations Sustainable Development provides country-level statistics and policies on natural resources, pollution, social indicators, economics and decision-making procedures.

CRIME

Planners seeking information on this crucial quality-of-life indicator have a variety of international, national, state and local sources to investigate. The United Nations is the principal source of comparative crime and justice statistics internationally through its Office of Drug Control and Crime Prevention (UN ODCCP). Its primary report is known as the *World Crime Survey,* a country-level look at types of crime and policing. Within the UN ODCCP, Internet-based international crime data are maintained by the United Nations Crime and Justice Information Network. This site links the user to both national and comparative data collections, summary reports and annual surveys.

Other sources for international data on crime include the INTERPOL, which publishes crime statistics annually for member countries in its *International Crime Statistics,* and the World Justice Information Network, which provides an Internet-based system for sharing crime data across countries.

Official country Web sites maintained by national governments also provide good starting points when tracking down crime statistics.

In the U.S., five agencies within the Department of Justice collect and publish data on crime. The FBI compiles the *Uniform Crime Reports* from local government data. Its hallmark publication, *Crime in the United States,* details types of crime for places of 10,000 or more. Its *Sourcebook of Criminal Justice Statistics* is available for purchase in paper and is free on the Internet from the State University of New York at Albany. The *National Crime Victimization Survey* monitors trends in types of crimes perpetrated on types of victims. The Bureau of Justice Statistics, in cooperation with the Inter-University Consortium for Political and Social Research, also sponsors the *National Archive of Criminal Justice Data.* Microdata on crime, victimization and corrections from the county to the international level can either be downloaded for manipulation with statistical software packages, such as SAS or SPSS, or manipulated on line using the Data Analysis System.

The Drug Enforcement Administration conducts multipronged initiatives to reduce drug demand and intercept drug dealers. The Department of Homeland Security operates the U.S. Border Patrol and prosecutes or removes those who overstay their visas. The Federal Bureau of Prisons issues a directory of all its own facilities.

The National Crime Justice Reference Service (NCJRS) publishes numerous reports analyzing crime data and control. The full text of many of its

In the U.S., five agencies within the Department of Justice collect and publish data on crime.

publications is searchable from the main Web site. The NCJRS also publishes an Abstracts Database of reports and journals, which can be purchased once they are identified.

The Bureau of Alcohol, Tobacco and Firearms enforces regulations and provides statewide guidance in handling criminal activities. HUD maintains a State of the Cities Data System that provides information on a variety of quality-of-life issues, including annual FBI crime data for cities and suburbs.

Local crime data are reported to the FBI via the Uniform Crime Reporting Program. This information is gathered from individual police agencies including police and sheriffs' departments and specialized policing units, including campus and transit police. Local police departments may also have unpublished, neighborhood-level crime statistics on a weekly basis and are often willing to provide this information to interested citizens.

Private firms also conduct analyses of local areas based on crime data. Various commercial Web sites exist that allow users to type in their home zip code and see quality-of-life information, including rankings based on public safety and crime.

Hate crimes motivated by race, gender, sexual orientation, immigrant status and other characteristics are of particular concern to local governments, especially as communities become more diverse. Both governmental and nongovernmental organizations track and report hate crimes. The FBI's Hate Crime Statistics provides national, state and local data by motivation. The United Nations is a good source

internationally, and state departments of civil rights provide good state-level data.

At the local level, county and city human relations commissions, many of which were established to quell unrest between racial groups in the 1960s, continue to promote harmony in diverse communities. They are also a good source for local data on hate crimes. Many nongovernmental groups gather and analyze hate-crime data, including the Southern Christian Leadership Conference, the Asian Pacific American Legal Center and the Anti-Defamation League.

GOVERNMENTAL ACTIVITIES

The first source for information about local, county and regional governments is the government itself, and your local telephone book is the best tool. Some local governments have Internet sites, but they may publish selectively and often remove the older editions of a report when a newer edition is issued. A better route may be to visit the city or county clerk's office where printed versions of reports are available. The second step for a planner is the community library, which frequently archives publications of the municipality. The third step is the local newspaper, which carries articles about community problems and politics.

You can assume that other localities have faced planning issues similar to yours. The International City/County Management Association (ICMA) publishes the *Municipal Yearbook*, a printed directory of the officials in cities over 2,500. The ICMA, the U.S.

Conference of Mayors, the National League of Cities, the National Center for Small Communities and the National Association for Counties publish special studies on local government planning issues.

The National Association of Regional Councils links to regional planning councils in each state. Many of those councils have Web sites with data and program guidance on the planning process. Although there are many Web directories that list travel or real estate Web sites for a given city, the best list for municipal governments appears under the name of the state in Piper's State and Local Government on the Net. Some large universities subscribe to the *Index to Current Urban Documents*, which indexes the publications of large cities, counties and regional governments by geography and subject.

Book of the States, issued biennially in paper copy by the Council of State Governments, compares states on current legislative issues, government powers, election procedures, tax rates and a surprising number of useful facts. The National Governors' Association publishes numerous "best practices" guides on subjects ranging from brown field development to welfare reform. States have developed excellent Web portals combining reports, statistics, directories and interactive e-government with their citizens. The most recognized index, arranged by state, is Piper's State and Local Government on the Net. Piper also includes national associations of government officials by area of interest. StateSearch is a subject approach to Web sites of all state agencies.

Several universities have attempted to develop regular surveys and reports on governmental activities in local and metropolitan areas, although these tend to be dependent on available financial support. Notable among these has been a series on metropolitan planning activities and studies published by the Nelson A. Rockefeller College of Public Affairs and Policy at the State University of New York in Albany.

Many states issue some form of state yearbook or manual giving information about the principal officers in state and local governments. Such sources sometimes provide election statistics from recent local, state and national elections.

At the federal level, the Census Bureau publishes extensive files on government organization, finance and employment from the federal to the local level in its quinquennial Census of Governments. It also issues a *Consolidated Federal Funds Report* that reports federal expenditures on grants, direct payments and procurement contracts by state and county. The American Council on Intergovernmental Relations is the successor to the Advisory Commission on Intergovernmental Relations, which produced numerous studies on taxation efforts and characteristics of state and local governments.

Moody's Investor Service issues an annual publication with semiweekly supplements on local and state governmental activities for potential investors in state and municipal bonds. Occasional studies of governmental activities are published by organizations such as the National Bureau of Economic Research, the University of Michigan's Survey

The National Association of Regional Councils links to regional planning councils in each state.

Research Center and the Republican and Democratic National Committees.

LAWS, LEGISLATION AND REGULATIONS

Some city and county governments publish their municipal codes on the Internet.

Some city and county governments publish their municipal codes on the Internet. Many of them are linked from the Municipal Code Corporation's Web site. An alternative is locating the main city Web site through Piper's State and Local Government on the Net. The city government offices and the local public library are the obvious next steps. City council minutes may be available on the city Web site or from the clerk or council's offices.

Most state governments provide a portion of their legislative bills, laws and regulations on the Web free of charge, but there are surprising gaps. One of the best ways to identify them is the Washburn University Law School's Web site, which lists state legislatures, laws, regulations and court decisions. Large universities may also have access to *State Capital Universe*, a database that indexes laws across states as well as within them. A companion source, *Academic Universe*, also contains federal and state court decisions as well as laws within states.

There are numerous commercial sources for identifying federal legislation, but some of the best are free public sources. *THOMAS* indexes federal bills since 1973 and provides bill status, with the full text from 1989. It also indexes the full text of the *Congressional Record* (floor debates) since 1989. Congressional committee hearings are transcripts of testimony by experts and lobbyists on proposed legislation or oversight of existing programs.

Many federal depository libraries have the full text in paper or microfiche. Some are available on the Internet, but the coverage is irregular. *The Legislative Source Book* by the Law Librarians' Society of Washington, D.C. is the most comprehensive source for identifying what is freely available on the Internet.

GPO Access is the best source for new laws (public laws), laws-in-force (U.S. Code), proposed regulations (Federal Register) and regulations in force (Code of Federal Regulations). While a commercial source, *Academic Universe*, is the most comprehensive source for U.S. decisions, the U.S. Courts Web site directs users to individual Web sites with the most current opinions.

FEDERAL INFORMATION SOURCES

Approximately 60% of all federal government publications are available on the Internet free of charge. The FirstGov Web site is the official gateway, but many people prefer Google's UncleSam for indexing purposes and the Louisiana State University locator for an agency approach. Your most important resource could be your local government documents librarian, who can guide you through "too much information"; supply alternative paper, CD-ROM and microfiche reports; and interpret many of the nuances. GPO Access provides a searchable directory of federal depository libraries on its Web site.

STATE INFORMATION SOURCES

In approaching a search for sources of state information, the first step is a check of the state's Web site using Piper's State and Local Government on the Net or StateSearch. Considerable variability exists among the types of information gathered and published by state agencies. Many states have agencies that roughly correspond to national agencies and collect similar information from smaller geographic areas of special interest to planners. Changes of administration at the state and national levels often result in the reorganization of agencies. It may take some hunting to find which office contains which sets of data.

Most states issue some form of annual agricultural statistics, which might include information on forests, fisheries and wildlife, depending on whether such activities are located with a department of agriculture or in some broader agency like a department of natural resources. Similarly, information on minerals, mines, natural gas and oil is usually available, but may be published by either a department of natural resources, a state department of energy or a department of mines.

Most states have some kind of department of education, which issues annual statistics in categories such as public education, school enrollments, state aid to education by local jurisdictions, teachers and salaries. In some states, these departments also issue annual reports on college and university activities.

A department of labor, possibly in conjunction with a department dealing with employment services, usually issues monthly and annual reports, and projections on labor force characteristics and employment levels, for local areas and specific industrial groups. A state highway department or department of transportation usually issues monthly and annual statistics on categories such as travel characteristics, gasoline sales, miles of highways built and maintained, condition and traffic of railroads, volume of traffic in airports and local population projections.

A state department of social services or welfare provides annual reports on numbers and economic conditions of the population, together with information about the kinds and levels of public assistance provided. State health departments provide information on births, deaths, diseases, marriages and divorces, and sometimes on levels of hospitalization and mental health levels and treatments. Frequently, the state health department is one source of current population estimates and population projections for the state and localities within the state. Similar agencies often provide data on numbers of doctors, nurses and other health professionals practicing in local areas within the state.

Information on vehicle registration, traffic accidents and drivers' licenses are usually provided in reports by either the department of state or possibly the state police department. Information on state and local government organization and financial levels is usually maintained and published by a state-level department of state or by a bureau or agency involved in municipal assistance, planning

In approaching a search for sources of state information, the first step is a check of the state's Web site using Piper's State and Local Government on the Net or StateSearch.

coordination or similar type of information and advisory activities. A state housing authority may provide information on housing stock, condition and new construction.

LOCAL
INFORMATION SOURCES

Each locality keeps records for both private and public purposes. While many of these records are technically open to the public, in practice they may be inaccessible because of the way in which they are kept and stored. While it is the norm to keep information on computer files, it can be a challenge to retrieve such files unless the event concerned is fairly recent or significant. This is a case where contacting a local public employee who has a long institutional memory is particularly valuable.

Some cities keep current and historical data in an organized and easily accessible fashion, but not all. Even with the ubiquitous use of computers, ledger books, 3 × 5 cards and old cartons filled with file folders in dusty corners may contain information not yet entered into a computer system.

Although information kept by local business firms may be better maintained, it is often more difficult to obtain due to the concern of protecting company secrets as well as preserving customers' privacy. Careful approaches, plus clear and unimpeachable guarantees of anonymity of individual records, are usually necessary before such information will be made available. A number of sources of local information might provide useful for planning purposes:

Some cities keep current and historical data in an organized and easily accessible fashion, but not all.

- *Tax and assessment records in local governmental offices:* These usually provide data on ownership, size and type of building; property uses; assessed value; condition; recent improvements or additions; a record of recent sales; and sometimes photographs of the property in question.

- *Building inspectors' records:* These are usually combined with tax and assessment records but may be more current, giving the characteristics and cost of recent improvements, results of any recent inspections, and possibly current information on occupancy characteristics of buildings.

- *Local real estate board:* These agencies usually maintain extensive files on properties recently put up for sale. Occasionally, the records are maintained over many years, providing a handy historical source of sales information as well as detailed descriptions of most of the locality's buildings and properties. A county or township plat book—especially useful when working in rural areas—is often published at low cost by such organizations to assist in real estate sales. Such a book, taken from public ownership and plat records, provides detailed maps and descriptions of the ownership of larger land segments throughout the local county or township.

- *Police or sheriff's office:* Such offices usually maintain elaborate records of complaints and crimes by place of occurrence, residence of the offender and type of crime. These records are sometimes difficult to gain access to because of practices protecting the individual's privacy. However, a cooperative arrangement to obtain such information for small geographic areas may be possible with some careful preparation.

Information in these records may provide useful indexes of problem areas in the city within which some kinds of planning activity may be more or less appropriate. For example, a concentration of residence of offenders in one area and occurrences of the same offenses in a different area may reveal a commuting pattern of local offenders that should be taken into consideration by both local law enforcement and local planning agencies.

- *Fire departments and fire insurance records:* Considerable information is usually maintained by most fire departments about the size, layout and condition of many buildings, especially larger commercial and residential structures. These data are often recent due to periodic fire inspections, and may prove valuable in preparing preliminary surveys and evaluations of certain sections of the city. However, many fire departments are hesitant to release such information to others since disclosure might make future inspections and cooperation much more difficult.

Fire insurance reports and ratings often reflect a combination of information on building condition and use with availability and quality of fire prevention and fire-fighting equipment. Combined with other, more detailed information on land use, such data might provide a useful, evaluative device for areas of the city or a relatively independent cross-check of the quality of other information.

- *Water and sewer departments:* Often combined in a single department, these agencies have records of the number of meters installed and volume of water consumed by individual house or address by month or quarter. While obtaining such information for individual households or businesses is unlikely, arrangements could probably be made to obtain aggregate data on water usage by district or neighborhood of the city. Since such aggregated data are of limited utility to most water and sewer departments, the planner must expect to pay for or provide most of the effort required to obtain the information.

Water usage is surprisingly stable and can give a good indication of the population of an area for which usage figures are known (as mentioned in the section entitled "Population and Demographics"). However, differences in social values and lifestyles are reflected in practices of watering lawns and gardens or in washing cars. Such variations produce significant seasonal differences in consumption patterns in various parts of the city related to social class and must be taken into account in making population estimates.

Water usage is surprisingly stable and can give a good indication of the population of an area for which usage figures are known . . .

In states and localities that collect sales taxes, information on receipts is frequently reported by local political jurisdiction.

- *Electricity and gas companies:* These companies are often privately owned and operated. Although they have information on the number of meters installed, and usage rates for individual households and other buildings, most companies are reluctant to release information to other companies or public agencies.

  A carefully prepared approach is warranted, with guarantees of nondisclosure of information on individual houses or units. Providing the background work for tabulating their data in larger geographic areas will almost certainly be necessary. As with water usage, consumption of electricity and gas is a relatively constant ratio to number of persons or types of activity, but seasonal and socioeconomic variations must be controlled.

- *Sales tax receipts:* In states and localities that collect sales taxes, information on receipts is frequently reported by local political jurisdiction. Total receipts, as well as receipts for individual types of commodities, may be a useful indicator of total population size as well as the economic condition of the population (as discussed in the sections entitled "Population and Demographics" and "Economics"). Receipts for basic necessities such as food or clothing are generally more reliable indicators, but these commodities are often exempted from sales taxes to minimize the impact on lower income families.

  When using sales taxes as an indicator of changes over time, pay particular attention to both the effects of inflation on increasing the volume of receipts as well as to changes in the tax laws regarding what kinds of commodities are to be taxed and the tax rate.

- *County health office:* The local county health office is the principal data-collection and referral agency for almost all information about births, deaths, diseases, accidents and a variety of other vital statistics, which are ultimately reported by state and federal agencies. Some assistance in handling the basic records of the health office could establish the basis for a useful, long-term, cooperative arrangement between local planning and health offices that share a number of interests and problems.

- *County extension programs and the soil conservation service:* Although these agencies focus primarily on rural and farming issues, they share a number of interests and information needs with local planning agencies, particularly with county planning agencies. These agencies usually have detailed records of the ownership and type of crops raised of most local farms as well as detailed information on soils, slope, drainage, wildlife, farm ponds and hunting areas. Of particular interest to local planners may be their usually well-maintained supply of aerial photographs and soil surveys of local areas. Such agencies often have copies of a number of the publicly available earth satellite photos of local areas, some taken with infrared and other techniques.

- *Local school boards:* As discussed in the sections entitled "Population and Demographics" and "Education," most local school boards maintain some form of school census, often required by state law. This census provides a basis for anticipating future demands for educational facilities by determining the number of young children living in individual school districts. Conducted by teachers or members of the local Parent-Teachers Association, such censuses are often quite accurate albeit highly limited counts of local population. Adults are generally ignored except as the parents of children, and childless households tend to be dropped from the counting process quite early.

    With some advance preparation and cooperation, significant improvements in the school census operation and its utility to the local planning office are possible. School administrators are usually willing to release these data on a district-by-district basis, although individual household information is usually not released. School enrollment data can be useful to local planning offices in making population estimates and estimating local migration patterns. These data are often easily available from local school districts or boards of education.

- *Automobile registration and drivers' licenses:* State offices usually maintain these records, but information for local areas can often be obtained. Both registration statistics and the number of drivers' licenses issued provide information about the numbers of local drivers, as well as age and sex information and some data on types of automobile ownership. The cooperation of state agencies in providing such data to local offices is problematic.

- *Local advertisements and want ads:* Commercial advertisements in newspapers and the Yellow Pages of local telephone directories are frequently overlooked as a source of information. Although obviously biased toward only those establishments that choose to pay for advertisements, such information can be used to provide a relatively sensitive picture of local activities and short-term trends. Some initial calibration is needed by noting the type and volume of advertisements occurring during a period with the actual volume and type of business activity known from some other source. Calibrating during census years—particularly the economic censuses—is the obvious solution.

    Once these first benchmarks are established, short- and long-term trends can be charted in a number of areas of activity. Possibilities include housing vacancies, jobs and unemployment, rental and sales values for houses and apartments and number of doctors, dentists and nursing homes. Carefully constructed and maintained over a number of years, such indicators can prove to be useful and sensitive barometers of local activities.

- *Local social service agencies:* The number of applicants and payments to the local population for

Commercial advertisements in newspapers and the Yellow Pages of local telephone directories are frequently overlooked as a source of information.

A number of regional agencies are to be found in most localities, usually combining the data and concerns of several local governments . . .

agencies such as welfare, Aid to Families with Dependent Children, unemployment compensation and Refugee Cash Assistance can provide useful information on the state of the local economy and its short-term impact on lower income or special-needs people. These data are available in aggregate form and some prior arrangements with local offices to aggregate statistics in the appropriate form are necessary. Even without statistical information, systematic observation of the number of people in line at such agencies is a simple and sensitive indicator of short-term trends in the local economy.

- *Chambers of commerce:* These groups collect and maintain elaborate files and datasets on local businesses. Reasonable access is usually possible since the information is intended for the public. Lists of local businesses by type and estimates of local sales volumes are the kinds of data that might be found in these organizations.
- *Local newspapers, magazines and libraries:* Such organizations usually maintain extensive files and archives on local events. These often include newspaper clippings, photographs, minutes of meetings, newsletters and correspondence. Many local newspapers have online editions and some maintain archives of past issues searchable by key word. Local planning offices may have their own archives and files including copies of old plans, proposals, and working documents on zoning hearings and subdivision reviews.

- *Economic development districts, councils of government and similar agencies:* A number of regional agencies are to be found in most localities, usually combining the data and concerns of several local governments, and relying heavily on federal sponsorship to establish and maintain their local legitimacy. The utility and the existence of such agencies fluctuate tremendously from region to region, as well as with whoever is in control of the national presidency and Congress.

However, one or more such agencies are often found locally and can provide additional sources of information for local planning officials. Frequently, such data are merely compilations collected from more localized authorities; sometimes they are reported more clearly and consistently than the same data maintained by local offices from which they originated. These regional agencies also tend to provide a ready basis for comparing local performance of a number of communities at once. They may also have better and more consistent access to state and federal data sources than the local office or library can provide. Becoming familiar with their files and library services is worthwhile as a potential adjunct to information maintained in local planning offices.

CONCLUSION

The information provided in this chapter only begins to scratch the surface of the kinds of data sources available to knowledgeable and imaginative local planners. A few hours in the library, on the Internet and on the phone can save weeks of effort and thousands of dollars once a planner knows where to find high-quality data. A strategy that uses both primary and secondary sources, carefully targeted to resolve a specific planning problem, will help a planner assemble background information. The next step is to analyze and then present this information using techniques described in the remaining chapters of this book.

APPLICATIONS

1. Choose a neighborhood in your city and determine the census tract (or tracts) within which it lies. Compile basic demographic statistics on this neighborhood (total population by age, sex and race) for the latest decennial census and compare that to the previous census statistics for this neighborhood. How have things changed in this area? What might be the planning implications of these demographic changes?

2. Create a fact sheet on environmental quality issues in your community. Visit the EPA Web site to see if there are national Superfund sites, air quality issues and other hazards in your city. Using a mapping program, map these hazards and compare their concentrations to demographic data on race, income and school-aged populations.

3. Visit the local chamber of commerce and determine what information it can provide on the number, type and size of local businesses over the last five years. What does this information begin to reveal about your local economy?

4. Obtain information from the local human relations commission (city, county or state) on hate crime incidents in your city over the past year. Map the incidents and see which neighborhoods have experienced the most or the worst type of conflicts.

BIBLIOGRAPHY

General Guides to Secondary Sources for Planners

American Planning Association (APA)
(www.planning.org)

APA provides guidance on the planning process and links to a number of publications and useful planning Web sites.

Hoch, Charles J., Linda C. Dalton and Frank So, editors. *The Practice of Local Government Planning.* 3rd ed. Washington, DC: International City/County Management Association, 2000.

This updated and venerable "Green Book" comprehensively covers planning topics in each of its chapters, and includes sections on secondary sources and a data-quality checklist.

Jeer, Sanjay. *Online Resources for Planners.* Washington, DC: American Planning Association, Planning Advisory Service, 1997.

This is a guide to Internet Web sites of interest to planners, including tips for navigating the information super highway and reviews of over 900 Web sites. Chapters are organized by planning topic.

PLANetizen (www.planetizen.com)

This Web site is designed for the urban planning and development community. It contains an online planning journal with current planning-related articles from a large selection of traditional magazines and newspapers, along with announcements and a calendar of events.

Maps on the Internet

Environmental Systems Research Institute (ESRI) GIS.com Web site (www.gis.com)

With a plethora of Web sites offering access to data and maps for Geographic Information System (GIS) usage, it is the most logical starting point with a good portal that provides useful links. Run by the private company ESRI, this Web site provides both educational examples to familiarize users with a GIS and its potential for local communities, and access to data and maps across the World Wide Web.

National Cartographic and Geographic Information Systems Center (www.info.usda.gov/nrcs)

A division of the Natural Resources Conservation Service, this center's Web site gives access to data for mapping, such as soil survey geographic databases at the national and state levels.

National Environmental Satellite, Data and Information Service (NESDIS) of the National Oceanic and Atmospheric Administration (NOAA) (www.nesdis.noaa.gov)

NESDIS's site contains U.S. and international weather records.

National Imagery and Mapping Agency (NIMA) (164.214.2.59)

NIMA is a government agency that was formed from the Department of Defense and serves as an arm of the U.S. intelligence community. It provides geospatial data to the public in the form of products for sale and for download on their Web site. Products include topographic maps, declassified satellite photos, aerial photos and other data useful for planning professionals.

National Oceanic Data Center (NODC) of the NOAA (www.nodc.noaa.gov)

NODC's site maintains a vast repository of oceanographic data, including environmental event satellite images, sea levels and pollution levels for mapping, as well as international data.

National Ocean Service (NOS) of the NOAA (www.nos.noaa.gov)

NOS's site provides harbor and coast charts, coral reef maps, an environmental sensitivity index and a plethora of maps and data through its Mapfinder program.

Neighborhood Knowledge Los Angeles (NKLA) (nkla.sppsr.ucla.edu)

NKLA is one example of many community-based, online projects that gather a wide range of public data in one place for easy access. Information such as property tax delinquency, building permits and building code complaints can be combined with local demographic and economic data in provided mapping programs. This gives the user the ability to visualize the assets and problems in their neighborhood.

U.S. Census Bureau (www.census.gov)

This site provides census data in the form of Topologically Integrated Geographic Encoding and Referencing (TIGER) system files that allow direct retrieval and mapping down to the block level of census geography. It also provides links to publicly available printed maps; free, downloadable maps; and online mapping for American Factfinder and State and County Quick-Facts data.

U.S. Census Bureau State Data Centers (SDCs) (www.census.gov/sdc/www)

SDCs are located in every state, the District of Columbia, Puerto Rico, Guam and the U.S. Virgin Islands. Generally state and local government agencies, they partner with the Census Bureau to disseminate data and provide special services to census data users including small area profiles, marketing research, studies on issues of local importance and access to thematic maps for local areas.

U.S. Environmental Protection Agency (EPA) (www.maps.epa.gov)

This EPA site permits users to create their own maps displaying local watersheds and polluters.

U.S. Geological Survey (USGS), U.S. Department of the Interior (www.usgs.gov)

The nation's premier map maker, the USGS offers a Web site with links to a number of products and data for mapping including Digital Elevation Models (DEMs) for topographic maps, land satellite data (LANDSAT), national wetlands inventory (NWI) data, and several free GIS programs to construct local maps for planning analysis.

U.S. Census (data sources and guides to using the data)

KIDS COUNT Census Data Online (www.aecf.org/kidscount/census)

This Web site, operated by the Annie E. Casey Foundation, compiles indicators of the well being of children in the U.S. from the 2000 census. Data are available at the national, state and some local levels including counties, large cities and metropolitan areas.

The Municipal Yearbook. Washington, DC: International City/County Management Association, multiple years.

These annual publications present census and other data about local U.S. governments in accessible formats. Each yearbook includes directories to local government officials in tens of thousands of American cities.

Myers, Dowell. *Analysis with Local Census Data. Portraits of Change.* San Diego: Academic Press, 1992.

This is a guidebook that demystifies the use of census data for local area analysis. It pays special attention to measuring change over time, and uses census data to understand housing and other practical planning issues from a "bottom-up" perspective. Examples are pulled from the 1990 U.S. Census, but techniques remain relevant.

Public Data Queries (www.pdq.com)

This site provides access to historical Census Public Use Microdata Samples (PUMS).

University of Minnesota's IPUMS/USA project (www.ipums/umn/edu)

This site provides access to historical U.S. Census PUMS.

U.S. Census Bureau (home page) (www.census.gov)

This is the U.S. Census Bureau's official Web site and is the best, most comprehensive source of data from the Decennial Censuses of Population and Housing, the Economic Census and the American Community Survey. The site offers access to maps, summary tables,

Public Use Microdata, state and county quick facts, and many other tools and special reports. The American Factfinder section is a useful starting point for planners as it provides detailed data, reference maps and thematic maps to the block level for the entire nation.

U.S. Census Bureau. *County and City Data Book.* Washington, DC: U.S. Government Printing Office, multiple years.

Published every four years, this resource contains the latest official statistics from the Censuses of Population, Housing and Economics for all U.S. counties, cities with 25,000 or more people and places of 2,500 or more people. Available in print, online at the University of Virginia (fisher.lib.Virginia.edu) and on CD-ROM.

U.S. Census Bureau. *State and Metropolitan Area Data Book.* Washington, DC: U.S. Government Printing Office, multiple years.

These books contain census statistics on the social and economic conditions of the U.S. at the state and metropolitan levels. They provide a guide to sources of other data from the Census Bureau, other federal agencies and private organizations. They are available in print, on line at the Census Bureau's Web site and on CD-ROM.

U.S. Census Bureau. *Statistical Abstract of the United States.* Washington, DC: U.S. Government Printing Office, multiple years.

These publications provide annual national and selected international data on social and economic conditions from the U.S. Census and other sources. They serve as a guide to sources of other data from the census, other federal agencies and private organizations. They are available in print, online at the Census Bureau's Web site and on CD-ROM.

Population and Demographics

Ameristat (www.ameristat.org)

Developed by the Population Reference Bureau, in partnership with the University of Michigan's Social Science Data Analysis Network, Ameristat gives you instant summaries—in graphics and text—of the demographic characteristics of the U.S. population.

Centers for Disease Control (CDC) Wonder (wonder.cdc.gov)

CDC's Wonder site provides natality and mortality data for every state and county.

City Population (www.citypopulation.de)

This site displays data for the world's largest cities through easy-to-use maps.

Claritas International: Consumer and Business Marketing Information, Demographics, Segmentation (www.claritas.com)

Claritas is a private company that offers for purchase access to mapping programs, local area population estimates and projections and special queries on variables that may interest planners.

Earthlights (www.cojoweb.com/earthlights.htm)

This site illustrates population density through nighttime photographs from a National Aeronautics and Space Administration satellite.

Human Relations Commissions at the state, county and city levels

Originally established in the volatile climate following the urban race riots of the 1960s, many human relations commissions continue to operate at various local levels. Their missions and data collection vary widely from place to place, but the better funded commissions collect data on ethnic and racial minorities, hate crimes and demographic change in their local areas.

Metropolitan Life Insurance Statistical Bulletin

This is a journal with articles on longevity, mortality, mortality due to particular diseases, population, accidents, and economic and insurance aspects of mortality. Check the local research or medical library for this bulletin.

National Center for Health Statistics. *Vital Statistics of the United States.* Hyattsville, MD: U.S. Department of Health and Human Services, multiple years.
(www.cdc.gov/nchs)

These annual reports of demographic information, such as natality, mortality, marriage and divorce, are available in large public and university libraries. They are based on data collected from county health departments and reported to states.

Office of Refugee Resettlement, U.S. Department of Health and Human Services (www.acf.dhhs.gov/programs/orr)

This agency publishes reports on refugee populations resettled in the U.S., including statistics by states and selected cities. Their Web site contains contact information for state refugee agencies and nonprofit advocacy groups along with grant applications for refugee service provision at the local level.

Polk Research Sampling (www.polk.com)

This private sector R. L. Polk Web site provides links to demographic data for purchase, including household data that can be used to design sample populations for local surveys.

Population Reference Bureau (www.prb.org)

This is a nonprofit group that tracks international and U.S. trends in demography, and publishes studies on topics ranging from migration to children's well being to elder care. It also provides demographic statistics at the national and state levels. It is a useful source for planners looking for the connection between demographic change and local resource needs.

United Nations (www.un.org)

This Web site for the United Nations contains a plethora of links for international demographic information including comparative social indicators and population counts. Of special interest to planners are demographic databases and mapping resources. See especially *Global Statistics* (a directory of links to national statistics, organized by country) and the *United Nations Demographic Yearbook* with data for the world's largest cities.

U.S. Census Bureau's International Population Data Base (www.census.gov)

This is a wonderful information source for international demographic data.

U.S. Census Bureau SDCs (www.census.gov/sdc/www)

SDCs are located in every state, the District of Columbia, Puerto Rico, Guam and the U.S. Virgin Islands. Generally state and local government agencies, they partner with the Census Bureau to disseminate data and provide special services to census data users including annual and five-year counts of state populations.

U.S. Bureau of Citizenship and Immigration Services (www.immigration.gov)

This INS Web site includes links to order and download publications about the demographic characteristics of international migrants in the U.S. It provides data on the places immigrants settle by states and selected cities.

World Health Organization (WHO) (www.who.int)

WHO's site provides statistics on international populations.

Housing and Construction

Construction Weblinks (www.constructionweblinks.com)

This portal provides links to a number of construction-related sites and publications including the *Dodge Construction Contract Statistics*, the *Engineering News-Record* and a plethora of private groups and government agencies that track construction data.

International Union for Housing Finance (www.housingfinance.org)

This nonprofit group's Web site contains a variety of publications and statistics on housing finance issues in the U.S. and abroad.

National Housing Institute (www.nhi.org)

This nonprofit organization examines affordable housing and community economic development issues, including how poverty and racism intersect with access to housing in the U.S. It publishes *ShelterForce, The Journal of Affordable Housing and Community Building*, with articles across a wide array of housing topics, including case studies of special interest to planners.

United Nations Human Settlements Programme (UN-HABITAT) (www.unhabitat.org)

UN-HABITAT's site provides access to statistics and reports on housing indicators across nations and in select urban areas.

U.S. Bureau of Labor Statistics (www.bls.gov)

This detailed Web site contains links to housing and construction information, including housing as part of the Consumer Price Index (CPI), new housing starts and building permit activity.

U.S. Census Bureau. American Housing Survey. Washington, DC: U.S. Government Printing Office, multiple years. (www.census.gov)

This bureau collects data every other year on the nation's housing units of all types, and every four years on housing units in selected metropolitan areas in the U.S. Both surveys are based on samples and are conducted by the U.S. Department of Housing and Urban Development. Panel data are available.

U.S. Department of Housing and Urban Development (HUD) (www.hud.gov)

Through HUD's site, users can access useful information tailored to private citizens, government groups and nonprofits. It includes a series of special topic reports and links to useful housing sites across the World Wide Web, as well as a special section on community development and planning.

Economics

American Chamber of Commerce Researchers' Association (www.accra.org)

This organization publishes a quarterly Cost of Living Index that provides selected price data and comparative living costs for over 300 cities.

U.S. Bureau of Economic Analysis (BEA), U.S. Department of Commerce (www.bea.gov)

BEA's site contains data on personal income for states, counties and metropolitan statistical areas. It also provides access to historical data for local areas.

U.S. Bureau of Labor Statistics (www.bls.gov)

> This is a detailed Web site that contains information on several economic indicators by local area and industry, including wages, employment and unemployment, CPI, layoffs and injuries. It also contains national and international data.

U.S. Census Bureau. *County and City Data Book.* Washington, DC: U.S. Government Printing Office, multiple years. (www.census.gov)

> Business and labor force data are available on this site for all U.S. counties, cities with 25,000 or more people and places with 2,500 or more people.

U.S. Census Bureau. *County Business Patterns.* Washington, DC: U.S. Government Printing Office, multiple years. (www.census.gov)

> This annual report provides data for local areas by industry. It is useful for both private sector and government planners in analyzing economic changes over time and economic activities in their cities.

Transportation

Association of State Highway and Transportation Officials (www.aashto.org)

> This Web site identifies the Web sites of its members (state departments of transportation) and provides a wealth of regional transportation data.

Bureau of Transportation Statistics, U.S. Department of Transportation (www.bts.gov)

> This site contains links to data at different geographic levels on a variety of transportation topics of interest to local planners.

Federal Highway Administration (FHA) (www.fhwa.dot.gov)

> The FHA publishes national and state data on road miles and vehicle miles traveled, as well as state and local highway finance data.

U.S. Census Bureau, American Factfinder (www.factfinder.census.gov)

> Data is provided from the Decennial Census on means of transportation to work and commuting time from the national to block group geographic levels.

U.S. Census Bureau Commodity Flow Survey (www.census.gov)

> Traffic flow data is provided on the volume of commodities shipped, from a sample of industries. It is organized by means of transport, size, origin and destination of shipments.

Health and Welfare

Agency for Healthcare Research and Quality (www.ahrq.gov)

> This agency offers training and workshops on community health issues for local planners.

American Hospital Directory (www.ahd.com)

> This directory provides free access to summary data on individual hospitals and more detailed information for a fee.

Centers for Medicare and Medicaid Services (formerly Health Care Financing Administration (HCFA)) (www.hcfa.gov)

> These centers issue state and county data on Medicare enrollment, some state data on Medicaid eligibility and performance plans for the State Children's Health Insurance Program.

Community Health Status Indicators Project
(www.communityhealth.hrsa.gov)

> This project has compiled comprehensive county-level data such as birth rates, death rates and behavior risk factors, including the Healthy People 2010 goals.

HealthWeb (www.healthweb.org)

> This is a searchable database of the best Web sites on medical topics and health care administration.

International Red Cross (www.ifrc.org)

> This site provides international health data.

Joint Commission on Accreditation of Healthcare Organizations (www.jcaho.org)

> A searchable directory of accreditation reports for hospitals, nursing homes and behavioral care facilities is provided.

Medicare Web site of the U.S. government
(www.medicare.gov)

> This site allows users to identify and compare local nursing home and dialysis facilities.

StateSearch (www.nascio.org/stateSearch)

> Identification of state health and social service agencies that provide heath-related data is provided.

U.S. Census Bureau, Summary File 3 (www.census.gov)

> This sample data file from the Decennial Census identifies people with physical and mental challenges and public assistance income to the block group level.

U.S. Department of Health and Human Services
(www.hhs.gov)

> This Web site contains extensive information on topics that may concern local planners, including links to minority health sites. A broad range of agencies, including the CDC, the National Center for Health Statistics and the Administration for Children and Families, can be contacted through this portal.

World Health Organization (WHO) (www.who.int)

> WHO's site provides international health data.

Education

ERIC Database (ericir.syr.edu)

> This is the index to the U.S. Department of Education reports and journal articles since 1966.

National Center for Education Statistics (NCES)
(nces.ed.gov)

> Access to a variety of reports and datasets about schools in the U.S., NCES's site includes information on the challenges facing urban school systems. Much of the data is national in scope, but certain variables and topics cover the state and local areas as well.

Quality Education Data (www.qeddata.com)

> This private sector company provides both for-purchase and free databases on a variety of education issues by state and selected city levels.

United Nations Educational, Scientific and Cultural Organization (www.uis.unesco.org)

> This site provides international education data.

U.S. Department of Education (www.ed.gov)

> Data and reports on school performance, campus crime and a number of other education issues at the local level are provided.

Environment, Natural Resources and Recreation

Bureau of Land Management
(www.blm.gov/nhp/index.htm)

> Information on public lands and park resources, including maps, is presented.

Bureau of Mines (minerals.usgs.gov)

This site provides data on mineral, coal and petroleum production.

Bureau of National Affairs. *Environment Reporter*, multiple years. (www.bna.com)

This private company produces a number of reports on planning-related issues, including the *Environmental Reporter* (available on the Web site). This reference manual covers developments in legislation, regulation, legal and policy sectors related to environmental issues. It is valuable in keeping planners current on the policies affecting their local areas. The Bureau of National Affairs also publishes data and reports about international environmental topics.

National Climatic Data Center (lwf.ncdc.noaa.gov)

Daily weather information is issued on this Web site.

National Park Service (www2.nature.nps.gov)

Data on park use, natural resources in national parks, information for park planners and a plethora of other useful guides and datasets are presented.

National Recreation and Park Association (www.nrpa.org)

This site contains a catalog with numerous publications of interest to local recreation planners.

United Nations Environmental Programme (www.unep.org)

This site contains the *Global Environmental Outlook* report that relates environmental problems to social, demographic and economic factors throughout the world.

United Nations Sustainable Development (www.un.org/esa/sustdev/csd.htm)

This site provides country-level statistics and policies on social and demographic conditions, natural resources and pollution, economics and decision-making.

U.S. Census Bureau. *Census of Agriculture*. Washington, DC: U.S. Government Printing Office, multiple years. (www.census.gov)

This is a comprehensive report on the state of agriculture in the nation, in each state and in each U.S. county.

U.S. Department of Energy (www.energy.gov)

Various agencies with reports on nuclear energy sources, electrical energy generation and natural gas production and consumption are linked to this site.

U.S. Environmental Protection Agency (EPA) (www.epa.gov)

This site provides a wealth of information at the local level, including the "Where You Live" tool that allows users to search for environmental information by zip code. The EPA releases reports about environmental violations at the county and community levels.

U.S. Fish and Wildlife Service (www.fws.gov)

This site provides information on forests, fisheries and wildlife.

U.S. Forest Service (www.fs.fed.us)

This site provides information on forests, fisheries and wildlife.

U.S. Geological Survey (USGS) (www.usgs.gov)

Local data on earthquakes, water resources and other environmental issues are maintained on this USGS site.

World Resources Institute (www.wri.org/wri/index.htm)

This organization publishes national-level data on endangered species, water and air pollution and sanitation in its *World Resources Report*, its *EarthTrends* database and individual research monographs.

Crime

Human Relations Commissions at the state, county and city levels (for example, see: humanrelations.co.la.ca.us)

Originally established in the volatile climate following the urban race riots of the 1960s, many human relations commissions continue to operate at various local levels. Many collect data on hate crimes in their jurisdictions and publish reports about race relations.

International Criminal Police Organization (INTERPOL) (www.interpol.int)

The INTERPOL, a private company, publishes crime statistics annually for select countries along with special reports on crimes, such as smuggling people across borders.

National Criminal Justice Reference Service (NCJRS) (www.ncjrs.org)

NCJRS publishes numerous reports on crime and control.

Southern Poverty Law Center. *Intelligence Reports*, multiple years. (www.splcenter.org)

These quarterly reports of the Southern Poverty Law Center (a venerable, nonprofit, antiracism group) track hate groups and hate crime incidents across the country down to the local level.

United Nations Office of Drug Control and Crime Prevention (UN ODCCP) (www.undcp.org)

UN ODCCP's Web site provides links to international crime data and reports.

U.S. Department of Housing and Urban Development (HUD), State of the Cities Data System (socds.huduser.org)

Information on a variety of quality-of-life issues, including FBI crime data for cities and suburbs through the State of the Cities Data System, is provided.

U.S. Department of Justice (www.usdoj.gov)

This site provides links to five agencies that collect and publish data on crime, including the FBI, the Bureau of Justice Statistics and the Drug Enforcement Administration.

Governmental Activities

Council of State Governments (www.csg.org)

Book of the States, published biennially, compares states, governmental powers, election procedures, tax rates, legislative issues and other useful categories.

Index to Current Urban Documents, Vol. 1 (1972/1973—). Westport, CN: Greenwood Publishing Group.

This document indexes city, county and regional government publications by broad subject heading and place name.

International City/County Management Association (ICMA) (www.icma.org)

ICMA publishes the *Municipal Yearbook* (a printed directory of the officials in cities with populations of over 2,500) along with special studies on local government planning issues.

National Association for Counties (www.naco.org)

Special studies on local government planning issues, especially as they relate to counties, are presented.

National Association of Regional Councils (www.narc.org)

Links to regional planning councils in each state are provided.

National Center for Small Communities (www.smallcommunites.org)

This organization publishes special studies on local government planning issues.

National Governors' Association (www.nga.org)
Numerous "best practices" guides on a range of planning subjects are published by this organization.

National League of Cities (www.nlc.org)
Special studies on local government planning issues are available.

Nelson A. Rockefeller College of Public Affairs and Policy (www.albany.edu)
This institution conducts and publishes reports on surveys and studies of governmental activities in local and metropolitan areas.

Piper's State and Local Government on the Net (www.statelocalgov.net)
This site is considered the best list for municipal governments.

StateSearch (www.nascio.org/stateSearch)
A subject approach search engine, which links to all state agencies, is maintained on this site.

U.S. Census Bureau. *Census of Governments.* (www.census.gov/govs/www)
This site provides quinquennial data on the organization, finance, employees and tax collections of federal, state, county, municipal and township governments as well as school districts.

U.S. Census Bureau. *Consolidated Federal Funds Report.* (harvester.census.gov/cffr/index.htm)
This is a searchable database of federal funds provided to individual state and county governments through grants, loans, direct expenditures and procurement contracts.

U.S. Conference of Mayors (www.usmayors.org)
Special studies on local government planning issues are presented.

Laws, Legislation and Regulations

Government Printing Office (GPO) Access (www.access.gpo.gov)
GPO Access's Web site is an online, CD-ROM and printed matter source for new laws, laws in force, proposed regulations and regulations in force, as well as links to many governmental agencies.

The Legislative Source Book (www.llsdc.org)
This publication, by the Law Librarians' Society of Washington, D. C. is the most comprehensive source for identifying what legal documents are free on the Internet.

Municipal Code Corporation (www.municode.com)
Links to many city and county governments' municipal codes are provided.

Piper's State and Local Government on the Net (www.statelocalgov.net)
This site provides links to the Web sites of local governments.

THOMAS (thomas.loc.gov)
Federal bills since 1973 and the full text of the Congressional Record since 1989 are indexed on this site. It also provides bill status.

U.S. Courts (www.uscourts.gov)
This is a comprehensive source of current legal opinions.

Washburn University Law School (www.washlaw.edu)
State legislatures, laws, regulations and court decisions are listed here.

Federal, State and Local Information Sources

FirstGov (www.firstgov.gov)
> This is the official gateway to locating federal government publications.

Google's Uncle Sam (www.google.com/unclesam)
> This is a gateway to locating federal government publications.

Government Printing Office (GPO) Access (www.access.gpo.gov)
> GPO Access's site provides a searchable directory of federal depository libraries.

Louisiana State University (www.lib.lsu.edu/gov/fedgov.htm)
> Links to federal agencies by hierarchal or alphabetical order, many of which offer federal government publications, are provided.

Piper's State and Local Government on the Net (www.statelocalgov.net)
> This is a directory to state and city government Web sites.

StateSearch (www.nascio.org)
> This is a directory to state government Web sites.

Information Organization

between peers involved in analysis,
ideas exchanged and negotiations

Collected information must be analyzed, processed and understood before it is useful to planners. The chapters in this part describe how planners organize information so that it makes sense and is professionally useful. They consider analytical methods, their use in certain contexts and new and evolving techniques in the area.

Chapter 4 describes analytical methods employed in planning.

Chapters 5 and **6** deal with process. Chapter 5 covers the interpersonal skills and techniques of working effectively in small groups. Chapter 6 describes aspects of involving the community in planning.

Chapter 7 describes the role computers can play in information gathering, analysis and communication.

Analytical Methods in Planning

Richard Crepeau

THE NEED FOR ANALYTIC METHODS

Information cannot usually be disseminated in the same form in which it is collected. Data and observations must be organized and processed to make them understandable to both the planner and to the audiences for whom they are intended. Important findings must be separated from unimportant ones and presented in a clear, convincing and understandable manner.

A number of highly sophisticated and powerful analytic methods are available; however, for most planning purposes, only a few elementary techniques are necessary and appropriate for preparing information for dissemination. The quality of the data, the sophistication of the audience to be addressed and the abilities of the person organizing the data all combine to dictate a fairly simple and commonsense approach to analyzing and digesting most information prior to attempting to communicate it.

Finding and choosing the proper technique for a particular communication requires a careful balancing of sophisticated background and simplicity of approach. This chapter presents a broad array of many of the simpler techniques appropriate to planning problems. Some knowledge of elementary statistics or mathematics is necessary for some of the techniques described, but an understanding of the *analytic choices available* and how they match the requirements of the communication problem being faced is the most critical ingredient for the successful organization and presentation of information.

At the simplest analytical level, communication consists of *descriptions* using numbers and percentages. How many vacant houses, how many houses in deteriorated condition, of what proportion of all houses does each of the groups consist and their location are all questions likely to arise in a neighborhood redevelopment situation such as that described for Mid-dlesville. Simple measures of distribution and composition are usually adequate for most such analyses.

At a slightly more sophisticated level, it may be desirable to know how many deteriorated houses are vacant or occupied. A two-way table presenting the appropriate cross-tabulation is required. However, before such a table is presented to an audience, it is sometimes desirable to be certain that the *apparent relationship* between housing vacancy and deterioration is real (i.e., that it is not merely one that could have occurred by chance). This calls for a test of *statistical significance,* possibly accompanied by some measure of *association* describing the strength of the relationship. Several tests and measures of association are described in this chapter.

A multiple cross-tabulation may sometimes be necessary in order to eliminate the effect of a third attribute on the relationship being examined. This might occur in Middlesville if it were suspected that older houses differed from newer houses in level of deterioration regardless of vacancy status. On rare occasions, it might be appropriate to examine and demonstrate the interrelationships of three or more variables with one of several types of *multivariate analyses.* Such techniques, however, are usually well beyond the quality of the data available, as well as beyond the understanding and appreciation of the audiences for whom the information is being organized.

Finally, it is sometimes desirable to demonstrate how a particular *process* operates. Although a number of highly sophisticated mathematical modeling techniques are available for such purposes, several nonquantitative techniques, such as simulation/gaming and scenario writing, may be more appropriate to the communication problems being considered here.

Feldt, Allan and Mitchell Rycus. *The Planner's Use of Information.* 1st ed. Chicago: American Planning Association, 1988, pp. 73-74.

Planners use many methods—both qualitative and quantitative—to assemble and analyze information. This chapter emphasizes *quantitative* methods. One characteristic that qualitative and quantitative methods share, once the study or analysis is done, is the need to tell a story. Reflecting on interviews or participant observation may be directly related to storytelling, but there is also an art in reflecting on the patterns and summaries inherent in analytical methods. Every analysis leads to an important story; rather than letting the numbers "speak for themselves," an analyst should be able to interpret the results in a manner understandable to those who consume those results (i.e., policy makers, fellow planners and the public). It is in this spirit that this chapter is written.

Analytical methods have a needed role in planning—and most planners will eventually have to use them. One can expend much energy successfully avoiding the task of crunching numbers; however, at some point, one will face the task of needing to sensibly consume the product of someone else's data and their analysis of it. For many applications, planners need quantitative information and useful summaries and discussions about the data. Results of qualitative analyses may be summarized numerically, and cartographic and general graphic display of quantitative information requires some knowledge of the strengths and weaknesses of quantitative methods to accurately communicate results.

In the rational planning process, analytical methods play an integral role in the deciphering, organizing, processing and summarizing of the data (e.g., for current conditions of housing or transportation). This in turn can be used to inform the public as part of the process of clarifying goals and objectives. When feasible and proper, the future impacts of the plan and its alternatives are forecast and compared to determine which of the outcomes best address the goals and objectives stated earlier in the process. Under more common circumstances, planners employ analytical methods during the development review process. Reconciling the design, layout and intensity requirements of city ordinances with proposals of permit applicants and their consultants require a basic understanding of applied analytical methods.

While it is easy to get mired in the detail and complexity of quantitative analysis, its connection to qualitative analysis cannot be overstated. Any analysis or modeling must be done for a purpose, and this purpose is generally guided by theory. To a great extent, theory developed through qualitative analysis is validated by empirical analysis. Viewed from another perspective, the specification of complex analytical models requires a theoretical context, usually conceptualized by qualitative means. Analytical methods are not practiced in a vacuum.

Qualitative methods also benefit from analytical methods. General analytical findings may support or refute findings based on field or ethnographic research. Shortcomings observed through the analysis of qualitative data may lead to improved qualitative technique. While there are many who favor one form of analysis over the other, it is folly to assume

While it is easy to get mired in the detail and complexity of quantitative analysis, its connection to qualitative analysis cannot be overstated.

DATA TO TELL A STORY

Assistant Planner received a call from Thomas, who was responsible for facilitating a citizen's group in the City of Middlesville. This citizen's group had the task of proposing alternatives for the transportation plan. This required quite a bit of information about Middlesville, ranging from travel patterns and usage of roadways, to an understanding of historical trends of demographics, the economy and land use patterns. He got on the task right away.

When Assistant Planner returned with his report, he expected Thomas to sing his praises. Instead, as Thomas browsed the report, he frowned, scratched his head and told Assistant Planner that the report really doesn't make sense to him, not to mention what the citizen's group might make of it.

"It's Greek to me," said Thomas. "Can you make it more relevant to the citizens? Give them something to talk about?"

"I really didn't want to 'dumb it down," he said. "I'm sure I would either be condescending to them or leave important information out."

"Nonsense," Thomas said. "Our citizen's group needs to spend more time on the task at hand rather than puzzle through your tables and output. You really had two jobs. First, you needed to find the data and sift through it.

continued on page 129

that one method is superior to the other. It all depends on context. They reinforce each other and can be complimentary.

PRELIMINARY CONSIDERATIONS

The following issues are important to consider prior to any detailed exposition of analytical methods. Of these, the first (related to spatial considerations) are particularly important for most analyses conducted by planners.

Space, Scale and Boundaries

Throughout much of its history, planning has been a spatially oriented discipline. As such, it is important to be aware of the special issues that space brings to the analytical table. Unfortunately, many introductory statistical texts ignore these effects. The following section intends to introduce basic issues of space.

Space: Space indicates geography, location or distance; there is little with which planners are concerned that doesn't involve some phenomenon that occurs in space. This can be in a natural region, administrative or political boundary, or a region or boundary determined by the individual analyst. The interaction of humans and the environment can be analyzed separately or jointly in a spatial context (such as the social interactions of communities across space, the effect of geographically separate landforms on one another or the effect that landforms may have on the social interaction of communities). Some examples of planning questions that are inherently spatial include:

- How many housing units are allowed per square mile?
- What is an appropriate population density?
- What is the proper separation of residential and employment uses?
- Where are the activity centers of my city?

The first three questions apply directly to the issue of space; the fourth addresses "space" in two manners (i.e., location, and space as a construct to define what has been termed as a socially constructed environment). Ask yourself:

- How would I draw a boundary around a neighborhood?
- How would I define the boundaries of an ethnic community?
- How would I locate the spatial extent of the real downtown?

In some circumstances, this is difficult without knowledge of the social structure of an area. In many instances, neighborhoods, communities and other areas fit neatly into other predetermined geography, such as political, administrative or census boundaries; however, that is not always true in other circumstances. With a greater understanding of the impact that space has on your research (and vice versa), your findings will be more robust and better able to withstand scrutiny.

Space also impacts our analysis of typical statistical phenomena (e.g., rates of poverty). Rather than existing as isolated pockets, areas of poverty exist in part because they are proximate to other areas of poverty. The concept of spatial autocorrelation describes this characteristic. One could say that spatial autocorrelation explains the mantra of real estate agents: "Location, Location, Location." Location matters. Real estate principles suggest that it is best to buy a cheap house in an expensive neighborhood rather than an expensive house in a cheap neighborhood, because your house is likely to change values based (in part) on its vicinity. Viewing your house as an investment, the value of your home will likely be greater (all other factors being equal) in an expensive neighborhood simply because it is proximate to expensive homes.

Scale: How data are aggregated or collapsed spatially in a study affects how scale will impact the results. In most circumstances, the variation or differences among areal units systematically changes as the specification of those units change in levels of aggregation. Many of the data used by planners come from the census or other governmental sources that use census geography. (See Chapter 3, "Information from Secondary Sources.")

As Figure 3-2 in Chapter 3 illustrates, when a planner changes the scale of analysis, they might change the unit of analysis (as dictated by census geography) from the block to the block group, or from the block group to the census tract. As the planner moves from block to census tract, variation in the data diminishes, thereby distorting the observations of particular phenomena. In the most extreme cases, the average value of, for example, per capita income may not change much as the planner aggregates the study area, while the variation of per capita income

about its mean value is likely to decrease. If (as in most situations) we are interested in differences and variations in a phenomenon, aggregating data reduces the differences we would be observing. Reducing differences could lead to outcomes and decisions dictated by biased information.

If a planner wants to analyze the pattern of points, which may indicate incidence of an observed phenomenon (e.g., substandard housing), then scale plays an important part in the analysis. In Figure 4-1, the same pattern of points is to be found in "A" and "B." However, they "read" as exhibiting different characteristics—dispersed in "A" and clustered in "B." The only difference between them is the difference in scale of "A" and "B" and the boundaries of the area under scrutiny.

Boundaries: Planners never work under conditions where time and money are unlimited resources. If a planner collects primary information or organizes secondary information gathered by others to conduct a study, certain limits must be placed on the scope of the study. Determining the study area and delimiting its boundary is one such limit. However, planners must recognize that the boundary may bias the results of a study, or that incorrectly determined boundaries could be responsible for incorrect information.

Aside from time and money issues, the planner must delineate study area boundaries based on the research question at hand. If the question is, "What proportion of land area is devoted to current and potential brown field development?", one reflexive response would be to focus on the central city areas

continued from page 128

Summarize it into something meaningful to you."

"I did that," Assistant Planner replied.

"You did a good job but you failed at your second task. You needed to tell a story with this mess of numbers you created," said Thomas. "I could direct you to any table or chart in this report and ask you about it. I'm positive you would know that table inside and out, what's behind all those numbers, and you'd be able to explain it to me in a way I can understand.

"But you didn't really explain those numbers in this report," Thomas pointed out. "You seem to have let the tables speak for themselves. Every chart and table tells a story, but they rarely do so without a storyteller.

"When you do so, you are providing a guide to your readers who don't have your analytical skills. For those in the citizen's group who are better equipped to understand what goes on behind those numbers, I'm sure they appreciate not having to switch gears every time they encounter a table just so they can digest the numbers. Like me."

"I never thought of things in that way," said Assistant Planner.

"Well, neither did I," said Thomas, "until someone told me about it."

because that is where most brown field development occurs. However, the planner is not considering the *total* land area of the city and will likely be overstating brown field development.

This dilemma is similar to the Modifiable Area Unit problem, which is likely to occur in situations where the analyst defines the study area boundaries absent census geography. Different schemes for delineating subunits in the study area may yield different results—not because the data have changed, but because the spatial units have changed. Is there an optimal scheme for any given delineation of a study area? Most certainly, but it may not be evident. The careful planner should simply be aware of the impact that different schema have on the subject of study.

Precision, Accuracy, Validity and Reliability

One axiom of analysis is "garbage in, garbage out" (i.e., the results of any sort of planning study depend on the quality of the data used). In planning, being mindful of these inputs is very important because the public may be wary of "number crunching." Given this possibility, planning analysts must ensure results that withstand critical scrutiny. The first step in ensuring quality results is collecting and using quality data.

Precision: One goal of data measurement is to have precise data; however, precision does not guarantee data that reflect the phenomenon as it exists in the real world. Many urban areas in the U.S. monitor the quality of their air with ambient air monitoring systems.

These complex instruments continuously measure levels of carbon monoxide and ozone. Precision is directly related to how well the instrument is calibrated (e.g., if one monitor is able to measure carbon monoxide within 50 parts per billion and another monitor is able to measure carbon monoxide within 25 parts per billion, then the latter monitor is considered more precise). This measurement, though precise, may not reflect the overall air quality of the region but only at the location of the monitoring device.

Accuracy: If a planner can measure a phenomenon without systematic bias, then it is measured with accuracy. However, a very precise measurement may be inaccurate due to a manufacturing defect or calibration error. Extending the example of the air monitoring system, it may be that an instrument consistently records carbon monoxide levels as 3% higher than they actually are. This systematic bias makes the instrument inaccurate.

Validity: The data that a planner collects can be considered valid if it measures the phenomenon it is supposed to be measuring. On the face of it, this sounds simple—or is it? If someone prepared a summary of typical annual traffic conditions in a beach resort, which was precisely and accurately measured only during the month of July, how valid would you suppose the data are? During the summer, there are likely to be more travelers with purposes completely different from the residents. It would be incorrect to use the findings from July in a beach town as representative of traffic during the rest of the year.

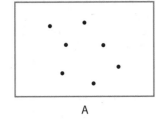

4-1. Scale, boundaries and reading of point patterns

Sometimes analysts cannot collect specific information simply because it doesn't exist or it is too expensive to gather. A proxy (a reasonable substitute) could be an acceptable alternative to the originally desired information—if it were valid. Other analysts create a composite or index of many pieces of information that could represent something like "community character" or "sense of place." In order for this index to be accepted, it should measure as much as possible those things we attribute to community character or sense of place.

Reliability: Professions that rely on census data must be concerned with the reliability of the data. Data are reliable if they are based on categories or definitions that change little over time. Those who analyze census data should be aware of changes in boundaries of Metropolitan Statistical Areas (MSAs) or census tracts from decade to decade. Census definitions of ethnicity also change (e.g., comparisons of "Hispanic" populations using census data over time are not necessarily reliable).

Measurement

Different types of phenomena or data are measured differently. The categorization of data by type or level of measurement helps determine the type of analysis or statistical technique. These levels of measurement are *nominal, ordinal* and *interval/ratio* or *continuous* (Figure 4-2).

Data measured on a *nominal* scale are primarily qualitative in nature—names, titles, places and descriptions. Land use classifications are measured on a nominal scale. Some typical categories could include residential, commercial, retail and open space.

Each category is mutually exclusive, so that a category could never be both residential and retail at the same time. What if an area is both residential and retail? You may want to create another category called "mixed use" that would include areas that are both retail and residential. This classification is considered nominal because the difference is based on description or name. Absent a context, residential is not "better" than commercial because it is listed first, nor are commercial uses twice as good as open space.

Sometimes, numbers are used as nominal classifications. Federal Information Processing Standard (FIPS) codes use numbers to identify states, MSAs, counties and census tracts. The number merely

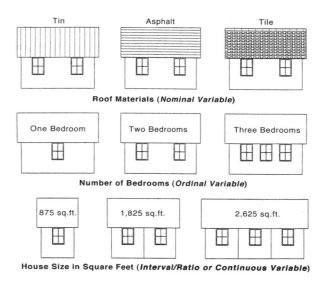

Roof Materials (*Nominal Variable*)

Number of Bedrooms (*Ordinal Variable*)

House Size in Square Feet (*Interval/Ratio or Continuous Variable*)

4-2. Data measurement and examples

identifies the geographic entity, not a numerical value. (Mindlessly calculating the average census tract number is certainly possible but entirely meaningless!)

Ordinal data are ordered. For example, if we rated land based on an index or composite of indicators to yield one number of "usefulness" for tracts of land, then the numbers associated with land would have order. In the same example, depending on the composite, numbers closer to 10 might indicate more useful land and numbers closer to 1 might indicate less useful land. Ordinal variables are considered discrete because there is no measurement between category 1 and category 2.

Such ordinal variables can be weakly or strongly ordered. Categorizing information with many unique values can derive weakly ordered variables. The U.S. Census usually categorizes age groups into five-year cohorts (ages between 0-4 years, 5-9 years, 10-14 years, etc.). The information is still ordered from youngest to oldest, but the information is collapsed into categories. One should note that collapsing data in this manner presents the same problems discussed in the section on "scale": it reduces the ability of the data to reflect the true phenomenon. While the average value of age may be similar, the variation within "age" would likely decrease.

Interval/ratio variables are commonly referred to as "continuous" variables because there is little incremental change from one possible value to the next. Theoretically, there are an infinite number of possible values that range between the numbers 1 and 2, so interval/ratio variables vary continuously. The dif-

ference between interval and ratio variables depends on the arbitrariness of "zero." If zero cannot be interpreted as the absence of the phenomenon under consideration, then the variable is measured on an interval scale.

Temperature, which is a measure of the flow of energy from a hotter body to a cooler body, is the classic example of an interval measurement. A temperature of zero, as measured on the Fahrenheit or Celsius scale, does not indicate the lack of a transfer of heat. On the other hand, with a ratio variable, zero actually means the complete absence of whatever is being measured. A household with zero income means the complete lack of income.

Figure 4-2 illustrates how an object of inquiry can be described by various methods of measurement. Using housing as an example, one can describe roofing materials—a nominal variable—to describe different types of housing. While one may prefer one type of roofing material over another, one can also argue that one type of material is not better or worse than another. As such, there is no ability to rank materials; they are merely named.

If we further describe housing units by the number of bedrooms each contains, we have an ordinal variable (one bedroom, two bedrooms, three bedrooms, etc.). We may rank our housing units by number of bedrooms, and one-bedroom houses (generally) are smaller than two bedroom houses, so there is an ability to order units described by this variable.

In addition, it would be hard to argue that any housing unit could have between two and three bedrooms; therefore, this ordinal variable measures discrete units. On the other hand, we may describe these housing units with a continuous variable, such as size as measured by square footage.

STATISTICS

Many times, planners need to summarize their information in a methodical and understandable manner; other times, planners would like to draw meaningful conclusions about the information they've collected. In either case, statistical methods make these objectives a reality. Two simple summary statistics are:

1. measures of central tendency (what is the typical value?)
2. measures of dispersion (how much variation is there in the data?)

In order to draw meaningful conclusions from the data drawn from a sample, a planner must be aware of underlying probability distributions in order to arrive at conclusions about meaningful differences one sees in the data.

Measures of Central Tendency

Can we describe a typical value for the data we've collected? Of course we can, but how do we describe it? There are three measures commonly used to summarize the information into a number that best describes the typical, or central, value: (1) the *mode*; (2) the *median*; and (3) the *mean*.

The *mode* identifies the value that occurs most often in the data. In fact, an alternative definition for mode is "that which is fashionable." In a sense, the mode is the most prevalent value for a given variable. The mode does not always accurately describe a typical value. In some instances, there is no mode because all values may be unique. In other instances, two values could occur most frequently; in this case, the variable is bimodal. In either circumstance, can you describe one typical value?

The median, by definition, is the middle value. Otherwise known as the 50th percentile, this is the value where there is an equal number of observations of lesser value and greater value. If, for example, we have a dataset with 25 observations and sort them in ascending order, the 13th observation will have 12 observations of lesser value and 12 observations of greater value than whatever value describes the 13th observation. Whether a planner describes housing units, persons, family income or the number of trips a household makes, the 13th value is the median.

The mean—perhaps the most widely known measure of central tendency—is also known as the "average" or "arithmetic mean." A planner can easily calculate the mean by adding up all values for a given variable and dividing this sum by the number of observations or cases in our dataset. The arithmetic mean is most useful with interval/ratio data. However, we may not want to use it in all circumstances.

The arithmetic mean is easily influenced by unusually high or low values, which is expected when a variable is characterized by a specific probability distribution, such as the normal distribution, as opposed to the median, which is a summary statistic

In a sense, the mode is the most fashionable value for a given variable.

that is not dependent on any sort of probability distribution (e.g., when summarizing income or housing prices).

A person could purchase a house for a price far above the typical values in the neighborhood. If we calculate the average housing price after this purchase, the mean gets "pulled up" by the high price reflected by the new purchase.

How do we avoid or minimize this effect? Use the median value. Let us assume that our dataset of 25 observations described housing values. In our ordered set of data, any reordering or drastic changes in value at the top end of the scale will have little to no influence on the median value; any change in the median value will be minimal.

Measures of Dispersion

While indicators of central tendency describe a typical value, they do not indicate the amount of variability or spread associated with the variable.

While indicators of central tendency describe a typical value, they do not indicate the amount of variability or spread associated with the variable. This is important because we would like to know if many values are clustered about the mean value, or if the values are dispersed (an indication of the precision of our estimates of typical values). Measures of variation include the *range, interquartile range (IQR), variance* and *standard deviation*.

The range merely describes the distance between the smallest and largest value of the data. The range can be considered volatile or easily influenced by extreme observations. Because of this, the range is rarely used except as a way to review the data for atypical minimum and maximum values.

Instead, many use the IQR as a simple, yet informative, measure of dispersion. The IQR describes the range of the middle 50% of data, or the distance between the 25th and 75th percentile. Regardless of extremely high or low values, the IQR reports a fairly robust measure of dispersion in our data.

More sophisticated measures that indicate variation about the mean value (the arithmetic mean) include the variance and standard deviation. Unlike the range and IQR, the variance and standard deviation rely on data that are distributed normally. Both indicators of variation provide information about the overall deviation of observations in relation to the mean. The formulas for these measures are:

Variance

$$s^2 = \frac{\sum\limits_{i=1}^{n}\left(X_i - \overline{X}\right)^2}{n-1}$$

Standard Deviation

$$s = \sqrt{\frac{\sum\limits_{i=1}^{n}\left(X_i - \overline{X}\right)^2}{n-1}}$$

where:

n = the number of observations

X_i = the value of variable X for a given observation i

$\overline{X}$ = the average value of variable X

You will note that the standard deviation is the square root of the variance. The variance is seldom used as a statistic to describe data, but it should be known that the variance is a measure of variation that includes all data. The reason we use the standard deviation is that the variance is measured in squared units. (Imagine telling your boss that the amount of variation in housing prices is measured in squared dollars.) By taking the square root of the variance, the standard deviation proves to be more useful as a descriptive (and understandable) statistic. Usually, just over 68% of the observations in your data lie within ±1 standard deviation of the mean; about 95% of the observations lie within ± 2 standard deviations of the mean; and about 99% of the data lie within ± 3 standard deviations of the mean.

As shown in Table 4-1, the typical household in renter-occupied units in Mecklenberg County, North Carolina (1989), as measured by the arithmetic mean, spends just under 24% of its household income on rent. Comparing the mean with the median, we note there is little difference between the two. The standard deviation tells us that 68% of the observations fall within a range of (23.72 – 4.09) and (23.72 + 4.09), meaning 68% of renters allocate between 19.63 and 27.81% of their household's income to rent.

Using the standard deviation may be suitable if we are discussing a single variable in isolation. However, what if we wish to compare variation among variables (e.g., per capita income and gross rent as a percentage of income)? (See Table 4-2.) Each has very different metrics: per capita income is measured in dollars, while gross rent/income is in percentages. How do we compare differences in variation between them? By using the coefficient of determination (CV),

we can create a common metric for comparison. The CV is nothing more than the size of the standard deviation in relation to the mean for that variable:

$$CV = \frac{s}{\bar{X}}$$

In a sense, we cannot compare apples and oranges (the variation in terms of dollars and percentages), so we create grapefruits out of both and then compare!

As Table 4-3 shows, there is a much greater variation in rent-to-income than the other variables. Indeed, housing values vary the least, even though the standard deviation is by far the largest of the three (the magnitude of the housing value numbers gives the impression that it varies more than per capita income).

Sampling

Sampling provides for a systematic way of obtaining incomplete, yet representative, observations for analysis. Why is it desirable to have incomplete information? As a planning office, we may not have the time, money or manpower to collect information from every citizen in town for our analysis. Therefore, we require methods to extract a representative sample.

Knowing that this information is incomplete requires the use of inferential statistics in order to provide an answer that incorporates the possibility that our sample isn't as representative as we hoped. (For a discussion of sampling theory and techniques, please refer to Chapter 2, "Survey Methods for Planners," which emphasizes random selection

TABLE 4-1	
Descriptive Statistics for Gross Rent/Income, Mecklenberg County, North Carolina	
Mean	23.93
Standard Error of the Mean	0.39
95% Confidence Interval	
Lower Bound	23.16
Upper Bound	24.71
Median	24.00
Variance	16.71
Standard Deviation	4.09
Minimum	10.00
Maximum	35.10
Range	25.10
Interquartile Range	3.70
Skewness	0.14
Kurtosis	1.71

among a group of potential respondents.) This section is meant to extend that discussion of sampling to include techniques for sampling areas or places rather than people (i.e., spatial sampling).

Spatial sampling: Spatial sampling helps to ensure random selection among a group of areas under study. Two methods are discussed here: *simple random point sampling* and *traverse sampling.*

As an example of spatial sampling, consider that we wish to determine the amount of impervious surface in a study area. Impervious surface does not allow water to penetrate into the ground, thus increasing the amount and velocity of water runoff. In turn, erosion on land and sedimentation in streams increase dramatically with greater proportions of impervious surface. These surfaces include asphalt or concrete paving and rooftops.

How can we determine the proportion of impervious surface in an area? One option is to hire thousands of people and have them inspect and measure every square foot of land in the study area. This, of course, would be foolish and expensive. Another option is to inspect an aerial photograph of an area that has sufficient resolution to allow us to discriminate impervious from pervious surfaces. By measuring and calculating the different surfaces as shown in the photograph, we could determine the percentage that is impervious. However, even this effort could be too time-consuming; therefore, we might choose one of the two sampling methods described here:

- *Simple random point sampling:* As the name implies, this is a method of choosing random samples from the image for calculation of percentage of impervious surfaces. The image measures 255 mm by 205 mm. We may create a coordinate system where x ranges between 0 and 205 and y ranges between 0 and 255. Using a random number generator available in computer spreadsheets, we can create a predetermined sample size of random x and y coordinate pairs that vary between 0 and 205 for x and 0 and 255 for y. The selection is random, because the location of an x or y coordinate is

---

TABLE 4-2

Household Data for Mecklenberg County

	Minimum	Maximum	Mean	Std. Dev.
Per Capita Income	3,171.00	50,676	15,996.95	8,051.88
Median Year Structure Built	1939	1987	1967.77	12.74
Gross Rent/Income	10.00	35.10	23.93	4.09
Median Housing Value	35,500.00	279,900.00	88,304.59	47,125.92

TABLE 4-3

Coefficients of Variation for Select Variables for Mecklenberg County

Variable	Calculation	CV
Per Capita Income (1989)	15996.95/8051.8820	1.987
Gross Rent/Income	23.9345/4.0879	5.855
Median Housing Value	88304.59/47125.9156	1.874

not dependent on the value of a previously selected *x* or *y* coordinate.

The planner then plots each *x* and *y* coordinate pair, determining whether or not that point lies in an area of impervious surface. Figure 4-3 shows the plotting of one coordinate pair, with a dashed white line. After all coordinate pairs are plotted and the determination is made, the planner then has an estimate of the proportion of impervious surface.

- If we record an impervious surface as "1" and no impervious surface as "0" for each coordinate pair, then sum the 1s and 0s and divide by the number of coordinate pairs we plotted, we arrive at our estimate of the proportion of impervious surface. For example, if we plotted 25 coordinate pairs and 14 of them landed on impervious surfaces, 14/25 or 56% of the study area is estimated to be covered by impervious surface. We may not want to rely on just one sample but repeat this procedure and average the results we get.

- *Traverse sampling:* Rather than using points, traverse sampling uses lines to help us measure the incidence of spatial phenomena. Conducting our analysis with the same aerial photo, and continuing to use the 205 mm × 255 mm grid, we select a predetermined amount of *x* and *y* values. For each pair, we conduct the analysis in this manner:

  1. Draw a vertical line across the photo where the *x* value lies.

  2. Determine the length of the line segments that cross impervious surface.

  3. Draw a horizontal line across the photo where the *y* value lies.

  4. Determine the length of the line segments that cross impervious surface.

  5. Add the two totals of impervious surface and divide by the total length of the two lines.

  6. Repeat for the next pair of *x* and *y* values.

Figure 4-3 shows the plotting of traverse sampling in solid black.

The more technically astute observer will wonder, "Why bother with the pencil and paper for this method when one can do this with a GIS?" Consider that, with a GIS, you will need to get the image into a suitable digital format. Then you will need to

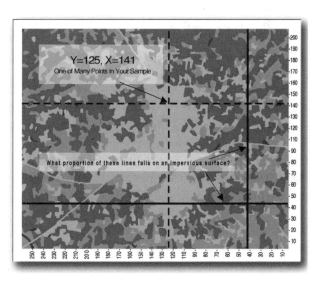

4-3. Aerial photograph with spatial sampling in progress— Simple Random Point (dashed line) and Traverse (solid line)

instruct the computer which color(s) are associated with impervious surface (and hope that each color uniquely describes each type of surface). (See the "Bibliography" in Chapter 7, "Computers and Planning.") When one considers the work necessary to make it all happen, it may very well take more time than just doing it by hand.

Probability

Probability distributions allow the analyst to be more precise in the estimates made from sampled data.

Probability distributions allow the analyst to be more precise in the estimates made from sampled data. Sampled data are incomplete data, although every measure is taken to assure ourselves with a degree of certainty that the sampled data accurately reflects reality. Different types of phenomena are described by different probability distributions.

The most common probability distribution is the normal distribution; however, other types of data with which planners deal can be characterized as having a binomial, poisson or other probability distribution. For the purposes of this chapter, we will focus on the most commonly used and relied upon distribution for planners: the *normal* (or *gaussian*) *probability distribution*. If we know (or assume) that the sampled data come from a population that is normally distributed, then we can make assumptions about the error associated with the estimates we make from the sample.

A *point estimate* is an estimate that describes one value. The point estimate of the mean is the sample mean we've calculated, which we hope represents the population mean (represented as μ; refer to the section entitled "Inferential Statistics" in this chapter for further discussion of population parameters). If we use this point estimate, we are placing a lot of faith in how representative this single value is of the population.

As an alternative, we may wish to calculate an interval of possible values and state a level of confidence that the actual value lies within this interval, assuming the variable is distributed normally. To do so, we can create a confidence interval, which we derive by calculating the following formula:

$$CI = \overline{X} \pm Z\sigma_{\overline{X}}$$

where:

CI = confidence interval
$\overline{X}$ = point estimate of the sample mean
Z = standard score
s = standard deviation
n = sample size

$$\sigma_{\overline{X}} = \frac{s}{\sqrt{n}} \quad \begin{array}{l} \text{= standard error of the} \\ \text{estimate of the mean of } X \end{array}$$

To determine the confidence level of our estimate, we adjust the standard score. To be 95% confident, our Z will always be 1.96; if we wish to be 99% confident, then we will specify our Z as 2.53. The rest is a matter of placing the numbers in the formula and performing the calculation. We can translate this number sentence to read, "The confidence interval about the mean of *X* is $\overline{X}$ plus-and-minus *Z* times the standard error of the estimate of *X*." An example of the use of the confidence interval can be illustrated in the context of "Issue #2 (City/County Scale): Transportation Plan for Middlesville" in the chapter entitled "A Planning Case Study."

In response to the article in the City of Middlesville's newspaper, which inaccurately stated that the new highway alignment would be cutting a swath through one of the city's poorest neighborhoods, Assistant Planner's boss wanted him to quickly make a determination of what the household income would be surrounding the planned highway site. If his critics were right, then perhaps the alignment should be reconsidered.

On the other hand, if the critics were incorrect, it would be best to present this information to the public. Rather than electing to conduct the more accurate, but time-consuming, study of collecting income information for all households, Assistant Planner decided to randomly sample households in the area and make a determination based on that information.

After Assistant Planner's quick survey of 200 households, he concluded that the average household income in the vicinity of the highway's alignment was $37,500—a modest figure, but perhaps not representative of the city's poor families. Of course, since Assistant Planner knew he was working with incomplete information (although it was collected using a proper random sample method), he couldn't report the average household income to his boss because it may be inaccurate.

He decided to construct a confidence interval around his sample estimate for average household income. Using the formula above, he assembled the required information (mean–$37,500; standard deviation–4,000; sample size–200). Still, he needed to decide how confident he wanted to be in the confidence interval he will construct.

Although a 95% level of confidence (using a *Z* of 1.96) is considered to be perfectly acceptable among his peers, he knew that the public would be skeptical of most answers coming from the planning office. Therefore, he wanted to be as confident as possible in his answer, so he chose to be 99% confident (using a *Z* of 2.53).

With this information, Assistant Planner was now able to go to his boss. Rather than just showing the numbers, he decided to also communicate the following information:

"We randomly sampled 200 households in the vicinity of the proposed highway improvements. We determined the mean household income to be $37,500, and that roughly 2/3 of our surveyed households fell within $4,000 of that mean (the standard deviation of 4,000). We can't rely solely on this number because there are households from which we did not get information. We got our information from a sample of households; therefore, it would be best to make our determination based on a range of values from which we can feel confident. To remain as conservative as possible in our estimation, I chose to be 99% confident in my estimate. I can say with 99% confidence that the true average household income lies somewhere between $36,770.28 and $38,229.72."

If his critics were right, then perhaps the alignment should be reconsidered.

TABLE 4-4
Confidence Level Calculations for Household Income in the City of Middlesville

Inputs to Analysis	Intermediate Calculations	Final Calculations
$\overline{X} = \$37,500$ $s = 4,000$ $n = 200$ $Z = 2.53$	$\sigma_{\overline{x}} = \dfrac{s}{\sqrt{n}}$ $282.84 = \dfrac{4,000}{\sqrt{200}}$	$CI = \$37,500 \pm 2.53(282.84)$ $CI = \$37,500 \pm 729.72$ $CI = \$36,770.28 \Leftarrow \mu \Rightarrow \$38,229.72$

Assistant Planner's boss can now meet with the citizens concerned about impacting low-income neighborhoods.

Inferential Statistics

Hypothesis testing further utilizes probability distributions. It also helps the analyst determine the possibility of making an error in stating that the differences observed in sample statistics reflect differences found in the real world. In its simplest form, we utilize hypothesis testing to make assertions when comparing summary statistics between two variables.

In inferential statistics, we state a null and alternative hypothesis. The null hypothesis generally assumes no difference between the two variables one is comparing. The alternative offered and tested for is that, indeed, the two samples are significantly different from each other. Continuing with the spatial sampling example, the null hypothesis could be stated as follows: "There is no difference in the esti-

In inferential statistics, we state a null and alternative hypothesis.

mates of impervious surfaces based on sampling technique"; the alternative hypothesis is: "The estimates of impervious surface are different based on sampling technique."

Why is hypothesis testing necessary in this case? Remember that the summary statistics came from samples and sampled information is incomplete information. There is the chance that any conclusion regarding the similarity or difference at which we arrive based on our point estimates may simply occur due to chance.

T-tests: The most common application of a t-test is to test differences in mean values. The comparisons can be between a sample mean and a known population parameter, two independently sampled means and two means matched by pairs across space or time. In order to apply a t-test, we must assume that the data came from random samples (and random independent samples in the case of the latter two t-tests). In addition, the variables selected must be normally distributed. The conclusions are that the mean values are equal or different. While this explanation used a summary statistic such as the mean, t-tests can also be conducted on tests for differences in proportions.

To extend the example used for the confidence interval in the scenario of "Issue #2 (City/County Scale): Transportation Plan for Middlesville" in the chapter entitled "A Planning Case Study," Assistant Planner can use a t-test to determine if the average household income, determined by his sample of households in the vicinity of the highway improvement, is significantly different from what is considered to be "low income" in the City of Opportune.

In fact, if Assistant Planner and his boss wished to convince the public that the households being impacted by the highway are not low income, extending the analysis of the confidence interval to include a t-test would be prudent and would probably convince more citizens that vulnerable citizens are not being targeted.

Regression analysis: Regression analysis is an extremely useful analytical tool for planners. Regression analysis attempts to explain variability in one factor by relating it to a reasonable set of other factors. The variable we wish to explain is the dependent variable; the factors we believe are associated with variation in the dependent variable are the independent variables. Two examples of regression models are "hedonic pricing" models, which describe the effects that certain factors have on the price of a house, and "travel demand" models, which describe the effects that factors have on how much an individual or household travels.

Regression analysis allows a planner to make a statement much more informative than "personal income affects how many trips a person makes on a typical day." The results of regression analysis allow us to expand upon this statement by suggesting the direction of the relationship and the amount of change in trip making that can be attributed to variation in income. While this tool is very useful, it can also be very complicated; it requires many assumptions to be met in order for the results to be meaningful. As a result, the complexity of the analysis makes the task harder for planners to interpret and communicate the results to the public. The use of regression analysis in the social sciences provides an unusually good example of the need for qualitatively grounded theory.

While it is easy to say that a set of independent variables "cause" the independent variable to change or vary, it would be folly to state causation with any degree of certainty. However, theory provides a good guide that would suggest some sort of causal relationship. While cause and effect might be clear cut in the physical sciences, the nature of social data requires planners to be much more cautious.

Regression analysis attempts to explain variability in one factor by relating it to a reasonable set of other factors.

DETERMINISTIC AND STOCHASTIC MODELS

Analytical modeling generally uses statistical and other quantitative techniques to create a mathematical abstraction of reality, not necessarily to create a representation of a phenomenon or behavior that is perfect in all respects. As an analogy, an architectural model of a building is an abstract representation of that building, but not necessarily a perfect copy. First, its size is smaller because fiscal and physical constraints prevent a full-scale replica from being constructed. Second, it isn't necessary to include every conceivable detail to the scaled-down model, but just enough to give the impression of its use and "feel"—allowing one to make an educated guess about its overall impact.

If you apply these aspects of an architectural model to an analytical model, you will find the fit to be appropriate. Analysts approximate physical processes and human behavior with mathematical expressions because fiscal and physical constraints prevent us from measuring and collecting information on all the factors that contribute to the choice someone makes (e.g., about taking the bus).

Additionally, since analytical models are, by nature, quantitative, how do we put a number on a feeling such as, "None of my friends ride the bus, so I don't use it much either." Analytical models, on the other hand, don't require perfect explanation. (In fact, a model that explains a phenomenon as nearly perfect is suspect!) One strives for adequate explanation of a phenomenon within the constraints of time and money.

Modeling attempts to explain or predict physical processes, human behavior or the choices we make individually or as a group. Analytical models can be either *deterministic* or *stochastic*. A model is deterministic when, in some sense, an outcome is determined for an individual based on their characteristics and surroundings. The choice to drive or walk to the store can be based on a number of factors, such as income level, education and neighborhood characteristics; based on prior observations, an analyst can create a model that explains the choice people generally make.

A deterministic model might use utility theory to explain the choice. Utility theory tells us a choice that provides the most benefit (or utility) to the individual will be the choice that is made. After applying the model to individual circumstance, the outcome is determined. Very little is left to chance.

Stochastic models, on the other hand, introduce the possibility that the unforeseen occurs. While the likelihood of a person with a low income, living near the CBD, will take the bus to work is high, there is always the chance that they won't, even if that means they won't maximize their utility by doing so. Since planners are continually faced with the fact that people sometimes don't maximize their utility, assigning a probability of less than 100% to a choice may be more realistic than a deterministic model where everyone is assumed to behave logically.

Analytical Models

Long-range planners tend to use analytical models to estimate values and forecast trends in populations, the economy and other, more specialized topics. Most of the techniques discussed here are more of a strictly quantitative nature and are not necessarily "statistics." This discussion is meant to be informative and not necessarily instructive. The reader is

Modeling attempts to explain or predict physical processes, human behavior or the choices we make individually or as a group.

well advised to consult texts that treat the analytical methods (and the previously discussed section entitled "Statistics") in a more rigorous and in-depth manner. Even if your job does not require you to be deeply immersed in these methods, you may be supervising analysts and might require a cursory background in what these methods should and shouldn't accomplish.

Demographic Models

Long-range planners tend to utilize these more complex and sophisticated methods of analyzing present populations and forecasting future ones. The more simplistic methods treat the population as an aggregate, using historical trends to extrapolate changes in the future. Others take a more pragmatic approach and recognize that any population is a composite. Future predictions should recognize this by incorporating such factors as age, gender, fertility and natural increase, as well as in- and out-migration.

Growth models and extrapolation: Growth models analyze historical trends in population changes and extrapolate those trends into the future. The process begins with a series of population data, typically provided by the census or other similar data extracted from other sources (see Chapter 3, "Information from Secondary Sources"). Growth models fit a "best fitting" line (or a line that best describes the existing historical pattern), then extends that trend into the future.

There are different diagnostic procedures that determine how well the fitted line matches existing historical observations and how well the estimated trend matches predetermined trend patterns (e.g., linear, exponential and logistic). In this sense, extrapolation is part science and part art. Sometimes the analysis suggests that a given pattern (such as an exponential trend) is most appropriate, but common sense or your knowledge of the data tells you that this trend may not be the most appropriate.

For example, population generally increases and your analysis may suggest that the best-fitting trend indicates exponential growth. Is continued exponential population growth over the long term a wise conclusion? Probably not. Therefore, the analyst must determine which best-fitting line also suggests a story that is believable or consistent with the circumstances. Although spreadsheet programs (such as Excel) have functions that allow a planner to conduct such analysis easily, there is very little direction given by these programs about the appropriateness of which method fits the data best. Klosterman's (1990) treatment of these growth models and their assessment is extremely valuable in this regard.

Example: Watauga County in northwest North Carolina is a rural county experiencing a tremendous amount of growth pressure, due in part to the presence of a large regional university and because the environmental amenities make it attractive as a place for second-home development. A planning analyst can employ a number of projection techniques. For the purposes of this example, we will use a historical trend of data (1975–1995) at five-year intervals and project population to the year 2010.

Growth models analyze historical trends in population changes and extrapolate those trends into the future.

TABLE 4-5

Population Projection for Watauga County, North Carolina

Year	Observed Population	Linear Regression	Geometric
1970	23,404	24,943	25,215
1975	29,800	28,151	27,896
1980	31,666	31,360	30,863
1985	35,071	34,568	34,145
1990	36,952	37,776	37,777
1995	40,890	40,985	41,794
2000	—	44,193	46,239
2005	—	47,401	51,157
2010	—	50,610	56,597

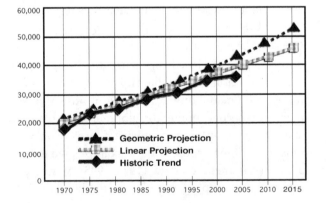

4-4. Population projection, Watauga County, North Carolina

Table 4-5 shows the results of the analysis and Figure 4-4 is a composite chart showing the historical data and all projections.

You will notice that the two methods for projection not only estimate future population, but the data for the historical period (1975–1995) are also estimated, based on the characteristics of the actual trend and the characteristics of the type of projection we are calculating. The determination of which projection to choose is both art and science. A set of statistics allows us to make a numerical interpretation of the "error" associated with our projection—this is the "science." The "art" suggests we employ something akin to the "smell test" when we observe our numbers and look at the chart. Does the projection with the least amount of error produce a set of numbers that are logical or believable? There might be circumstances where projections show 200% to 300% growth over a short period of time. The statistics might show this to be "reliable"; in reality, this projection may not be possible at all.

Figure 4-4 shows (in solid black) the historic trend of population growth in Watauga County. The solid gray line is the linear growth projection showing, as expected, a straight-line historical and projected population growth, assuming growth to occur by a constant amount from period to period. The geometric projection (dashed black line) shows a slight upward curve, indicating an assumption that population growth will be occurring at a constant rate (e.g., rather than increasing by 1,000 persons per period, the increase is 2% per period).

In the short term, the geometric curve may be more accurate and realistic; if we continue to assume a constant rate over the long term, we may soon be experiencing growth at unprecedented and unrealistic levels. Slightly more sophisticated projection techniques take into consideration factors such as "limits to growth" that mitigate projections of "uncontrolled growth."

Population pyramids and cohort-component analysis: While most growth models consider an area's population in the aggregate, we know that the "population" is more than a monolithic entity. The population of any jurisdiction is made up of people of different ages, sexes and other characteristics. Some areas see tremendous population growth because it is a popular destination; other areas experience growth because the resident population may be very fertile.

Some areas, such as in rural America, are "graying" because there is little hope or opportunity for the younger residents, who end up leaving for better opportunities elsewhere. Treating the population one dimensionally—as the extrapolation models do—masks the complexity of an area's population. Revealing this complexity is very important for planners whose role it is to suggest policies or strategies that anticipate future demands on infrastructure and other public services.

Cohort-component analysis uses a pyramid to describe this complexity. The pyramid displays the distribution of the population by age (the cohorts) and by sex (the component). Population pyramids are very useful tools that describe a given area on the basis of age and sex distributions. They also allow for

consistent comparison of a given area in two time periods, or even allow for consistent comparison of two areas in the same time period.

The age cohorts are broken into equal intervals, typically five years (with an open-ended top category). A line down the center is zero and the distance from the center (either to the right or left) indicates the proportion of that cohort that is male or female. Also, by convention, the population of each cohort illustrates the proportion of the total population rather than the absolute population size. Why? If we are comparing the same area, then it may not make a difference, but using proportions make comparisons of areas of different sizes easy and more sensible.

Figure 4-5 shows a series of stylized population pyramids that illustrates the communicative power of population pyramids. A "male dominant" pyramid shows a proportionally greater bar area on the male side as opposed to the female side of the pyramid. Conversely, a female dominant pyramid shows the opposite relationship between male and female populations. In general, a population pyramid that is skewed to one side or the other suggests a population that is disproportionately male or female. A pyramid that is youth dominant shows greater area towards the base of the pyramid and gradually tapers toward the top. The elderly dominant pyramid is "top heavy," suggesting a population that is predominately senior.

In the real world, however, the population pyramids created for areas diverge from the stylized examples of Figure 4-5. Either the relationships

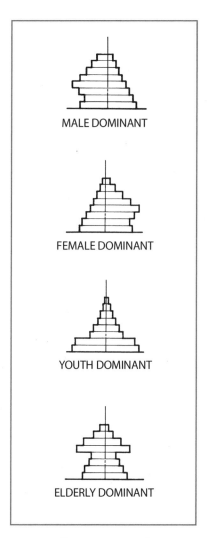

MALE DOMINANT

FEMALE DOMINANT

YOUTH DOMINANT

ELDERLY DOMINANT

4-5. Illustrative population pyramids for four different types of populations

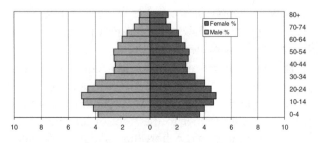

4-6. Population pyramid, United States (1975)

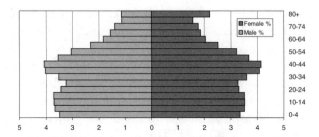

4-7. Population pyramid, United States (2000)

between males and females or age cohorts aren't as cut and dried as the stylized examples, or a compound relationship exists between different age cohorts and gender. Population pyramids from actual data require knowledgeable interpretation. One useful exercise is to examine the pyramids constructed from actual data, which follows in the next section.

As shown in Figure 4-6, the age-sex distribution of the U.S. in 1975 exhibits a fairly typical distribution for industrialized countries: slightly tapering, with some evident "humps" that suggest a population boom, then a later "repeat" boom—the progeny of the earlier cohort. In addition, it is evident that females tend to outlive males, as suggested by longer bars at older ages for females than for males.

Figure 4-7 shows the age-sex distribution of the U.S. 25 years later (2000). The lower "bulge" from 1975 (centered around the 15-19 age cohort) has now moved up 25 years (centered around the 40-44 age cohort). By comparing these two pyramids, two interesting factors are suggested: the parents of 1975 had larger families than their kids did, and the eld-

erly compose a larger share of the total population in 2000 than in 1975 (especially women).

An analysis of population pyramids is useful at the local level and important for planners. Figures 4-8 and 4-9 compare two regions in North Carolina. Figure 4-8 is from a region in northwest North Carolina—a very rural area in the Blue Ridge Mountains of southern Appalachia. Figure 4-9 is from part of the "Research Triangle" region of North Carolina and capital of the state.

The "triangle" area pyramid suggests (as one might expect) a thriving metropolitan area with a healthy economy that attracts young professionals and young families. This younger cohort is less distinct in northwest North Carolina and indicates a "graying" population in the mountains—a factor that further research shows to be due to out-migration of young adults rather than to a particularly healthy elderly population.

Why is this detailed analysis of the population important to planners? Think of the types of services that each of these populations demands: younger

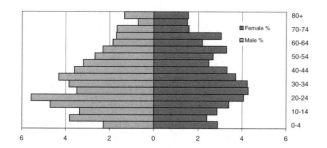

4-8. Population pyramid, North Carolina Public Use Microdata Area (PUMA) 0500 (northwest rural area) (1990)

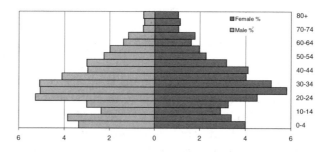

4-9. Population pyramid, North Carolina PUMAs 1901, 1902, 1903 (Wake County) (1990)

families require funds and planning for recreation facilities, schools and infrastructure that accommodates both residences and places of employment. On the other hand, the rural area will likely require health and social services that cater to an elderly population rather than spending on schools, etc. In addition, this type of research would lead to other questions of interest to planners: Why are the youth leaving the region? What can be done to stem the out-migration and actually attract people to the region?

We can also create a dynamic representation of population growth. This method then shows how the age cohorts travel along the pyramid through time. An example of this is shown in Figure 4-10.

In this example, our age cohorts are divided into intervals of 15 years. Note that the elapsed time between each pyramid corresponds to the width of each age cohort. All members of each age cohort thus migrate "up" into the next cohort.

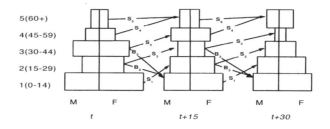

4-10. Cohort-component analysis (after Krueckeberg and Silvers, 1974)

The flows indicated in the figure show how the cohorts are populated from one time period to the next. The "S" illustrates how surviving members of the younger cohorts move into the older cohorts in the next interval (e.g., those who have died in the intervening 15 years are dropped). The oldest cohort (S_5) cannot migrate any further and remains at the top.

Estimates of deaths can be determined by rates of mortality, usually determined by the state demographic analysts. The "B" flow indicates births coming from fertile females from the second and third cohorts. The amount of natural increase is a function of fertility rates and the number of fertile females in each cohort.

This figure lacks a demonstration of how in- and out-migration affect populations in the age cohorts. In-migration increases populations in all age cohorts (whereas natural increase will only affect the youngest cohort); out-migration decreases populations in all age cohorts. Estimates of fertility, mortality and migration can usually be supplied by state demographers. However, most state demographers estimate these figures statewide and not for individual counties or cities. If you use statewide estimates, you are assuming that the fertility, mortality and migration characteristics of your local area reflect statewide trends.

Diversity and segregation: Two simple measures of diversity and segregation are the *Gini Coefficient* and the *Lorenz Curve*. Both measure inequality, typically in terms of income distribution.

The first step to calculating both measures is to rank-order your data, then divide it up into quantiles (divisions that contain an equal number of observations). In the case of income, the total income of each quantile is added, then the proportion of total income is determined for each quantile. An example is shown in Table 4-6.

For each year, the population is divided up into five equal parts (20% of the population in each category) based upon how much income is earned (the "lowest fifth" in this example means the lowest 20% of income earners). In 1994, the lowest fifth of the population earned 4.2% of the nation's income; the highest fifth of the population earned nearly 47% of the nation's income. If income were distributed equally in the U.S., each fifth of the population would earn 20% of the nation's income. The Gini Coefficient and Lorenz Curve illustrate this information numerically and graphically.

The Gini Coefficient is calculated using the following formula:

$$G = (0.5)\left(\sum_{i=1}^{k}|x_i - y_i|\right)$$

where:

G = The Gini Coefficient

x_i = relative frequency of x for quantile i (percentage of population)

y_i = relative frequency of y for quantile i (percentage of income)

k = the number of quantiles

For each quantile, we take the absolute difference of the percentage of income and percentage of popu-

TABLE 4-6

**Distribution of Income by
Quantile in the U.S. (1992-1994)**

Year	Lowest 20%	Second 20%	Third 20%	Fourth 20%	Highest 20%
1994	4.2	10.0	15.7	23.3	46.9
1993	4.2	10.1	15.9	23.6	46.2
1992	4.3	10.5	16.5	24.0	44.7

lation, then sum the answers of all quantiles and multiply by 0.5 (or, divide in half).

The possible values of the Gini Coefficient range from 0 (complete equality in the distribution of whatever one is measuring) to 50 (complete inequality in the distribution). In Table 4-7, the data for U.S. incomes in 1994 yield a Gini Coefficient of 30.2.

The Lorenz Curve uses the same data to determine the cumulative relative frequency of population and income. The cumulative relative frequency is calculated by accumulating the percentages from one quantile to the next. Then we plot the x and y coordinate pairs on graph paper, comparing this curve with a line of perfect equality (which is a line drawn at 45 degrees from the origin).

See Figure 4-11. Note that the Gini Coefficient corresponds to the area between the Lorenz Curve for these data and the line of equality.

Economic Models

Determining the conditions and characteristics of the local economy is an important part of planning, but no single figure provides the analyst with all necessary information. Three questions that might be asked in making planning decisions related to economic conditions are:

1. What are the basic and nonbasic industries in the area (location quotients)?
2. How might those industries change over time (shift-share analysis)?
3. What are the flows of commodities into and out of the area (multipliers)?

TABLE 4-7

Data for Gini Coefficient and Lorenz Curve (U.S. 1994)

Quintiles	Population (X)	Income (Y)	|X-Y|	Cumulative Population (X)	Cumulative Income (Y)
5	20	46.9	26.9	20	46.9
4	20	23.3	3.3	40	70.2
3	20	15.7	4.3	60	85.9
2	20	10	10	80	95.9
1	20	4.1	15.9	100	100

$$\sum_{i=1}^{k}\left|x_i - y_i\right| = 60.4$$

$$G = (0.5)(60.4) = 30.2$$

The three methods discussed in this section accomplish all these objectives.

Location quotients: Basic industries are those that tend to be net exporters of their products. By exporting goods, these industries import dollars into the local economy that circulate locally. Identifying basic (and nonbasic) industries allow economic planners to determine how best to allocate resources to economic development.

After identifying what industries are basic to a local economy, are these consistent with goals identified by the public? Are there industries considered to be "basic" yet the analysis doesn't bear this out? Basic industries are not consistent among local

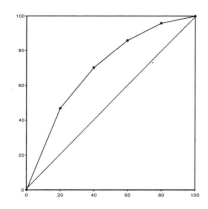

4-11. Lorenz Curve, U.S. (1994)

economies. Some economies are based on manufacturing industries; others rely heavily on tourism; still others base their economies on retirement income.

Calculating location quotients for economic sectors is a quick way of identifying which industries are basic and which aren't. The formula for a location quotient is:

$$LQ = \frac{\% \; Local \; Employment \; in \; Sector \; X}{\% \; National \; Employment \; in \; Sector \; X}$$

The *location quotient* indicates whether an economic sector employs proportionally more people locally as compared with that economic sector's share of employment nationally. While we might compare the local economy to regional or state figures, convention dictates a national comparison because the national economy is considered to be self-sufficient. Therefore, we are comparing our local economy to a self-sufficient standard.

A separate location quotient is calculated for each economic sector. These sectors are identified by the Standard Industrial Classification (SIC) code, or more recently by the SIC's replacement, the North American Industrial Classification (NAIC) code. Traditional economic sectors include manufacturing; construction; agriculture; wholesale trade; retail trade; services; finance, insurance and real estate (FIRE); and transportation, communications and utilities (TCU).

Because this is a ratio, the location quotient is equal to 1 if a sector's share of local employment is equal to the self-sufficient standard. If the value is less

Calculating location quotients for economic sectors is a quick way of identifying which industries are basic and which aren't.

than 1, one can assume that the sector is not sufficient to meet local needs (and therefore must import goods produced by that sector, thereby exporting local money outside the local economy).

Even in an era of globalization, local economies—especially rural—are sensitive to the export of their dollars, and planners worry about a location quotient less than .75. Location quotients greater than 1 indicate that the economic sector is producing more than enough to meet local needs, suggesting that those goods are exported and providing outside money to the local economy. A value of 1.25 or greater represents significant export activity. Once identified, a sector is then deemed as basic (LQ $\geq$ 1.25) or nonbasic, and economic planning can take place accordingly.

Shift-share analysis: Location quotients provide a static picture of the local economy's basic industry. Of course, one can calculate and compare location quotients over time, but perhaps an easier method of comparing local economic growth with national trends is through the use of *shift-share analysis*.

Shift-share analysis determines if local growth or decline is:

1. stimulated by national growth or decline;
2. due to a local concentration of businesses in relatively faster or slower growth economic sectors; or
3. due to the local establishment of more or less competitive firms as compared to the national average for that sector.

To conduct the shift-share analysis, we need to calculate:

1. a National Growth component;
2. an Industrial Growth component; and
3. a Competitive Share component.

To calculate the National Growth component, we take the base year local employment for each sector and multiply it by the average employment growth rate that has occurred nationally. Assuming the local economy has been similar to the national economy, the resulting number is the amount of growth in each sector that can be attributed to growth in the national economy.

$$E_i^r g^n$$

where:

E_i^r = base year employment of sector i in region r

g^n = growth rate of national economy

We determine the Industrial Growth component by multiplying base year local employment in each sector by the difference we see in the national growth rate in each economic sector and the general growth rate for the national economy. The industrial growth mix indicates that a majority of local employment is in sectors that are growing faster than total employment nationally (a positive industrial growth mix) or a majority of local employment is in sectors that are growing slower than total employment nationally.

$$E_i^r \left(g_i^n - g^n \right)$$

where:

E_i^r = base year employment of sector i in region r

g_i^n = national growth rate in sector i

g^n = growth rate of national economy

The Competitive Share component is calculated by multiplying a sector's local employment by the difference in the growth rate of that sector nationally and locally. A positive Competitive Share indicates growth above and beyond that attributable to the national economy. The opposite can be said of a negative Competitive Share.

$$E_i^r \left(g_i^r - g_i^n \right)$$

where:

E_i^r = base year employment of sector i in region r

g_i^r = regional growth rate in sector i

g_i^n = national growth rate in sector i

Multipliers: As discussed previously, basic industries help import money into a local economy. This new money circulates locally and, to some extent, stimulates other economic activity in an area such as employment. We can be precise in determining the *multipliers* for income and employment. For the purposes of this discussion on multipliers, we will focus on the employment multiplier.

Export industries create connections in local economies. The money that export workers earn is spent locally for goods and services; the money that export

To calculate the National Growth component, we take the base year local employment for each sector and multiply it by the average employment growth rate that has occurred nationally.

firms make is also spent locally. More jobs in export-related industries lead to more jobs in the local economy that support activity in the export sectors.

The employment multiplier helps us estimate the effect an export industry has on local employment. The employment multiplier can be calculated with the following formula:

$$Employment\ Multiplier = \frac{Total\ Employment}{Export\ Employment}$$

This average employment multiplier tells us how many jobs are created, potentially, for every new export job attracted to the area. Getting total employment is a fairly simple matter, but how do you determine the amount of export employment? For each sector, we use the following formula (after determining the location quotient)

$$Percent\ Export = \left(1 - \frac{1}{LQ}\right) \times 100$$

and apply this percentage to the total employment for each sector. By summing the percentage of employment theoretically devoted to export purposes, we have an estimate of total export employment.

OTHER PLANNING METHODS

Transportation Planning

The most widely used process for analyzing the impacts of transportation policies is through the Urban Transportation Model System (UTMS). The

OBJECT-ORIENTED PROGRAMMING AND CHAOS MODELING IN PLANNING

Chaos modeling—or its more formal designation, "complex, nonlinear, dynamical systems"—has been around for a number of years and planners have been introduced to these models before (see Cartwright 1991; Batty and Longley 1994). However, there has been a more recent increase in land use modeling using models that have evolved through the complex systems literature.

One such example was developed at the Centre for Advanced Spatial Analysis, located in University College London (www.casa.ucl.ac.uk/contact.htm). They have developed a model called SprawlSim, which is, in part, a multiagent system model combined with a geosimulation model, and was "designed as a tool to help researchers, the public, planning agencies, and public policy developers to experiment with ideas about suburban sprawl" (quoted from the Web site as accessed on December 20, 2001).

Nonlinear dynamics and agent-based models have also made it into the mainstream with applications serving policy purposes. TRANSIMS is an agent-based model developed by Los Alamos National Laboratory, which helps regions satisfy Clean Air Act and Transportation Efficiency Act for the 21st Century requirements for air quality and transportation objectives. Other agent-based models include those that evaluate land use and demographics, which include the ability to test very specific land use policies using economic, social, environmental and spatial data. Still others help planners understand pedestrian flows in urban environments.

Through the use of agent-based models, the traditional analytical perspective shifts from the aggregate to the individual. Agent-based models simulate decisions made by individuals in response to their environment as well as in response to the decisions of other agents (individuals). The common denominator of these examples is the ability to model human-environment interactions at a very fine level of spatial detail.

Contrast this with the traditional modeling paradigm in which analysts summarize these human-environment interactions into zonal aggregations and thereby restrict themselves to analyzing general outcomes as opposed to the detail that agent-based models provide.

In order to fully appreciate these models, planners who are interested in this type of analysis are learning to use object-oriented programming methods. The dynamics of agent-based models flow from rule-governed behavior within the frame of a complex dynamical system (here, cellular automata, multi-agent systems and complex adaptive systems are all included as agent-based models). It would appear that these models are best suited for describing current land use pattern behavior and forecasting future land use characteristics.

One can get started in the area by simply doing an Internet search (using Google or another search engine) on land use, cellular automata and/or agent-based models. Currently, there are several sites that offer examples of systems (such as Sprawl-Sim, described above) as well as a variety of economic-, transportation- and geographic-based models that are also described by complex systems behavior. The Santa Fe Institute (see Waldrop 1992 for an excellent history of the Santa Fe Institute and the emergence of chaos science) is currently involved in research on the use of complex systems modeling for environmental problems. They will no doubt become more involved in land use models in the future.

Zoning remains the key policy tool that planners use to organize urban and regional areas. Most states require some type of a zoning process and a corresponding map to establish land use guidelines for an area. However, given the constant tensions and conflict over appropriate zoning regulations, variances, takings, smart growth initiatives and other general issues associated with sprawl, it appears that better methods are needed to help planners shape their regions.

Land parcels have attributes that characterize their form (e.g., current zoning, past zoning, soil type, vegetation and existing structures) and that characterization may change over time depending (to a great amount) on the attributes of neighboring and nearby parcels. (In the jargon of agent-based modeling, land parcels are called *agents* and their attributes are called *states*.) If rules governing those changes can be developed (e.g., the probability that a parcel zoned agriculture will be rezoned residential when surrounding parcels are zoned residential), then agent-based modeling should be able to predict future land use characteristics.

Agent-based models—using current and historic land use patterns, current and historic zoning, fragile land overlays and even community policies (along with other measures the programmer may choose to consider, such as land ownership and land value)—may prove to be a better forecaster for future land use characteristics than we currently use. If such models are tied into a Geographic Information System with modern 3-D graphic packages, then planners will be in a better position to make reasonable recommendations and offer better visualizations to communicate these to their communities.

They might also offer better tools that allow citizen participation in decisions regarding how a locality could be zoned and to assist in visualizing what communities might look like under various planning initiatives. Planners have tried to do this in the past; however, with the aid of modern complex modeling programs and high-speed, high-capacity computers (available at a relatively low cost), planners will be able to do this type of forecasting and visualization more accurately and with a higher level of detail than ever before.

—Mitchell J. Rycus

Batty, Michael and Paul Longley. *Fractal Cities.* London: Academic Press, 1994.

Cartwright, T.J. "Planning and Chaos Theory," *Journal of the American Planning Association,* Vol. 57, No. 1. Chicago: American Planning Association, Winter 1991.

Waldrop, Mitchell. *Complexity.* New York: Simon & Schuster, 1992.

UTMS is also known as the "Four-Step" model, which accurately describes the process of forecasting transportation within an area or region. While the mathematics of this forecasting procedure can be very complex, the process that the model represents is very straightforward and actually very intuitive.

The four steps of the UTMS are:

1. trip generation
2. trip distribution
3. mode choice
4. network assignment

Each of these four steps is actually a separate analytical process, and the results of one "step" are used as inputs for the following steps. The UTMS can also be considered an "iterative" process (i.e., the model can repeat itself a number of times). The number of iterations generally depends upon how far into the future we are forecasting travel.

The UTMS requires two basic pieces of information before it can do its job. The information provided by the Land Use/Activity System Model lets the UTMS know about the character and patterns of land use within the study area. This information, which is divided into analysis zones, can include the general types of land use in the region, the intensity of their use, and the demographic and economic activity within the zone. Planners also provide information about the transportation network for the region. This information includes the location and layout of the network as well as the characteristics of the network, such as speed limits, turning restrictions at intersections and whether streets are "one-way" or "two-way"

UTMS is also known as the "Four-Step" model, which accurately describes the process of forecasting transportation within an area or region.

streets. Once this information is provided, the modeling procedure for travel begins.

Trip generation: This first step of the model asks the question, "How much travel is being generated by this zone?" Trips can be generated by a zone in two ways: by producing trips and by attracting trips. A zone produces trips through its "native" population and land uses. Typically, most trips are produced by households and are primarily home based. The purposes of the home-based trips are varied and include commuting, shopping and socializing; however, economic activities also produce trips (e.g., deliveries and service provision).

Trips are also attracted to zones. The primary trip attractors are economic uses. Zones attract trips because they are places of employment, they attract commuters and they are places to do business (e.g., retail and commercial centers).

Trip distribution: The second step asks, "Where are those trips going?" Once the UTMS has determined the amount of travel produced by and attracted to a zone, the next task is to distribute those trips throughout the study area. For each zone, the UTMS allocates those trips among all other zones (including itself); it links origins and destinations of trips. This is determined by a number of factors, including how attractive a zone is to travelers or how accessible that zone is with respect to the number of activities that can be conducted there. Another factor is called "friction" (i.e., the ease of travel between two zones). The more friction, the less likely that interaction exists between two zones. Friction is a catch-all term that can include distance, speed limits and stops between two zones.

Mode choice: The third step asks, "What mode of transportation is being used by the travelers?" Through the UTMS, we now know how many trips are being generated; we also know where those trips are going. It is very important to determine the mode by which those trips are being made. The mode choice step of the UTMS predicts the share of travel by mode; generally, this prediction is split between automobiles and transit, although more sophisticated models can be more realistic and take into account carpooling and different types of transit trips.

The estimated choices are determined primarily by two factors: cost and socioeconomic characteristics. The cost of a trip, or a certain type of trip, influences the choice to make that trip and influences the mode we might choose in order to make that trip. The cost of a trip can be explicit (i.e., it can cost money out of our pocket); the cost can also be implicit (i.e., the axiom that "time is money"). To a great extent, socioeconomic characteristics can determine the choice that is made. Affluent households may rely more on automobiles because of their convenience and they may perceive their time as more valuable. As a result, these affluent households may not wish to spend time waiting for a bus or train, nor are they willing to take a less direct route to their destination.

Network assignment: The last step asks, "By what route are these trips traveling from one place to another?" As any traveler is aware, there is more than one way to arrive at a destination. The choice of route is influenced by a number of different factors, such as time of day, weather conditions, street conditions and characteristics and perceived safety. This step of the model considers all alternative routes among zones as well as any characteristics that can be attributed to those routes. Some models assume that all trips are made at the same time; others are more realistic as they incrementally make assignments that allow for the possibility of deciding a route based on congestion conditions.

CONCLUSIONS

This chapter has only scratched the surface of the many analytical and quantitative techniques available to planners. Hidden behind these descriptions are many built-in assumptions, and it would behoove the planner to be acquainted with some of these assumptions in order to properly use these and more sophisticated techniques.

Some directions that analytical techniques have recently taken deal with the concepts of *complexity* and *chaos*—two terms used to describe aspects of a very technical field called *nonlinear dynamics*. The idea behind chaos theory and complexity is the fact that what used to be called random "noise" (phenomena for which no discernible pattern can be found) actually has some level of predictability given the right analytical techniques. Policy analysis and planning techniques are making forays into using nonlinear dynamics as a way of describing urban patterns as well as the cause and effect of decisions in a process. While the study of nonlinear dynamics

The cost of a trip can be explicit (i.e., it can cost money out of our pocket); the cost can also be implicit (i.e., the axiom that "time is money").

will likely never enter the "mainstream" of planning thought and practice, it is just this sort of research that finds itself "under the hood" of forecasting and predictive analytical programs.

The purpose of this chapter is not to make the reader an analyst, but rather to familiarize the reader with a survey of techniques that is useful to planners. As well, the reader should gain an appreciation of these techniques. More importantly, the inaccessible nature of quantitative analysis requires the ability to translate these numbers into a story—not only for your own sake, but for the sake of the people you are serving. For further reading, see the annotated "Bibliography" at the end of this chapter.

> *. . . the inaccessible nature of quantitative analysis requires the ability to translate these numbers into a story—not only for your own sake, but for the sake of the people you are serving.*

APPLICATIONS

1. Using information from the U.S. Census Bureau, calculate or obtain the average and standard deviation of housing value for your county. Then summarize that information by municipality and unincorporated area. Similarly summarize the information by census tract and finally by block group. What sort of pattern do you notice in the mean and standard deviation of housing value as your summary level moves from county, to place, to census tract, then to block group?

2. Create a thematic map of property values by parcel. Conduct a simple visual analysis. Do you notice any patterns? What phenomena can explain this pattern?

3. By selecting any sort of phenomenon that interests you (travel, poverty, real estate, etc.), formulate a conceptual model of what might influence that phenomenon. Restrict yourself to phenomena for which you can actually collect data. Be able to tell someone how you think these individual factors will affect the dependent variable (i.e., are the relationships positive or negative?).

4. Using Table 4-5, tell a story with the numbers presented in the table. How do the numbers change from period to period (absolute changes and percentage changes)? How would you describe the difference between the linear projection results and the geometric projection results? Take a stand: which one might be the most reliable number?

BIBLIOGRAPHY

Burt, James E. and Gerald M. Barber. *Elementary Statistics for Geographers.* 2d ed. New York: The Guilford Press, 1996.

> This text provides a great background in basic and intermediate statistics, both of a nonspatial and spatial variety. All of the concepts are explained in a straightforward manner with many diagrams and examples. In addition, many of the examples are those with which planners are familiar (e.g., housing and transportation). This text is valuable because its discussion of spatial statistics is at a high enough level to be useful, yet still be accessible.

Fotheringham, A. Stewart, Chris Brunsdon and Martin Charlton. *Quantitative Geography: Perspectives on Spatial Data Analysis.* London: Sage, 2000.

For those who wish to dive deeper into spatial analysis, this text provides the conceptual material necessary to begin that journey. This is less a "textbook" and more of an in-depth overview of the many facets of spatial analysis. Topics of note are "Spatial Data," "The Role of Geographical Information Systems" and "Exploring Data Visually." The text covers the traditional spatial techniques such as point pattern analysis, spatial regression and statistical inference. However, there are few examples of analysis that take the reader through from start to finish.

Kennedy, Peter. *A Guide to Econometrics.* Cambridge, MA: MIT Press, 1994.

Kennedy's text is a must-have for analysts—primarily for those using regression techniques. The guide is a true reference, useful for finding out quick bits of information about analytical techniques. Perhaps most important, Kennedy summarizes the advantages and disadvantages of the techniques along with many of the assumptions underlying these techniques, as well as the threats to validity.

Klosterman, Richard E. *Community Analysis and Planning Techniques.* Savage, MD: Rowman & Littlefield, 1990.

This is an excellent introduction to population and economic analysis techniques. The first half of the book discusses population projection and cohort-component analysis; the second half focuses on economic base studies. It is very well written and quite accessible for most people—even those who are scared of formulas and other assorted Greek notation.

Klosterman, Richard E., Richard K. Brail and Earl G. Bossard. *Spreadsheet Models for Urban and Regional Analysis.* New Brunswick, NJ: CUPR Press, 1993.

Not only does this text discuss various analytical techniques in a fair amount of detail, you can readily use these techniques if you have a computer and a spreadsheet program. Contributors to the text provide easy-to-use spreadsheet macros for the analysis of demographic and economic data, as well as environmental analysis and decision-making tools. The spreadsheet models are available in Lotus 1-2-3 and Excel. The authors also discuss how to begin designing your own tools for custom applications.

Krueckeberg, Donald A. and Arthur L. Silvers. *Urban Planning Analysis: Methods and Models.* New York: John Wiley and Sons, 1974.

Oppenheim, Norbert. *Applied Models in Urban and Regional Analysis.* Englewood Cliffs, NJ: Prentice-Hall, 1980.

A mid-level text, this book provides an excellent overview of the techniques discussed in this chapter in a suitable level of detail. The examples are informative and accessible, at least for those who feel comfortable with matrix notation. Even ignoring the math, the discussion is accessible enough to make this text valuable.

Plane, David A. and Peter A. Rogerson. *The Geographical Analysis of Population: With Applications to Planning and Business.* New York: John Wiley & Sons, 1994.

Plane and Rogerson provide an excellent text for those interested in demographic techniques. This text blends theory and practicality almost seamlessly and provides the reader with numerous examples and sample problems at the end of the chapters. Topics covered include population composition, demographic change, migration, forecasting and an excellent discussion that puts these techniques into perspective for the practicing planner.

Schofield, John A. *Cost Benefit Analysis in Urban & Regional Planning.* London: Allen & Unwin, 1987.

This is an admittedly dry, yet very useful, text for cost-benefit analysis. If you have an aversion to economics or the neoclassical way of thinking, then perhaps this isn't for you. However, if you wish to learn about the connection between economic thought and planning, then this book is an excellent resource. The first part of the book covers some basics in economics—namely welfare, distribution, surplus, etc. The second part provides a methodical application of cost-benefit analysis to topics such as urban renewal, land use planning, transportation and recreation facilities.

Stokey, Edith and Richard Zeckhauser. *A Primer for Policy Analysis.* New York: Norton, 1978.

As the title suggests, this book is intended for those who wish to provide themselves with an introduction to the quantitative side of policy analysis. The authors provide the reader with a suitable background in the mathematics required for the text (relatively minimal) as well as a background in some of the economic principles inherent in policy analysis. Topics include project evaluation, valuation, public choice and decision analysis.

Studenmund, A. H. *Using Econometrics: A Practical Guide.* New York: Harper Collins, 1992.

If you already feel comfortable with basic statistics and would like an introduction to regression analysis, Studenmund provides the reader with an excellent background. I really like this book because it describes some fairly sophisticated techniques in a very accessible manner. Aside from Ordinary Least Squares (OLS) regression—the most common and simplest form of regression analysis—the author takes you through diagnostic techniques to test assumptions, time-series, logistic regression and simultaneous models. Many examples and practice problems are also included, as well as a copy of ECSTAT (a statistics program).

CHAPTER 5

Working With Small Groups

Peter Ash

The executive officers of a private consulting firm, Planning Solutions, having just signed a contract with the States of Hiatonka and East Victoria to survey energy options, treated themselves to a self-congratulatory lunch. Over coffee, they discussed how to proceed. The senior members of the firm thought that work groups should be formed to evaluate options for energy alternatives to fuel oil and that Senior Planner should be the leader of the group (the Water Group), which would examine using water power to generate energy.

Groups like the Water Group are common in planning. This chapter considers issues relevant to the effective use of small groups by planners. It will focus on small groups of fewer than 10 members, meeting repeatedly with a fairly stable membership, with a leader clearly defined and with a task articulated at the outset. The emphasis will be on how to work with such groups rather than on the abstract theory of groups. The Water Group will provide illustrations of many of the techniques.

GROUP PROCESSES AND THE GROUP TASK

Tasks

Planning groups are work groups; they are set up to fulfill particular tasks.

Planning groups are work groups; they are set up to fulfill particular tasks. At their lunch, the executive officers of Planning Solutions had the task of deciding the necessary steps in order to survey energy options. One of their decisions was to create the Water Group. The Water Group has a different task: to examine using water power for production of energy. Another group may have a highly technical task (e.g., to do a physical survey of a dam site).

Planners also use groups to carry out nontechnical tasks, such as achieving greater cooperation among members of the planning firm. In such groups, the outcomes are not decisions, but rather attitudinal changes among planners that will facilitate their working together. Another type of attitudinal change group is one whose task is to develop acceptance for an already determined plan. There

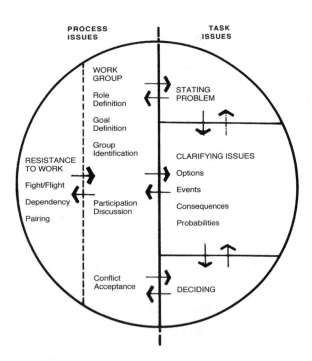

5-1. Group process and group task

are many public hearings that have this task as a covert function.

The Water Group is a problem-solving group whose task is to provide options and discussion to the planning firm, who will then weigh recommendations in the context of other reports from similar groups. The task of the Water Group is to produce a report that elaborates on the options for using water power to generate energy and evaluates the consequences of these options. The report will go to the executive officers of Planning Solutions and will be one basis for the firm's recommendations to their clients.

The group is defined by its task. The task must be clear, and the group must accept it as its work or the group will not be able to carry out its assignment. The group task can be broken down into smaller problems (see the sidebar entitled "Components of a Group Task") involving three objectives:

1. stating the problem
2. clarifying issues
3. choosing among alternatives

These steps may be iterative. For example, clarifying preferences and choosing among alternatives may lead to changing the definition of objectives in the original problem statement and raise new issues that need to be clarified.

Process

The interactions of the members during the problem-solving steps define and form the group process. Group process is sometimes discussed in terms of an individual member's actions, motivations and feelings toward other members and the group as a whole. Group process is also conceptualized by considering the group as a whole. Groups seem to take on a life of their own, which becomes more than the accumulation of individual experiences. If one thinks of the group as a machine that processes problems in an effort to arrive at solutions, the group process is the description of the interworkings of machine components, while the actual steps have to do with the function performed by each component.

Group process issues are discussed at a conceptual level different from that of task issues. For example, while the group process issue of goal definition is usually foremost at the problem statement stage, it may also surface at the decision-making stage. Issues of group process are often associated with particular task steps, but nevertheless span the range of problem solving as well as being relevant when groups resist doing the work. Figure 5-1 shows these interactions schematically.

The overt goal of the group process is to perform the group task. However, groups have another, usually covert, task: to achieve identity as a group. This is not to say that groups always work to perpetuate themselves (although many do), but that they strive to maintain a group identity and may do so in ways that interfere with the performance of the task. For example, if members fear that new ideas will upset a leader who has authority to disband the group, they will tend not to be innovative. In this way, they try to promote the group's continuance at the expense of not producing new ideas.

COMPONENTS OF A GROUP TASK

1. Stating the problem
   a. Exposition of the problem
   b. Delineating objectives of a solution

2. Clarifying issues
   a. Clarifying options for both information gathering and final actions
   b. Clarifying external events that may occur
   c. Judging consequences of various courses of action
   d. Estimating probabilities of uncertain events
   e. Clarifying preferences

3. Choosing among alternatives
   a. Comparing outcomes of options
   b. Making trade-offs among values
   c. Reporting the decision

When a group is manifestly not carrying out its task efficiently, it is always appropriate to wonder what group process goal it is trying to achieve. In well-functioning groups, the achievement of the task improves group morale, which in turn leads to improved group functioning and better task performance.

This chapter describes how to affect group process to improve small-group problem solving. Since the leader generally has more influence than any other member on group processes, most of the suggestions are directed to techniques the leader might use. Members may use many of these same techniques.

ESTABLISHING A GROUP

Why a Group?

A person (or another group) with a task to be completed must decide whether to use an individual problem solver or a group. Planners use groups largely to bring together varying expertise; to help accumulate data; to lend legitimacy to the decision-making process; and to provide a range of alternatives, options and ways of thinking not available from one person. Not all decisions are put to a group because group work is time-consuming; someone in authority already knows what they want to do or is satisfied that they can figure it out; or the problem solver is concerned that, in trying to satisfy disparate group members, poor decisions will be made.

Plan for a Group

Once a task is defined, a group can be established. Discussing the nature of the leader, the membership and the external factors relevant to the group can specify its structure.

Leader: Most planning groups will specify a leader. The leader may be appointed, may set up her own group or may decide to form a group that will elect its own leader. In our example, Senior Planner was designated by the executives in her firm to establish and lead the Water Group. It is a natural tendency of groups to want leaders; even so-called leaderless groups tend to assign certain organizing functions to one person.

To see how strongly a group will try to obtain a leader, one need only look at psychotherapy groups in which the therapist actively stays out of the leadership role. In such groups, one quickly sees anger toward the therapist for not fulfilling the group's expectations that they lead. Some groups rotate members through the leader's role, either because no member wants the continual chore of leading or because the group is afraid one leader will become too powerful. The potential difficulty with changing leaders is that a group will spend a large portion of its time re-establishing role definitions, expectations of how the group will operate and modes of interaction.

Group leaders have a number of decisions to make in organizing the group:

- What kind of a leader are they going to be?
- How much authority will they wield?

- Can they, as leader, constitute a majority of one and outvote the entire group?
- Do they see the group as advisory to them?
- Are they going to run a formal group according to *Robert's Rules of Order* or allow a more informal exchange?
- Do they relish loud, heated discussions or would they prefer courtesy and decorum to be maintained at all costs?

Many of these decisions will be made without thinking and will seem to the leader to be determined by previous experience, outside expectations of the nature of the group and the leader's personality. They are decisions that often have an "of course" quality, although groups are potentially capable of working effectively with widely varying leadership styles. Still, it is useful, particularly for beginning leaders, to be clear about these various dimensions because these answers will affect the choice of members as well as giving the leader a clear expectation of what their role will be.

Regardless of the sort of authority the leader intends to wield, it is of crucial importance that she is clear about and identify with the group's task. If her leadership is seen as facilitating the work, the group will identify with her. In many planning groups, the leader has primary authority to make decisions. As far as the group goes, however, the leader's major role in the group process is to facilitate the group's carrying out its task. This role is different from whatever power prerogatives she carries. A leader with authority must be both facilitator and decision maker. She will do better if she acts as a facilitator most of the time.

Some leaders temperamentally have difficulty setting aside their authority to help promote group discussion. Such people in authority might well ask another group member to act as discussion leader and facilitator, so that the authority can participate actively in the discussion without having to be concerned about the dampening effect their comments would have were they also the facilitator.

Even as a group member, a person with authority needs to focus on facilitating the group and defer decision making until the group has made its opinions known. Groups do not work well when they feel their contribution is undervalued. If they are to meet simply to rubber stamp decisions the authority will make independently, their task—properly defined—is only to legitimize (rather than produce) solutions. The most common reason for unproductive meetings is that the leader fails to recognize that her primary responsibility is to help the group work on its task. This does not mean she forfeits the powers of decision making, but rather that she suspends them until after full group discussion.

Because of the role as group facilitator, the leader must be prepared to suppress expressing her own feelings. Other members may show anger at a disruptive member but, for the leader, such feelings are properly expressed only if they serve to help the group as a whole function effectively. The higher the leader's status in the organization relative to other

Even as a group member, a person with authority needs to focus on facilitating the group and defer decision making until the group has made its opinions known.

VOTING AND NONVOTING MEMBERS OF A GROUP

A group may consist of members who have voting privileges and those who don't. It is a good idea to define these roles at the outset. Voting members not only have a vote but their opinions have weight in arriving at a group decision through discussion. Nonvoting members may be present solely to perform functions in support of the group's task. These individuals should not expect to vote or to express opinions in group discussion except when asked for one within the context of their role.

Nonvoting members of the group may be termed "staff" or "resources." In the Water Group, Staff Assistant may be present to take notes but would rarely be expected to speak, except perhaps to help in logistics such as identifying likely dates for the next meeting. In some groups, unlike the Water Group, an attorney might be present to give legal opinions but not

continued on page 165

group members, the more important it is that she remain impersonal in the group.

Membership: The membership (types of expertise and individuals) and size of the group will have an important impact on the way the group functions. Groups larger than 10 become unwieldy and more formal. If the number of experts needed is larger than 10, it is wise to set up several small groups. Groups of five or fewer are so small that the absence of one member can bring the group's progress to a halt.

Since the executives of Planning Solutions had full confidence in Senior Planner, she was given the authority to pick the members of the Water Group. Leader (as we will now call her) has some preliminary ideas about who should be in the group. Planner B, another member of the firm, has wide expertise in energy planning. Leader thinks that a water-planning engineer will be necessary and that a member whose expertise is on legal aspects would be useful.

Leader needs to consider the role the nonplanners will have in the group. Members from Planning Solutions are interested in the overall task of the group. Representatives of particular interests, such as the members from each state's water ministry, are stakeholders and have an allegiance to the groups they represent.

Whether to include stakeholders as voting members of a group (as opposed to bringing them in to obtain their points of view but not allowing them to have a voting presence) is a strategic decision. It involves considering how much conflict different

stakeholders are likely to have among themselves; the likelihood that they will use their positions to frustrate the group's larger aims; and the usefulness of having a stakeholder participate in the decision-making process, both to illuminate what are likely to be acceptable compromises and to legitimize the group's decision in the eyes of the constituency the stakeholder represents.

Leader enjoys lively discussions, does not anticipate that stakeholders will frustrate the group's work, and wants to be able to continually check whether the options being formulated will be controversial. She decides to include stakeholders as full members of the group. The final list of roles on the committee is:

1. Leader
2. General Planner (general expertise)
3. Water Planner (outside water consultant specialist)
4. attorney
5. representative of regional Natural Resources Board
6. representative of energy department (Hiatonka)
7. representative of energy department (East Victoria)
8. representative of environmental action group
9. representative of utility company

Leader, having decided what roles she wants in the group, now chooses the particular people. In this task, she will be guided by several considerations. First, how well do members get along? In determining the other planners in the group, Leader has already decided on General Planner, a planner with general expertise. She chooses Water Planner because of his specific skills. Leader, having worked with both planners in her firm before, is confident that they get along well.

However, it is not necessary that members know each other. In fact, if a significant subgroup is well acquainted outside the group, they may bring ways of interacting with one another that lead other members to feel excluded. This is a potential pitfall for the Water Group because the three planners are friends and have worked together many times before, so Leader plans to watch for the formation of coalitions.

Group cohesion increases with personal, positive feelings between members. Leader might face a choice between, for example, Mr. Gruff of the Natural Resources Board, who has a great deal of expertise but an abrasive personality, and his assistant Nat Resources, who has slightly less expertise but whom everyone likes. It is not simply a matter of personal preference to choose the likable Nat Resources; the quality of group performance will increase if the meetings are pleasant and cooperative. One hostile member can make work so unpleasant for the rest of the group that productivity falls drastically. Leader decides she will arrange a side meeting among Mr. Gruff, Nat Resources and herself to make use of Mr. Gruff's expertise without including him in the group.

The energy departments are picking their own representatives, Hiatonka and Victoria, so Leader has no choice there. The environmental action group frequently sends Mr. Slowfeet to planning meetings. Leader has reservations: Mr. Slowfeet is often absent and, when he comes, he comes late. Groups tend to regard such behavior as a member's voting with his feet on the group's worth, with a consequent lowering of morale.

Leader wants the group to go well. She invites Environ, who accepts the appointment. Mr. Noisome, the in-house planner for the utility company, is known for his loud blustering at everyone who disagrees with him, so Leader invites his assistant, the equally competent but more temperate Utility. The Water Group membership is therefore as follows:

1. Leader (planner)
2. General Planner (planner)
3. Water Planner (planner)
4. Knowlaw (attorney)
5. Nat Resources (representing natural resources board)
6. Hiatonka (representing Water ministry)
7. Victoria (representing Water ministry)
8. Environ (representing environmental action group)
9. Utility (representing utility company)

External factors: While specifying the members and the leader defines one side of the group's boundary, external factors (those persons or agencies not in the group but relevant to it) define the other side.

Planning Solutions, who set up the Water Group and defined its task, is one such external factor. The directors of the departments of energy, to whom a copy of the final report will go, are others. Because the nature of a planner's work affects outside

continued from page 164

to otherwise participate. Other individuals might be called in on a temporary basis to present information useful to the group's deliberations. In that case, it is clear that they will not vote or contribute to the decisions of the group.

However, the issue gets more confusing in other situations. A common example is when professional planners, who are responsible for background work on the topic under discussion, are members of the group on an ongoing basis to support the appointed members of the group. The planning staff and perhaps other members of the group are likely to consider their opinions highly relevant. On the other hand, these staff members may be viewed as having a vested interest in the outcome or as being too resistant to the opinions of the appointed members. It is a good idea to establish at the beginning of a group process whether such staff are voting or nonvoting members.

groups, planning groups must take cognizance of such external factors.

All members of the Water Group serve as members as well as liaisons to outside groups. Since planning groups often take part in preparing reports and recommendations for other groups, ascertaining the activities, expectations and preferences of external groups are essential. Planning groups often use members as representatives of their constituent groups, both to obtain varying points of view and to legitimize group decisions.

It is important that members be selected whom the constituent groups will acknowledge as representative. For example, the Water Group might point to the participation of Utility to rebut a charge that their final report did not properly consider the utility company's position. If the utility company did not consider Utility to represent their viewpoint, his membership could not be used in this way.

External factors can operate to the detriment of the group. For example, political intrigue at Planning Solutions could lead to the Water Group's disbanding, or members of the group may fear that the two energy departments will not use their report regardless of its content. Such difficulties interfere profoundly with a group's work. In such cases, the group may need to address itself to the external factors to ensure its own survival and usefulness. On the other hand, anticipating that a report is eagerly awaited and that a great deal depends on it can help bring meaning to the group's work, increase the group's cohesion and improve dedication to the task.

A group identity must be formed to some degree before the group can begin work on its task.

THE FIRST MEETING

When a group is chosen, it exists only in the minds of the leader and its members. At the first meeting, it becomes an active group. The group has two jobs: the first (and obvious) one is to work on its task; the second one (less obvious, but in some ways more powerful) is to keep itself going and maintain a group identity.

A group identity must be formed to some degree before the group can begin work on its task. The identity will continue to develop over the life of the group, but initially the group needs to share a sense of roles, power and the task at hand. This process often takes place without being noticed, but it becomes highlighted when consensus breaks down. The structure of a group may be compared to the effects of wearing eyeglasses. Most of the time, the wearer is not aware of their glasses, although they greatly affect what is seen; they become aware of them when they fall off, get dirty or no longer function properly. Structure is not noticed as long as it is shared. As the group goes along, it may become evident that certain elements of structure, which were thought to be shared, are not.

Suppose, at the first meeting, Utility does not recognize that Leader should lead and insists the group elect its own leader. The group has several options (e.g., to follow his idea, to reject it, to table it or to vote Utility out of the group) but they cannot easily ignore his statement. A challenge to the existing structure must be addressed before work can proceed.

Setting

A comfortable setting is important for the group's work and refreshments can help foster informality.

Leader has use of a conference room at the central offices of Planning Solutions, which are located within easy reach by most members. She knows that the room has adequate seating, a good conference table, good lighting and ventilation and is appropriately sized for the group (i.e., neither too large for easy communication nor too small for this size group). The room is equipped with slide and computer presentation equipment and is set up for Internet access. Leader decides to have drinks and snacks available.

Building Group Identity

Making introductions: The group's first meeting has a great influence on setting the tone for meetings that follow. In a group of people who do not already know each other, the leader's style has considerable impact on the group's style. While the planner members of the Water Group work together every day, they are relatively unfamiliar with the stakeholder representatives.

It is useful for Leader to go around before the meeting formally starts, welcome each stakeholder and shake their hand. (There are regional variations for this and other social behavior: in parts of the southern United States, failing to use this personal touch—paying one's respects—is considered almost rude; in the north, such behavior is less common but more effective for being unusual.)

Once the meeting formally begins, the group will probably start by making introductions. Instead of having each member state name and title, Leader can say why she wanted the person in the group, and go on to ask the member to expand on their background, tell the group why they are there and say what they hope to get out of being a member. This introduction helps the group get to know each other and encourages members to begin to define their own roles in the group. Additionally, it is a way for Leader to make clear that she values the particular contributions of each member—a message she will wish to give in a number of indirect ways. After introductions are made, she may wish to make further clarifying comments about how she anticipates the group will work. At times, the person or entity that has organized it does not chair a new group. In such cases, the leader might introduce members by their affiliation and the important attributes they bring to the task being addressed.

Recorder: Most groups should have a recorder to summarize the group's major points of discussion and distribute notes by the next meeting. Notes allow members to refresh their memories about the previous meeting. Perhaps more importantly, notes acknowledge members' contributions and let them know whether they were properly understood. Groups differ in their need for formal documentation to present later to clients, other planning groups or outside agencies. Some members may want only decisions recorded, thinking that discussion will be freer if it is off the record; others may wish for more

The group's first meeting has a great influence on setting the tone for meetings that follow.

MAKING DECISIONS: CONSENSUS, *ROBERT'S RULES* OR HYBRID?

The Water Group is an example of a planning group assembled to perform a specific task over a defined period of time. In this case, Planning Solutions (a private firm) created the Water Group to bring various constituencies together to examine a specific option for energy policy.

There are other types of small groups that planners will encounter in the public sector. One is a task force appointed by an elected board or council and charged with creating a policy, or set of approaches, to deal with a specific problem—again, usually in a defined period of time. Another is a standing committee or subcommittee of an elected or appointed board or commission, delegated to review specific issues or proposals. The choice of a decision-making process needs to be a deliberate and strategic one for the organizers of the group, as it will have an impact on both the group dynamics and satisfaction with outcomes.

The two major ways decisions can be made in a group are by *consensus* or by *voting*, using parliamentary methods, especially *Robert's Rules of Order*. Each has its strengths and weaknesses.

The Water Group used the consensus method in which brainstorming may be used to establish a list of options or proposals that are discussed by the group. In discussion, the leader might call on members to speak or allow spontaneous discussion. Over time, the major topics are agreed upon and the leader may restate the group's position on each, writing them down in note form or displaying them on a flip chart. The group is thus explicitly or implicitly asked to agree. If no one contradicts a position, or if only one or two members do and are not able to gain any support, the group is considered to have come to consensus on that point.

With a formal voting procedure using *Robert's Rules of Order* (see the sidebar entitled *"Robert's Rules of Order"*), a motion to approve a proposal or document is put forward, discussion occurs and a vote is taken. If the group is not unanimous in approving the proposal, the numbers of votes for and against it are recorded. The document may be amended or altered, again by majority vote, before the final vote is taken. Appointed standing or ad-hoc committees—which report to an elected or appointed board or commission, and which review and make decisions on proposals presented by other individuals or agencies—are best run by *Robert's Rules*. A vote is recorded that may be referred to in future decisions and discussions.

Advantages and Disadvantages of the Consensus Method

- The informality of this method provides a warmer atmosphere and helps to build a small-group identity.
- Creative work by a group is best fostered by freewheeling discussion.
- If group dynamics go well, a strong group identity is more likely to emerge using this method.
- Less vocal members of the group may feel inhibited, or if a member receives poor feedback for their contribution, they may stop participating in the discussion. The views of the more articulate and aggressive members may dominate the final decision and, in the end, the "disappointed minority" may simply feel that they were not heard.
- Some decisions may be revisited time and time again if strong voices persist in bringing them up.
- The statement of the group decision as articulated by the leader may be manipulative in that members will be put in the position of objecting to a statement that has been identified as a group decision. There is pressure not to fracture the group identity.

Advantages and Disadvantages of the Parliamentary Method

- The formality of the method makes for a more orderly discussion. Less aggressive members of the group may feel more empowered to speak in their turn.
- The ability to offer amendments allows changes to be made or rejected and each viewpoint to receive its fair hearing: if the change attracts enough votes, it prevails; with the consensus approach, if no other person speaks up for it, it will fail.
- Once voted on, a matter is disposed of and no further discussion is necessary.
- There is less opportunity for the leader or others to manipulate the opposition in support of a particular statement, as even the weakest member can vote and may be able to persuade others to vote for their viewpoint. The "disappointed minority" will thus have a numerical rating of the support they received.
- The formality may appear cold or bureaucratic to some and be less conducive to establishment of a group identity.
- Discussion, because it is more orderly, is less freewheeling. By the time a member is recognized to speak, several unrelated topics may have followed the statement that they are addressing.

Using *Robert's Rules of Order* is probably not appropriate for a group engaged in a creative task. However, a group that must produce a final document or product might use a hybrid approach. A consensus approach might be used in producing a draft document. The group could then vote on the various provisions. If the document is advisory to an elected body, the vote will add credence to the document.

—Vivienne N. Armentrout

detail. The first meeting is a good time to raise this issue explicitly for group discussion. Leader has Staff Assistant who will staff the group and will also act as recorder.

Agenda: Agendas are useful for small work groups, especially at early meetings. They help to give a sense of direction and set goals for the meeting. By identifying goals, agendas can help forestall getting stuck on one issue. The agendas may not need to be distributed to each member but could be put on a chalkboard. At an early meeting, a group should consider its use of agendas.

Some leaders prefer to have a formal agenda to which it must adhere and use it to control meetings. Other groups use agendas as skeletons for structuring meetings and are open to additions during meetings. Informal groups usually do better when members feel free to add items to the agenda. Agendas for the first meetings often encompass such issues as setting priorities and directions for later meetings. As it develops, the group should also consider its longer agenda—the overall flow of its work—in order to fit its work efficiently to external time constraints.

Setting forth of group task: In a relatively brief manner, Leader now sets forth the group task. Assuming the group made self-introductions, she has some sense of how the group task fits in with members' expectations. In specifying the task, she will also want to set down relevant external parameters, such as how much time the group has to prepare its report, how often and where it will meet,

ROBERT'S RULES OF ORDER

Robert's Rules of Order is the basis for most parliamentary process in the United States. Most elected or appointed public bodies and many civic groups explicitly state in their bylaws that *Robert's Rules* will be followed in their deliberations. The application of these rules can seem arcane and elaborate to the uninitiated; indeed, many organizations have an appointed parliamentarian to interpret them. However, they are a very practical and functional means to guarantee a fair process, avoid confusion and deliver a result that can claim to reflect the will of the majority.

The basis of *Robert's Rules* is the making and voting on of motions. Motions govern the business of the day and are the means by which decisions are made. The rules provide for which types of motions take precedence and how proposed amendments may be made or rejected. All business is done through the chair, who calls on members in turn. An important feature of the rules is to allow (and then terminate) debate in an orderly and fair manner. Usually, motions are carried by a vote of the majority of those present.

Groups often have their own special rules or bylaws that alter or apply the general rules delineated in *Robert's Rules of Order*. For example, some organizations may allow proxy voting (by members not present) while many do not. Some may require a majority of the entire membership (not just those present) for a motion to pass. Usually, there is a "quorum" defined, so that at least some proportion of the membership must be present. Some groups may require a two-thirds vote or other "supermajority" vote for certain types of motions. A famous example is the 60 votes required in the U.S. Senate to cut off debate on a motion.

There are dozens of versions of *Robert's Rules* available in book and leaflet form, all based on the original by General Henry Robert, first published in 1876. Many are interpretative and contain hints on conducting meetings. There is at least one software product aimed at perfecting one's skill through simulations. (Skilled users can wield a lot of power in some groups.) At the base level, the rules are very simple: be courteous, be clear and whoever has the votes wins.

This annotated bibliography/resource for *Robert's Rules of Order* may be useful for a more detailed exposition of the method:

Robert III, Henry M., William J. Evans, Daniel H. Honemann and Thomas J. Balch. *Robert's Rules of Order, Newly Revised*. 10th ed. Cambridge, MA: Perseus Publishing, 2000.

> This is the "official" and up-to-date revision of the original (first published in 1876), as issued by the heirs of the original author, General Henry Robert. It now includes many modernizations, including discussions of the use of the Internet and video conferencing

Rozkis, Laurie E. and Ellen Lichtenstein. *21st Century Robert's Rules of Order*. New York: Dell Publishing, 1995.

> An inexpensive and modernized paraphrase of *Robert's Rules* written in modern colloquial language with explanations of the use and application of various rules and procedures.

www.parliamentarians.org/parlipro.htm

> This is a discussion of parliamentary procedure based on the *Robert's Rules of Order, Newly Revised*, 10th ed.

www.constitution.org/rror/rror--00.htm

> An online reproduction of the 1915 version, complete with charts, is available at this site.

—Vivienne N. Armentrout

whether funds are available for doing studies and how long the report is expected to be. After briefly discussing the task, she should encourage the group to respond.

> During the introductions, Water Planner says he has been in numerous groups writing reports of this sort before. "Speaking as a planner," he says, "I know that many reports get filed in the circular file. I'd be a lot happier if I knew who was going to read our report." When Leader then specifies the group task, she can take particular care to identify who will be reading the report and, in the ensuing discussion, should check with Water Planner to see whether he still has concerns about this.

Speaking to members' concerns and then asking for their response is useful even if the information does not allay the concerns. If members feel understood, they feel an affinity with the group and its task even if they do not get what they want. This principle is of central importance in group decision making because it allows members to compromise their individual preferences in favor of a group decision. If Water Planner were dissatisfied with Leader's answer, Leader could then take the next step and note that the person or entity to whom the report goes should be considered a problem with various options to be explored. This step serves to underline that Water Planner's contribution has been heard and may, in fact, lead to better use of the group's report.

In this first meeting, members should have time to react to each step. The group will likely see some testing between members and subtle jockeying for roles, position and influence. The less familiar members are with one another, the more time is needed to allow for this initial testing. Allowing the group process to develop in this way does not mean delaying the task, but recognizes that a group needs to establish an identity before it can work. At the same time, group identity grows stronger when a group does meaningful work. After members have introduced themselves, explained their goals and discussed the group goal, the group will move to problem solving.

FACILITATING PROBLEM SOLVING

Using the problem-solving outline introduced earlier (see the sidebar entitled "Components of a Group Task"), two examples will illustrate how group process affects the performance of problem-solving steps.

A Process Problem: What Should the Group Do Next?

Stating the problem: Leader would like each member to bring to the next meeting a three- to five-page memo of the relevant concerns in that member's area and considers simply asking each member to do this. Such a directive runs the risk of causing the members to feel ordered about, incapable of deciding and devalued. An important principle in working with groups is to try to turn individual decisions into group decisions, so Leader asks the group specifically how it should proceed.

The group will likely see some testing between members . . . time is needed to allow for this initial testing.

Clarifying options: At this early stage in the group, Leader is particularly attentive to setting the tone of discussions that will follow.

Promoting informality: Small groups tend to work best if they proceed informally. Using first names, for example, helps promote free and open discussion. Reinforcing members for their contributions helps promote informality and reduces anxiety about contributing. The leader should recognize that groups generally wish to promote harmony and positive group feeling and are often responsive and ready to accept encouragement in this direction. In informal groups, shifts to formal procedures (e.g., a move to parliamentary procedure) generally indicate the existence of unresolved conflict.

Encouraging participation: For groups to work well, it is important that all members participate. Promoting informality is intended to encourage participation. Members will participate when they feel the group values their contributions. Everyone has had the experience of saying something and having no one respond—one feels rather like the cartoon character who runs straight off a cliff and is sustained in the air until they realize they are no longer on solid ground.

Reactions to members' comments (such as overtly appreciating them, restating them, clarifying them and integrating them with what others have said) all promote participation. For members who hold back making comments, active solicitation of their ideas by the leader is often helpful. One easy and useful method for integrating ideas is to write them on a marker board.

Leader asks for suggestions and writes the following on the blackboard in response to members' comments.

1. We don't need any hydroelectric power; people could conserve.
2. Do a stream-flow analysis to ascertain whether the Pleasant River has enough energy to be worth damming.
3. Prepare three- to five-page memos.
4. Begin a more detailed site analysis of Eagle Point (in response to Nat Resources, who thinks, from his own work, that this is where a dam should probably go).

Leader writes these suggestions on the board without criticism and without specifying names. This serves to define the ideas as group ideas; when one is turned down, it is the group that is discarding one of its own ideas rather than rejecting a particular member's contribution.

Clarifying consequences of options: The group then turns to look at the implications of each suggestion.

1. Environ's suggestion about conservation would lead the group to disband. A member comments that this suggestion should be redefined as describing a trade-off problem. Leader comments that this will need to be addressed later.
2. A possible consequence of stream-flow analysis is that no dam may be feasible.

Small groups tend to work best if they proceed informally.

3. Memos (Leader's hoped-for result) would allow the group to begin exploring a wide range of issues.
4. The consequences of a site analysis would be high cost and significant time required.

It often happens that a group feeling positively about itself will set goals beyond its capabilities. Water Planner, having just completed a report on dams in the two states, says he will prepare an abstract of dam usage for next week's meeting. Hiatonka and Victoria, not to be outdone, promise to have ready detailed reports of all water usage for energy in their respective states. General Planner, having recently worked with the state water departments, fears that a complete survey of current usage cannot be completed in a week and is concerned about the effect on the group if the first deadline it sets for itself is not achieved.

He proposes, therefore, that the three members instead begin to collect relevant data and report their preliminary impressions to the group at the next meeting. Leaving the performance of the first task somewhat open-ended allows the members to try to achieve what they had initially stated, but does not carry the penalty of failure should that project prove too ambitious. However, it is often useful for a group to set out a timetable for completion of component tasks.

Choosing among alternatives: Having clearly specified the consequences of the four options, the group rapidly reaches the consensus that a stream-flow analysis has to be done. They also think short reports are useful, and decide to table the site analysis pending further study, and to delay discussions of the value trade-offs inherent in the suggestion about conservation. Had Leader overlooked or been unaware of the need for a stream analysis, or had she specified that other members should bring in reports, she would have at least delayed getting the stream-analysis data and run the potential risk of the group's proceeding without that crucial information.

A Technical Problem:
Effects of a Dam at Eagle Point

Problem statement: Several meetings later, the group has located various possible sites for dams and is now considering Eagle Point. The members seem to agree that they need to give this location special attention and the problem has become one of determining the consequences of putting a dam at Eagle Point. The problem statement also includes a specification of likely outcome criteria, such as power generated, cost and environmental impact.

Option clarification, external events and judging consequences: During this phase of problem solving, the group collects and weighs information. They set out the possibilities before arriving at a decision. The greatest danger for the group in this phase of problem solving is to reach early closure and move into the phase of making choices without fully setting out all relevant parameters. One of the greatest advantages of groups is the potential for generating diverse ideas; one of the greatest problems is that the group process might prevent this from occurring.

It often happens that a group feeling positively about itself will set goals beyond its capabilities . . . it is often useful for a group to set out a timetable for completion of component tasks.

Groupthink: Janis (1972) coined the term *groupthink* for the phenomenon that occurs when groups become so harmonious that diversity is lost and new ideas do not surface. This can occur when groups seek conformity, when conflict is seen as too dangerous or for other reasons. The leader's primary job in this phase of problem solving is to prevent premature closure.

The Water Group has listed four topics—engineering questions, environmental impact, cost and community relations—and appears ready to move on to discussing other sites. Leader suggests that the group consider in more detail possible adverse consequences of a dam at Eagle Point.

The group lists a number of possible consequences and members start mentioning other dam locations. Leader, concerned about premature closure, asks, "What might we have left out?" As the discussion proceeds, Water Planner, who was saying that a detailed flow study should be done (at significant cost), is reminded that the U.S. Army Corps of Engineers might have done a low-level engineering study. If they did, the Corps' report would save a great deal of the group's time.

Environ questions whether there might be an archeologist studying Native American ruins that would be flooded by a dam, with major implications for overall feasibility. Nat Resources raises the possibility that the need to retain water in a reservoir behind the dam would limit generating power. The Water Group cannot anticipate all such problems but will have a much better chance of finding them if it occurs to someone to look.

In addition to keeping open the search for more options, Leader has some other techniques available for promoting discussion of a range of ideas.

Brainstorming: Brainstorming is a technique that generates new ideas by expressly forbidding any evaluative comments of ideas until all ideas are listed. It is often conducted by asking members for ideas and listing them on a marker board or a large pad on an easel. Seeing others' ideas, members are encouraged to respond however they wish; these remarks are listed without evaluative comments.

In groups where some members are much more verbal than others, a further way of promoting ideas is to have members write thoughts down anonymously. This prevents less assertive members from being interrupted and adds anonymity to the safety of no evaluation. Notes are collected, the ideas listed and another round of idea-generating is conducted. The primary difficulty of brainstorming is that it seems gimmicky in situations in which members do not fear others' comments.

Devil's advocate: The leader challenges group thinking as a matter of principle, not necessarily because they believe in or are committed to the position they are espousing.

Evaluation of progress thus far: Often the group can look back on its prior decisions, try to find problems with them and consider whether these problems are fully represented in the current list of options.

Conflict: By bringing together a diversity of views, groups can obtain a synthesis that a single

In groups where some members are much more verbal than others, a further way of promoting ideas is to have members write thoughts down anonymously.

person could not produce. Conflict is useful in helping to bring these diverse ideas forward. As members marshal their arguments, new and varied points will be raised. The danger is that conflict will become so heated that productive work ceases. Members will begin to use their ideas as supportive arguments rather than for illumination.

There are wide variations in the level of conflict indicated by a particular behavior, and the understanding of conflict can require considerable social skill. There are groups in which the comment, "Perhaps you could be so good as to give us a report next week," can mean, "Why haven't you finished that yet?" Groups in which members are more familiar with each other generally can tolerate more overt emotion than groups of relative strangers.

The resolution of unproductive conflict is a major concern of the group. Generally, conflict can be tolerated to the extent that it does not threaten the group's identity. For this reason, early sessions are much more sensitive to disruption by conflict than later ones.

> At the first meeting, Environ and Utility, having battled elsewhere, begin to discuss rather heatedly the trade-offs between environmental protection and resource utilization. Leader, wanting to build group identity, notes that there is clearly disagreement, summarizes the issues raised by the two members and comments that the group will need to work through this conflict at some point. She states, however, that for now she would like to move to the next point on the agenda. Leader's intervention recognizes the existence of conflict while affirming the importance of both positions by stating that the group will take up the issues, but delays discussion until the group is more cohesive.

When emotional conflict (as opposed to disagreement or differing points of view) erupts, the leader will serve a number of managing functions. The primary goal is to keep to the subject at hand. The leader wants to discourage personal attacks, to integrate the material with earlier group work and to defuse emotions if the discussion becomes heated. In the Water Group, Leader accepts the presence of conflict but attempts to limit its scope to useful discussion.

> As the group is discussing the pros and cons of a dam at Eagle Point, Environ and Utility take up the discussion they left in the first session. Utility begins, stating, "All the environmentalists want to do is lie down in front of the bulldozers." As Environ starts to redden, Leader asks Utility why he thinks the environmentalists might do this in the specific case of the Pleasant River Dam. This comment defines the issue as task-related and prompts Utility to role-play the environmental position. Before Utility can respond, Environ remarks, "People like Utility dream with glee of driving bulldozers into mountains of environmentalists."

At this point, Leader has a choice: she can try to stay in a problem-solving mode or she can decide that the personal animosity needs to be addressed immediately; the group cannot handle both issues at once. Let us suppose that she decides the personal animosity is not great, that the group members are taking up established rhetorical positions and that

The resolution of unproductive conflict is a major concern of the group. When emotional conflict . . . erupts, the leader will serve a number of managing functions.

the feelings involved can be discounted for the present.

Leader says Environ does not know Utility's dreams. This defines Environ's remark as inappropriate. Leader then returns to Utility with another request for his understanding of the environmental objection to the Eagle Point Dam. Utility says he thinks environmentalists want to canoe on the Pleasant River. Environ responds that this is only one of the difficulties and lists three others.

Leader then turns to Water Planner, who has recently completed a dam survey, to see what effect earlier dams had on recreational use, which integrates this discussion with an earlier issue. After getting a response, Leader summarizes the sense of Environ's objections to the dam, and invites Environ to discuss with her environmental action group which of these issues is most relevant, thus identifying the next procedural stage for resolution of this conflict.

Conflict at an emotional level is handled somewhat differently. Ignoring or discounting it seldom leads to resolution.

Conflict at an emotional level is handled somewhat differently. Ignoring or discounting it seldom leads to resolution. The group may sense that the conflict is too disruptive and shy away from it; it may also feel that a good statement of feelings would be useful. In the example, after Environ makes her comment about Utility's dream, Leader may choose to involve the group in the decision about which level to work on, saying, "There seem to be some strong feelings involved here. I wonder if we need to get them out in the open before going on," and then waiting for the group response.

If the group moves to discuss feelings, it leaves the level of problem solving on the issue of the dam and moves to the level of group process. The central principle in dealing with conflicting feelings is that feelings should be accepted, not criticized or externalized. Thus, if Environ goes on to say, "All Utility does is bicker, put down environmentalists and want to get his own way," the important thing on which to focus is Environ's feelings and their clarification, not whether Utility is really that particular way or not.

A group member might say, "You get angry when you think Utility is out to provoke you." The focus remains on Environ, not on Utility. Utility may chime in, with a denial or acknowledgment, and the group can then take the same approach with him: "You feel strongly about this" or "Did Environ's response to what you said surprise you?" The leader should avoid taking sides. Some groups will try to scapegoat one member, and it is then quite important for the leader to support the scapegoated member without attacking the group. Generally, people feel better after they have expressed their feelings and felt someone else has understood, even if the external reality is unchanged. If the group continually needs to discuss these kinds of conflicts, it should try to identify why these feelings continually emerge.

Conflict between a member and the leader has special characteristics. As a member of the group, the leader may want to speak her mind, but she must realize that she is also the leader; if she abandons the principles of keeping conflict impersonal and encouraging group discussion even when the group disagrees with her, she will have a major adverse impact on the group. Leaders need to clarify and promote full discussion in their role of group facilitator, at the cost of not exercising some of the privileges of group membership.

The examples of conflict presented thus far concern two people. Conflicts sometimes arise among three or more people and the general principles for handling them are the same. Disruptive conflicts tend to reduce to a succession of two-sided conflicts (e.g., with A, B and C all disagreeing, leading to A and B against C, and then A against B).

Group responsibility for group process: In these examples, Leader has taken the primary responsibility for managing the group process. In well-run groups, the leader as well as each member learn to share responsibility for the smooth operation of the group. Members may learn by watching the leader and modeling themselves on their ways of facilitating the group's work. For example, when the leader says "I don't want to take sides" as she responds to a conflict, she makes her technique explicit. The leader can encourage members to facilitate the group by commenting positively on their actions when they promote the group process. The leader may also ask the group at the end of the meeting how they thought the meeting went and, if there were difficulties, how the group might better handle such problems. This last technique may seem gimmicky with some groups, particularly those that have worked together for some time.

Victoria begins the meeting by reporting that Leader called her earlier to say she was ill and could not attend today's meeting. The group appoints a temporary chairperson and goes on with their discussion of the Pleasant River Dam. As the discussion seems to come to a premature closure, Victoria takes a devil's advocate position. This leads to a heated conflict, which Knowlaw defuses by restating the work-related issues involved.

The members were able to take over Leader's functions in her absence. Perhaps they can also carry out many of those same functions when Leader is present.

Choosing among alternatives: After clarifying options and consequences, the group comes to the point of decision. Planning groups frequently do not make final decisions on issues requiring value trade-offs and consequently are prone to feel that their conclusions carry little weight. For instance, they will not make a final decision about whether the power a dam at Eagle Point could generate is worth the negative environmental impact and expense of constructing a dam. Such decisions are usually made in the political arena.

Groups can be helped to be more comfortable in their advisory role by fully discussing the decision-making mechanism both in and out of the group. The task of an advisory group is to decide in specific terms what recommendations they are making to the final decision maker. To maximize the usefulness of the report, it is important for the group to understand

MEMBERSHIP PRESENCE AT MEETINGS

Not all work needs to be done with all members present. Some other structures include:

- *Subcommittees:* useful if there are component tasks, especially those requiring the expertise of only a few members
- *Temporary or visiting members:* those with special knowledge brought in for a brief period
- *Meetings between leader and one member:* often to explore or resolve a particular issue
- *Negotiation sessions:* if two members have a conflict, the leader may try to mediate the issue without the full group's presence

The general principles that apply to groups also apply to these smaller group structures.

the process by which a decision will be made after the report is sent.

From a group process perspective, such discussion helps clarify the external factors of the group's structure. This can help the group to formulate recommendations in a way that will directly address the concerns of the decision maker. Some group members will have other relationships with the decision maker and will be in a position to undertake some political activity after the report is sent. In the Water Group, for example, Hiatonka and Victoria work with the directors of their respective departments of energy; therefore, each can describe how their departments use reports from outside consultants.

They will also be able to discuss the report with decision makers after those departments receive it.

Most groups wish for spontaneous unanimity in their decisions and, failing that, will try to arrive at a compromise consensus. This tendency derives from the group's wish to have members think alike and is closely tied to the group's wish for cohesion. Since a decision not accepted by all members highlights that views are not shared, groups tend to avoid making these differences manifest out of concern that those with different ideas will feel excluded. Groups can tolerate some decisions in the face of continuing disagreement; however, if this becomes frequent and the opposition vocal, the group's identity tends to be threatened. If the group does not agree, a useful first step is to elucidate those issues on which the group can agree. Often a group can agree on technical assessments but not on value trade-offs.

> Environ and Utility both read the ornithology reports and agree that a high head dam would likely lead to a 40% reduction in the number of eagles nesting at Eagle Point. This does not bother Utility, while Environ is quite upset and mysteriously predicts, "God gets even!"

Even if the group knows that it will not be making the final decision about whether to build a dam, it can still emphasize or de-emphasize the importance of a 40% reduction of eagle nests. The next step is to fully air the group's concerns about the reduction. Often, if members believe they have had a chance to make their points, they can accede to the consensus, perhaps by stating, "The report should have a few

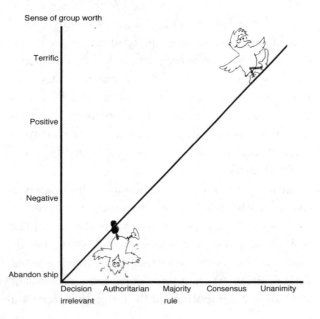

Relations between feelings of group worth and decision mechanism

lines about the eagles' plight." They may even go on to support the idea to their constituent groups by saying, "It's not so bad. At least we prevented wiping out the fiddlefish." Members do not come to the group expecting to get everything they want. What is important is that they feel that the decision process took them into account. In planning groups, a minority that feels strongly, if outvoted, may nevertheless be allowed to submit a minority report.

GROUP RESISTANCE

Leader is becoming uncomfortable with the group. Everyone is friendly, cheerful, cooperative and kind but, with something of a jolt, Leader realizes that for the past several weeks no progress has been made. Leader thinks back: at the last meeting, the group had a long discussion about how the fuel industry lobbies were working to get their oil deregulation bill through Congress. The group had much imaginative discussion about how they could stymie the lobbyists if only they were the congressional subcommittee acting on the bill. Since they were not, the discussion led to no useful work. After that protracted discussion, the group moved on to gossip about the personal life of the governor of East Victoria. It was quite an absorbing discussion but not useful. Previous meetings had been similar. What was wrong?

When groups move away from their task, they have left the work group mode and moved to another level of functioning. The first step—often the most difficult—is to recognize that this has happened. The difficulty stems from the level of absorption that can be present in the group while discussing matters not related to the task. Often the recognition that the group has made such a shift will come from a sense that nothing is being accomplished although the discussion seems relevant. Once this is recognized, the leader or any group member can move to a different point of view: the perspective of group process.

When groups are functioning well, the group process is not at the forefront of attention. Instead, the group is working with the issues that need to be resolved to accomplish the task. Looking at the group process arises out of a need to account for and deal with resistance to working. This shift in perspective can be likened to a visual shift in perspective. Those not familiar with the illustration in Figure 5-2 will, at first glance, often see a young woman. If told that there is another way to see the picture, some people can find it alone; for others, it helps to know that there is a picture of an old woman in profile. In groups, to see the group process, one needs to shift away from the more usual level of focusing on individual interactions.

Types of Resistance

Differing theorists have delineated many different perspectives of group process. W. R. Bion (1974), from his work with psychotherapy groups, has set forth one way of conceptualizing group process. Bion speaks of groups, when they are not working, as having a purpose other than solving the group task. This purpose is usually not conscious. Bion describes three types of purpose, which he calls *basic assumptions*, as the most common.

5-2. On perception (after Boring, 1930)

The group is gossiping about the fuel lobbyists. General Planner bemoans their pernicious influence on legislation. Nat Resources mutters about possible bribery. Environ is sure they will work to suppress the group's report. Knowlaw relates some juicy tidbits of one lobbyist's recent divorce.

Fight/flight group: In the above interactions, the group is eagerly talking about the fuel lobbyists, focusing on "those baddies out there" in a way that uses the group's time but accomplishes little. Bion refers to a group operating in this way as having the basic assumption of *fight/flight*, because the group views its responses as either to destroy the danger or to flee it. These responses may be couched in terms of wishes or intentions rather than planned actions. Such a group needs to be distinguished from a working group discussing, for example, what review process the group's report will undergo, perhaps considering the possibility that lobbyists might affect that review.

A group can move to a fight/flight mode and spend hours bemoaning the inadequacies of the reviewers and fantasize about ways to get even with them for their supposed incompetence, rather than discuss, in a work-oriented mode, what factors about the reviewing committee need to be considered.

One of the signals that a group is in a fight/flight mode is that members talk of the group as though it is the home of all things good, while the external force or agency is seen as the embodiment of badness and devoid of any redeeming qualities. The group, however, can itself achieve cohesion in the process of focusing on a perceived external danger. At times, the group's need for an external danger is so strong that it will create one in the group mind, even if none exists. Presumably, this is useful for the Water Group, although why the group needs to do this is not yet clear.

At the next meeting, the group again picks up its discussion of the lobbyists. Leader says this discussion is interesting, but she does not see how it directly affects what the group needs to do next, which is to assess the effects of damming the Pleasant River. The group agrees, with some chagrin, that she is right.

Leader has clarified the basic assumption of fight/flight, pointing out its essential unreality, and this allows the group to change.

After a pause, Leader suggests the group take up the next issue on the agenda, preparing the assessment of the dam. Nat Resources says he does not know what form the report should be in and looks to the rest of the group for help. Other members also seem to have no idea what form would be most appropriate, and one by one they suggest that Leader should guide them. Leader, attempting to be helpful, raises several possibilities, all of which the group finds faulty. The group seems to agree that it cannot solve this problem and needs direct instructions from Leader. Leader begins to have the feeling that she is leading a group of helpless children.

Dependency group: A group engaged in the above interactions is an example of what Bion calls a *dependency group*. Dependency groups often depend on the

leader, although a group may see itself as dependent on an outside force. When Utility says, "We can't write the report until the energy department tells us how" (even though it should be clear that the department has less idea of what the relevant factors are than the Water Group), then the group is acting as a dependency group. Leader says the group seems to expect her to do all the work and points out that General Planner, Water Planner, Nat Resources and Utility have all worked on similar projects before and probably have a good deal of experience in writing these reports. Everyone agrees and members begin to talk about what formats have been used in the past.

> After some profitable discussion, Environ and Utility get into a long, repetitive argument about the effects of damming the Pleasant River. The group has heard this many times before and hardly any new information is being offered, but the group nevertheless patiently sits back and listens as this discussion goes on and on. Twenty minutes later, it is still going on, with no end in sight. Environ and Utility are discussing the issue more heatedly, although what is being said is repetitive. The rest of the group looks intensely interested, although exactly in what is not clear.

Pairing group: Bion refers to this phenomenon (i.e., two people taking center stage as the rest of the group sits back and watches) as a *pairing group*. The basic assumption in a pairing group is that two people have taken over the group's functions; the rest of the group acts as though they were waiting for some-

thing productive to come out of the interaction, although there is little evidence that this will occur. The group fantasy is nevertheless quite strong and serves to hold other members back from participating. Leader, recognizing what is going on, says that she thinks the group as a whole should express its comments on what format to use and what considerations about the dam are relevant.

Working with Group Resistance

In these examples, Leader is like a physician who makes a diagnosis and intervenes in a way that reduces symptoms, but the symptoms are then replaced by another difficulty. Leader's interventions help to get the group back on the track for a time, but as she goes home, she has the uncomfortable sense that something is still not quite right. After each intervention, the group shifted into some other form of resistance. Why?

The group's shifting away from a work group to a fight/flight dependency, or pairing group, represents resistance to the task at hand. The causes of such resistance are not always easy to find, but it is useful to bring them into the open. Repeated moves out of the work group state usually indicate that some feelings are being avoided. The work group leader, considering the problem, decides to take action.

> At the next group meeting, Leader finds that, within five minutes, the group is having another jovial discussion about the governor of East Victoria. Not knowing whether this is social pleasantry, Leader waits several

The group's shifting away from a work group to a fight/flight dependency or pairing group, represents resistance to the task at hand.

Groups tend to blame difficulties on individuals.

---

minutes and finds the group still on the topic. She then verbalizes her concern that the group is having a problem accomplishing much, not only now, but over the past three meetings, and suggests that something is going on in the group to cause this, but she does not know what. Members, on reflection, agree.

After a pause, Utility says he finds himself a bit confused at the meetings since he does not get agendas ahead of time. An underlying theme in his tone of voice says he is resentful that the group does not think enough of him to get the agendas to him on time. Environ says she is annoyed that Knowlaw does not come to meetings but is still a member and feels tired of always waiting for her. Leader suggests that maybe Knowlaw is staying away from something that is going on in the group.

After a lull, Nat Resources remarks that several meetings ago, he submitted a preliminary report that the group had quietly, but strongly, criticized. He said he felt all his effort had gone unappreciated. General Planner says he tossed out what he felt were some good ideas and no one seemed to care. Leader says she had been concerned when she heard the head of Planning Solutions say, "Who cares about the damn water anyway?"

When a member voices the idea that individually each member was feeling unappreciated, there is a general nodding of heads. Water Planner then points out that the group is on schedule with its preliminary assessments, that he personally likes all the other members and that he wants the group to do a good job. Other members begin to cite the group's accomplishments and start to express positive attitudes toward continuing.

In this example, Leader keeps inviting the group to reflect on feelings that might be getting in the way of useful work. After the members are able to voice feeling unappreciated and isolated, the group is able to move attention to its successes, reconstitute the collective group self-esteem and move on with some hope of productive work.

PROBLEM PERSONALITIES

Groups tend to blame difficulties on individuals. Such a view does not consider that what looks like problematic individual behavior may be symptomatic of an assumption the group is making. When Environ and Utility are arguing, it can appear as though two people are in conflict. Such a view neglects to consider the role of other group members who are allowing the argument to go on. One may see group involvement more directly by picking up instances of covert encouragement.

During a pause in Utility and Environ's argument, Water Planner mildly says he supposes Environ does not understand Utility's point, when it is clear that Environ had understood but simply disagreed. Utility accepts Water Planner's statement and begins to recite again his views for the alleged benefit of Environ, who already understands perfectly well. Here, Water Planner, as a representative of the group, can be seen to facilitate the continuation of a pointless and repetitive argument. Victoria, who apprehends the group process, says she thinks the group understands Utility's view and notes that some members disagree with it.

At times, however, disruptive individual behavior needs to be handled directly. These problems occur particularly in groups that are afflicted with members whose personalities grate on the collective group nerve.

Hiatonka continually interrupts the statements of others, makes personal and derogatory comments, challenges Leader's authority and skips meetings. The group becomes increasingly resentful. Consider Victoria, who likes to pick fights whenever she can; or Knowlaw, who is chronically late to all appointments, the Water Group included. Leader, who knows these three socially, knows their behavior is not specific to the group; they always act that way.

Fortunately, groups exert great power over their members and a cohesive group can often manage problem personalities as a matter of course. Everyone has had the experience of saying something and getting no response. The speaker usually has a sense of not being there and is then hesitant to say anything further. People who are difficult in their interpersonal relationships tend to require a counterpoint for their actions and groups are capable of avoiding that reciprocal role.

By focusing on the group's task, the leader can sometimes steer clear of the pitfall of pointless haggling. If the group process does not curb the problematic behavior, the leader has three options: to focus the group on controlling the difficult member, to focus on the interpersonal conflict in the group or to confront the member individually. The range of

maneuvers in these options is endless and much depends on the leader's personal style.

It is helpful for all planners who work in small groups to become aware of their own coping styles. Many people think direct, individual confrontations are powerful interventions; in fact, the most powerful interventions are those that mobilize group pressure. Among these are statements that discourage what the problem person is saying or disallow it as a relevant contribution. As an extreme example, groups of psychiatric patients with a psychotic member can often stop that member from acting crazy in the group when any psychotic statement is defined by the therapist as irrelevant to what the group is talking about. The group gives the message, "If you're going to be like that, we'll have nothing to do with you."

A threat of exclusion from the group, expressed or implied, has powerful effects on behavior. If the leader's statement does not suffice, they may encourage the group to confront the particular member about their way of relating. Usually, if severely disruptive behavior continues in the face of confrontation by the group, the group can be encouraged to ostracize the member. Difficulties such as chronic lateness or absence can often be controlled when the group discusses their disruptive effects in the presence of the offending member.

Another type of problem arises when one member is relatively weak and is not participating fully in the group's work. The usual response of groups is to expect less of that member and not push for that person's working up to the group's standards.

Groups tend to be more tolerant of aberrant behavior than the leader or another individual member might be.

A group handles an instance of interpersonal conflict generated by a problem person much the same way it handles other instances of interpersonal conflict; however, with problem members, such conflict is more frequent. At an individual level, the leader or another member may meet with the problem member outside the group to discuss the difficult behavior. This produces less embarrassment than confrontation by the entire group. It is often less effective but may be a useful first step. Group confrontation can always follow.

TERMINATION

Most planning groups end after they have finished their task. In an effective and cohesive group, a positive group spirit and positive individual personal relationships will have been formed. The dissolution of the group will therefore be attended by feelings of sadness and loss, as well as feelings of satisfaction for a job well done. It is useful to allow time for the expression of feelings about termination, and give members a chance to review what has been accomplished, comment on the successes and failures of the group and say good-bye to one another.

SUMMARY

Small groups perform specific tasks in planning. The leader has a particularly crucial role to play in shaping the group and the way it works, in structuring the group, formulating problems, leading discussion, resolving conflict and facilitating decisions. When group resistance against working becomes manifest, shifting attention from the task to the group process itself offers the best way of dealing with the resistance. Understanding group process is a potent tool for working on tasks as well as for solving interpersonal difficulties that arise in the course of a group's work.

APPLICATIONS

1. Think of a small group of which you have been a leader or a member.
   a. How would you characterize that group's structure? What was its task?
   b. What issues of group process were problems for the group?
   c. Recall several instances of conflict. How were they resolved? How might they have been better resolved?
   d. What ways of encouraging discussion were particularly effective in that group? What ways did not lead to more discussion?
   e. Can you recall discussions in which the group left the work group state and became a fight/flight dependency or pairing group? What was the transition out of such a state?
2. How is a group of students working on a task different from a working group of planners?

BIBLIOGRAPHY

Berne, E. *The Structure and Dynamics of Organizations and Groups.* New York: Ballantine, 1963.

Berne offers a readable discussion of the structure of groups of all sizes.

Bion, W. R. *Experiences in Groups*. New York: Ballantine, 1974.

This is the classic exposition of basic assumption groups derived from Bion's work with psychotherapy groups. Psychotherapists have studied groups in which the group task is to facilitate personal change and understand group processes. Such work tends to emphasize emotional issues, often with elucidation of the individual's unconscious processes and fantasies.

Boring, E. G. "Apparatus, Notes: A New Ambiguous Figure." *American Journal of Psychology* 42:444-445, 1930.

Carr, C. *Team Leader's Problem Solver*. Englewood Cliffs, NJ: Prentice Hall, 1996.

Carr's how-to manual includes many examples of problems for a leader in running a group, each with a number of solutions.

Fisher, R., W. Ury and B. Patton. *Getting to Yes: Negotiating Agreement Without Giving In*. Boston: Houghton Miflin, 1991.

This classic in negotiation literature is a very readable discussion of techniques to promote negotiation and agreement.

Freud, S. *Group Psychology and the Analysis of the Ego*. Translated by James Strachey. London and Vienna: International Psycho-Analytical Press, 1922.

Freud presents the original psychoanalytic theory of groups.

Janis, I. *Victims of Groupthink*. Boston: Houghton Mifflin, 1972.

———. *Crucial Decisions: Leadership in Policymaking and Crisis Management*. New York: Free Press, 1989.

This book describes procedures for making sound decisions and offers ways to avoid poor processes.

Raiffa, H. *Decision Analysis: Introductory Lectures on Choices Under Uncertainty*. Reading, MA: Addison-Wesley, 1968.

In this excellent introductory text on decision analysis, decision theorists have focused on problem-solving stages and extending problem-solving paradigms from the individual to the group level.

Zander, A. *Making Groups Effective*. San Francisco: Jossey-Bass, 1994.

This work by a leading social psychologist analyzes some of the practical aspects of working in small groups.

Public Participation

Elaine Cogan

WHY INVOLVE THE PUBLIC?

On the one hand, the answer to this question for planners is an easy one: "They make us do it." "They" are the countless federal agencies such as the EPA, U.S. Forest Service, Department of Transportation, U.S. Army Corps of Engineers and many others that require some form of public involvement before key decisions are made. At the local level, many states, counties and municipal governments also require a modicum of public participation. Many times, citizens become involved spontaneously when issues that concern them arise.

On the other hand, planners with little or negative experience may be reluctant to undertake anything more than is legally required, under the mistaken notion that public involvement is an impediment, not a help, to the planning process. To the contrary, well-designed and well-implemented citizen participation can provide tangible benefits to the entire planning process by:

- providing valuable insights into citizens' values and preferences
- developing and nurturing an environment of goodwill and trust
- helping to avoid or mitigate protracted or costly delays and conflicts
- providing information about public perceptions and concerns that planners and policy makers may have overlooked
- providing citizen support for a final project or strategy

- engendering a meaningful, two-way dialogue between the public and the planners
- leading to understandable and consensus-driven decision making
- developing a reservoir of understanding and goodwill
- increasing faith in the democratic system

The purposes of this chapter are to:

- help planners understand and support the importance of public participation as integral to the success of most public projects
- evaluate the broad array of tools that may be used to meet specific needs and circumstances
- learn how to evaluate the outcomes, learning from our mistakes as well as our successes

Even the most dedicated practitioners may need to rethink many of their techniques and assumptions to be successful in an increasingly multicultural environment. For example, spoken and written English is not the language of choice for many citizens who nevertheless are anxious to be involved in public issues, especially on the local level. Cultural differences and expectations must be accommodated if public participation in the 21st century is to reach all the people who should be involved.

Public Participation:
An End in Itself or a Means to an End?

The EIS has become so institutionalized by the federal government and many states that it may indeed seem that public involvement is an end in itself. The rules are so proscribed as to the number of days

Even the most dedicated practitioners may need to rethink many of their techniques and assumptions to be successful in an increasingly multicultural environment.

TABLE 6-1

Likely Contribution of Citizen Participation at Different Levels of Government

Planning Action	Level of Government			
	Federal	State	Regional	Local
Goal formulation	A	Δ	Δ	Δ
Data collection and analysis	—	A	A	A
Alternative policy definition	A	A	Δ	Δ
Alternative policy evaluation	—	—	A	Δ
Policy selection	—	—	—	Δ
Policy implementation	—	A	A	Δ
Monitoring and evaluation	A	A	A	Δ

Potential contribution:

Δ = High   A = Moderate   — = Low

Source: Cogan, Sharpe and Hertzberg (1986)

public comment is allowed on a given subject, the form of that comment and how the agency will respond that public participation may seem to be running on its own track while the technical analyses continue unabated. None of these impediments deter savvy special interest groups who know exactly how to make their opinions known. However, they can constrain the average citizen who may be totally baffled and discouraged when form appears to supersede function; when, in striving for the end (just to say we did it), we lose sight of the means (applying the best techniques to help influence the decision).

The most successful public participation is a means to an end, and that end is more informed public policy. Whether the involvement is substantial or minimal, members of the public should have various opportunities to be heard; if their comments are taken seriously, the eventual decision or solution should be stronger and more supportable. The likely contribution of citizen participation to planning processes of various levels of government is illustrated in Table 6-1.

While it is important for planners and decision makers to listen, it is just as important that citizens understand that public participation is not a means by which they will always "get their way," nor should the planners or decision makers expect to get what they want all the time. The most valuable outcome is when all parties have had sufficient opportunity to *understand and reason with each other.*

Though public participation has a role throughout the planning process (as noted in Table 6-1), it can be especially effective in the stages of goal formulation and policy definition. This is the time when it is most important to understand community values as they relate to goals, objectives and policies of a particular issue. It can also be the most challenging because there are no concrete alternatives or options to test with the public.

These stages require the planner to exercise sound listening and interpretative skills. While it may appear to be somewhat less useful during the data collection and analysis phases, planners have to be careful about making assumptions that the public is unsophisticated or does not know enough to have any meaningful contribution at these times. Public input can be especially valuable in local matters such as traffic control, zoning and parks, where people may call attention to matters that planners overlook. Generally, the more reliant the project is on community values, the more important it is to check in with the public each step of the way.

The Difference Between Public Relations and Public Participation

A fatal flaw in any planning process is to assume a selling mode, that all one needs to do is "educate" the public on the "truths" of the project and they will gladly assent to whatever the conclusion or outcome may be. While education, in the sense of informing the public, is an essential part of the process, it is only one part. Information, including text and graphics, should be presented in an unbiased fashion. If the subject is controversial, it may be helpful to present the issues at the beginning—a question-and-answer format is sometimes useful. Avoid slogans and phrases that appear to trivialize or direct the public's concerns. We are not selling soap or breakfast cereal. We are engaged in serious dialogue with people over issues that merit their attention, but it

does not mean that materials should be unattractive or that we cannot have some fun.

Another important point stressed in this chapter is that one format or technique does not fit all. Few citizens stay with the project throughout. Many tend to be most active on matters that immediately concern them. Luckily, there is a vast array of tools (see Figure 6-1). Planners must choose the best fit for each situation and consider resources, project goals and public needs and expectations.

Above all, planners should recognize that, while public participation and involvement may be a somewhat routine part of their jobs, citizens have other options. They do not have to read the materials, go to the meetings, log on to the Web or take any notice at all. They may choose to vote as the only way of voicing their opinions or ignore even that privilege. However, as the democratic process is best served when the citizens find it in their interest to participate, and do so constructively, it is the planner's obligation to be clear about the purpose and goals of the public involvement requested and respond positively when it occurs.

THE BEGINNING

Defining the Public

The first, and essential, step in designing a public participation process is to ascertain which members of the public you need to reach for each particular situation. Without that essential definition, the whole process can be stymied. The materials may be

Avoid slogans and phrases that appear to trivialize or direct the public's concerns.

designed for the wrong audience and never reach the "right" one. You may say or do inappropriate things.

In defining that audience, ask yourselves these basic questions: who, individually or in a group, is likely to:

- be most affected by the decisions or policies that will be made?
- have influence over the decisions, formally or informally?
- be responsible for making the final decision?

6-1. Primary communications functions of public involvement mechanisms

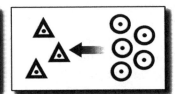 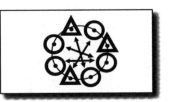

Presentation	Receipt	Exchange
Newspaper articles	Public hearings	Workshops
Radio and TV programs	Survey questionnaires	Special task forces
Speeches/presentations to groups	Public inquiry	Interviews
Field trips	Media balloting	Advisory boards
Exhibits	Public meetings	Informal contacts
School programs		Interactive cable TV
Films		Study group discussions
Brochures		Gaming/simulation
Newsletters	▲ Planner	
Reports		
Letters	◉ Public	
Conferences		

Source: Warner, Katharine P. "Public Involvement as Planning Communication," *The Planner's Use of Information.* 1st ed. Chicago: American Planning Association, 1988, p.131.

- have already indicated an interest?
- want to be involved?
- represent a perspective that should be heard?

Be inclusive in this initial screening and list all who fit those definitions. You may want to divide the list into categories of those who are most likely to want to be more actively or passively involved as the process proceeds. Avoid the temptation to create an enemies list (i.e., those who you or others assume are opposed, even before the project begins). While it is important to be realistic in assessing the degree of controversy or difficulty, start with the assumption that people are willing to cooperate under the right circumstances. This, of course, does not assume that everyone will be satisfied with the conclusion. Eventually, people may have to agree to disagree. The objective of public participation is to help them feel confident that the process has been fair and has treated them fairly.

In answering the above questions, your list of potential participants is most likely to include the following:

- *Elected public officials:* They have their own networks and may even have taken a position on the issue before the process begins. Still, they want to know what their constituents are saying and be apprised of any real or perceived controversies. Sometimes, they may be willing to designate a representative to an advisory or steering committee. They often will want private briefings. Keep them informed through whatever means they request.

- *Public agency staffs:* Seldom can one agency do it all. You may need help from the frontline troops of other public bodies. Often, they will agree to participate on technical advisory committees whose work complements or is parallel to the public participation process. They are the keys to information, data and funding. Treat them with respect.

- *Respected opinion leaders:* These may include the League of Women Voters and similar civic groups well known and respected in your local community or community of interest.

- *Special interest groups:* Care should be taken to include representatives of as many as you can identify people on all sides of the spectrum and not just those who agree with you.

- *Any others:* There are others who may add value to this particular process. Do not neglect well-respected "elder" statespeople, poets, writers, historians or others with a unique perspective.

Identifying Members of the Public

How do we identify those members of the public who have a stake in the community or project, or who have special insights or skills? Every community has its activists and public-spirited citizens— people who can be counted on to volunteer for yet another committee or cause. Many have strong opinions. While it is important to include them in the process, it also is vital to cast a wider net. To make sure your list includes all the interests that need to be part

of the process, you may want to consult the local newspaper editor, elected officials or other activists. If you do your work properly, the variety of interests may surprise you.

Publicize the public involvement process and opportunities for participation through notices in the media, your Web page, newsletters, direct mail or other means. Even if several hundred people have responded, it is important that they are contacted somehow after they have taken the trouble to show an interest. Reply by phone, e-mail or letter, and ask them the best ways they want to be involved. Some will want only to be informed either personally or for their organization; others may be willing to give you their mailing list or ask to be on a steering or advisory committee.

As laborious as these first steps may seem, they are really shortcuts to an effective process. You have now identified all the sectors of the public that should be involved and compiled an initial database of interested groups and individuals.

Defining Adequate Resources

The many components of a successful public participation program can be broadly divided into human and financial resources. Each contributes to its success. It is important to have sufficient people to help carry out the process, which includes leaders as well as workers. You certainly need more numbers if you decide to put leaflets on every doorstep than if you use a mass-mailing service. In the latter case, however, you need more money. Volunteers from citizen

SPECIAL CONTRIBUTIONS FROM THE PUBLIC

In one community undertaking a future visioning process, two invaluable members of the steering committee were a writer who had written a town history and a new, young artist who saw the community with a creative eye. Each added a special quality to the deliberations and the final product.

IDENTIFYING PUBLICS

Information about potential partici-pants can come from different sources:

- *Self-identification:* Interested persons are encouraged to make them-selves known directly through let-ters, telephone calls, visits, testimony and other avenues. Those opposed to certain actions may announce themselves through peti-tions, protest demonstrations or even lawsuits.
- *A listing of appropriate population groupings, organizations and individ-uals:* Sources include organizational membership and officer lists, social and economic profile statistics for an area (which could form the basis for special surveys or publicity efforts), newspaper files and city directories.
- *A particularly well-informed person, organizational officers and others:* Such third-party references may con-siderably expand the potential num-ber of participants. However, to guard against professional biases, it is important to consult a diverse set of reference people.

Warner, Katharine P. "Public Involvement as Planning Communication," *The Planner's Use of Information.* 1st ed. Chicago: Ameri-can Planning Association, 1988, p. 129.

groups or youth service organizations can help extend the reach of paid staff, but they need direction and follow-through. Sometimes, expensive bro-chures and fact sheets may be rejected by a wary public as wasteful and profligate; more modest mis-sives will do as well or better.

Whatever your human resources and budget, you need adequate time to get the job done right. That means ensuring that the process is timed so that the results of public involvement are considered before key decisions are made. Public participation pro-grams are too often orphans or add-ons after the budgets and schedules for every other part of the project have been set. Planners may find that the best way to make the case for adequate funds and staff is after a crisis has occurred. Hopefully, a well-conceived public involvement process will win sup-port before panic erupts.

PUBLIC INVOLVEMENT TECHNIQUES

There are many ways to involve the public in a meaningful way as the summary of involvement techniques, which is provided in Figure 6-2, illus-trates. No one technique fits all circumstances. The methods described in this figure—in terms of pur-pose, strengths and weaknesses—are not mutually exclusive, and should be mixed and matched as needed. Their relative success in terms of number of people who can be reached, degree of two-way com-munication and level of staff effort are noted by accompanying symbols (as noted in Figure 6-2).

Choosing the right method for eliciting participa-tion in a given context requires care and thought. Avoid the one-size-fits-all approach, especially if a particular technique has been successful in a different project. Choose the appropriate tools after answering these questions. Which one or more of the methods:

- reaches our targeted audience(s)?
- is within our budget?
- provides information from the public that we need?
- gives the public the information it needs?
- best utilizes staff and volunteer resources?
- satisfies our public participation goals?

HOW TO PUBLICIZE THE MEETING

Citizen-unfriendly notices are common roadblocks to successful public meetings. Too often, when there is sparse attendance at a meeting, public agency per-sonnel complain that "people don't care." They will care and they will come if they understand the pur-pose of the meeting, how the outcome affects them and the role they are expected to play in helping reach a decision. Planners cannot justify poorly writ-ten or unclear notices on the grounds of statutory requirements for content. You can meet the legalities and still use understandable, concise English. Pro-vide a translation into another language if the audi-ence warrants it.

Before composing any meeting notice that will be delivered to the public, give thought to what people need to know to be motivated to attend. This factor must take precedence over what you think they

6-2. Summary of public involvement techniques

ADVISORY COMMITTEE	Purpose	Strengths	Weaknesses
◒ ■ ▲ Group of 12-25 stakeholders who meet regularly during the course of the project	• Advise about design and progress of the project • Discuss pertinent issues • May sponsor public event(s) • Possibly make policy recommendations	• Forum for detailed discussion • Environment for two-way dialogue • Builds relationships to the community	• Requires ongoing staff commitment • Some cost for supplies and refreshments • Risk of low attendance if meetings are not productive • Involves relatively small number of people

BRIEFING	Purpose	Strengths	Weaknesses
○ ◒ ▲ Meeting with one or more stakeholders or the media	• Provide information about specific program or projects • Receive limited feedback	• Opportunity to reach specific groups and answer individual questions	• Involves relatively small number of people • Limited public exposure • Little control over what the media chooses to report

BROCHURE/FACT SHEET	Purpose	Strengths	Weaknesses
● □ ▲ Publication(s) describing project and/or citizen participation process	• Provide general information to a wide variety of audiences	• Easy to read • Cost-effective way to reach numbers of people	• Little opportunity for two-way dialogue (mail-back questionnaire may mitigate this somewhat) • May be costly to produce • No guarantee that information will be read • Professional layout/design may be best • Not always reader-friendly

CORRESPONDENCE	Purpose	Strengths	Weaknesses
◒ □ △ Response to comments from stakeholders/public; may be by letter or e-mail	• Receive information about specific concerns that may not be raised elsewhere • Give individual attention to those who write	• Message conveyed that you take concerns seriously • Understanding of one or more individuals increased	• Little opportunity for two-way discussion • Replies may be misconstrued • May be time-consuming • Possibility of mass-mailing campaign

KEY
- ● maximum targeted audience
- ◒ possible targeted audience
- ○ minimum targeted audience
- ■ high degree 2-way communication
- ◒ some 2-way communication
- □ minimum or no 2-way communication
- ▲ extensive staff effort
- △ reasonable staff effort
- △ minimum staff effort

DIRECT MAIL	Purpose	Strengths	Weaknesses
Notices or other materials sent to individuals, businesses or organizations	• Provide information to select audiences	• Relatively inexpensive to produce • May be distributed widely, or targeted to specific demographic or geographic audiences	• One-way dialogue; mail-back questionnaire or form may mitigate this • First-class mail expensive; third-class unreliable

ELECTRONIC VOTING	Purpose	Strengths	Weaknesses
Test of people's opinions through use of individual keypads	• Obtain speedy information about preferences and priorities	• Fun! People like to use technique • Instant results	• Trained operator required • Superficial results that lack depth

EXPERT REVIEW PANEL	Purpose	Strengths	Weaknesses
Group of recognized experts or special interests	• Provide outside expertise and oversight, particularly at points of crisis or impasse	• Opportunity for a neutral perspective • Helpful in reviewing complicated data	• May be expensive • May be difficult to assemble and coordinate • May encounter disagreement over who is an "expert"

FOCUS GROUP RESEARCH	Purpose	Strengths	Weaknesses
Small group (10-20) of people specifically chosen to represent populations/interests	• Gauge reaction of representative groups of people to specific plans or concepts	• Useful for testing reactions before presenting to public • Tool for generating new ideas	• Limited number of participants • Requires professional recruiting, organizing and facilitating • May be expensive

INTERNET	Purpose	Strengths	Weaknesses
Electronic communication about a project or process	• Involve individuals who may not come to meetings or otherwise participate in public process	• Use of "cutting edge" technology • Engagement of people who may be alienated from public discourse	• Requires staff involvement and monitoring • Technology not yet familiar to vast numbers of the public

MEDIA	Purpose	Strengths	Weaknesses
Written releases, briefings or interviews to representatives of radio, television and newspapers	• Communicate information to the general public	• Opportunities for exposure to people who may not otherwise be involved	• Limited control over content • Not likely to promote two-way dialogue with the public

NEWSLETTER	Purpose	Strengths	Weaknesses
Periodic publication	• Provide ongoing information to general or specific audiences • Update stakeholders and/or public on status of project	• Convenient to read and use as reference • May be targeted to specific people or groups	• Must be reader-friendly • May be costly or time-consuming to produce and distribute • One-way communication: questionnaire needed to solicit direct input

OPEN HOUSE/COMMUNITY FAIR	Purpose	Strengths	Weaknesses
One-day event over a period of time (usually 4 to 6 hours) to provide information and receive comments from a disparate audience	• Meet people informally to discuss issues and receive input before decisions are made	• Target to broad audience • Opportunities for two-way dialogue • May provide useful feedback	• Generally a one-time event; ongoing dialogue or follow-up often needed • Requires significant staff involvement • May be difficult to generate public interest

PERSONAL INTERVIEWS	Purpose	Strengths	Weaknesses
Discussions with specific stakeholders	• Inform selected individuals • Obtain in-depth opinions and reactions	• Better understanding is facilitated • Valuable information is provided	• Involves limited number of people • Requires skilled interviewers administer and interpret results

PUBLIC DISPLAY	Purpose	Strengths	Weaknesses
Information placed in community gathering places (e.g., libraries, grocery stores and banks)	• Provide information that general public can understand without personal explanation	• Relatively low maintenance • Limited staffing • Convenient to public	• Little to no opportunity for two-way dialogue • Must be well produced, maintained and updated • May be perceived as promotional

PUBLIC HEARING	Purpose	Strengths	Weaknesses
Formal process before final decisions are made	• Comply with legal requirements	• Opportunity for the public to hear what decision makers say about the project • Preset agenda and formula is followed	• Little to no opportunity for two-way dialogue or new information to emerge • Public perception that decisions have already been made

PUBLIC MEETING	Purpose	Strengths	Weaknesses
Meeting with general or specific audiences to present information and answer questions	• Provide information and address issues and concerns before decisions are made	• Flexible format • Opportunity to engage in some two-way dialogue	• Little opportunity to explore issues in depth • May be attended only by groups or individuals with specific agendas • Difficult to generate significant turnout

PUBLIC WORKSHOP	Purpose	Strengths	Weaknesses
Interactive meeting to address/solve specific issues/problems	• Provide information • Engage in collaborative discussions	• Potential for meaningful, two-way dialogue • Opportunity to generate ideas/solve problems	• Significant staff time and resources required • May be attended only by groups or individuals with specific agendas

QUESTIONNAIRE	Purpose	Strengths	Weaknesses
Unscientific survey of general public or selected individuals or groups	• Obtain information about opinions on specific issues	• Relatively low cost • Can be widely disseminated where people congregate (e.g., libraries, schools and shopping centers)	• Does not allow for two-way dialogue • Respondents do not necessarily represent general public • Requires skilled staff to develop questions and interpret results

REPORT	Purpose	Strengths	Weaknesses
Written account of process or project	• Provide information about the project or sum up specific efforts or issues	• Detailed information is provided • Potential for broad use and distribution	• May provide more information than general public wants to know • May be too technical for average public to understand

SCIENTIFIC SURVEY	Purpose	Strengths	Weaknesses
Query of random sample of given population	• Obtain information that is statistically reliable	• Representative opinion of specific demographic groups • Administered by professional polling organization	• Does not allow for two-way dialogue • Relatively costly to design, administer and interpret

SPEAKERS BUREAU	Purpose	Strengths	Weaknesses
Presentations to selected groups in the community	• Inform specific organizations about plans or activities • Obtain opinions or ideas	• Convenient; representatives go out to people • Opportunities for some two-way dialogue • May draw in volunteers	• Does not reach broad public • Requires significant staff time to organize, train and carry through

TASK FORCE	Purpose	Strengths	Weaknesses
Committee charged with accomplishing specific mission in specific amount of time	• Make decision or recommendations about one or more issues	• May represent a variety of perspectives • Opportunity for meaningful two-way dialogue	• Involves small number of people • Requires significant time commitment of staff • Limited scope

TOUR	Purpose	Strengths	Weaknesses
Orientation to physical site for invited stakeholders/public	• Improve understanding with "hands-on" experience • Helpful when written descriptions are not enough	• Opportunity to showcase project • May attract media	• May require special safety or other precautions • Difficult to organize • Only a few people involved

VISUAL AIDS	Purpose	Strengths	Weaknesses
Graphs, charts, overheads and computer-assisted graphics	• Explain concepts or ideas to lay audience	• May help people understand technical information • May be relatively inexpensive	• Often misused, poorly executed or too complicated • Requires skilled presenter(s) • Less is often best

WEB PAGE	Purpose	Strengths	Weaknesses
Graphic display of information available to computer users	• Provide information to individuals who may not otherwise be reached by other techniques • Obtain comments and reactions	• Of interest to growing segment of the public • Moderate set-up cost • May be used to facilitate e-mail communication or review of specific documents	• Precludes use by those without computers • User must take initiative to access information • Expertise needed to establish and maintain • Requires periodic updating and monitoring of responses

MAKE THE PURPOSE OF A MEETING CLEAR

Planners in a growing metropolitan area were having trouble getting people to attend a series of meetings titled "Urban Issues That Confront Us." When they sent out a notice announcing a "Summit Meeting to Solve Our Pressing Regional Problems," the attendance doubled.

should know or what you are required by law to tell them. The information should be presented in the general order given below.

- *Purpose of the meeting:* Citizens rightly become distressed if they show up at a meeting expecting an open session at which they can give testimony, only to be told that just the staff and "expert witnesses" are allowed to speak. Similarly, the public will feel cheated if the notice leads people to believe that a definitive decision will be made before the meeting ends, and they find out that the purpose of the meeting is to gather opinions for a later decision to be made behind closed doors. Planners must first make sure that everyone participating in the meeting agrees on its purpose, then state that purpose accurately in the written notice. Experiment with attention-getting headlines: "Street-widening Proposal" will encourage more citizens to read on than the bureaucratic "Notice for Potential Vacation of Certain Streets for Purposes of Accommodating Traffic."

- *Action to be taken:* What will happen as the result of this meeting? More meetings? Definite recommendations? A tax increase? Be clear and unambiguous.

- *Date, time and place:* Do not bury this information somewhere toward the end of the notice; put it right up front. Recipients can thus consult their calendars and be spared having to read further if they are busy at the appointed time. On the other hand, with the purpose of

the meeting stated so clearly and compellingly in the first paragraph—followed by the date, time and place—they may decide to change their schedules because of the importance of the event.

- *Financial implications:* What, if anything, will the proposal under consideration cost? Will this street widening, annexation, park acquisition, solid waste regulation or other matter require the public to pay more money? Say so, and in terms that taxpayers can understand. Translate property tax millage rates and other esoteric governmental jargon into increased taxes for a typical middle-class household; if you are talking about sales or excise taxes, translate it into so much per dollar of purchase.

- *Citizen participation:* Are ad hoc comments acceptable or must people sign up in advance to testify? Can they register by mail? Is there a time limit? Failure to make all the rules clear in the notice may cause misunderstanding and hostility that will ruin the public meeting. If citizens accidentally or purposely misunderstand their role and insist, "No one told us that we have only three minutes apiece," the planner can point out the clear, unambiguous statement to that effect in the invitation.

- *Optional additional explanatory material:* Attach simple maps or charts to illustrate complicated land use or other matters. If there are several illustrations, employ consistent symbols such as crosshatching. Always include a north arrow and mark streets or other familiar landmarks clearly. Do not use a surveyor's dim pencil sketch annotated with scrawled notations that are impossible for laypeople to decipher.

- *Legal reference:* Include legal justification only if you must, preferably as an attachment that citizens can ignore if they wish without missing anything important.

Put all the above (with the exception of legal requirements, maps and other extras) on one double-spaced page (two pages only if absolutely necessary). An outline, as suggested above, can be standardized on the computer so that staff can fill in the blanks. Avoid verbosity and jargon. Give careful attention to format as well: wide margins, short paragraphs and double-spaced text increase the likelihood that your notice will be read and taken seriously. The example in the sidebar entitled "Traditional Notification Form" shows how even a legislative notice can be made more "reader-friendly." Compare this to an even lighter touch (see the sidebar entitled "Revised Notification Form") that still presents all the needed information.

PRESENTING INFORMATION EFFECTIVELY

Whether preparing a newsletter, meeting summary, media release, brochures or reports, or speaking to a few or to many people, it is essential to communicate your messages succinctly and in terms your audience understands. The following techniques help tell your story clearly and convincingly.

Write for Public Understanding

Many planners, particularly those with a technical background, are not adept at writing for the public. Their written prose may be grammatically and technically correct but is often stilted, redundant or verbose. Either assign this task to someone who is professionally qualified or learn to write in a simple, direct style. Follow these guidelines to improve the readability and effectiveness of your written materials:

- Avoid the use of jargon. Use technical terms sparingly, if at all; write at a level that speaks to the understanding of your audience. Do not use acronyms unless you define them or include a glossary of terms.
- Use active language. Avoid the passive ("The city wishes to announce a public meeting") in favor of being more direct ("Come to a public meeting to discuss plans for a new roadway").
- Be succinct. Avoid long words and complex sentences. Be clear and concise.
- Illustrate clearly. Choose graphs and charts that are uncluttered and visually attractive.
- Strive for brevity. Less is more as far as the general public is concerned. Provide more detailed back-up materials to those who may request them.
- Write for your audience. If needed, translate into a language other than English, and include a contact person and telephone number for those who want more information.

Strive for brevity. Less is more as far as the general public is concerned.

TRADITIONAL NOTIFICATION FORM

Notice of Hearing to Rezone Property

Regarding Petition No. 1789222 PB, related to former Petition No. 5589167 PB, tax parcel 089507-214-576. The city is entertaining said petition from Thomas McIntire, owner of property at 2900 Elm Street, to rezone said property from RS-2, Single-Family Residential, to PS-1, Public Service.

The city's planning and zoning commission will hold the first public hearing on this petition on February 28 at 6:30 PM in the third-floor auditorium of City Hall. The planning and zoning commission on March 9 at 6:30 PM in the third-floor auditorium of City Hall will hold the second public hearing.

Following these public hearings, the planning and zoning commission will either vote to instruct the city attorney to draft a new zoning ordinance for the property, deny the petition or continue the hearing in order to obtain additional comments and information.

The permitted uses for this property are single-family dwellings and customary accessory buildings incidental thereto. The permitted uses of the proposed zoning are libraries, senior and community centers, museums and art galleries and public golf courses. Petitioner proposes to erect a senior or community center.

As a property owner within 400 feet of said property, you may make your views known to the planning and zoning commission by appearing in person at one or both of said hearings, or by writing a letter to be received on or before the date of the second hearing. Other citizens may also testify.

If you have any questions or desire to review this request in detail, contact the Department of Planning and Zoning, City Hall, Room 725, or call 811-555-1155.

Cogan, Elaine. "Getting the Word Out," *Successful Public Meetings: A Practical Guide.* Chicago: American Planning Association, 2000, p. 41.

REVISED NOTIFICATION FORM

Proposal to Change Use of Residential Property to Allow Senior or Community Center
[attention-getting title]

Thomas McIntire, living at 2900 Elm Street, is asking the city to rezone his property from residential use (RS-2) to Public Service (PS-1), to allow construction of a senior or community center. **[purpose of the meeting]**

The city's planning and zoning commission may either allow or deny this request and is holding two public hearings to obtain citizen comments.   **[action to be taken]**

Both hearings will be held in the third-floor City Hall auditorium, February 28 and March 9 at 6:30 PM   **[date, time and place early in the notice]**

If the property is approved as proposed, it will be used by a nonprofit corporation, which will not pay property taxes. The remaining property taxpayers in the city will be required to make up the difference. The current property taxes paid by the owner are approximately $1,500 per year.   **[financial implications]**

All citizens who own property within 400 feet of this property are invited to testify in person or write to the planning and zoning department before midnight of the second hearing (March 9). Any other interested parties may also participate in the hearing or in writing.   **[citizen participation]**

For more information, contact Hortense Allen, Project Planner, Department of Planning and Zoning, City Hall, Room 725, or call Ms. Allen at 811-555-1115.   **[optional additional information]**

Please refer to the accompanying map for specific site information. The legal petition for this case is on file as #1789222 PB and #5589167 PB.   **[legal reference]**

Cogan, Elaine. "Getting the Word Out," *Successful Public Meetings: A Practical Guide.* Chicago: American Planning Association, 2000, p. 41.

Speak Clearly

Many technically trained planners are not adept at giving effective presentations. This is a learned skill that is essential when communicating with the public.

- Tailor your message to your audience. What do they want to know about a particular subject before they can offer an informed opinion?
- Prepare well in advance. Allow sufficient time to outline the information needed, obtain needed data, choose the best presenters and rehearse sufficiently.
- Arrive early enough to test the microphone and any other equipment, such as a slide or overhead projector.
- Employ only those visual aids that can be used with ease and that advance your message.
- Limit the spoken part of the program to no more than 30 minutes, with several presenters. This requires discipline to choose only that information of interest to each audience.
- Be yourself. Tell a joke only if it fits your personality and the setting.
- Leave sufficient time for audience questions.

Answer All Questions

Except for formal hearings where public comments may either be severely limited or not be welcome at all, always leave time for questions at the end of your presentation.

- Make sure the entire audience hears and understands the question. Repeat or paraphrase when necessary.

- Answer directly and to the point.
- Talk to the level of the whole audience; avoid answers that are specific to only one individual. If questioners need more information, arrange to see them afterward.
- Never argue; answer critical questions politely and firmly.
- Do not be afraid to say you do not know. Ask questioners to see you afterward so you can obtain their names and phone numbers. Follow up promptly.
- Summarize at the end by repeating the points you want the audience to remember, including anything of relevance you learned during the question-and-answer period.

Value of Nonverbal Communication

Studies show that how we say things—our tone of voice and the body language we use—is at least as important as what we say. Be aware of the importance of how these communicate to the audience.

- Make eye contact with as many people as possible; do not focus only on one individual or point in the room.
- When answering questions, show you are listening and are open to new ideas. Do not scowl, cross your arms, put your hands on your hips or use other body language that says you have made up your mind or do not agree.
- Wear comfortable clothes that are neither too formal nor too casual for your audience.

Except for formal hearings where public comments may either be severely limited or not be welcome at all, always leave time for questions at the end of your presentation.

- Do not fiddle with your hands, pens, pencils, keys or coins in your pocket.
- Relax. Smile. Enjoy yourself.

Use Audio-visual Materials Well

Graphics should enhance, not replace, your presentation. Follow these basic guidelines for how to use them effectively:

- Choose the medium, size and scale that will make your message more clear or meaningful to each audience. For example, slides or a video in a small room with about 20 attendees can be overwhelming, while overheads or flip charts may be more appropriate. Conversely, flip charts are not readable by large audiences.
- Make all your graphics simple and unambiguous.
- In all lists, use phrases rather than complete sentences.
- Paraphrase written information; never duplicate pages from a text.
- Bring your own equipment, including spare light bulbs, extension cords, marking pens, masking tape and other necessities.
- Distribute handouts only when you refer to them, or give them to the audience as they leave.
- If anything goes wrong, do not apologize or spend precious time trying to repair the equipment. Extemporize or go directly to the question part of the meeting.

For more hints on effective public presentations, see also Chapter 8, "Speaking Skills for Presentations," and Chapter 10, "Graphic Communication."

How can the media help advance the public participation process?

POSITIVE MEDIA RELATIONS

The contribution of the media to the success or failure of any public participation process cannot be overestimated. Even today—when newspaper readership is shrinking, when most people get their information from radio and television "sound bites" and what they can glean from the Internet—media people are still leaders in their communities. What they do not choose to say about your program can be as influential as what they do say. Some planners mistakenly consider the media to be a necessary evil at the best; at the worst, dangerous and adversarial. The media, on the other hand, consider themselves as guardians of the public's right to know, and the conveyors of truth and information that may otherwise be hidden.

How can the media help advance the public participation process? First, it is important to recognize that there are important differences among the forms of media. Television is primarily a visual medium. Pictures are expected to tell the story, augmented by fast-talking anchors and reporters. They gravitate to public meetings where there is shouting and controversy and may not be as interested when things appear to be going smoothly. Still, you can probably interest them in human events, especially anything involving children or animals.

If you have graphs or charts, use short phrases and bright colors that can be picked up by the camera. Most importantly, practice reducing your message to 30 seconds. That's only about 10 words, but it's as much as most television program producers will give you.

Explore the opportunities of broadcasting over local cable. In many communities, they do more than just transmit signals and may be interested in programming your issue in some depth. The range of audience may be somewhat limited, but you can write and produce a show of a half hour or more and involve the people who will advance the issue. In some areas, cable can be a valuable public participation tool where viewers are involved to phone in comments or questions.

Radio is the most intimate of the media. It is most often background to whatever else its audience is doing (e.g., driving in the car, being in the bathroom or kitchen or working in the office or workshop). Most communities have one or more local talk shows with certain types of followers. There should be at least one show willing to interview a spokesperson for your project with some degree of civility. If you have a budget for advertising, radio is the least expensive of the media; the staff can help you target the audience you want to reach. If you have funds, place ads to invite participation in public events, or encourage people to call in for more information. Radio and television may give you reduced rates or free public service announcements.

As noted, local newspaper editors are still influential in their communities, although fewer people are actually reading what they say. Meet with them early to inform them of your sincerity in mounting an effective and open public process. An editor who has lived in the community for some time probably has strong views about what has failed before and warn-ings about how to succeed this time. Listen carefully. You may learn something. Inquire about the best way to keep them informed of the process; depending on their resources, they may want to assign a reporter as a primary contact. Continue to keep them apprised and enlist their cooperation in publicizing important milestones and events.

Do not overlook the minority media—those that are in contact with important ethnic communities or segments of the population such as seniors. They often have readers you cannot otherwise reach and may be willing to give you more space or air time, especially with stories of interest to their audiences.

In summary, be friendly and open with the media, but do not expect them to be your friend. They have a job to do and may be critical of what you are doing, but they are an important conduit to the public you want to serve.

STEP BY STEP

Successful public participation is a complex and iterative process that requires constant and careful management and attention. Each stage of the project has its own rhythm and needs. There is no ideal time span, though anything that lasts much more than a year risks a burnout factor as key people may move away or lose interest. On the other hand, if it is over in less than six months, you may give the impression that important decisions are being made elsewhere.

The ideal process is long enough to follow the project through, giving citizens ample time to be informed, to comment and to participate. It also is

Do not overlook the minority media— those that are in contact with important ethnic communities or segments of the population such as seniors.

SELECTING THE RIGHT METHOD

The challenge that planners face in involving the public is deciding what method of all those available (see Figure 6-2) will be successful in a particular case. In both of the following situations, planners were innovative and ultimately successful because they asked themselves, "What is the best way we can convey our information and have a productive dialogue with the public?" instead of "How can we get public involvement with the least effort to ourselves?" The results were satisfying to all parties.

How to Welcome All and Prevent Grandstanding by a Few

The planners in a suburban community of about 10,000 people completed the first draft of a new transportation systems plan. They had worked about six months on an ambitious set of options under the direction of the mayor. To their surprise, just when they were finished with the draft, the incumbent mayor was defeated by a newcomer to the community, who campaigned successfully on a platform to overturn much of what the previous mayor had favored, wanting more freeways and "less kowtowing to the ped and bike lobby." The planners revised the draft plan to meet all these objectives—more roads as well as more paths for riding and walking. The result was a very controversial document that seemed to please no one.

Traditionally, the department held "town hall" meetings on such subjects where citizens can say anything they want for as long as they want. Though some people favored this as "democracy in action," others realized that very little is accomplished as the meetings often deteriorate into shouting matches among people with strong opinions. The new mayor told city staff to find a better way to involve the public and find out their opinions.

Reviewing the matrix of public involvement techniques in this chapter (Figure 6-2), staff chose a *combination* of a *briefing* and *open house/community fair*. They met separately with the mayor and the influential editor of the local newspaper to brief them about key issues in the draft report and answer questions. They found the mayor less dogmatic in private (compared to her public persona) and willing to go along with the open house/community fair method of communicating with the public. The editor agreed to summarize the main points of the report in the paper and urge people to attend the public event.

The open house was held from 4:30 to 8:30 PM on a weekday in the local school cafeteria. As people entered, they were invited to view the various displays about the draft transportation plan and the several options, to talk with staff people stationed at tables around the room and to write down their opinions on newsprint placed on easels. Twice, people who were particularly interested in one part of the plan—new roads or bike paths, for example—were invited to have more in-depth discussions with staff at sections of the room partitioned for that purpose. Everyone was invited to fill out a written questionnaire. A surprisingly large number of people (about 250) came and went; some stayed for 10 minutes and others for several hours.

There were only two negative comments—both from zealots who were angry that there were no opportunities to address a large crowd. Most people said they appreciated the informal opportunities to get their questions answered and to express themselves in a nonthreatening environment. Other than having to be on duty for so many hours, the staff was delighted that they were able to discuss the issues with a variety of citizens. They recognized many new people who did not ordinarily come out to the traditional public meetings and said the feedback they received was constructive and enlightening.

The mayor stayed the whole time to shake hands and take credit for this "new way of doing things in our town."

When to Go to the People Instead of Waiting for Them to Come to Us

The city's draft comprehensive land use plan was completed. As most plans are, it was both very complicated and simple. There were many legal code amendments that had to be dealt with, as well as important zone changes that tended to get lost in the verbiage. The city held a few public meetings, but only a few citizens and a fair number of developers and their lawyers showed up. Planners were frustrated, asking themselves, "Don't people care about what could happen to their community?"

Reviewing the matrix of techniques, planners decided to go out to the public rather than wait for people to come to them. They put together a list of the most influential local service, civic and business clubs, and sent them each a letter offering to provide a speaker on the proposed plan at a future meeting. After receiving a surprising number of positive responses, they realized they had to tackle the hard part: organizing 20- to 25-minute presentations of the technical material in laypeople's language, choosing the appropriate visual aids and enlisting staff members to make the presentations.

The work was labor-intensive but very satisfying. People from all over town thanked them for coming out to them and talking about these important issues. Carrying their outreach a step further, the planners designed and updated a Web page with the pertinent information on the comprehensive plan, thus reaching out to an even broader segment of the public. When the formal hearings were held, the citizens who did come out were as complimentary about the process as they were about the plan.

flexible and able to adjust to technical, political or other detours or delays. Though general citizen participation in government is the ideal, the most effective processes are most often related to specific projects. In all cases, it is important that participants reach milestones they can celebrate.

Planners should follow these steps, no matter the time or specific project:

- Choose the public participation team with all the skills needed for success. These include people able to communicate well with the public, as well as those with technical expertise.

- Set the goals and objectives, key milestones and decision points early in the process.

- Agree on the primary and secondary audiences and develop means to involve them.

- Be inclusive.

- Decide on the type of participation that best suits the needs of the project and your audience. Is it mainly passive (presenting information) or primarily active (strong emphasis on sending and receiving information and feedback)? The most effective process has some of both, with the degree varying as needed.

- Develop and publicize a time schedule that is ample to affect the outcome of the project and flexible to respond to crises and unexpected events.

- Make sure that top management is informed and participates at key junctures.

- Assign appropriate spokespeople for the media.

- Give sufficient time and attention to all written materials—brochures, fact sheets, media releases and displays—so that they fit the needs of the project and expectations of the audience.
- Hold staff meetings regularly to assess progress and make corrections or changes as needed.
- Be willing to come to closure, admitting success and learning from failures.

HOW TO EVALUATE SUCCESS

The best measure of success is when the public and the decision makers reach general agreement or consensus on a plan of action. Continued contention or disagreement may be an indication that something is awry.

Advisory Committee or Task Force Participation

Be willing to come to closure, admitting success and learning from failures.

Regular attendance from at least 75% of the participants is a positive indicator. Dwindling attendance is a sign that the format, agenda or results are not meeting the needs or expectations of participants. If attendance is lagging, call nonattendees or discuss the issue with the regulars. Is the meeting time inconvenient? Are participants being given enough opportunity for meaningful influence? Are some members simply overextended?

Ask for a frank appraisal of the problem and take corrective action accordingly. It may require revisiting the meeting schedule, providing more emphasis on meaningful dialogue and decision making or replacing the nonattending members. The latter merits serious consideration. If the process is nearing completion, a new member may disturb or unbalance the relationships and levels of trust that have been carefully built up with the rest of the participants. In other cases, the need for continued representation by a specific group or interest may outweigh these concerns. As with everything else related to public participation, individual considerations are the key.

Survey Responses

The percentage of surveys returned—either in terms of people in the relevant group or community, or as a proportion of the total number contacted—is a quantitative and qualitative indicator of public interest. For a community survey distributed by mail, through the local media, the Web or other such means, and conducted without a significant follow-up effort, 1% is a good response rate and 2% is very good. For a survey targeted to a specific group of stakeholders, followed up with telephone calls, a 5% response rate is highly successful.

If too few people respond to give an accurate sense of stakeholder opinion, it may be necessary to undertake more staff-intensive activities, such as random or targeted follow-up telephone interviews or surveys of specific community representatives.

Public Meeting Attendance

Numbers do not tell the whole story. A relatively few, highly engaged people can hold a very productive, useful meeting. Measure success against the size of the directly and indirectly affected community, their known perceptions of the importance of the issue

AN EFFECTIVE PUBLIC PARTICIPATION PROCESS

An effective participatory planning process should enable planners to test the social acceptability of their assumptions and program proposals, as well as enable involved members of the public to express their preferences among potential management alternatives. To date, there have been few attempts by planning agencies to define performance criteria for evaluating the effectiveness of public involvement activities. Such a list might start with the following general criteria:

1. The planning process should provide opportunities for members of the public who choose to participate.

2. The public should be made aware of the availability of such participation opportunities so they can make a choice.

3. Sufficient information should be made available to the public so they can participate effectively.

4. Planning agencies should be able to respond effectively to the inputs and activities of public participants.

There are no hard-and-fast or best procedures for structuring public involvement. Those arrangements that will work most effectively depend to a great extent on the specifics of each situation, such as the focus and geographic scope of the planning effort, the resources available to planners, the history and seriousness of planning problems in the area, the types of areas in which civic and special interest groups are active and the degree of importance they attribute to the planning efforts.

Building an effective public involvement process is more an art than a science. Planners need to develop the best program communication mosaic for each situation. Care should be exercised to maintain program balance and openness to different opinions so as not to screen out certain interest groups. Ignoring either the noisy or silent opposition only postpones the conflict and often increases its later intensity.

To build an open and effective framework for public involvement, the planner needs a variety of communication skills, including the ability to:

1. write reports, articles, brochures and press releases clearly

2. use graphics of all types to illustrate the kinds of information being presented either verbally or in writing

3. verbally present the essential facts behind planning recommendations

4. frame alternatives or planning options in a manner that enables people to respond meaningfully and state their preferences

5. formulate, carry out and analyze surveys so that they provide useful planning information

6. listen to people and answer questions in a manner that is both sensitive and responsive

7. participate productively in group discussions

8. recognize and understand the social and political implications of various planning contexts

Warner, Katharine P. "Public Involvement as Planning Communication," *The Planner's Use of Information*. 1st ed. Chicago: American Planning Association, 1988, p. 137.

and the extent of the notification process. A turnout of about 1% to 2% of those contacted is average.

It is not easy to ascertain why stakeholders or the general public did not attend what you thought was an important meeting. Ask your advisory committee or other stakeholders these questions:

- Was the time or location inconvenient?
- Was publicity and notification adequate?
- Are the issues really as important to stakeholders or other members of the community as you thought they were?

Plan the next event in accordance with what you learn, or conduct other outreach activities that are more likely to be successful.

Informal Feedback

The most common forms of informal feedback include positive or negative newspaper editorials, letters to the editors, phone calls or e-mail. The breadth and depth of such responses can be anecdotal evidence about how well you have succeeded in the public participation process. Give less credence to form letters or e-mail from special interest groups.

Public participation should be ongoing as well as specific. While individual projects may not be as successful as you would have liked, the reservoir of goodwill may be deep and sustaining. Never give up!

APPLICATIONS

1. In "Issue #1 (Neighborhood Scale): Urban Development in Middlesville" under the chapter entitled "A Planning Case Study," a developer and his team of planners and architects had progressed to where schematics for a 50-unit construction that would involve a zoning change from R-1, C-1 were being reviewed by the city planning office without any significant public participation. The university's student organization heard about the proposed development "through the grapevine" and mounted a noisy protest campaign. What should or could the planning office have done to find out if anyone in the public would be interested? What should they do now?

2. In "Issue #2 (City/County Scale): Transportation Plan for Middlesville," what type of process should the planning department have followed before the public hearing so that all points of view could have been acknowledged and understood? What educational or informational materials should have been produced beforehand? What should they do now?

3. In "Issue #3 (Regional Scale): Energy Planning for Hiatonka and East Victoria," decision makers in the governors' offices are beginning to hear from a disparate group of constituencies with various points of view. They are complaining that the consultants did not check with them and are writing a technical study "in a vacuum." State representatives and others are also getting angry phone calls, letters and e-mail from their constituents. The study is in jeopardy of being quashed. Can this project be saved? Is there a way to attempt to reach common ground?

Should state planners sit back and let the politicians handle it? What does this say about how planners can affect important policy decisions?

BIBLIOGRAPHY

Bernstein, T. M. *The Careful Writer.* New York: Atheneum, 1965.

Bernstein presents a succinct and complete guide to good writing.

Carpenter, S. L. and W. J. D. Kennedy. *Managing Public Disputes: A Practical Guide to Handling Conflict and Reaching Agreements.* San Francisco: Jossey-Bass, 1988.

This guide helps planners be aware of existing help for public agreements that may appear insurmountable.

Cogan, A., S. Sharpe and J. Hertzberg. "Citizen Participation." *The Practice of State and Regional Planning.* Chicago: American Planning Association with the International City Management Association, 1986.

This publication provides basic information from reliable sources and makes a convincing case for the value of citizen participation in helping resolve important governmental issues.

Cogan, E. *Successful Public Meetings: A Practical Guide.* Chicago: American Planning Association, 2000.

Cogan offers a comprehensive discussion of the topics in this chapter.

Cogan, E. and B. Padrow. *You Can Talk to (Almost) Anyone about (Almost) Anything.* Portland, OR: Continuing Education Publications, Portland State University, 1984.

This book describes basic information about how to prepare for and make winning presentations.

Doyle, M. and D. Straus. *How to Make Meetings Work.* New York: Berkley, 1984.

This provides practical ideas that can be used in a variety of situations.

Fletcher, W. *Meetings, Meetings.* New York: Morrow, 1984.

As the title indicates, this provides an overview of techniques for dealing with many different kinds of meetings.

O'Hayre, J. *Gobbledygook Has Gotta Go.* Washington, DC: U.S. Government Printing Office, 1966.

O'Hayre has written a witty, irreverent, invaluable guide on how *not* to write for the public.

Race, Bruce and Carolyn Torma. *Youth Planning Charettes.* Chicago: American Planning Association, 1998.

This is a complete guide to helping young people participate in community planning.

Robert, H. N. *Robert's Rules of Order.* New York: Bell, 1907.

The classic work on how to lead a formal meeting. It is somewhat archaic in style and has been republished and paraphrased in many different titles. Two well-known examples follow.

Robert III, Henry M., William J. Evans, Daniel H. Honemann and Thomas J. Balch. *Robert's Rules of Order, Newly Revised.* 10th ed. Cambridge, MA: Perseus Publishing, 2000.

This is the "official" and up-to-date revision of the original, as issued by the heirs of the original author. It now includes many modernizations, including discussions of the use of the Internet and videoconferencing.

Rozkis, Laurie E. and Ellen Lichtenstein. *21st Century Robert's Rules of Order.* New York: Dell Publishing, 1995.

Rozkis and Lichtenstein provide an inexpensive and modernized paraphrase of *Robert's Rules* written in modern colloquial language, with explanations of the use and application of various rules and procedures.

Stacey, W. S. *Business and Professional Speaking*. New York: William C. Brown, 1983.

This includes everything one needs to know about speech making.

Strauss, B. and F. Strauss. *New Ways to Better Meetings*. New York: Viking, 1952.

Ideas to enlarge the scope of possibilities for meeting management are included in this book.

CHAPTER 7

Computers and Planning

Richard Crepeau

ACCESSING AND DISSEMINATING INFORMATION

Assistant Planner was given the problem of litter on Main Street in Middlesville on a warm Friday afternoon. After he had surveyed the situation in person and made some notes, he needed some information about the trash pickup schedule. However, the public works department closed early on Fridays.

He turned on his laptop computer while sipping iced tea on his patio late Sunday evening. The computer dialed up a phone connection to Assistant Planner's local Internet service provider. After starting his Web browser, he navigated to the Web page for Public Works and used his mouse to click the phrase "refuse pickup schedule," which appeared on the computer screen.

A new Web page appeared that prompted him to type in a street and location within the city. He typed in "Main Street" and "Downtown," and clicked on a button that said "enter." The city's Public Works data processing computer received the request and searched for all records on trash pickups along downtown's Main Street. After finding the pickups, the data processor collected and delivered them to the computer screen on Assistant Planner's patio. He discovered the locations of all stops along downtown's Main Street as well as the fact that all trash pickups along Main Street occur on Tuesday.

Acting on a hunch, Assistant Planner returned to the Web page for Public Works and found a prompt for "day of pickup."

He typed in "Friday, Saturday" and clicked the "enter" button with his mouse. After a couple of seconds, his computer screen displayed a list of all stops made in the city on Fridays and Saturdays. A button on the Web page prompted him to "sort by street," so he clicked on it and the computer screen changed to display the same information sorted by street name. Assistant Planner scrolled down to confirm his hunch that streets close to Main Street had trash pickups on Friday and Saturday.

Assistant Planner opened the word processing program on his computer and quickly wrote a memo to his supervisor detailing his recommendation for moving trash pickup along downtown's Main Street from Tuesday to either Friday or Saturday. He pointed out that not only will the businesses be pleased with this change, but services may be more efficient for Public Works.

After saving the document, Assistant Planner opened up his e-mail program and addressed a message to his supervisor requesting a meeting for early Monday morning. To prepare her for this meeting, he attached the word processor document to the e-mail and sent it, so that the message and document will be waiting for the planning director when she arrives on Monday morning.

Assistant Planner sipped the last of his iced tea, logged off of his Internet connection and turned the computer off. He still had an hour or two of lazy sunshine left to enjoy from his hammock.

INTRODUCTION

Computers allow planners the control of and access to large amounts of information. Recent breakthroughs in prices, size, speed, capacity and intercommunication among computers have "democratized" computing and information technology. As the vignette about Assistant Planner illustrates (see the sidebar entitled "Accessing and Disseminating Information"), a laptop computer can allow a planner access to information from their patio in a few moments on a weekend. Previously, this might have taken an entire afternoon of walking around to various city offices. Large databases of all types of information, some of which were noted in Chapter 3, "Information from Secondary Sources," are also readily available. In the past, obtaining these might have required weeks of archival research.

In addition, computers have increased the efficiency and ease with which planners can accomplish any number of tasks (e.g., forecasting population, creating maps, organizing permit information or creating presentation graphics for public meetings). It almost seems that a planning office would fall apart without computers. It is easy to forget that, not very long ago, computers were nowhere to be seen in a planning office; even today, there are planning offices in the U.S. that do not have the expertise or funding to incorporate computers in any meaningful way beyond word processing, simple database management and minimal mapping functions.

Before we discuss the application of computers to planning, it is helpful to pause and reflect on the rapid advance of this technology (as shown in the sidebar entitled "History of Computing"). From its early days (when computers consisted of vacuum tubes, blinking lights and mechanical switches) to contemporary computers (which can perform hundreds of millions or more calculations per second), the trajectory of computer technology is a marvel.

Why go through this brief history of computing? Only to warn the reader that "obsolescence" goes hand in hand with computer technology and, as time goes on, this chapter may seem antiquated. With that in mind, the goal of this chapter is to highlight the basic concepts of computers and the applications planners are likely to use with computers, rather than discuss specific technologies or computer applications.

The use of computer technology in planning can be discussed as applications in four different contexts: computation, data storage and information management, presentation and the distribution of public information.

Computation

Computers have become indispensable tools for planners. Economic forecasts, transportation analyses and spatial analyses, as currently practiced, require the power computers offer us. The presence of computers has also affected the operation of a planning office. Twenty to thirty years ago, requests for computationally intensive tasks were sent to a centralized data processing center, and the wait for output could be up to a week, depending upon the

Computers allow planners the control of and access to large amounts of information.

HISTORY OF COMPUTING

Computation, per se, is nothing new. The abacus from Asia Minor has existed for thousands of years. Blaise Pascal (French philosopher and mathematician) invented a mechanical computer in the mid 1600s and Charles Babbage's Analytical Engine of the mid 1800s was designed to be a steam-powered computing system. However, electronic computation is distinctively a 20th century phenomenon that has evolved ever faster, fueling a growth in trade and human interaction.

Early electronic computers, such as the Mark I in the 1940s, used electricity as a way to move mechanical switches (much the way the abacus uses fingers and the Analytical Engine used steam). The Mark I took 3 to 5 seconds to perform each mathematical operation. The Electronic Numerical Integrator and Computer (ENIAC) increased operating speeds by nearly 1,000 times, but this came at a price: the ENIAC consisted of 18,000 vacuum tubes, 70,000 resistors and over 5,000,000 soldered joints. It is said that the ENIAC would consume so much electricity (roughly 160 kilowatts) that the lights of certain portions of Philadelphia would dim during operation.

Still, computers could not store information (i.e., instructions and data had to be input on a job-by-job basis) and the results could not be stored within the computer for future retrieval. The Electronic Discrete Variable Automatic Computer (EDVAC) and Universal Variable Computer (UNIVAC) in the late 1940s solved the "memory" problem by constructing magnetic matrices that stored information. In addition, the EDVAC and UNIVAC were the first computers to be used for general (i.e., nonmilitary or academic) purposes. The U.S. Census Bureau and General Electric used the UNIVAC for their operations. Election predictions were first made with the help of computers during Eisenhower's election in 1952.

The size of computers shrank considerably with the introduction of more sophisticated electronic components. Smaller transistors replaced the bulky vacuum tubes; more sophisticated storage devices enabled computers to become faster, more reliable and more flexible. Due to this flexibility and sophistication, as well as the fact that computers were becoming more affordable and energy efficient, commercial enterprises adopted computers to automate many tasks.

In the 1970s, integrated circuit technology allowed computers to become smaller and faster. Integrated circuits (i.e., silicon chips) squeeze the functions of thousands of separate electronic components (e.g., transistors and resistors) onto a component no larger than a dime. The explosion of computer technology in the San Francisco Bay Area at this time created a hot spot of economic activity that is still known as Silicon Valley.

Since the 1970s, computers have become ever smaller and faster. Computers, which once occupied entire floors of offices, became appliances that are at home on a desktop. At this time, computers have become tools for research and business, as well as for enhancing personal productivity, interaction and entertainment. Where once 10 years passed between the Mark I computer and the UNIVAC, improvements in computer technology are now marked in months rather than in decades.

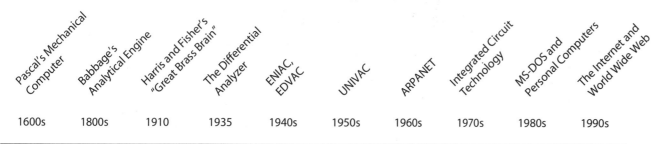

BALANCING NEEDS AND DESIRES

The use of a Geographic Information System (GIS) provides an excellent illustration of balancing needs and desires. GISs became the rage among planning departments because they could store spatial information, analyze data and create wonderful maps. Without considering how complex these applications can be, many agencies purchased a GIS at great expense, only to realize how difficult such systems could be in order to make them operational for specific contexts.

Assistant Planner recently spoke with an old friend who worked in the planning department of a nearby city. She related a story about her city's experience with a GIS. A software vendor convinced the city manager that a GIS could integrate the planning department with public works, taxation and assessment and environmental services. Conceptually, this sounded like a great idea and the city manager purchased the software. Soon, the city manager found out that the GIS was not streamlining operations.

The public works department was the first to state that none of their employees could adequately use the software; other departments mentioned the same problem. It was dis-

continued on page 219

queue. Now this can be done in house, with the human user as the major time limiter.

Data Storage and Information Management

Organization and manipulation of information are the major uses for computers in most administrative contexts. A tremendous amount and variety of information must be stored either in long-term archives or in ways that allow near-instantaneous access. However, just as with a "paper" filing system, the information needs to be legible and organized. How many times have planners searched through one of the agency's file cabinets to find a document, only to find the file drawer in disarray, not find the file in the drawer at all, or find the file but be unable to understand the scribbling in the file?

Computers can help any agency organize its information; however, as with any such system, supervision and oversight on the part of the users determine its success. Computers are excellent tools for collecting, storing, creating and analyzing information; however, to be effective, the organization of that information is critical. Good file management and documentation are essential.

Planners use information to achieve a number of goals. One such goal is creating a more efficient work environment. Computers can easily manage information on permits and actually track the process any given permit undertakes. Information on client contact, site inspections and violations can be attached to permits and recalled at a moment's notice. Retrieving addresses of property owners for public notifica-

tion is also a simple matter. Few planners can now imagine running a planning office without relying on computers for handling information. Computers have enabled planners to deal with multiple pieces of information more easily and effectively.

Presentation

Through the display of information on a computer screen, or printing information on paper or slides, visualizing for analysis and for communicating information is an important task for planning agencies. Many concepts in planning require more than one way to get the point across and computers have become versatile tools for enabling a myriad of ways for visualization (see Chapter 10, "Graphic Communication").

With computers, planners may create graphics for public meetings that summarize or distill a complex process into one or many simple pictures. Creating, recreating and amending graphics is nearly instantaneous compared to the laborious, time-consuming and expensive processes of the past. Assistant Planner's littering problem could quickly and effectively be communicated by digitizing photos of the litter and arranging those photos for a public presentation, or by inserting them in an e-mail to supervisors and decision makers.

Computers also allow us to create maps and analyze the spatial information that maps contain. Simply, we can create maps that show use zoning districts, the extent of municipal services and the distribution of sensitive environmental lands. On a more complex level, we can also create computer environments that allow us to examine the visual impact of a proposed development.

Distribution of Public Information

The American public increasingly demands accountability and transparency of their government. This is particularly true of local governments where planning decisions affect most everything a citizen experiences (see Chapter 6, "Public Participation" and Chapter 11, "Planning in the Political Context"). Computers allow planning agencies to provide information to citizenry. Whether this interaction is active or passive depends a great deal on the type of information requested.

An *active* interaction environment is one that allows a permit applicant to find out the progress of their application. We can think of this interaction as active in that a user queries a computer's database for specific information and the computer delivers this information to the applicant. An active interaction could also include construction of "what-if" scenarios from different assumptions or starting points provided by the user.

A *passive* interaction environment could be a series of Web pages devoted to providing general information about a long-range planning process (e.g., purpose, current status, findings and future meetings), a department's permit process or a public body's meeting schedule and agenda. A process like this is passive because the information is on the Web

page, waiting for a user to access it. The information does not change from user to user. '

DESIGN OF THE COMPUTING ENVIRONMENT

The administration of computers in a planning context can be deceptively complex. The key is to determine the requirements of the planning unit and the essential criteria to meet those requirements. The second step is to organize the equipment and applications within the unit. Many systems fail because the requirements and capabilities were not properly anticipated.

Needs Versus Desires

It is easy to fall into the trap of keeping up with the Joneses. The Joneses could be similar planning offices in other jurisdictions or sister agencies within the same jurisdiction. If the reason for requesting a specific computer or application is because "other people use it," then one must reconsider their priorities. If the request comes from recognition that the computer or application will improve the efficiency of the office—or increase the interaction among individuals in the office, the governing body and the public— then the priorities are likely well thought out.

In order to avoid problems, such as those described in the sidebar entitled "Balancing Needs and Desires," determining an agency or firm's requirements can be accomplished with a rational planning model as follows:

continued from page 218

covered that quite a few workers had used a GIS before—even the same GIS that the city purchased—but there was a big difference between using a GIS and actually developing a system of acquiring, analyzing and presenting the spatial information that a GIS uses. In order for the city to actually implement the GIS, at least two new employees needed to be hired. The city did not have the budget for this.

The tax parcel data that existed in electronic format was not readable by the GIS; the public works information, such as power, sewer and water main locations, did not exist in electronic format at all. The parcel data could be purchased elsewhere, or special software could be developed that translated the parcel data, but both options were expensive. The public works data had to be digitized into a file that the GIS could read.

Even if the data and manpower were available, the city would have to purchase peripheral equipment such as scanners, plotters, digitizers, larger computer monitors and computer systems that had the necessary computing power and storage space.

In the end, the city decided to shelve the idea of integrating departments with a GIS.

- *Define the problem*. Why do you need this computer system? To help manage information? To respond to citizen or client inquiries more quickly?
- *Clarify values*. For whom are you doing this? The agency, the city, the citizens or perhaps to attract a more diverse client base?
- *Select goals*. Distill the problem definition and clarification of values into specific, achievable goals.
- *Formulate plans and alternatives*. Given your office's resources, how can you best meet your goals? Are you looking for a short-term impact or for gradually improving your capabilities over time?
- *Forecast alternatives*. Try to determine what the outcome would be for each plan (e.g., the costs, benefits and efficiency gains).
- *Evaluate outcomes*. Given the costs, benefits and efficiency gains, what are the comparative strengths and weaknesses of each plan?
- *Develop detailed plans for implementation*. Which plan maximizes the benefits at a cost that is acceptable to all parties involved? Choose that plan and implement it.
- *Review and evaluate*. Continually monitor the effectiveness of your program and modify the implementation to address unforeseen circumstances.

Stand-alone Computers Versus Networks

In the example thus far, we have discussed the conceptual "what" of computers in the planning office.

Continually monitor the effectiveness of your program and modify the implementation to address unforeseen circumstances.

The "how" remains: Will the agency provide these resources in a centralized or distributed fashion? In other words, will the computational strength of the planning agency be in the form of a network or as a collection of stand-alone computers?

How are the computing resources to be allocated? Is it more efficient to have them distributed autonomously among all planners or should the planning unit have the ability to centrally locate all resources? The goals and values of the institution and unit context determine the right model.

Stand-alone: In the case of a "stand-alone" computing model (Figure 7-1, Option A), consider each computer to be an extension of a person's desk. Under most circumstances, the papers and pencils on the desktop or in the drawers remain the property of the person who owns the desk. The stand-alone computing environment operates in the same manner: what is in one's computer remains the "property" of the computer's owner or operator. In this environment, if a planner wanted to retrieve an electronic file from a co-worker, they would walk to the co-worker's desk, ask for the document, have the file copied onto a diskette, take the diskette back to their desk and transfer the file into the computer's hard drive.

Some may find this cumbersome, especially in a working environment where constant interaction and cooperation is necessary. However, in smaller working environments, this may not be much of an obstacle. In the stand-alone model, each computer is a self-contained unit. The computer provides its own operating system, applications software and data storage capabilities. This sort of system integrity provides a tremendous amount of computer security (one needs to be physically at the computer to access the data in the computer) and minimizes the risks of passing along computer viruses. However, this isolation comes at a cost by reducing beneficial interaction among co-workers and increasing the complexity of managing the computer system(s).

Networks: If electronic documents, computer programs and computing resources (such as storage devices and printers) can be shared among many computers, then the system itself can be much more efficient. In many situations, it is easier for someone to manage a single network of computers rather than a collection of individual computers. The term "network" is used to describe a collection of computers and the peripherals necessary to make the computers work together. Each computer or connection is defined as a "node" or point in the network where information converges or disseminates. A network can either be a Local-area Network (LAN) or a Wide-area Network (WAN).

LANs typically connect computers and computing services within an office or building by means of special software and equipment. LANs can be differentiated by the means in which the interaction occurs, in either a *peer-to-peer* or *client-server* fashion.

In a peer-to-peer environment (Figure 7-1, Option B), all nodes or computers are treated as equals. Documents and data can be shared among all members of the LAN. Many types of peer-to-peer software

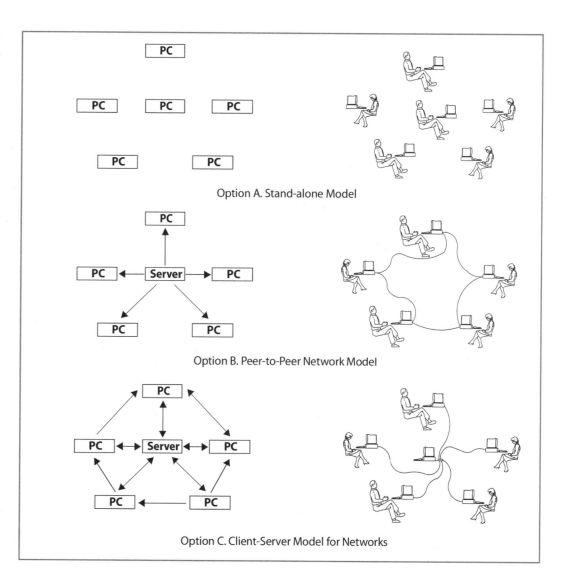

Option A. Stand-alone Model

Option B. Peer-to-Peer Network Model

Option C. Client-Server Model for Networks

7-1. PC network server models

allow users to interact with each other in more sophisticated ways (e.g., electronic messaging, scheduling and connecting with other networks). Note, however, that this interaction is not completely open. The networking software enables the administrators to designate parts of an individual's computer as private and inaccessible to the other members of the network. In a peer-to-peer framework, there is no central node as all computers are equal.

By contrast, the client-server network (Figure 7-1, Option C) describes a network in which one computer (the server) provides services to all other computers in the network (the clients). In the most extreme example, the server provides all computer applications (e.g., word processing, spreadsheets and a GIS) as well as most data storage capabilities.

To an individual client or node, being part of a network may not be apparent until limitations of the hardware or software have been reached or there are more users trying to access a program than are allowed. During these times of peak usage, many network clients experience congestion and the computer may not be as responsive. To eliminate these problems, proper planning is necessary to determine the demands for services provided by the network. One possible solution is to create a hybrid system in which day-to-day applications (e.g., word processing and graphics production) are provided locally and data-intensive applications (e.g., GIS, mapping and large database operations) can be served via the LAN.

In contrast to LANs, the scope of service for WANs is defined regionally or even internationally.

In contrast to LANs, the scope of service for WANs is defined regionally or even internationally. Whereas LANs deliver information via cables within an office building, WANs use telephone lines, fiber-optic cables, microwave transmission and satellites to distribute information. The most visible WAN is the Internet, which enables large corporations and individuals alike to distribute information.

Some WANs are private and exclusive; others are public. A private WAN might be a Web page accessible from any location but limited to designated users with passwords. For example, the Middlesville environmental engineering department could have a scheduling or calendar page intended only for employees of that department. Even though Assistant Planner might be an employee of the city, he might not have access to this internal information; however, as in the vignette at the beginning of this chapter, he did access the public WAN (as any citizen could) and was still able to access useful information.

Many planning agencies participate in both LANs and WANs and utilize the capabilities of each. Internally, planning agencies must efficiently transfer information, data and documentation among many users. As a permit moves through the approval process, the information must be accessible to all departments involved (e.g., planning, the public works department and public safety). Being part of a network allows all parties to access this permit information without the need for traveling from office to office. A planning agency may also wish to disseminate information on a WAN, allowing permit applicants to view the progress of their applications or provide an alternative means for contacting the planners responsible for shepherding the permit through the development review process.

COMPUTER HARDWARE AND SOFTWARE

Hardware allows the user to interact with the computer (input and output devices) as well as provide the engine for the computational process (the central processing unit, or CPU). Software, at various levels, tells the computer how to use the hardware, acts as translator between the user and computer and provides detailed instructions for specific jobs (e.g., graphics, word processing or statistical analysis).

Hardware

Hardware can be organized into three categories:

- *input devices* (such as the keyboard, mouse, scanners and digitizers, which create an avenue of communication from the user to the computer)
- *computation hardware* (such as the CPU and a variety of storage media, which manipulate and archive data)
- *output devices* (such as monitors, printers and sound devices)

Input: The *keyboard* is the workhorse of the computer. It consists of alphanumeric keys, function keys, cursor keys and numeric keys. Alphanumeric keys are the standard letters, numbers and symbols. The function keys (F1 through F12) access preprogrammed commands for some computer applications. (While some consistency exists among computer applications as to what a given function key does, it is not universal.) Cursor keys allow the user to move the cursor around the monitor. Numeric keys offer a convenient alternative for intensive numerical input. Other keys include the "enter" key, which either executes commands or introduces line breaks, and the <Alt>, Shift and <Ctrl> keys, used in command functions in combination with other keys.

The *mouse* has evolved from a tool used mostly by graphic designers (because it allowed for fluid motion across the screen, like a pencil on a piece of paper) to an input device that is required for most computer applications. While a keyboard's cursor keys allow the cursor to move in discrete horizontal and vertical units, the mouse moves the cursor in a continuous motion at any angle. The left button on the mouse typically acts as the "enter" key; in most programs, the right button invokes "pop-up menus" for shortcut access to many functions. However, many skilled computer users also learn keyboard shortcuts to functions, thus avoiding continual use of the mouse.

Scanners convert images and text into digital formats. The image or photograph is translated electronically and stored in a specific file format on the computer. However, scanning text can be quite complex. There is a fundamental difference between scanning the *image* of the text on the page and actually copying the text into a format understandable to word processing applications (such as a symbol or letter of the alphabet).

Hardware allows the user to interact with the computer (input and output devices) as well as provide the engine for the computational process (the central processing unit, or CPU).

Storage media generally refers to long-term storage or a place to store data and programs.

Through the use of Optical Character Recognition (OCR) software, the image of text is converted into binary code so that the collection of letters can be understood by and manipulated with a word processor. What if Assistant Planner had to redraft a section of the city's zoning ordinance but the ordinance existed only on paper? He could scan the ordinance into a computer but, without OCR software, the ordinance would merely be pictures of pages of the zoning ordinance and completely uneditable. The OCR software translates the image into text by recognizing the patterns of letters on the page. Once scanned with OCR software, Assistant Planner can edit away, as if someone had typed the document for him.

Digitizers allow a user to input lines and shapes into the computer. In contrast to a scanner (where an image or text is "copied" from paper or photo), a digitizer can be viewed as a sketch board. These input devices are most handy for digital cartography and a GIS. Digitizers can be as small as a paper tablet or as large as a chalkboard. By either using a pen or a "puck" connected electronically to the board, a user can enter information depicting rivers, roads, blocks and boundaries that can later be mapped or analyzed spatially.

Digital cameras, video recorders and voice recognition software are other examples of input devices.

Computation: Computation hardware for data processing and data storage is much more powerful today and provides better integration of these two functions than in the past. While it is tempting to think of the CPU as the brains of the computer, this term is misleading. The CPU is merely the hardware (mostly integrated circuits) that coordinates all activity within the computer (e.g., performing arithmetic and logical operations, interpreting input from the user for the computer's operating system, retrieving data from storage and delivering output to the user via the computer monitor or printer).

Memory and *storage media* can be distinguished from one another along the time dimension. Memory generally refers to short-term or "volatile" memory that disappears when a calculation is finished or the computer is turned off. Storage media generally refers to long-term storage or a place to store data and programs.

Read-Only Memory (ROM) is an exception to the above rule: it is nonvolatile memory borne on integrated circuit chips. It consists of commands and instructions the CPU uses to operate. These commands and instructions cannot be changed or altered. Random Access Memory (RAM), also on integrated circuit chips, is volatile and temporary. Portions of most computer programs and the data they use are stored in RAM, which works with data much more quickly and efficiently than storage media such as floppy and hard disks, where friction plays a factor in slowing the transfer of information. The more RAM a computer has, the more likely it is to work smoothly. RAM is volatile because any data or instructions that exist in it disappear when the power is turned off.

Floppy disks, hard disks and compact disks are all current examples of storage media that are used to hold archived data and programs. Floppy and hard disks are primarily magnetic media. The storage of these data was meant to be permanent, but there are weaknesses inherent in magnetic media. The data stored on disk are subject to the same electromagnetic forces that initially placed them there. Much data have been lost by accidentally placing diskettes on or near magnetic devices.

The strength of magnetic force weakens over time, thus degrading the quality of data. CD-ROM—or more recently, Compact Disk–Read-Write (CD-RW)—technology has addressed the drawbacks inherent in magnetic media storage. CD technology relies on light (provided by a laser) and the physical topography of the recorded surface. Initially, CDs were read-only (a type of portable ROM device) and the ability to record data on a CD was limited; then, the CD could only be recorded a single time. CD technology has evolved so that a CD-RW allows multiple "writes" onto a single CD. The clear advantages of CD. technology are robust storage, more capacity and faster data transfer rates.

Output: Output devices create an interface, providing either text or images that communicate prompts to the user for further input or commands, or final products such as reports, posters and other graphic images. *Monitors* or "screens" provide immediate feedback from the computer. While there used to be a distinction among monitors that could accommodate graphics or just text, the dominant computing environment is now a graphical user interface (GUI, or "gooey"). The choice now is how sophisticated you wish your graphic output to be (i.e., how many millions of colors are displayed, how fine the screen resolution is, how much animation and video capabilities you want, whether you want a cathode-ray tube or a liquid crystal display). The choice of monitor is usually determined by budget and also by whether the eventual use will be graphic-intensive (e.g., graphic design, mapping and a GIS) or not.

Printers provide a permanent product for the computer user, either in the form of a document or graphic. The choice of printer is determined by its eventual use. Some printers print documents very quickly but may not be good for graphic output; other printers may be very good at graphic output but are much too expensive if used primarily for printing reports. Color printers are especially useful for GIS reports and for graphics (such as charts) where color is used in presenting data. Plotters can be classified as printers for large output, such as maps and charts for public meetings and presentations.

Planners have a wide choice of printers from which to choose. The basic difference is between ink-jet and laser printers. The quality of ink-jet printers has improved quite a bit, so most choices are based on cost. At first glance, ink-jet printers are inexpensive; however, ink cartridges can be very expensive, especially for color ink. Laser printers have a steep up-front cost; in the long term, they may be very economical. Laser toner cartridges may be recycled and

The strength of magnetic force weakens over time, thus degrading the quality of data.

future cartridge purchases may be discounted accordingly.

If one were in a position to choose among printers, the decision can be made simpler if the choice is between a personal or public printer; or the choice is between a text- or graphic-intensive output. Ink-jet printers are good for personal use; laser printers are dependable workhorses for a public, office-based printer. Ink-jet printers are perhaps best suited for text-based output. Although ink-jet printers produce color graphics, the output isn't generally considered publication quality because the ink jet itself prints one line at a time and may "streak" across the page. It may very well be a wise investment for a planning office to purchase a color laser printer, keeping in mind the added expense of color toner.

The trend towards system integration has led to many crossovers, such as Linux, that have found a home among many PCs, replacing the Windows operating system.

Software

Software tells the computer what tasks to perform and how to perform them. Communication ranges from simple (transferring data from one storage medium to another) to complex (simulating the choice a traveler makes given the arrangement of roads and a set of trip purposes). Much software is available as prepackaged applications. A proficient operator can create (or program) a tailor-made application for special needs. Planners don't generally devise their own applications as the range of "canned" or preprogrammed planning applications is quite bountiful.

Operating systems: Basic Input Output System (BIOS, pronounced *bi-oss*) is not really software. It is stored in a ROM chip that the computer accesses after the power switch is turned on. The BIOS, in actuality, wakes the computer up, allowing the CPU to communicate with the rest of the computer's hardware, such as the monitor, printer, memory and hard disk. While the BIOS "introduces" the CPU to the rest of the computer, operating systems provide a means for the computer to control the hardware and process application software. The most important function of operating systems, however, is managing the directory of files and file configuration.

Different computer architectures require different operating systems, although there is a trend towards integration. Most personal computers (PCs) use a variant of the Windows operating system, while Macintosh computers use System X. There are a multitude of types of the UNIX (actually, UNICS: Uniplexed Information and Computing Service) operating system (UNIX, HP-UNIX and Linux) that primarily operate on larger mainframe computers. However, as PCs have become more powerful, the more technologically savvy users exploit the strength and versatility of UNIX in a nonmainframe environment.

The trend towards system integration has led to many crossovers, such as Linux, that have found a home among many PCs, replacing the Windows operating system. The different operating systems each have a vocal and loyal following. Windows is appreciated because of the wide range of applications designed for its use; illustrators favor a Macintosh system because it was built primarily as a graphics-based system; scientists, programmers and academics favor UNIX systems.

Many people discuss Disk Operating System (DOS) and Windows in the same breath because Windows grew out of DOS in response to the popularity of Macintosh's GUI. DOS is a command-line operating system, in which the computer prompts the user to type in a command via the keyboard, typically with the "C-prompt," which looks like "C:\>."

The commands either move, copy or delete files; perform various disk or system maintenance tasks; or alter the directory structure. The user may also type the name of a program they wish to use. The command line is also common in UNIX systems. Windows has superseded DOS as the dominant PC operating system. Windows began as a DOS "shell" or graphical interface between the user and the command line. It has now *become* the operating system.

The Macintosh computer and associated operating system was developed in 1984, when it was heralded as a new paradigm in computing. By borrowing concepts developed at Xerox, a GUI was used for the first time in a commercially available PC. The distinction between the Macintosh and the DOS/Windows environment is generally categorized in this way: Windows is a graphical interface superimposed on the DOS environment; Macintosh is a true, graphically oriented operating system.

The UNIX operating system was developed at AT & T's Bell Laboratories in the early 1970s and, in a sense, was the first "open source" program (i.e., the source code is free and open to anyone who wishes to use it). Because UNIX began as an open source operating system, many people and organizations altered it to suit their needs. UNIX soon became the workhorse of (then) modern computing in government, academia and industry.

Today, UNIX is still used extensively as an operating system, although many versions of UNIX are no longer free or open source. One notable exception is Linux, which still operates under an open source license. While an open source license generally allows unlimited access and "ownership" to the source code, the use of the source code for personal profit is disallowed, and any alterations to the program should be documented and made public.

Programming: Software applications (compiled programs) are created by programming. The simple diagram in Figure 7-2 illustrates the steps taken when creating a program:

- Conceptualize what needs to be done and determine the best approach to achieving the goal.
- Write the code that accomplishes the task.
- Debug (a type of proofreading to be sure that the syntax is correct) the code.
- Compile the source code into an executable program, which can then be used to accomplish the task for which it was designed.

Of course, this is a simplified example of a computer program; in fact, the same program may be written with a script (discussed in the next paragraph; see also the sidebar entitled "Scripts"); sometimes the task determines which program language to use. A few programming languages

SCRIPTS

Many Geographic Information System (GIS) technicians use scripts (such as Avenue) to create an interface for specific users or specific uses with ArcView GIS. Out of the box, ArcView does many things—perhaps too many things for a planner. The GIS technician can create an Avenue script to remove buttons that execute irrelevant tasks or create new buttons that provide functionality for planning-specific tasks.

One such example could be a script that creates a button that, when pressed, asks the user to specify a parcel of land belonging to an owner applying for a conditional use permit. When specified, ArcView then determines all parcels that are within 100 feet of the property and returns a list with the names, addresses and other contact information for those parcels identified. The GIS technician can further automate this process by asking for a file that lists all properties undergoing a process that require public notification, while separate reports are prepared for each individual property.

In short, the script creates new functionality to a program or application that was not anticipated by the software developer but is greatly needed by the planning office.

remaining from the earlier days of computing are BASIC, FORTRAN, COBOL and C. Of these, only C remains in widespread use, but it is sure to be surpassed by C++ (the "++" meaning "increment one" in the C language), Visual Basic and Java in popularity, if not versatility. A full-fledged computer application is likely to be made up of a number of compiled programs—some to control the flow of information, some to analyze numbers, some to display data and graphics and still others to coordinate these subprograms.

Relatively few planners have the time or interest to create compiled programs. However, computer users are sometimes confronted with a vexing problem: they need to perform a task that a program cannot do "out of the box." Such tasks could include passing information from a database to a word processor or the repetition of common keystrokes for data input or editing. These tasks are too simple to write a program for, but are perhaps too esoteric for a software developer to include as an option in a word processing program. Being aware of the availability of *scripts* or *macros* can make a planner's work much easier.

Scripting languages have the reputation of providing the glue or duct tape to modern computing systems and are thus the unsung heroes of computing. Traditionally, scripts or scripting languages (such as Perl and Tcl) provide a means for a programmer or systems administrator to automate mundane tasks, or provide a communications link between the operating system and applications programs. Newer scripting languages (like JavaScript) provide a certain amount of programming flexibility to existing program applications. Macro languages, included with most programs known to casual computer users, could be included within the category of scripts. Once created, rather than being compiled, the script is sent to an interpreter. The interpreter acts as the filter between the script and the CPU, telling the CPU how to perform the tasks being requested by the script.

What is the conceptual difference between a compiled program and an uncompiled script? It is not size, as there are huge scripts and miniscule programs. Compiled programs tend to be general purpose compared to task-specific scripts. A compiled program could very well be a statistics package

```
[File: hello.c]
#include <studio.h>
int main
{
Printf("Hello Planners!\n");
return (0)
}
```

7-2. The process of programming

designed to calculate a number of routines for a number of purposes. A script might only read a file of data, calculate a mean value of a prespecified set of fields and return that number into another file.

Both programs "do" statistics, but one is all purpose and the other is very limited. Compiled programs must go through a compiler, which creates an executable file out of the programming language. Scripts often automate repetitive tasks, such as passing information between programs, sorting items in a list and searching a number of files for records that meet specific criteria and collect the information into a single file. In this manner, traditional scripting languages are utilities. Admittedly, the typical planner will not incorporate scripts or macros into their everyday work, but knowledge of scripting can certainly help one out of a jam or create a sense of self-sufficiency in the workplace.

Some of the newer scripting languages sit in the middle ground between scripts and compiled programs. Languages such as Avenue (for ESRI's Arc-View GIS), Arc Macro Language (AML for ArcINFO) and Visual Basic for Applications (VBA for Microsoft's Office products) provide an opportunity to simplify and execute repetitive tasks and customize the user interface for specific purposes. (See the sidebar entitled "Scripts" for an example.)

HTML, Dynamic HTML (DHTML) and Extensible Markup Language (XML), found in Web-enabled documents, are examples of *markup language*. While not a programming language per se, markup language instructs Web browsers how to place and render text and images on the screen, as well as coordinate the delivery of information between the user and the computer server. At its simplest, markup languages format text or provide background imagery that one sees on a Web page. Surrounding text with HTML "tags" provides instruction to the browser to treat that text accordingly. Table 7-1 provides examples of italics, bold and underscore tags surrounding a phrase. Note that the author of the Web page codes the tags, but the result, as seen in a browser, is the rendering of the text formatting and not the instructions themselves.

Markup languages have become increasingly sophisticated, evolving from a language that formats text to one that enables interaction between computer users and remote computer systems. For example, markup syntax (such as "forms") sends queries to database programs and returns the results to you through the browser.

Knowledge of markup languages or "Web authoring" tools has become increasingly integrated with the function of planning. Many planning agencies deliver quite a bit of information over the Web, allowing citizens and developers information about zoning and subdivision ordinances, comprehensive plans and permit tracking, and providing a means for delivering brochures and blank applications.

Why should a planner know about such technology? An uninformed computer technician may make wonderful Web pages, but many times the information provided by planners exists in sensitive political and social contexts. Therefore, it is advised that

TABLE 7-1 **Hypertext** **Markup Language**	
HTML	**Result**
<i>Hello, world</i>	*Hello, world*
Hello, world	**Hello, world**
<u>Hello, world</u>	<u>Hello, world</u>

SUITES OF APPLICATIONS

A *suite* is a collection of applications, typically consisting of a word processor, spreadsheet, database and graphic presentation programs. In most instances, suites are a marketing device that allow a user to buy all necessary programs as a bundle at a lower price than purchasing each program individually. To date, there are no fully featured suites that are integrated as one application—each application stands on its own. However, great strides have been made to integrate the separate applications as much as possible, allowing information to be passed almost seamlessly among them; however, such integration is not unique to suite applications.

planners keep as much control as possible over such subtleties as the presentation of information, including what is contained on Web pages, that are accessible to the public.

COMPUTER APPLICATIONS

Computer applications (applied, compiled programs) with which planners need to be familiar range from word processors to a GIS. While a planner may never use all the applications discussed here, a certain level of familiarity is useful. Beyond the traditional uses of word processors, spreadsheets and databases, the knowledge a planner brings to these applications is very important. For example, planners create and distribute many forms, such as those related to permit applications and reports to planning boards. Knowing that a word processor can automate a process will save time and ensure a consistent, quality product. Knowing that word processors allow a planner to create a report template also saves time by having language and formatting that is identical, from month to month, already stored in a "new" document.

Word Processing

The primary functions of word processing applications are to allow easier text editing and layout formatting during the creation of written documents. Many word processors are sophisticated enough to enable the user to create documents that emulate professional typesetting and are of publishable quality.

Most of today's programs operate on a "What You See Is What You Get" (WYSIWYG) basis (i.e., the screen representation resembles the printed product). Where once a writer or editor had to retype or rewrite entire sections of a piece in order to accommodate an addition, deletion or alteration to text, word processors allow writers and editors to move, copy and rearrange text with great flexibility so that the remaining text shifts to accommodate these changes.

Chapter 10, "Graphic Communication," provides some hints on report production, text formatting and font styles; Chapter 9, "Written Communication," offers tips on writing appropriate and persuasive text. Additionally, the writer/editor has access to various tools, such as spell checkers, that can scan an entire document, identify spelling errors, suggest corrections and make grammatical suggestions. However, tools such as spell checkers are not a substitute for a proofreader. There are many words and parts of words that spell checkers will pass on merely because they meet specific criteria in the dictionary, not because the word is the appropriate one for that context.

Spreadsheets

Spreadsheets, such as Excel, provide the ability for users to format and lay out sets of numbers in an organized and visually pleasing manner. They allow the conduct of "what if" scenarios, calculation of a specific series of numbers and many other organizational and analytical operations. In this manner, spreadsheets can be considered a scratch pad of sorts and their power as a "number cruncher" allows sophisticated users to build financial and analytical applications.

A spreadsheet is organized in a row-by-column (or "R × C") fashion and is displayed as a grid of rectangles or "cells." Each cell can be located by its row and column coordinates. By convention, most row coordinates are numbered and column coordinates are lettered. This coordinate reference system is important and integral to the strength of a spreadsheet. Aside from entering numbers from the keyboard, users also create formulas to represent a calculation or outcome. A formula will use cell references as opposed to the number in that cell for three reasons:

1. It is easier to type "B4" as a reference to the contents of a cell instead of "1,437,150" or a larger, more complex number.

2. Cell references are "relative" (i.e., if a user copies and pastes a formula from one cell to another, the reference to other cells also moves in relative location to the cell).

3. Formulas are dynamic (i.e., if a user changes the value of a cell's contents that are referenced in a formula, the result automatically changes to reflect new values).

Databases

Planners use a great deal of information or data, both assembled within the planning office and acquired from other sources or agencies. Just as the organization of files in a computer system is critical, so too is the organization of data within those files. Database applications provide a way to organize and access what may seem a limitless amount of information. A database management system such as Access enables the organization of data with two separate models: single-table or "flat-file systems and relational database management systems (RDBMS).

A flat-file system stores all database information in a single table. In some respects, flat-file databases are easy to understand. All the information a planner needs is contained in a single file. One can think of a database as a large spreadsheet, where observations or records exist in rows and information related to those records is organized along the columns. An example of a small flat-file table is shown in Table 7-2.

TABLE 7-2

Example of a Database Table

	I.D.	Neighborhood	HH Inc	Rent/Apt
>	1	Sugar Grove	11,481	152.98
	2	Vilas	9,392	197.42
	3	Boone	8,074	154.7
	4	Hilltop	8,353	231.64
	5	Watauga	11,658	220.74
	6	Council Heights	9,295	202.47
	7	Eastbrook	10,798	248.69
	8	Tracy	7,730	231.37
	9	Poplar Hill	10,989	256.56
	10	Maple	8,135	190.93
	11	Northwest		195
	12	Southeast	8,622	168.26

* (Auto Number)

This small database includes information on 12 neighborhoods including the neighborhood name, average household income and average rent per apartment. The power of database management is the ability to "query" the data (i.e., ask the database program to report on those cases that fall within the parameters that interest the user). A query is somewhat different than a "search" function. One can search for a specific neighborhood or average household income, but the usefulness of a search function is limited. By querying the data, we can locate neighborhoods that meet certain criteria.

Most queries are structured as logical arguments. If Assistant Planner wanted to identify all neighborhoods where the average household income is less than $9,000, his logical argument may look like:

show if "HH Inc" < 9000

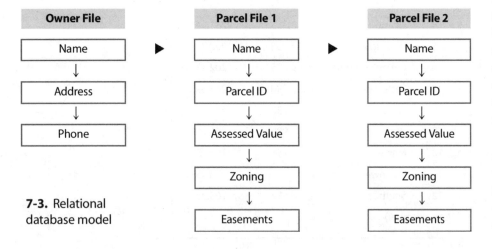

7-3. Relational database model

which translates into "keep all records if the variable 'HH Inc' is less than 9000." If he wished to identify those neighborhoods where the average rent per apartment is between $195 and $225, inclusive, his logical argument may look like:

show if "Rent/Apt" >= 195 & "Rent/Apt" <= 225

which translates into "keep all records if the variable 'Rent/Apt' is greater than or equal to 195 and less than or equal to 225."

In many circumstances, a flat-file system is adequate; however, there are times when having too much data actually get in the way. If there are circumstances when a particular company or individual owns multiple parcels, information such as the name and contact information must be retyped for each duplicate.

If individuals with the same name are in the database, how can one tell them apart? In these circumstances, an RDBMS is useful. In essence, an RDBMS links multiple files together with fields that are common to the files. Separate databases are related to one another with common elements or variables. Instead of one extremely large and complex data file, Figure 7-3 shows that the RDBMS is a shell that uses smaller, more manageable files.

If an address is changed in a file, that single change is reflected whenever other information is linked to that file in a "one-to-many" relationship (e.g., if Joe Smith Inc. owned 15 parcels of land, this information could exist in a file that contains information on property owners and in another file that describes the property owned). Joe Smith Inc.'s contact information exists as one record in the "owner" file, and a *reference* to that record (such as a unique identification (ID) number) is duplicated for every parcel the company owns in the "parcel" file. If Joe Smith Inc. changes its name to Joseph R. Smith Enterprises, this change need only be made once in the owner file (and not in the reference to that record in the parcel file). The 15 parcels that Joe owns are connected to the owner file, so it will reflect the new name without having to change it 15 times.

Desktop Publishing

Many times, a planner may need to place graphics in a report with a tool that allows for a more sophisticated "layout" of text and graphics. Such "desktop publishing" applications enable a computer user to create the look and feel of a magazine or quarterly report rather than a term paper. Planners often find themselves in the position of distributing the findings of community task forces or "blue ribbon" committees. Knowing how important perceptions are, planners may want to have a professional feel to their reports.

Desktop publishing programs can be very flexible in terms of layout features such as text columns and positioning, combining pictures and text wrapping. While this is possible with word processing programs, most desktop publishing programs integrate input (text and pictures) with output (printing and lithography) by allowing the computer user to specify such things as color separation. (For a more in-depth discussion of graphic arts and the production process, see Chapter 10, "Graphic Communication.")

Internet and E-mail

The Internet has enabled distances to shrink as no other technology has since the telephone. In its infancy (1969), the Internet served military and academic institutions that supported military research. The Advanced Research Projects Agency Network (ARPANET) provided a means of communicating and transferring data across the country. Aside from an alternative means of communicating and transporting data, the ARPANET incorporated dynamic routing—what is now known as Internet protocol (IP)—which slices data being sent from one computer into smaller packets of information. These packets get sent to the destination by different routes and are reassembled by the receiving computer. "Dynamic routing" means that if a section of the Internet is disabled (initially anticipated as a military interruption, but now possibly as a result of congestion or a disabled computer server), the packet can be automatically rerouted and arrive at the destination computer.

By the late 1980s, the Internet lost its military and academic focus and became available for general public consumption. By the early 1990s, the World Wide Web had materialized as a network of linked documents and data, and had gradually evolved from a hobby pursued by computer aficionados to encompass a significant portion of our nation's economic activity. In the 21st century, it is making infor-

The Internet has enabled distances to shrink as no other technology has since the telephone.

TABLE 7-3

Common Domain Names for the Internet

Top Level Domain	Description
.edu ~	Educational Institution
.gov ~	U.S. Governmental Institution
.mil ~	U.S. Military Institution
.net ~	Internet Service Provider
.org ~	Nonprofit Organization
.com ~	Commercial Organization

mation from around the world available to the world. (See Chapter 2, "Survey Methods for Planners" and Chapter 3, "Information from Secondary Sources.")

A user "surfs" the Internet with the use of a browser. The browser interprets and displays HTML, DHTML and XML documents and their associated images and data. This global network is a client-server relationship, where a server provides documents and serves them to clients that access the site. In order for someone to access these documents, they must first have access to the Internet through such a server. Internet Service Providers (ISPs) provide the gateway to the Internet for many homes and small businesses. Planning and other governmental agencies may have their own server and network hardware and architecture or may contract with a provider for them.

Web sites are an important means for planning organizations to communicate with the public. Each Web site has an address associated with it and must be requested from a central controlling organization. The address describes a hierarchy separated by periods that describe a "domain." The top-level domain (the last string of letters in the domain name) generally describes the type of institution operating the Web site. Table 7-3 describes most generally accepted top-level domains.

The second-level domain is chosen by the organization, typically by name. A first-level domain could differentiate different servers if an organization operates more than one. The domain is preceded by the trans-fer protocol associated with that type of data, and this combination is referred to as the Uniform Resource Locator (URL). The URL designated as "http://www.plansforall.com" uses the Hypertext Transfer Protocol (http) that is the most common way to access Internet documents. (It is not necessary to type in "http://" when searching for a Web site.) The "com" indicates that this is a commercial enterprise and the likely name for the company is "Plans for All."

Many planning agencies have harnessed the power of the Internet to serve the citizens of their jurisdiction. The Internet is an excellent way of disseminating information such as staff contact information, progress of specific planning efforts, distribution of draft documents and access to development ordinances and maps.

Just as the use of the Internet for accessing information has increased, so too has the use of electronic mail (e-mail). E-mail provides a convenient method for communicating with others, as well as a method for transferring documents and images. As with regular mail, one must correctly address the document in order for it to arrive at the proper destination. The syntax of an e-mail address for Assistant Planner at the firm Plans for All could be:

aplanner@plansforall.com

The domain is consistent with that of the Web site for Plans for All. The system administrator would designate the username "aplanner." The "@" ("at") symbol indicates that "aplanner" is a user (or has an e-mail account) at plansforall.com. Once we know how to get in touch with Assistant Planner, we can use a number of e-mail programs to contact him. Many Internet browsers come integrated with e-mail programs and e-mail programs may be acquired independently of Internet browsers.

One form of e-mail communication gaining currency is an Internet-based e-mail account. The advantage of an Internet e-mail account is that your e-mail is always accessible to you as long as you have access to the Internet. If you use an ISP-based e-mail account, you may not always have access because of software incompatibilities or a considerable expense due to long distance phone charges.

Geographic Information System

A GIS is a type of software tool with many uses by planners. A traditional pen-and-paper geographer or planner would create maps and overlay transparencies and then analyze relationships among different types of information that are delineated on different transparencies. The GIS tool has made this analysis much easier. The ability of a GIS to analyze and display large, complicated spatial datasets has made the work of a traditional geographer or cartographer more productive. The GIS has also expanded the analytical capabilities of geographers generally and planners specifically. To understand the strengths of a GIS, one must understand its mechanisms.

Data structures: A GIS uses mostly spatial data (i.e., data that can be located on a map). This may be combined with nonspatial information. For example, while the structural condition of a house is nonspatial,

its location on 125 Main Street *is* spatial. Two general spatial data structures are raster and vector formats (Figure 7-4). Both types of structures have their advantages and disadvantages and usually dictate the type of analysis or mapping one conducts. Fortunately, GIS software allows the analyst to convert data structures from raster to vector and vice versa.

Raster data is composed of grids (or rasters). Each raster has a value associated with it that describes the phenomena (land use type, slope or vegetation cover). If we are using raster data that describe retail, commercial and residential land uses, a raster coded

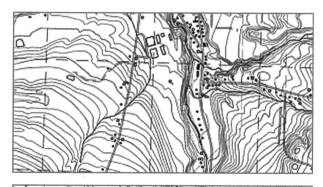

7-4. Raster and vector data models

"1" could indicate "retail," "2" could be "commercial" and "3" could be "residential." Depending on the resolution or detail of the data, a raster dataset could be recognizable as an area of study (or not). This is a disadvantage of raster data (i.e., where the raster is associated with a specific area in space). A raster can only take on one value, which is usually the dominant feature of that bit of land represented by the raster. If the actual inventory of land represented by a raster is 25% retail, 25% commercial and 50% residential, the raster will be coded "3" for "residential" because it is the dominant land use. For visual presentation, a separate color signifies a unique land use type.

Vector data structures are much more map-like and the generalization inherent in raster structures is minimized. Three types of vector data are:

1. *points* (indicating landmarks and other specific locations)
2. *lines* (representing roads, rivers, sewer and water mains)
3. *polygons* (representing areas such as census blocks, neighborhoods or metropolitan statistical areas)

One advantage of vector data structures is illustrated by the use of points. In raster data, the point is represented by a raster, which implies that the point occupies space; in a vector data structure, the point is merely a representation of exact map coordinates occupying no amount of area. Vector data also possesses "topology," or the ability to make connections with other data. Topology allows an analyst to define spatial relationships such as connectivity (of arcs or lines), contiguity (one polygon or tract abutting another) and designations of area or volume. Without topology, a "geographic" dataset may represent no more than a "graphic" because the spatial relationships among all the components of that graphic are not stated in a way that is understood by a computer program.

Cartography vs. spatial analysis: A GIS enables the user to create maps; cartography, which is the making of maps, is distinctly separate from spatial analysis. One can think of cartography as the placement, display and presentation of data on a two-dimensional surface. A spatial analyst attempts to quantify and summarize patterns over space and the relationships among the mapped phenomena. There are instances of a spatial analysis being conducted without looking at a map (i.e., one doesn't require a GIS to conduct spatial analysis; one merely requires the data that describe spatial phenomena such as location and distance).

This does not diminish the role of the cartographer (see also Chapter 10, "Graphic Communication") because the communication of this visual information is very important. In addition, a GIS may not be the best tool to create and publish maps. Many cartographers collect data with a GIS, but transfer the data to a computer program that is better suited to the manipulation of images.

Database functions versus spatial analysis: One of the benefits of a GIS is its ability to act as a spatial database. Earlier, we discussed an example of a planner collecting information for the purposes of public

A GIS enables the user to create maps; cartography, which is the making of maps, is distinctly separate from spatial analysis.

notification. This is a classic example of using a GIS as a spatial database. The fact that the information is spatial allows us to use a query stating

find if distance <= 100 feet

from the subject parcel. The GIS then determines which parcels exist within 100 feet of the parcel under consideration. As with other database functions, a query can ask for all parcels that meet a specific criterion, then create reports that provide more detailed information.

Planning Information Systems: Planning Information Systems are just now taking advantage of much of the technology discussed so far. These systems are not so much a new technology inasmuch as they are an integration of the GIS and other analytical tools (fiscal, economic and statistical). The goal of integration in these systems is different from the "suites" discussed earlier, but rather involves planners with the public they serve—making it easier to visualize the often complex dynamics of planning and development.

ETHICAL AND SOCIAL ISSUES

There are many peripheral issues associated with the use of computers in a planning office that don't directly bear on the mission of the office or how well suited computers are to the tasks performed by the planners:

- Who owns the computers or the information that exists on a given computer?
- How much privacy should an employee expect with regard to their employer?

- How does the use of computers affect the relationship between the office and the clients it serves?

The use of computers begs the issue of ethics, both as a user and as a potential administrator of computer systems. There is a certain amount of responsibility inherent in providing privacy, equity and access to computer users. On the other side of the coin, computer users must be cognizant of the constraints within which their employers or public servants operate, and those constraints must be respected.

One rule of thumb by which every computer user must operate is that the information they have on their computer should be considered public—or at least publicly available. Many noncomputing analogies apply to the link between expectations of privacy and office interactions. Are there conversations you don't have with a fellow planner in the hallway because the topic is sensitive or personal? If so, make the same decisions when you decide to send an e-mail that is sensitive or personal. Are there places you go that you wouldn't want your fellow planners to know about? Treat your Internet "surfing" in the same manner (i.e., keep it related to your tasks and research).

The level of privacy granted to employees is very limited: the computer equipment with which you work typically is not yours but the public's or your firm's. Court rulings support the notion that if computers and computer equipment are the employer's property, then the employee should not expect the information they store on that computer to be private. This means that the e-mail, pictures and documents

One rule of thumb by which every computer user must operate is that the information they have on their computer should be considered public—or at least publicly available.

stored on the computer are subject to search and inspection.

Given this value placed on the property of the employer, it is still the responsibility of the employer to provide clear and understandable guidelines for which employees will be held accountable. For example, Assistant Planner was reading an article in the regional planning newsletter about a planner whose e-mail was read by his supervisor. The management had a policy to periodically review e-mail generated by the office. As a result of one of these reviews, it came to light that this planner was apparently undermining the efforts of the planning office to develop a long-range plan because he disagreed with the strategic approach to land development. The detailed and abundant e-mail messages provided the management with an adequate paper trail to link setbacks in the planning process with ideas and statements made by the planner.

While it is a generally accepted principle that no person should be convicted based on their opinions (and the planner in question could very well be innocent of sabotaging the planning process), the fact that a link could be made based on the communication proved unfortunate for the planner.

As of this writing, the distribution of computer access is considered to be unequal. For example, affluent schools have greater access to computer terminals and the latest technology. Some public libraries within a city or county system do not have Internet connections while others do. The same could be said of planning offices or of the clients that

As of this writing, the distribution of computer access is considered to be unequal.

planners serve. To some extent, these disparities might be rationalized and the concept of equity might be subjective, but the consequences of inequity are long lived. Segments of society are put at a disadvantage if there is no exposure to technological advances. Computers can make education or access to public information more efficient and productive, so seeking parity in availability of, and access to, computers in education is an equity issue.

Consider the mistakes that a planning office could make by providing information only through a Web page (such as dates and times for meetings, announcements for critical planning issues, and other information and educational material). If the office determined that providing this type of information could replace traditional means of communication and public notification, think of who would be left out of the process: those who cannot afford a computer and those who have a computer but cannot afford an Internet connection. What are the implications for the city's planning process if segments of the population are ignored? Sometimes it is easy to forget that access to computers is not universal. Strategies involving the use of computers that impact the public should be mindful of equity issues.

Similar to issues of equity are those of access. Providing access to computers as well as to the information that computers deliver is extremely important. Accessibility can be a general concept: there are universities that feel it is important for their students to have access to the network from dormitories, or they will provide a sufficient number of computer labs that are open at all hours. This allows access for most people in most places at most times. However, what if a potential user had physical disabilities that prevented them from accessing computers that are otherwise ubiquitous?

Technology has advanced far enough to accommodate, for example, the vision-impaired through the use of voice-recognition software. Voice-recognition software converts the spoken work into text that is displayed in a document. Different phrases or sounds differentiate between text that should be added to a document and commands that should be executed in order to format text or manage files.

Creating Web pages should make one cognizant of people with disabilities. Not everyone can read small print; some may rely on a text interface rather than a graphical interface. How would your Web page look if it were accessed in a text-only format? Although no pictures can be displayed, are there descriptions of the pictures that could not be rendered? If the Web is truly for everyone, then one must be sure that everyone can access the information.

CONCLUSION

The use of computers in planning is at a threshold primarily because of the recent availability of reasonably priced computers and the extensive amount of software development. . . . This threshold is an important one because there is always the danger of becoming overcomputerized.

—RYCUS, MITCHELL. *THE PLANNER'S USE OF INFORMATION*. 1ST ED. CHICAGO: AMERICAN PLANNING ASSOCIATION, 1988, P. 153.

Mitchell Rycus' admonition about computers in planning is quite prophetic and this chapter has tried to illuminate this fine line. Computers are powerful and can make the business of planning very efficient. However, a lot of thought must go into the incorporation of computers into the planning arena. Information and computation is good, but there can be too much of a good thing. Computers can get in the way of planning—allowing technology and all the wonderful things we can do with computers obstruct our vision of the purpose of planning. In a nutshell, let planning dictate your use of computers rather than letting computers dictate your planning.

APPLICATIONS

1. The city manager of a small municipality calls you into her office to talk about the need for networking the planning department's computer system. Tell her, generally, why networking would be beneficial and why it would be costly. If she were convinced about implementing a computer network, what would be the most appropriate network for a small municipality?

2. Contact a private and a public planning agency and inquire about their current computer usage. Determine their projected future computer usage and how they expect to meet their needs. What differences, if any, are there between the two types of agencies?

3. A colleague is planning to implement a community survey. You know that you will be responsible for creating a database of the responses and

analyzing it. Do you wait for the data to arrive after the survey has been administered or should you consult with your colleague prior to or during survey development? Explain your answer.

4. During a monthly staff meeting, your supervisor stated that he wants the planning department to develop a Web site and move towards a "paperless office." How do you respond?

BIBLIOGRAPHY

Ceruzzi, Paul E. *A History of Modern Computing.* Boston: MIT Press, 1998.

Davis, Bruce. *GIS: A Visual Approach.* Santa Fe: Onword Press, 1996.

This is a "quick and dirty" overview of a Geographic Information System (GIS), for those who want a simple yet informative discussion. The approach of the book is very nontechnical, but that can be viewed as a benefit. While the reader may not be able to jump in front of a GIS and conduct a spatial analysis, the reader will be able to carry on an intelligent discussion of a GIS—its strengths, weaknesses, capabilities and issues related to spatial data.

DeMers, Michael N. *Fundamentals of Geographic Information Systems.* New York: John Wiley & Sons, Inc., 1997.

DeMers discusses the details of a GIS as generically applied to the technology and not to software. While the book is primarily an academic textbook, it could prove to be an invaluable desk reference for (adventurous) managers and technicians alike.

Gookin, Dan. *PCs for Dummies.* Foster City, CA: IDG Books, 1998.

While some may not think highly of the "Dummies" series, this book manages to supply the reader with a tremendous amount of information—hardware, software and peripherals—presented in a very nonthreatening manner (and with a sense of humor).

Rob, Peter and Carlos Coronel. *Database Systems: Design, Implementation and Management.* Cambridge, MA: Course Technology, 1997.

This textbook does a skillful job of explaining databases and goes into detail about the thought required of database management that has nothing to do with computers. Planning is everything and database software is merely an easy way to implement the project you have in mind.

Schwartz, Randal L. and Tom Christiansen. *Learning Perl.* Cambridge, MA: O'Reilly, 1997.

Perl has been around for a long time and will likely continue to thrive, no matter how sophisticated other applications become. In addition to teaching Perl, this book also teaches basic programming skills. For this reason, no other programming books are suggested in this bibliography. Most languages are changing rapidly, so if you are learning to program, why not start here?

Siefert, Marsha, George Gerbner and Janice Fisher, editors. *The Information Gap: How computers and other new communication technologies affect the social distribution of Power.* New York: Oxford University Press, 1989.

Information Communication

to experts, the public and other clients

Effective planning practice requires information to be gathered from relevant sources with appropriate and affordable methods. Information must be processed and analyzed so as to yield insight and strategy for effective action. Parts 1 and 2 of this book sought to provide guidance o nhow best to achieve these goals. However, practicing planners have repeatedly stressed that central to professional success is the ability to communicate this information effectively. Verbal, written, graphic and interpersonal modes of communications are all essential. The chapters in **Part 3** describe these modes, the relevant strategies to be considered and the delivery modes to be mastered. They address how planners can best communicate information by selective and careful choice of means of communication, level of content detail, venue, medium and mode.

Chapter 8 describes strategies to become an effective speaker and to make judicious choice of subject, length, delivery style and content of presentations.

Chapter 9 describes the numerous venues for which planners must write and provides guidance to shape this writing so that it is appropriate in detail, style and tone for the professional end that is sought.

Chapter 10 describes the centrality of various forms of graphics in planning and highlights the increasing importance and ease with which relevant visual information can be obtained and utilized in planning communication.

Chapter 11 stresses the need for a political acumen in choosing the medium, mode and means of communication for effective practice.

Speaking Skills for Presentations

Alfred W. Storey

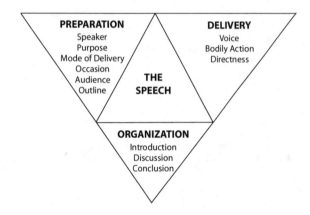

8-1. Three components of oral communication

Effective oral communication is an important skill for planners and can be learned through preparation, practice and reflection. A planner needs to be able to speak effectively in many settings:

- working in a large group or in a team setting
- conducting field interviews
- participating as a consultant to a subcommittee
- making an oral presentation to a planning commission or a city council
- speaking to a public gathering

Having effective oral communication skills greatly enhances a planner's ability to inform, convince or persuade—and that is what a planner wants to do.

To be an effective speaker, in addition to knowing the depth and substance of what is to be communicated, a planner must give careful attention to these three components of oral communication:

1. *Preparation* includes an analysis of oneself as a speaker, the occasion for making an oral presentation, the purpose of the presentation, an analysis of the audience, the time allocated, the place where the speech is to be given, the mode of delivery, the construction of an outline and the consideration of visual aids to be used.

2. *Organization* includes the introduction, discussion (body) and conclusion of a speech.

3. *Delivery* includes the use of voice, bodily action (including gestures) and directness (including eye contact).

Before discussing these three components in detail, it is useful to review Scenario 2 (see the sidebar "Two Scenarios" in the chapter entitled "Introduction"). Note how Assistant Planner took the "preparation" factors of speaker, purpose, time, audience and occasion into account when he prepared for his first meeting with members of the chamber of commerce. When he spoke to them, he told them how impressed the mayor was with their visit, how interested the mayor and city planner were about their concerns regarding trash pickup and how his task was to find a satisfactory solution to the problem. He gave attention to audience factors by studying with whom he would be meeting and by learning the name of each member of the delegation to the mayor. He also gave attention to purpose by gathering data through on-site visits, interviews, observations and cost estimates, so that an equitable solution could be found for the problem of trash build-up on Main Street.

The objective of this chapter is to provide the planner with ideas, tips and examples for becoming a more effective oral communicator by addressing the three components of oral communication outlined earlier.

PREPARATION

The more prepared you are, the less worried you'll be. The less prepared you are, the more worried you'll be. The more worried you are, the less effective you'll be. The more prepared you are, the more effective you'll be. If you know you're going to be effective, you won't worry. If you don't prepare, you will worry. So, be prepared.

—CHARLES OSGOOD

The Speaker

It is assumed that the planner who is called upon to make an oral presentation knows what issues need to be addressed and is knowledgeable about the material. The planner should be able to demonstrate expertise and project enthusiasm without becoming overly technical. It is important to find the right balance between accessibility and technical credibility.

That balance is often difficult to achieve if the speaker knows the material but has feelings of tension, anxiety (stage fright) or nervousness before speaking to an audience. Some speakers feel dryness around their lips, sweaty palms, a sinking feeling in their stomach, a pounding heart and quivering knees—all signs of tension and anxiety, which are the natural consequences of the fact that the speaker is getting ready to do the difficult task of speaking to an audience. Here are a few steps that will help reduce the feelings of anxiety and enhance the effectiveness of a speech:

- *Recognize the signs.* Some disturbance of mental, physical and emotional balance is normal in a speaking situation. Though a speaker is aware of these signs of stage fright, audience members seldom notice. Remembering this can help a speaker gain confidence and help control these feelings.
- *Be well prepared.* This is one of the most important deterrents to stage fright. Having a carefully prepared outline and writing out the first sentence of the speech will minimize feelings of uncertainty. Also, rehearse the speech several times to yourself or, even better, to a friend or colleague.
- *Become familiar with the surroundings.* Arrive a half-hour early to examine the room where the speech will be made and become acquainted with other participants in the program. It is important to make certain that any audio-visual equipment you plan to use is set up and is functioning properly and that your material has been loaded for the proper place in the program. If possible, turn on the projector and check it.
- *Just before speaking, breathe deeply.* Fill the lungs with air and take a brisk walk around the block. These activities help reduce muscle tension and calm the speaker's nerves.

The Purpose

Every speech should have a purpose and all the material included in the speech should be judged on the basis of whether it contributes to achieving that purpose. The purpose must be one that is attainable

It is assumed that the planner who is called upon to make an oral presentation knows what issues need to be addressed and is knowledgeable about the material.

When preparing to give a talk, a speaker needs to know how much time is allotted for the presentation.

within the amount of time allowed for the speech and appropriate for the audience and the occasion. Usually the planner will have one or more of the following purposes in mind:

- *Inform* (give the audience particular information about a specified item): In Scenario 2 (see the sidebar "Two Scenarios" in the chapter entitled "Introduction"), Assistant Planner gave a speech to "inform" when he met with the chamber of commerce in Middlesville for the first time. His purpose was to inform them of the various kinds of trash containers that were available. "He showed them catalog pictures . . ."

- *Actuate* (get the audience to take a particular action): After Assistant Planner informed the chamber of commerce members of the kinds of trash containers available, he added a second purpose to "actuate" to his presentation: ". . . to study the possibilities (keeping in mind cost and durability as well as aesthetics) and arranged to meet with them the following week to obtain their recommendations." Assistant Planner moved from a speech to "inform" to a speech to "actuate."

- *Convince* (bring the audience to a particular point of view): In Scenario 2, Assistant Planner recommended that the Board of Public Works (BPW) reschedule garbage collection in the downtown district for Fridays, or even Saturday mornings, to minimize weekend build-ups. "With the approval of the planning director, he made a PowerPoint presentation to the

chamber of commerce . . ." using his photographs, notes from his conversations (and other data he had collected) and a financial argument. In this way, Assistant Planner was able to "convince" members of the chamber of commerce that the new pickup schedule would solve the trash problem on Main Street.

The Time

When preparing to give a talk, a speaker needs to know how much time is allotted for the presentation. Knowing the time allocation helps the speaker select the type and amount of material that can be treated adequately within the time limit. It is important to be selective. Speakers can lose effectiveness if they overrun or ignore the allotted time. Audience members tend to become distracted, tired, fidgety or bored, especially if several speakers have talked on the same subject. You need to know when and after whom you will be speaking.

Plan to speak for no more than 60% or 70% of the time allocated (i.e., if the time allocated for the presentation is 30 minutes, plan to speak for only 20 minutes). Use the last 10 minutes for a question-and-answer period. That will give the audience members a chance to ask questions about the topic that will clarify points of information or give them additional information.

When preparing for a 20-minute speech, write 2 minutes in the left-hand margin of the outline, opposite the introduction; write 15 minutes opposite the body of the speech; and write 3 minutes in the left-hand margin opposite the conclusion of the speech. Then practice giving the speech from the outline—observing the time limits for each part of the speech—and add or detract information, examples and illustrations as needed. This will help you stay within the allocated time and get additional information to audience members, which is of particular interest to them, during the question-and-answer period.

The Audience

The speaker needs to know something about the proposed audience, such as their knowledge of the subject, educational level, position(s) on the topic being discussed, economic status and political views. What will be the size and age range of the audience? What do they expect from the speaker? Are they attending on a voluntary basis or as part of a training assignment or class? Will the audience be composed of city, county or township officials, planners or lay people?

Many of these audience factors are present in "Issue #1 (Neighborhood Scale): Urban Development in Middlesville" in the chapter entitled "A Planning Case Study." The audience in this case would vary widely in age, since it would include senior citizens, members of the chamber of commerce and students from the University of Hiatonka. Also, there would be several different vested interests represented in the audience, including members of a newly formed neighborhood coalition, two minority groups and the downtown business association.

Planning commission members may be attuned to the speaker's content, language and objectives, as they will have some particular expertise on the topic. Council members, on the other hand, would have a broader responsibility for city affairs and might be less able to understand the technical jargon and specific contextual, institutional and physical issues related to planning.

The Occasion

The planner needs to know the nature of the occasion for an oral presentation, which helps prepare the material in order to inform, actuate or convince the audience. Also, it is essential that the speaker know the makeup of the audience, why the audience is there, who the other speakers are on the program and the physical conditions surrounding the occasion (i.e., whether the speech is to be delivered indoors or outdoors, the nature of the acoustics and whether a public address system is needed).

Knowing the nature of the occasion helps the planner formulate a strategy, or plan, for identifying and dealing with the important issues. Knowing the nature of the occasion helps the planner determine whether the purpose of the presentation should be to inform, actuate or convince (persuade). An effective strategy, which may be used with any of these three purposes, is based on a well-known, logical procedure called the *reflective thought process*.

An outline for a speech using this strategy would include four steps, in this order:

1. definition of the problem, or issues;
2. analysis of evidence and information;

Planning commission members may be attuned to the speaker's content, language and objectives, as they will have some particular expertise on the topic.

3. consideration of possible solutions (pros and cons); and

4. selection of the final solution.

Steps 1 and 2 would be used in a speech to inform; Steps 1, 2 and 3 would be used in a speech to actuate; and all four steps would be used in a speech to convince.

The Mode of Oral Delivery

Two common forms for delivering speeches are the *manuscript speech* and the *extemporaneous (extempore) speech*. The manuscript speech is written out in its entirety and read orally from the printed page. It is perhaps the most challenging type of speech to deliver effectively to a visible audience because it is difficult to:

- maintain eye contact with both the text and the audience
- use gestures while holding the manuscript
- have natural vocal variety, vocal emphasis and variation of rate while reading
- use any bodily action when restricted to reading from the printed page

The manuscript speech is needed and useful in a situation in which the speaker has to be very accurate or when detailed, statistical data are required. Manuscripts usually are required when speeches are given over radio or television, so that the contents may be reviewed before air time and that restricted radio and television time limits may be met.

The extemporaneous speech is the form most useful to planners. In the extempore style of speaking, generally a work or sentence outline helps to give structure to the content and limit the amount of material to be presented in a given time. The speech is not written out in sentences and paragraphs; rather, words are chosen as the speech is delivered. Careful preparation is essential for this seemingly more "informal" mode of delivery.

The extemporaneous style of speaking offers several advantages:

- The speaker can be more direct with the audience with the use of voice, gestures and physical appearance.
- It is easier for the speaker to focus attention on the audience and maintain good eye contact because there is no manuscript.
- A speaker can use charts, drawings, maps, overhead projectors and other audio-visual material more effectively when speaking extemporaneously.
- It is easier for the speaker to make on-the-spot adjustments with ideas and words when not "tied" to a written manuscript or memorized speech.

The Outline

An outline of the speech can help a speaker in several ways:

- It helps one organize thoughts and information logically and sequentially.
- It helps the speaker deliver the proper amount of information within the prescribed time frame.

The extemporaneous speech is the form most useful to planners.

KEY WORD OUTLINES

Middlesville's Assistant Planner must make a presentation to Middlesville's planning commission on the zoning change requested by the developer in "Issue #1 (Neighborhood Scale): Urban Development in Middlesville" (see the chapter entitled "A Planning Case Study"). The purpose of the presentation is to inform the commission of the current conditions on the site, the changes proposed by the developer and other relevant city policies and planning issues. For this presentation, a *key word outline* might look like this:

I.   Current site conditions and structures
   A. Housing units
   B. Commercial structures
   C. Surrounding area
   D. Adjacent central business district (CBD)

II. Zoning
   A. R-1 (not in compliance)
   B. C-1

   C. Proposed zoning changes
   D. Preliminary master plan revisions

III. Infrastructure
   A. Parking
   B. Transportation
   C. Impervious surfaces and storm water
   D. Sewer and water
   E. Roads within project

IV. Housing supply
   A. Income ranges and affordable housing
   B. Historic structures
   C. Numbers of housing units

V.   Economic development
   A. Services available in area
   B. Obsolete buildings
   C. Tax base

VI. Staff recommendations
   A. Issues
   B. Integrate/master plan

- It provides a graphic picture of what the speaker plans to say.
- It forces the speaker to think through the ideas with some care.
- It helps the speaker avoid irrelevant materials.
- It serves as a memory aid during delivery of the speech.
- It helps the speaker coordinate any visual aids that are used.

The outline is based upon a few simple rules:

- Each unit in the outline should contain only one item or statement.

- The items included should be sequenced and logically subordinated.
- The logical relation of the included items should be made graphically clear with indentation, symbols and headings.
- The organization of the outline should be simple and clear.

The *key word outline* (which uses only sentence fragments) and the *complete sentence outline* (which uses only complete sentences) are the two kinds of outline best suited for delivering an extemporaneous speech. The *key word outline* is useful for the speaker who needs a guideline or must use notes. The key

COMPLETE SENTENCE OUTLINES

A *complete sentence outline* for the same presentation might look like this:

I. Current site conditions and structures

   A. The existing eight houses contain 19 housing units, all of which are rental. The physical condition of the structures is sound, though some repair is needed.
   B. The buildings on the remainder of the site are either vacant, low-intensity, industrial structures or used as storage of obsolete equipment. They would need to be gutted or demolished to support a current use. However, one building has a convenience store that is the only food store in the area.
   C. The surrounding area of low-density housing consists of small, single-family homes on small lots, approximately 55% of which are owner occupied.
   D. The adjacent CBD consists of small, light industrial buildings, some of which have been renovated to house small service businesses. There are few retail shops in the area.

II. Zoning

   A. The current zoning for the residential area is R-1, though most of the structures are not in compliance since they have been divided into rental units.
   B. The remainder of the site is C-1 (commercial zoning).
   C. The developer proposes R-4 (high-density housing) for the entire site.
   D. Community discussions about master plan revisions have so far focused on increasing services for local residents and the renovation or removal of obsolete indus-

trial buildings. The precise use for the current site has not yet been discussed.

III. Infrastructure

   A. Most parking in the area is on the street. The developer proposes to build an underground parking garage for 50 vehicles, which is one space per unit. The current city standard is two spaces per unit.
   B. Most local roads are two lane, with parking on both sides. Some congestion is experienced at rush periods where the residential streets empty onto the main route downtown.
   C. With new federal storm water regulations, the city is trying to limit impervious surfaces. The project would remove parking lots in the commercial area. The currently open ground in the residential area would be lost and new roads and driveways would be built. A new storm water collection system would be needed.
   D. The city water mains in the area were replaced 10 years ago. The sewer mains serving the site are at least 50 years old and were designed for a low-density population.
   E. The developer proposes private driveways within the project. Access for emergency vehicles needs to be considered.

IV. Housing supply

   A. The current residential structures are rented to families and individuals under the median income for the city. This qualifies them as "affordable housing" under state guidelines.
   B. Two of the residential structures date back to the 1890s and fall under the city's Historic Preservation ordinance for evaluation as historic structures.
   C. There are currently 19 housing units at the site; 50 units are proposed.

V. Economic development

  A. There are relatively few services in the area. The only convenience store would be demolished under the plan. There are many buildings in the nearby CBD commercial area, which are underutilized and where more services could be located.

  B. The light industrial buildings on the site are mostly beyond repair and present a visual blight to the area, including the nearby CBD commercial area.

  C. The current assessed value of the site is very low and would likely double (or more) with the proposed development, increasing the city's tax base.

VI. Staff recommendations

  A. There are a number of infrastructure issues for the site that should be resolved with the developer before site plan approval.:

    1. The costs of sewer main replacement and storm water collection are site-specific.

    2. The number of daily trips from the additional housing units will trigger a traffic study.

    3. Design and maintenance of the private roads/driveways should also be resolved.

  B. The proposed development plan is partly in accord with early master plan discussions with the surrounding neighborhood.

    1. These have emphasized increased services for the area and improved appearance with removal or better appearance of obsolete industrial buildings, including some in the adjacent CBD.

    2. Effects of the development should be evaluated as part of the planning process.

    3. Transportation and affordable housing issues also need to be evaluated.

words or phrases serve as a reminder of the order of the material but allow the speaker to choose words during the delivery of the speech. The *complete sentence outline* forces a clear organization of the materials, the proper integration and subordination of the ideas to be presented and reflects a complete preparation of the speech.

ORGANIZATION

The organization of a speech is an important element in effective delivery. The speaker must organize the thoughts and ideas to be presented in a meaningful pattern. This is analogous to a plan for a building or a map of a city, which makes the overall interrelationship of components clear.

There may not be a single, best way to organize a speech; however, the basic pattern that serves as a model for organizing most types of speeches is the three-part organization consisting of the *introduction*, *body or discussion* and *conclusion*.

The Introduction

Though it may seem unusual and counterintuitive, the introduction to a speech should be prepared last. The introduction functions as a brief "road map" of the speech and gives the audience an idea of what to expect. After the conclusion and the body or discussion have been worked out, the speaker will know what to highlight and incorporate into the introduction. Introductions need to be well planned and executed. Often, first impressions are strong, so what the speaker does at the beginning of the speech is important to the overall success and mission of the speech.

Four important functions of the introduction are to:

1. gain the attention of the audience
2. arouse the interest of the audience
3. present the theme or central idea of the speech
4. suggest, or state, the purpose of the speech

The first part of the introduction of any speech has the purpose of gaining the attention and arousing the interest of the audience. There are at least five ways of opening the speech:

1. by referring to circumstances attending the speaker's appearance in front of the audience
2. by telling a story (serious or humorous)
3. by alluding to a timely and striking statement
4. by alluding to a timely and important incident
5. by asking a question

To illustrate how these five ways of opening a speech might work, consider how Assistant Planner might have begun his first oral presentation to the chamber of commerce.

1. *Reference to attendant circumstance:* "Credit for what I have to say goes to Mayor Lorch and to those who went to see the mayor—Ms. B., Mr. Y., Mr. K. and Ms. L. You have brought an important matter regarding the health and appearance of our city to the mayor's attention. The mayor is in complete agreement with you and has asked the city planning office to work with your organization to find the best possible solution to the problem."

2. *Story (narration and description):* "It is a beautiful spring, Monday morning in Middlesville. On this day, our town is going to be visited by the state's Beautification Awards Committee. The car bearing the four committee members enters town from the north; crosses over our beautiful, winding river; and moves along the tree-lined Elm Street, with its well-cared-for homes and neatly trimmed lawns. As the car turns from Elm Street onto Main Street, the first sight to greet the committee's eyes . . ."

3. *Allusion to a timely and striking statement:* "'If the people of Middlesville will channel their requests for city improvement through the system, the system will be responsive.' Have you ever heard this statement? I am meeting with you today because Mayor Lorch and the city planning director believe . . ."

4. *Allusion to a timely and important incident:* "On Friday, the day after the city planning director asked me to meet with you about the collection of trash on Main Street, the mayor's office received word that the state's Beautification Awards Committee is scheduled to visit Middlesville some time next month. The timeliness of your visit to the mayor's office . . ."

5. *A question:* "Do you believe in the old saying, 'There is nothing that can't be done that can't be done.'"? I do. That is why the image of Middlesville . . ."

The closing part of the introduction should include the central idea of the speech. This is accomplished

> *The first part of the introduction of any speech has the purpose of gaining the attention and arousing the interest of the audience.*

by making a direct statement or by asking one or more questions that suggest the theme. In this way, the purpose of the speech is given and the introduction is drawn to a close. By using one of the five types of introductions, the speaker should be able to gain the attention and arouse the interest of the audience.

The Body or Discussion

The body or discussion is the heart of the speech. This is where the speaker does what the introduction says will be done. In the body, the main ideas are developed, the analysis takes place, the evidence is presented and the major statements and their subordinate points are presented. The length of time for the speech will determine how extensively the ideas are treated and developed.

Four ways by which a speaker may develop an idea in the body or discussion of a speech, including examples, are:

1. *exposition* (offering an explanation): the speaker explains the rules of the game of basketball or how to work a certain play
2. *argumentation* (defending one side of a proposition): the speaker attempts to prove that one basketball team is better than the other
3. *description* (telling how a particular point of view, a product, an object, a person or a situation appears to the senses—that is, how it looks, tastes, feels, smells or sounds): the speaker gives some of the details surrounding a tournament game that appeal to the senses, such as the attitude of the crowd, the activities of the cheer-

leaders, the colorful flags and banners, the pep band and whistles of the game officials
4. *narration* (telling a story): the speaker tells how a particular game was played from the opening center jump to the final whistle

Depending upon the role they are playing—and in what context or occasion, to what audience, the purpose of the speech and other parameters—the speaker must decide what form will be the most useful in developing an idea and whether to use logical and/or emotional appeals.

It is from the body or discussion of the speech that the listener determines the speaker's train of thought. Therefore, the speaker must have that train of thought well organized and well supported with illustrations, anecdotes, reasoning, emotionally evocative material and evidence to guide the audience.

The Conclusion

After the body or discussion of a speech has been developed, it should be rounded out, given a note of finality and brought to a conclusion. The conclusion should not be a perfunctory, tacked-on addition, but should serve as the climax of the speech. The conclusion is important because it represents the last opportunity the speaker has to make a point clear to the audience. The conclusion should be developed so the speech does not end abruptly. The conclusion should provide the speaker with an additional opportunity to reach the audience. It should be brief, simple and have both unity and energy.

In general, there are three types of conclusions:

After the body or discussion of a speech has been developed, it should be rounded out, given a note of finality and brought to a conclusion.

As the speaker develops the central idea of the speech, the listeners may say, in effect, "Yes, I see the point, but what should we do about it?"

1. *Conclusion of summary:* Designed to provide a bird's-eye view of the speech, this type of conclusion may consist of a formal summary, a pointed or epigrammatic statement or an illustration containing the essential idea of the body or discussion. While a formal summary may be adequate with regard to restatement of material, it may frequently be desirable to restate the substance of the speech in a new way. Hence, a brief paraphrase as well as a pointed statement or an illustration may be useful.

2. *Conclusion of application:* As the speaker develops the central idea of the speech, the listeners may say, in effect, "Yes, I see the point, but what should we do about it?" A speaker who expects the listeners to do anything should apply the central idea to the audience by doing one (or both) of the following two things:

   a. apply the theme and its subordinate idea to the interest of the listeners (e.g., the speaker should relate the ideas contained in the speech to the attitudes, ideals, vocations and avocations of the listeners)

   b. suggest procedures available to them (e.g., the speaker should ask listeners to do such specific things as sign, buy, investigate, vote, donate, write or whatever else is appropriate; the speaker should offer the audience a way to translate belief into action)

3. *Conclusion of motivation:* A speaker who wishes to do more than make ideas clear (conclusion of summary) or present a means of doing

something about it (conclusion of application) should appeal to the basic motives or desires of the listeners. The speaker needs to supplement logical appeal with a psychological appeal to such desires as self-preservation, reputation, affection for others, sentiment or property. The speaker should relate the central idea to one or more such basic motives, thus tapping the resources inherent in human means.

DELIVERY

The careful preparation and organization of a speech have been covered in this chapter in detail. Now, attention can be given to the third area of concern—delivery. Three of the most important skills a speaker can develop for effective oral presentation are the use of *voice, bodily action* (including gestures) and *directness* (including eye contact).

Voice

A clear, well-understood voice is a tremendous asset in oral communication. The voice describes the speaker and reflects the speaker's emotions. Often, the tone and nature of the voice tell us what an individual is like and whether that person is happy, angry or bored.

A good voice is one that calls little attention to itself. It promotes the communication of ideas. A disagreeable voice is likely to attract attention to itself and cause the listener to miss the communication of ideas. A speaker who wishes to have a good voice—so that listeners focus on the message rather than on the voice—needs to study and perfect at least two essentials of voice control: *audibility* and *vocal variety.*

Audibility: This refers to the use of an adequate volume that is adjusted to the room or situation. It is the speaker's responsibility at the outset to make sure that the volume of voice is sufficient for the size of the room or place in which the speech is given. This is a very important responsibility. There is not much point in refining and polishing a speech and then delivering it in a way that is inaudible for some of the audience.

To avoid this, it is useful at the beginning of a speech to call upon someone in the back row of the audience and ask if that person can hear what is being said. If the person indicates difficulty in hearing the speaker at that distance, the speaker must speak louder or use a voice amplifier, such as a microphone. Often, speakers prefer to speak without the aid of a public address system, but the system is a means of making certain that audience members hear adequately. A speaker should make a voice test with the microphone to ensure that the volume is satisfactory for the audience.

Vocal variety: To produce vocal variety, pitch, rate and loudness must change according to the mode and meaning of the message. A speaker can have immediate control over pitch, rate and loudness. In an oral presentation, vocal variety will make the voice more interesting to an audience, help hold the audience's attention and give more emphasis and meaning to the speaker's words.

In speech, *pitch* may be described as the tone of one's voice. In music, the pitch would be any given point on the musical scale; in speaking, pitch is the tone—or the point of sound on the speaking scale—in which the voice is heard. Nature provides individuals with differing ranges of pitch. Speakers must recognize their vocal capacity and work with it. Pitch can be controlled with conscious effort. Usually, one does not enjoy listening to a voice that continues on the same level or same plane. Pitch should be varied with the content of what is being said.

A speaker who does not vary pitch will not have a natural, pleasing and impressive voice. If the tone of voice rises to high, unnatural levels, the pitch becomes unpleasant. A natural pitch for a speaker may be at a high tone level or a low tone level. The best use of pitch demands upward and downward movement—or *inflection*—relieving monotony and serving to express and emphasize different thoughts and emotions. Inflection is controllable and, when given conscious effort, helps the intelligibility of thought.

The number of words uttered in one minute judges the rate of speech. Researchers have found that the average rate of speaking is 125 to 150 words per minute, although people can understand and assimilate words at the rate of 250 words per minute. The matter of whether a person speaks at the same rate is just as important as whether a person speaks too slowly or too rapidly. Most listeners dislike a dragged-out rate of speaking or awkward pausing, or speech that is so rapid that emphasis is impossible. Therefore, it is important to vary one's rate of speech.

The *pause* is an important element in varying the rate of speech. A variety of emotions will demand a

It is the speaker's responsibility at the outset to make sure that the volume of voice is sufficient for the size of the room or place in which the speech is given.

variety in the rate. The length and frequency of pauses are determined by the sentiment expressed. Pauses should be used knowingly to change the rate of speech to suit the speaker's intellectual and emotional modes. If the speaker is concerned with better communication of ideas, then attention should be given to variety in the speaking rate.

A third important component of variety is *loudness*. Speakers have control over loudness but often do not use that control to their advantage. Changes in loudness, or vocal force, may be used to relieve monotony and to secure interest and emphasis in speech. Some voices are too loud, but a far greater number are too weak. Generally, if one varies the pitch of the voice appropriately, loudness variations will be adequate.

Some people tend to decrease loudness near the end of a phrase or sentence so that the listener fails to hear the last words in the sentence ("dropping" the voice). Sometimes people associate loudness with emphasis and do not understand that a subdued voice can serve the same purpose. An increase in loudness does not necessarily mean a higher pitch. Though pitch may be raised with more force, that does not always occur.

Sometimes people associate loudness with emphasis and do not understand that a subdued voice can serve the same purpose.

Loudness means that one makes the voice more audible. The voice becomes louder as the need for emphasis or emotion dictates. It must be understood, however, that one may also gain greater emphasis with a decrease in loudness. In both cases, the movement of the voice for greater or less loudness adds variation to speaking. The variation in loudness must be in accordance with the size of the room, the occasion, the size of the audience and the emotional state of the speaker.

Bodily Action

An important aspect of delivery is *bodily action*:

- Does the speaker use body language to aid the sending of a message?
- Does the speaker appear to be at ease and physically comfortable?
- Is the bodily action of the speaker (i.e., facial expression, gestures, posture and general physical movement) helpful to the audience's understanding of the message?

Sometimes speakers inhibit their normal bodily action when speaking to an audience. If one's gestures are not synchronized with what is being said, such behavior will be distracting to an audience and detract from the content of the speech. If a speaker shuffles across the platform and does not appear alert and vital in both posture and bodily movement, audience members will assume that there is lack of conviction, preparation or commitment to what is being said. This will detract from the audience's acceptance of the speaker's message.

Effective bodily action prompts the communication process in several ways:

- It attracts the attention of listeners and helps them maintain an interest in the speaker.
- The oral performance becomes more attractive and interesting.

- The meaning of words and ideas is aided by the speaker's visual cues, which provide the audience with a means of evaluating the speaker's attitude and intention toward them.
- It serves as a transitional aid within the speech and helps to integrate the total speech performance. If bodily action is vigorous and alert, it will help make the voice vigorous and alert.

Most people use facial expression, hand gestures, head movements and other forms of bodily action when speaking in normal conversation, but they tend to freeze before an audience. Generally, experience and coaching help an individual to be as free with body movement when on the platform as when off the platform. The speaker who employs effective bodily action stands a better chance of winning and holding the attention of an audience than the speaker who does not.

Directness

No single action on the part of a speaker is more important than *direct eye contact* with the audience. As a speaker looks directly into the eyes of individuals in an audience, those people in turn feel a greater interest in the speaker and have a desire to continue to look at the speaker. Such attention improves the chances of having the audience listen to and understand more clearly the intent of the speaker's message. Audience members may be distracted by a speaker who stares above their heads or who looks at the floor or ground while speaking. A major reason for speakers to retain a high quality of directness through eye contact with audience members is that it lets the speaker know whether audience members are paying attention, whether what is said appears to be received by the audience and whether one's remarks are on target.

Direct eye contact greatly aids other forms of directness in a speaker's approach to an audience. For example, it would be virtually impossible for a speaker to look audience members directly in the eye without at the same time using gestures, head movements and other bodily action that coincide with what is being said. Direct eye contact also helps the speaker know whether all members of the audience hear the speaker's voice adequately. It fosters direct response from audience members and enhances the communication process between the speaker and the audience.

Developing good eye contact is not difficult. When two or more people are having a conversation with each other, they tend to look one another "in the eye," gesture with their hands to emphasize a point and vary their facial expressions as a way of showing how they feel about what they are saying. A speaker should amplify this "one-on-one" conversational approach when talking to an audience. This does not mean that a speaker has to look at every person in the audience on an individual basis. Rather, a speaker needs to look at different sections of the audience to find individuals with friendly, responsive faces.

As the speaker looks at—and talks to—those responsive individuals, other members of the audience will feel that the speaker is talking to them as well. With this kind of eye contact, the speaker will get "feedback" and a sense of how audience members

Direct eye contact greatly aids other forms of directness in a speaker's approach to an audience.

are responding to the speech; audience members will feel that the speaker is talking to them as individuals. When two people talk together on a topic of common interest, they do so genuinely and earnestly. Adopting this attitude with an audience is the most basic step in developing directness. In summary, it is one thing to talk *at* an audience and another to talk *to* it as individuals.

Here are some aids for becoming more direct:

- *Look directly at the audience and focus on individuals all the time.* Watch the audience and consciously record its reactions in an attempt to adapt your speech and manner to it. Audiences are as different as individuals and must be observed carefully while you are speaking.
- *Concentrate on communicating your ideas to the audience.* All movement should arise spontaneously from this concentration.
- *Maintain good posture and use gestures.* These suggest directness to an audience. Face an audience squarely, walk deliberately and stand deliberately still when you are not walking. Gestures synchronized with the words give added meaning and emphasis to what you say.
- *Cultivate a pleasant and mobile facial expression.* This is an outward expression of enthusiasm and earnest friendliness. Reflect your thinking with facial expression.

Some hindrances to directness are:

- *Self-absorption:* The speaker who worries about things such as personal matters while on the speaking platform cannot communicate directly

Watch the audience and consciously record its reactions in an attempt to adapt your speech and manner to it.

with the audience. Give attention to the message and to the audience.

- *Fear of making mistakes:* Theodore Roosevelt said, "Show me the man who does not make mistakes, and I will show you the man who does not do anything." If you make a mistake, don't try to hide it from your audience. Admit your mistake, correct it and move on with the speech. You will get additional attention from your audience and you will gain greater support. Your audience wants you to succeed.
- *Stage fright:* Some disturbance in the normal mental, physical and emotional balance is inevitable in the speaking situation. People who have spoken for years still experience some stage fright. A certain amount of tension can help the speaker make a more energized delivery.

Gestures, bodily action and directness may be improved by following the suggestions in Applications 1, 4 and 5 at the end of this chapter.

VISUAL AIDS

Often, visual aids help the communication process and have these important advantages:

- *Clarity:* Words may not always have the same meaning to both the speaker and the audience. If listeners can see what the speaker is talking about—as well as hear it—they are likely to understand more fully.
- *Audience attention:* An audience will generally show more interest and attention when visual aids are used. The longer a presentation is, the

more important the use of visual aids becomes for the purpose of maintaining the attention of the audience.

- *Memory:* An audience is likely to remember more of the material, and for a longer period of time, when visual aids are used. The aids also help the speaker remember what to say.

- *Poise:* Handling and pointing to visual aids give the speaker additional reasons for moving around and for developing poise. Maintaining poise can help ease tension for both the speaker and the audience and can help strengthen the impression the speaker makes on the audience.

Charts, diagrams, maps, graphs, flip charts, overhead projectors, slides, PowerPoint presentations and video recordings are important aids in explaining difficult or technical subjects. In some cases, a picture may be worth a thousand words. See Chapter 10, "Graphic Communication," for details of visual presentation methods. It addresses the use of computer-generated graphics and sound to provide visual flexibility. Use of personal computers, interactive desktop graphics and overhead projectors can be highly effective but can also be time-consuming and expensive. Use the technique that fits the content of the message, the size of the room and the characteristics of the audience.

Here are a few simple rules to follow and some obvious mistakes to avoid:

- Charts or other means of presentation should be large enough to be seen. Both graphics and lettering should be visible from the back of the room. Do not guess what the proper size is for making the presentation. Draw an experimental chart or diagram beforehand and test it out in the room in which the presentation is to be made to determine whether the lines of the chart or diagram can easily be seen in detail.

- Do not crowd too many details into one chart; this can lead to confusion. Avoid needless complexity. If there are several explanations to be made, or a series of steps in a process to be explained, do not try to put them in one diagram. Use a series of diagrams, each as simple as possible.

- Talk to the audience in strong, positive tones and not to the visual aid. Learn the art of keeping a pointer properly placed on the slide while looking at the audience.

- Do not stand between the audience and the chart or projection. As a speaker should not ignore an audience and talk to the visual aid, so should the speaker not ignore the visual aid while talking to the audience. If the audience is seated very close to the speaker, then the speaker should stand a bit to one side and, in most cases, use a pointer.

- Do not let an unused visual aid distract attention. If possible, they should be kept out of sight until needed and removed from sight when no longer needed. Audience members will look at a chart or picture as soon as it appears and try to figure out its purpose. If a visual aid is exposed to the audience before it is

DESIGN GUIDELINES FOR CREATING YOUR POWERPOINT, OVERHEAD OR SLIDE PRESENTATION

Legibility

To check how your presentation will look when projected, view it on your computer screen from a distance of 10 feet. If you are having trouble reading your monitor, the effect will be the same when projected.

Layout

- Simple and bold is best.
- Don't use busy backgrounds.
- Make sure there is good contrast between the text and background.
- Keep intense colors to a minimum.
- Text placement should be consistent.
- Don't overanimate with transitions.
- Select colors that are easy on the eye for several minutes of viewing.

continued on page 261

ready to be used, it may become distracting and prevent the audience from listening as attentively as possible to the speaker.

- If a microphone is necessary and visual aids are going to be used, a handheld microphone, or a lavaliere (worn around the neck) microphone, will give greater freedom and flexibility than a stand or lectern microphone. It is especially useful when the speaker is referring to charts and overheads and when moving around the room to get proximity and directness with various sections of the audience.

In summary, audiovisual aids are useful in successful oral presentations, but they require good preparation. The visual presentation should be well designed. Good color and font choice, proper size of fonts and the avoidance of overcrowded texts are important. The sidebar entitled "Design Guidelines for Creating your PowerPoint, Overhead or Slide Presentation" provides design guidelines for text on such visuals. Speakers should prepare their audiovisual materials well ahead of the speaking occasion and should be familiar with any audiovisual equipment they plan to use. It is extremely important that they *practice* both with the material they have prepared and with the equipment they plan to use long before the oral presentation is made.

The development of effective oral communication skills is essential to planners. How they gather and organize material; how they analyze the occasion, the audience and purpose of their oral presentations; and how they develop and use their voices, gestures, bodily action and eye contact can determine the success of their oral presentations. With these skills, they will inform, persuade and otherwise communicate with audiences in many different settings and for many different purposes.

APPLICATIONS

We can become aware of our own needs as oral communicators and improve our abilities by applying some of the suggestions offered here. Each of us has developed our own unique style of speaking and can become more effective speakers. We need to understand which parts of our speaking personality require improvement, know what techniques and skills we can apply to bring about that improvement and practice. We can become more effective and successful planners if we improve our verbal communication skills.

1. *Checklist to assess speaking skills and attitudes:* Rate yourself on the following statements with a 1, 2, 3, 4 or 5, where:

   1 = very seldom
   2 = about 1/4 of the time
   3 = about 1/2 of the time
   4 = about 3/4 of the time
   5 = almost always

Speaking

- When speaking, I pronounce words clearly to make it easy for listeners to understand.
- When speaking, I look directly at members of the audience.

- When speaking, I do not do other things (arrange papers, play with a pencil or pointer or jingle coins in my pocket) that may distract the attention of my audience.

Attitude
- I research my topic thoroughly and speak in a confident manner.
- I show respect toward the person(s) with whom I am talking.
- When I speak to audiences, I make certain that I understand them, their frame of reference, their situation and their environment.

2. Analyze a popular speaker on television, at a public meeting in your town or at your church. Ask yourself these questions as you listen to and observe the speaker in order to determine what was most effective and least effective. Did the speaker:
   - use their voice to the best advantage?
   - vary the rate of speech?
   - converse with the audience?
   - read the speech? memorize it? use notes?
   - use meaningful gestures?
   - use the body for communication?
   - use effective eye contact?
   - include an introduction, body and conclusion?
3. Prepare a 2-minute presentation on a planning project. Imagine an audience of 30 people. Put your speech on a tape recorder and listen to the playback. (Keep your tape recording to use in Application #5.)

- How does your voice sound? Does it have a monotone?
- Do you speak at an understandable rate?
- Do you use vocalized pauses (e.g., er, ahh, umm)?
- Do you have a meaningful, vocal emphasis on important words?

4. Practice the speech you prepared for Application #3 in front of a mirror. Observe your facial expression, gestures and bodily action.
   - Does your facial expression change as you give different emphases to various points in your speech?
   - Are your gestures synchronized with your words? Do they add meaning to your oral expression?
   - Do you move your head when emphasizing a point? Are you making eye contact with your imaginary audience? Do you occasionally move about, especially at transition points in your speech, to give visual relief to your audience and physical relief to yourself?
5. After you have practiced a speech before a mirror (as suggested in Application #4), give the speech in front of a mirror and simultaneously record it on tape. Compare this tape with the tape made in Application #3.
   - Do you notice any voice differences between the two tapes?
   - Is there more variety in tone, rate and volume in the second tape when compared to the first tape?

continued from page 260

Fonts
- Select simple, bold styles.
- Delicate serif fonts are difficult to read.
- All caps is very difficult to read.
- Headlines should be between 36 and 44 points in size.
- Subtext should be between 34 and 36 points in size.
- Use 24 to 28 point size for second-level text.
- Try to keep subtext to 7 lines.

**Data Projectors
(Liquid Crystal Display Panels)**

Data projectors are XGA (1024 x 768), compressed XGA or SVGA (800 x 600) resolution. Check that your data files are compatible.

Adapted from the American Planning Association's *PowerPoint Design Guidelines*, American Planning Association, 2002.

- Did your use of gestures and bodily action improve the effectiveness of your voice?

BIBLIOGRAPHY

Bjornlund, Lynda. *Ten Steps to Effective Presentations.* Washington, DC: International City/County Management Association, 1994.

   The preface to this publication states, "Many believe that public speaking is our greatest fear . . . Skills for speaking can be learned." The author then provides instruction for developing the introduction, body and conclusion; for analyzing an audience; for enhancing delivery skills; and for conducting question-and-answer periods.

Langworthy, Steve. *Planning Commissioners' Handbook.* 2d ed. Ann Arbor: Michigan Municipal League, 2000.

   This handbook has up-to-date information on such visual tools as digital cameras, video recordings and geographic information systems, their applications to planning and zoning processes and their uses to provide additional information about topics such as land value, zoning and ownership.

Leeds, Dorothy. *Power Speak: The Complete Guide to Persuasive Public Speaking.* New York: Prentice Hall Press, 1988.

   The author offers excellent strategies for opening oral presentations in a variety of settings. Pages 67 and 68 contain important factors for analyzing audiences and their settings.

Lewis, Thomas R. and Ralph G. Nichols. *Speaking and Listening: A Guide to Effective Oral-Aural Communication.* Dubuque, IA: Wm. C. Brown Company Publishers, 1965.

   This book attempts to coordinate the training processes needed for both effective speaking and listening. It includes exercises for practicing skills and for evaluating both speaking and listening effectiveness.

Martin, Howard and C. William Colburn. *Communication and Consensus: An Introduction to Rhetorical Discourse.* New York: Harcourt Brace Jovanovich, 1972.

   Chapter 4, "Understanding an Audience: The Listener's Alignment" contains an excellent discussion of audience analysis and assessment.

Och, Donovan J. and Anthony C. Winkler. *A Brief Introduction to Speech.* New York: Harcourt, Brace, Jovanovich, 1979.

   Part 2 contains helpful chapters on outlining, speech, construction, speech delivery and use of the voice. The material is presented in a direct and practical manner.

Osgood, Charles. *Osgood on Speaking.* New York: William Morrow and Company, Inc., 1988.

   This book contains excellent suggestions for facing and overcoming stage fright. Pages 65–85 offer personal tips on preparing oneself for the speaking occasion, including such items as sleep, eating and lung capacity.

Wheeler, Kenneth M., editor. *Effective Communication. A Local Government Guide.* Washington, DC: International City/County Management Association, 1994.

   This publication contains useful analyses of the target audiences with whom government officials must communicate. It provides additional information regarding the types of presentations, questions which need to be asked when preparing an oral presentation and advanced technical support tools for illustrative purposes.

Written Communication

Vivienne N. Armentrout

INTRODUCTION

Information is key to planning. This concept is illustrated in many of the chapters in this book. Planners collect information, search it out from secondary sources, analyze it and make plans with it. However, especially and essentially, they must communicate it. Effective communication is a necessity at many steps in the planning process. The written word is the primary means of communication when detail, clarity and specificity are needed.

Together with effective use of graphic methods (see Chapter 10, "Graphic Communication"), spoken presentations (see Chapter 6, "Public Participation" and Chapter 8, "Speaking Skills for Presentations") and the appropriate presentation of data (see Chapter 4, "Analytical Methods in Planning"), written communication enables the planner to inform, query or persuade the various audiences involved in the planning process. Written reports and records are also important in documenting planning intent and outcomes for future reference and for legal purposes.

In the sidebar entitled "The Planner Writes," Assistant Planner used a variety of writing products to address the issue of the littering in downtown Middlesville. He kept these in a folder as hard copies in addition to the electronic files stored on his computer. Since much of the information in the project was repeated from document to document, over time he was able to reshape and reuse much of what he wrote. However, he understood that since the different documents often had a different audience and

THE PLANNER WRITES

When Assistant Planner finished his assessment of the street littering problem in Middlesville (see the sidebar "Two Scenarios" in the chapter entitled "Introduction"), he assembled his field studies notes, surveys, photographs, information from the Board of Public Works (BPW) Web site and records of interviews and meetings with the chamber of commerce. He wrote a brief *e-mail* to the planning director summarizing his findings. She promptly e-mailed him back, directing him to draft a preliminary report to send to the mayor the next day.

The preliminary report was in the form of a *memo* addressed to the planning director, which contained a short, simple description, without graphics, of the information collected, as well as a bulleted list of observations and recommendations. Ordinarily, the planning director would have reviewed this and approved the next steps, but since this was a political issue, she sent it up to the mayor.

After a 5-minute review, the mayor agreed that the planning department should proceed in the direction outlined and requested that the plan be presented to the chamber of commerce. He reminded the planning director that, since the chamber's first impulse was to buy new trash receptacles, this idea needed to be addressed but not recommended. He also reminded her that if the chamber liked the idea of new garbage pickup days on Main Street, this would need to be approved by the BPW.

Assistant Planner e-mailed the secretary of the chamber and asked to arrange a meeting in two weeks. The secretary requested a brief *summary* of what the meeting would involve and a meeting *agenda*. Assistant Planner quickly reworked the preliminary report, removing the recommendations and softening the observations. He led with a paragraph emphasizing the need and value of citizen input, especially informed input such as that of the chamber, to community welfare. Without the chamber's intervention, this important problem might not have received the attention it deserved. The meeting was to explain options proposed by city staff who stood ready to provide service.

The summary was printed on planning department stationery with its prominent logo. As soon as the meeting time and place were finalized, Assistant Planner placed that information in large type on the bottom of a *one-page announcement* on department stationery and sent it for distribution to the chamber secretary as an e-mail attachment. He sent hard copies (paper) to the planning director and the mayor and posted it on the public meetings bulletin board in city hall.

Meanwhile, Assistant Planner began to rough out a *technical report* for the BPW. His outline noted the information or text that each section would require, including additional general information about the city trash collection system and the budgetary effects of shifting personnel to the proposed new schedule. He also obtained copies of earlier reports for the BPW for reference regarding format. He sent an e-mail to the BPW's administrative assistant requesting that the issue be added to next month's agenda.

The *Power Point presentation* to the chamber used digital images and laid out the facts in a few, simple bulleted sentences that avoided planning jargon. Included were an introduction to the problem, highlights of the chamber's role, site observations and the planning department's conclusion that a change in trash collection days might solve the problem. A *handout* of the presentation was accompanied by a separate sheet detailing the cost of purchasing new trash receptacles. The arguments the chamber of commerce had advanced for new receptacles were listed with a suggestion that they might be able to cover the cost for these from their Good Citizenship Fund.

The chamber of commerce members were persuaded. They endorsed the idea of the revised trash collection schedule instead of the purchase of new receptacles. Assistant Planner followed up with a *memo* to all attendees summarizing the meeting, especially the conclusion, and thanking them for their assistance. He carbon-copied (CC'd) the mayor and the planning director. Fortunately, most of the members were accessible by e-mail, so the memo could be sent electronically.

The *technical report* for the BPW was then finalized. It began with a *summary memo,* which described the action requested and the reasoning. The attached *full report*, written in technical language (with all appropriate jargon), included his field studies, surveys and selected photographs. It also included a summary history of litter efforts in other cities, references to the importance of clean streets to downtown economic development and a description of the interest and involvement of the chamber of commerce. It also included, for ease of reference, historical information about downtown trash pickup, a copy of the current pickup schedules and a description of how changing the pickup schedule would affect the budget and work schedules.

He drafted a *resolution* for the BPW to pass so that the proposed changes would be approved. Before sending this package to the BPW for their next agenda packet, Assistant Planner asked the planning director to review it. He also asked a friend in the BPW to look it over for any misstatements about that department's work. Before doing either of these things, he ran the document through his word processing program's spell check and proofread a printed draft.

Once the BPW had approved the plan, Assistant Planner wrote a *memo* to the mayor describing the changes in simple terms and when they were to begin. He characterized the effort as a case of concerned citizens helping to improve the economic climate of the city. The memo was CC'd to the chamber of commerce and blind-copied (BCC'd) to the planning director and the director of public works.

At the meeting with the chamber of commerce a month later, Assistant Planner presented photographs showing the clean downtown streets. The mayor was present to receive the congratulations from the chamber of commerce for a job well done.

The mayor wiped his brow and went home early. Assistant Planner went back to his office and archived all of his document files.

purpose, the tone and language he used had to differ from piece to piece.

Writing in a planning context is not a goal in itself. It is done to accomplish the specific purpose for which the piece was written, whether it is to call a meeting, elicit participation, propose a plan for land use, resolve a dispute over zoning, request funding for a project or approve an ordinance. Much of this writing will be expository (informational), some will be persuasive and some will be a consciously and judiciously chosen mixture. Planners usually work in a political environment (see Chapter 11, "Planning in the Political Context"). It is important at all times to consider the effect on the audience to whom the document is addressed and whether that effect will help to accomplish the intended purpose. The writing must be sufficiently clear and easily read to capture the reader. The language, style, content and presentation should be tailored to the desired result.

This chapter reviews some of the types of documents planners are routinely called upon to write and provides practical hints on how to use them most effectively. Sources for further study on language and style are cited in the text and in the "Bibliography."

GETTING STARTED

A number of considerations are listed that a planner should keep in mind when preparing to write any document. Many of these will be discussed at more length later in the chapter.

- What is the *purpose*? What is the specific information you are trying to communicate? Is it simple information, such as establishing a meeting date, or is it a statement setting down the parameters of a complex issue or analysis of data? Are you requesting information? Are you trying to make a case for a proposed project and thus writing to persuade? Are you hoping for or expecting a response or action from your reader?

- What is the *audience*? To whom are you writing? Are they your colleagues in the same department, the public, an appointed or elected commission or a client in the private sector?

- Based on the answers to the first two sets of questions, what is the appropriate *tone*? Should this be an informal, chatty note using colloquialisms or a formal, even didactic, report that will become part of the public record?

- The *format* of the document is itself a means of communication in that it conveys a sense of purpose to your audience. In addition, good format makes for a more readable document. This includes the use of appropriate sections (e.g., an introduction and a conclusion for a report) and the choice of fonts, margins, bold emphasis, bullets, titles and spacing. These and other techniques can help communicate what the writer deems to be key concepts. (See Chapter 10, "Graphic Communication," for more on the effects of format on perceptions.)

- The *length* of the document is often dictated by its purpose (e.g., a memo of more than two pages would be unusual and perhaps should

It is important at all times to consider the effect on the audience to whom the document is addressed and whether that effect will help to accomplish the intended purpose.

be replaced by a report with a cover memo; a site plan review one page long would look as though it might not be complete). When setting out to write, you should have a general idea of the appropriate length and try to format the document appropriately.

- Will there be *graphic illustrations* or *data tables or graphs* included? If so, plan to integrate them into the document. They can make a document more powerful (see Chapter 10, "Graphic Communication") but not if they are attached at the end as an afterthought or not well integrated into the argument. Also, they can be distracting if they are irrelevant.

- The *completeness* and *accuracy* of information and statements are each expected to be of high quality for any document produced by planning professionals.

- *Style* indicates both the language used—with your own way of putting words together to express a thought—and the correct usage for punctuation, abbreviations and format for certain documents.

- *Grammar, spelling* and *word usage* should be correct in the final document.

Many people find it difficult to write. For some, starting to write is the most difficult step. If you are one of these people, here are a few hints that might help:

- Make some quick *notes* about the purpose. What are you trying to do? Are there specific pieces of information that will be included? Are you making a point or asking a question?

- Make an *outline* if you can, but don't let the daunting task of writing a complete outline with sub-sub-subsections stop you. Just a rough outline with a few notes may be enough to get you started.

- *Begin at the top,* if that is comfortable. Perhaps you might find it easier to write out the core piece of information that belongs in the middle of the document. You can then finish up the introduction and conclusion later. Word processing programs are wonderfully convenient for moving sections and rearranging sentences. The important point is to begin composition.

- Don't be discouraged if your first attempts seem awkward. Just *get your thoughts down.* They can be polished later.

- Use similar letters, reports or reviews to suggest the appropriate *format* and even some of the language, especially for a routine type of document.

- Find someone at work or elsewhere who will read your work and comment on its use of *language* and *style,* not just correct typographical errors. Ask for frank opinions and suggestions.

- Word processing programs have useful *spelling checkers* and *grammar checkers.* However, if this is a problem area for you, ask your editing friend to watch for those errors, too.

- Give yourself plenty of *time.* Writing with a deadline is difficult, even for skilled writers.

Don't be discouraged if your first attempts seem awkward. **Just get your thoughts down.** *They can be polished later.*

MEMOS, LETTERS AND E-MAILS

As was illustrated by Assistant Planner's odyssey with trash receptacles, direct communication to individuals and groups via memos, letters and e-mails is important throughout a project. These forms are also often used to document facts or a position or to establish a paper trail. A few suggestions for document format and style for these means of correspondence are included in the following sections. For a more complete overview, please consult references on business writing.

Given that planners use these forms in their tasks of integration, synthesis and collaboration throughout a project, it is especially important to consider the audience, tone, purpose and subtle, implicit messages being conveyed with these everyday communications. As with other documents, format, language and style are all part of the total effect and effectiveness of memos and letters.

Memos and E-mails

Memos (or memoranda) are most often used *within* an organization. While at one time these were the standard means of communicating everyday details of business, e-mail has taken over much of this function. Now the issuance of a memo is often a *formal* request or a statement of position.

For example, Assistant Planner wrote a memo to the planning director summarizing the meeting of the chamber of commerce with city planners and the conclusion that a change in trash collection schedules was preferable to buying new receptacles. This

served as a formal *record* of the matter, which the mayor immediately faxed to some of his friends at the chamber in anticipation of the official report. It was also a request to proceed further with the project, which was granted.

A memo may also be the cover page to a report used as a means of documenting those responsible and the circumstances under which the report was prepared. This was the purpose of Assistant Planner's summary memo to the BPW. Other uses of memos within organizations might be to announce staffing changes, policy or rule changes and other announcements of interest to an entire group.

E-mails are now used in place of most memos in many organizations and groups for most day-to-day communication. Most of the comments here on memos also apply to e-mails to some degree. (See the sidebar entitled "E-mails" for some specific hints on e-mail use.)

Since the purpose of a hard-copy memo is so often formal with the advent of e-mail, the language should also be in a formal style. However, "formal" does not necessarily mean heavy, bureaucratic-sounding prose. As noted in the sidebar entitled "Writing Simply and Clearly," writing simply and clearly is much more likely to communicate effectively with your audience and will also show off your ability to be concise and direct.

With careful word choices, a memo can be a powerful vehicle for expression. Since memos by their nature are intended to be short documents (generally

E-MAILS

These days, e-mails frequently replace memos and letters or are used as a way to distribute them. As ubiquitous as this method of communication is, it is important for planners to understand e-mail etiquette and to become skillful in the nuances of e-mail usage. Here are a few suggestions:

- Although a certain casual style may be more appropriate for e-mail communication, it is wise to compose your messages carefully, avoid misspelling and grammatical errors, and pay some attention to format. Your message may be printed out and filed by many recipients. Give it the same attention you would for a hard-copy message.

- For emphasis, use asterisks or other punctuation marks rather than capitalization. Use all-capital-letter text very sparingly; it may be considered rude, like shouting.

- Information can be in the text of the e-mail itself or in an attached document. Computer systems vary widely. Some may have difficulty in opening or printing your attachment; therefore, it is often prudent to repeat important information in the text of the e-mail.

- Organizations using e-mail for important documents will sometimes eliminate all paper or telephone notification to group members. Before doing this, make sure that everyone in the group you are trying to reach reads their e-mails regularly and/or are able to receive them. Otherwise, you may offend some people in the group and fail to accomplish needed communication.

- E-mails are a very useful means to distribute information to a long list of people. Sometimes you want all recipients to be known to all others (e.g., members of a committee or various officials). However, at other times, such dissemination of all e-mail addresses may not be appreciated by some members on your list. It is possible to create lists in which the addresses of individual recipients are not shown. Learn how to do this in the e-mail program you use and exercise the option diplomatically.

- Be judicious when you forward or "blind copy" messages. Some people may be offended to learn that, without their permission or knowledge, another person has received their message or has been copied on a message you have sent to them.

- As with letters and memos, never commit to writing in an e-mail words that you do not want repeated or published widely. Do not assume that any e-mail is private. It is easier with e-mail to send an angry or compromising message before really thinking it over. Stop and think before hitting the "send" button. Messages can usually be saved as drafts. Take the time you need for reflection.

WRITING SIMPLY AND CLEARLY

When writing an official document, it is tempting to fall into a style that might be called "bureaucratese." While most of us would never use this style in writing for personal uses, it often appears in planning documents. Thus, Assistant Planner might write in his report to the chamber of commerce:

> It was determined through the direct observation of the population in the central business district (CBD) over both weekend and weekday time periods that utilization of the trash receptacles was uniform and that the total volume of the refuse discarded appeared to increase only by an insignificant increment on weekends. The causation of the observed deleterious littering in the CBD is thought to be the refuse removal schedule for the commercial business bulk refuse containers served by the city, which may leave little volume for additional disposal of refuse over the weekend.

There are several excellent texts (see the "Bibliography") that have sug-

continued on page 271

from one to two pages), spare and concise sentences that are easily scanned by the reader are most effective.

The standard memo format is as follows:

- *To:* (addressee, including group designations such as "all city employees")
- *From:* (one or more individuals, even a long list, but usually not a group; this makes these individuals responsible for the information and statements contained in the memo)
- *Date:* (spelled out in the format of "October 30, 2003")
- *Re:* or *Subject:* (a descriptive, short phrase is better than a single word or two)
- *CC:* or just *C:* (to whom copied)
- body or text in paragraph form

The underlying message of the *To:* line is that the direct addressees are those who are affected by the information and are expected to respond, if a response is indicated. The *CC:* or *C:* is used to inform others who are not expected to respond or to be directly affected, at least immediately. Assistant Planner might have written a memo to his planning director indicating that he was preparing a packet for the BPW meeting the next month and CC'd the BPW director.

Power relationships are often displayed by the use of the *CC:* line. It indicates which parties have a role in the deliberations and who has working relationships with whom. For example, if the chamber of commerce had responded to Assistant Planner's report with a memo indicating that the solution suggested was not acceptable and CC'd this to the

mayor, it would be a clear statement that they had direct access to the top and that he had better pay attention to their concerns. Some organizations also have distribution lists (expanded CC lists) at the end of the document; placement on this list may be a coveted position, both for status reasons and because individuals wish to be kept informed.

Blind copies (BCCs, sent to individuals who are not CC'd) are sometimes advisable or necessary, but carry a certain air of deception. By listing all recipients in either the *To:* or *CC:* lines, you are making an implicit statement that the communication is going to this limited group. If you wish to use the memo as a means of general distribution of information, one straightforward means is to place a statement at the end stating "This will also be released to the press" or "This will also be sent to all neighborhood organizations."

Depending on the politics of the organization, it may be convenient to blind copy memos to support staff or others who are not directly involved in the discussion but must prepare material, or for action based on the information in the memo.

The body of the memo should be organized like any good document, with an *introduction* (perhaps some history of the issue), a main section with a *discussion* of the issue and a concluding sentence or paragraph with the *action* to be taken or the *question(s)* asked. The memo from Assistant Planner to the planning director informing her of his work on the packet for the BPW might read:

To: Planning Director, City of Middlesville
From: Assistant Planner
CC: Director, Public Works
Date: August 13, 2010
Re: Approval of Refuse Collection
           Route Change by BPW

As you recall, we discussed the downtown litter problem in the public meeting with the chamber of commerce on July 29 and there was general agreement that a change in the downtown refuse collection routes would be a good solution to the problem. The mayor has also indicated his interest in pursuing this solution. It will require approval by the Board of Public Works (BPW). I am now working to obtain this approval.

The next meeting of the BPW is August 30. I have asked to have this matter placed on the agenda. In addition to a draft resolution, I am preparing a technical report that includes a proposed change i ncollection times and a budget analysis for their packet. I have requested permission to be present and expect to appear at their meeting to answer questions. The deadline for packet inserts is Friday, August 21. I will provide you with a copy of the report for your review by August 18.

Please let me know if there is further action you wish me to take before the BPW meeting or if you have any questions about the report. Thank you.

Note that most of the information in the memo was probably already known to the planning director from informal conversation. However, the memo documented Assistant Planner's intentions and the dates by which he proposed to accomplish them. If the planning director wishes, this is her chance to make changes. It also informed the BPW director of the history of the issue, as well as who was supporting the changes.

Letters

Letters are usually for communication to individuals *outside* the organization. A letter printed on good stationery and sent by mail carries the implication that it contains important information. Now that e-mail is used for so much informal communication, sending a letter has become even more impressive.

Some typical uses for letters that highlight this impressive quality are formal commendations and awards, notifications (e.g., that a zoning change review was pending), requests for specific information, thank-yous and invitations. Letters can serve as a means of documenting a regulatory decision or a complaint. They are likely to be produced in court trials, and sent to boards and commissions as evidence.

Most of the comments on language, organization and addresses on memos apply here. However, since letters are from a long tradition, some change in tone and style is appropriate. While sentences should be simple and the writing crisp, the language may be a little more expansive, especially for commendations and thank-yous. Traditional phrases and formal etiquette are more appropriate here.

Of course, the address and salutation should be in standard letter format. Generally, only one person will be addressed and all other recipients CC'd. Both

continued from page 270

gested solutions to specific errors in this style of writing. *Planning in Plain English* (2000) by Natalie Macris has step-by-step examples and alternatives to a number of common failings. Some of the suggested approaches are:

- using simple sentences rather than complex ones
- using simple words rather than complicated ones
- avoiding the passive voice in favor of the active voice
- avoiding jargon and acronyms
- using verbs instead of nouns to indicate action
- avoiding too many qualifying phrases

Fortunately, since Assistant Planner was well aware of the pitfalls of this kind of writing, and knew that he was writing to a general audience, his report actually read:

> Our survey of the people using the commercial area over the weekend and on a weekday showed that they used the available trash receptacles as often at both times. We believe that the littering is caused by the city refuse removal schedule for commercial dumpsters, which leaves them near overflowing just as the weekend begins.

A letter is no place for graphics, tables or long data analyses . ... Long letters are not likely to be read in their entirety ...

name and title (Dear Mayor Lorch) are appropriate in the salutation (use Mr., Ms., Dr., etc., if there is no position title). You may feel that only the first name should be used to indicate a personal connection. When it is a formal communication, a nice touch is to type out the full name and title, then mark it out with a pen and handwrite the first name. (This is only done among peers, of course. If you are Assistant Planner, you do not call the mayor "Orv" in a letter, even if you have talked with him at a party or know him well from another context.)

The salutation may be omitted if the letter is not being sent to a specific person. For example, a letter to "Department of Transportation, Planning Division" need not begin "To whom it may concern"; simply omit the salutation line. If possible, use Web sites and directories or make a phone call to obtain the name of the person who will read the letter.

The closing phrase above the signature, which concludes a letter, should be appropriate to the relationship between the recipient and the sender. Such constructions as "Very sincerely yours" appear quaint today. For most business purposes, "Sincerely" will do. For a close colleague in another department or agency, or someone such as an award honoree who merits more warmth in the closing, variations on "Best regards" and "Warmest wishes" are useful.

A letter is no place for graphics, tables or long data analyses. If the subject matter requires these, use a cover letter and refer to a separate enclosure. For example, a letter to residents of an area near a site being considered for a zoning change would include the basic information about the change, the time and the place of the public hearing, their rights under the law and the contact information (names, phone numbers and addresses of planning staff). An enclosure would have a map or diagram of the site and the specifics of the project being planned there.

If the letter is longer than two pages, review it to see whether some of the information can be extracted into an enclosed proposal, outline of action or summary of data, or whether the letter can be simplified and edited down. Long letters are not likely to be read in their entirety unless they contain information extremely crucial to the recipient.

REPORTS

Much of the real meat of a planner's work is in reports. At every stage of a project and at every level of detail and completeness, a report is likely to be generated. Examples of reports include plan, zoning or site plan reviews; studies and analyses of their results; summaries and analyses of small group or public participation proceedings; or plans.

As mentioned earlier in the "Getting Started" section, a good way to begin is to make an outline of the major points of the report:

- What is the purpose?
- What types of information are to be included?
- What data, graphics or other supporting materials will be used?
- Is there a conclusion or set of recommendations to be stressed?

The rest of the text should lead the reader through the arguments so that these conclusions or recommendations are the natural and obvious outcome. A detailed, step-by-step outline is nice; however, for some writers, a rough sketch of major points will be enough to launch the writing process. Start writing. With word processing programs, the sequence of the arguments can be changed at will.

Organization

The basic sections of a report are listed here. Depending on the substance and extent of the material, and the point in the life cycle of the project, a particular report may contain only some of these sections.

- *Title:* The title should be as completely descriptive as possible without being too lengthy. For example, "Zoning Request Review for the Middlesville Central Renaissance Project" and not "Review for Zoning Change Request #1066," or "Recommendations for an Alternative Energy Project for Hiatonka and Victoria" and not "Report of the Water Group."

- *Introduction:* This can be a short summary of the purpose of the report, which may include some background information, dates, locations and the people responsible. The reader should know what the report will be about after reading the introduction. The last few lines should pose the question or action that is to be resolved or at least addressed by the report. For example, the introduction to the Water Group's report (see "A Planning Case Study" and Chapter 5, "Working With Small Groups") might state that "this report examines potential alternative sources of energy for Hiatonka and Victoria." It is posing a question of fact or needed action, which will be methodically examined and analyzed in the body of the report and answered by the conclusion.

- *Background:* A more lengthy history and some technical details may be appropriate for some reports. For example, in writing the report for the Water Group's recommendations, Planning Solutions staff would expect an audience of two state energy departments, all legislators, news media, environmental groups, energy industry groups and economic development interests. Their information in the "Background" section would include: the history and current use of fuel oil for production of electricity in Hiatonka and Victoria, paired with projections of possible fuel shortages and price increases; a summary of the results of the governors' conference calling for joint action; a reference to the legislation establishing study groups; and the successful bid by Planning Solutions to consider alternative energy sources. None of this directly relates to the work of the Water Group, but it establishes the setting for it.

- *Body:* The body of the text contains all information and analysis. This includes the methodology, data collected and data analysis for studies. This is where the makeup of the Water Group, the data specific to the issue of hydroelectric

. . . the text should lead the reader through the arguments so that these conclusions or recommendations are the natural and obvious outcome.

power and the arguments for and against different alternatives were discussed by Planning Solutions.

- *Data tables, charts and graphs:* These are part of the body, but each should be self-contained to the extent that it will be understandable without reference to the text. Each table or chart should have a title. Coordinates, units and a legend explaining different lines, symbols, etc., should all be clearly indicated. It is usually best to number them and to use the number when referring to them in the text. The data and the conclusions to be drawn from them should also be summarized in the text. This allows the reader to understand how the data are being used to substantiate the author's argument.

- *Illustrations, including maps and plans:* These should also have titles or figure legends that explain their significance and origin as needed. They, too, should be referred to and discussed in the text, unless it is a purely decorative illustration. (See Chapter 10, "Graphic Communication," for a full discussion of the use of graphics.)

- *Summary:* A summary repeats the major points of the report. It may also contain a conclusion. Some reports may use only a summary at the end of the report, when the main intent is to present information. For example, a report from a public meeting might end with a summary of the major viewpoints expressed. The

Water Group's report did not include a summary, since it would have meant repeating the earlier paragraphs summarizing data and conclusions of their studies and discussion.

- *Conclusion:* Unlike a summary, a conclusion does not necessary repeat the information but rather draws the *important findings* of the report into a *concise statement*. This is especially appropriate when analysis is involved, as in a study where data are collected or in a plan review. The Water Group's conclusion was a recommendation for a dam on the Pleasant River at Eagle Point, which also acknowledged some of the environmental problems to be resolved. The final conclusion was that the energy departments of the two states should begin engineering studies for a dam, but should consult with the Hiatonka Department of Natural Resources on how to maintain a breeding habitat for eagles in spite of the disruption of the cliffs along the Pleasant River.

- *Executive summary:* For lengthy reports, an executive summary is highly recommended. It is similar to the abstract used for academic works in that it summarizes all sections of the document and is at the beginning of it, often on a separate page or two. The executive summary is often the only part of the report that is carefully read and serves as a guide to the points that will be investigated by the reader. It should be, whenever possible, just one or no more than two pages long. It should have an

A summary repeats the major points of the report.

introduction, a body (which refers to the methods, data and analysis) and a conclusion. It should be formatted for easy reading, with bullets and bold emphasis to highlight important points. The executive summary from the Water Group's report was one page long and placed immediately after the title page. It was later attached to a press release announcing the recommendations of the group. Much of it was quoted extensively in the press and in newsletters from special interest groups, such as environmental groups and energy companies.

- *References, sources or bibliography:* For most types of planning reports, a formal bibliography will not be appropriate unless for some reason it was necessary to cite references in the body of the text. Sources for further reading (or Web sites) are often appreciated when the report is a discussion of a broad topic, such as land use or transportation. Ordinances or state law citations are pertinent for certain types of reviews.

- *Appendices:* Material that is bulky, detailed and supplementary (rather than necessary to the understanding of the information and analysis in the report) is best included as an appendix. Examples are: a survey questionnaire or, if it is too long, the questions from it from which summary data are used in the report; very large tables of data, which are summarized in charts within the body of the report; or the complete text of comments from a public meeting. In

many instances, these may simply be omitted if the audience for the report is unlikely to refer to them. In some cases, for example, if the report is on a controversial subject, it may be necessary to include them as a defensive measure and as a way to support the position taken. Certainly, the Water Group's report was heavy in appendices, including items such as: a table showing details of an annual stream flow analysis of major rivers of the two states (the mean annual figures were in a table and chart in the body of the report); a 50-year history of fuel oil usage in the two states in tabular form (referred to in summary form in the background); and the resume of each member of the Water Group (to establish their credentials and thus support their conclusions).

Formats

The format refers both to the sections included and to the typographical presentation of the document. Departments and companies will frequently have templates or conventional formats with a standard style for the documents commonly produced in the organization. Here are a few elements to consider in format and typographical style. (See Chapter 10, "Graphic Communication," for a more comprehensive discussion of typography and fonts and their use in documents.)

- *Headings and subheadings:* The sections of the report should be clearly separated with headings. Headings can also be used to summarize

For most types of planning reports, a formal bibliography will not be appropriate unless for some reason it was necessary to cite references in the body of the text.

and separate thoughts or topics within the body of the report. Different levels of headings can be specified with different fonts or font sizes. Use of a bold font helps them stand out and emphasizes the separation between topics.

- *Bullets and lists:* If the information can be arranged in list form, bulleted or numbered lists will make it more easily read. Numbered lists are used for sequences or processes ("The following steps must be followed to obtain a zoning variance"), while bullets are used to list parallel points or topics ("These are the recommendations from the task force"). Bullets should not be used as a substitute for paragraphs or to break up text where there is no obvious common subject among the bullets. See *Planning in Plain English* (Macris 2000) in the "Bibliography" for a good discussion of the use of bullets and the methods used to determine parallel subjects.

- *Fonts:* With word processing programs and high-resolution printers, it is tempting to use numerous fonts for emphasis and variety. This is distracting to the reader and should be avoided. Serif fonts (such as Times Roman) are easier to read and are best for text. Sans serif fonts (such as Helvetica) are good for headings and titles if you want to provide a visual contrast. Italic fonts are useful for emphasis but are difficult to read as blocks of text, as are uppercase (all capitals) and script fonts. Bold fonts

are useful for emphasis in headings or within paragraphs.

- *Text boxes:* Insertion of boxes (lines around a block of text with or without shading) is useful to present asides or other material that does not fit into the smooth flow of text. They can also be used across the width of the page as an extreme attention-getting device. For example, if the minutes of a regularly held meeting include an unusual change of location for the next meeting, a box across the end of the page might announce this change. Boxes serve to break up solid text and provide visual interest. They also distract the reader from the main text and should not be overused.

- *Color:* It is now possible to add both background color and different font colors to documents. This should be avoided except for special cases. While colored graphics can enhance reports, colored or shaded backgrounds make the document difficult to copy and both font and background color are distracting. Remember that you want the reader to absorb the information you are presenting. This is related to the speed with which the eye is able to scan the text. Fancy effects slow this process down. For very special presentations (more likely to be proposals than reports), colored titles and a few discreetly shaded boxes might be justifiable. Color increases the size of documents and makes them more difficult to send as e-mail attachments. Also, color docu-

---

Bullets should not be used as a substitute for paragraphs or to break up text where there is no obvious common subject among the bullets.

ments are often later copied in black and white and information may be lost as certain colors do not reproduce well.

- *Margins:* Standard margin widths (usually about 1 inch all around) should be used. Too-wide margins make the document look pretentious and low-content; narrow ones look crowded.

- *Spacing:* Too much space makes the document look empty and too little looks crowded. Spaces between paragraphs are helpful. Word processing programs will let you adjust spaces between bullet items so that full line breaks are not necessary. Use consistent spacing throughout (e.g., two breaks between heading and paragraph, one between paragraphs and 6 points between bullet items).

- *Page numbering and dating:* Page numbers, usually in the footer, are essential. If the report is to be placed in a binder with tab dividers, it may be better to have each section numbered separately. The date of the document may be indicated only by the cover memo or title page. For reports with very time-specific purposes (on a planning commission agenda, for example), placing the date in the footer or header is helpful. If the document is still in draft form and is being circulated for comment, noting the date in the corner header or footer with the word DRAFT helps to track versions (e.g., DRAFT 8/18/01).

Language and Style

The fundamental attribute of all documents—regardless of purpose or format—beyond the factual material, analysis, graphics, tables and special formats is the writer's *style*. This is a difficult concept to explain, but the classic and beloved essay on style by Strunk and White (2000) has done it well.

> *Young writers often suppose that style is a garnish for the meat of prose, a sauce by which a dull dish is made palatable. Style has no such separate entity; it is nondetachable, unfilterable. The beginner should approach style warily, realizing that it is himself he is approaching, no other; and he should begin by turning resolutely away from all devices that are popularly believed to indicate style—all mannerisms, tricks, adornments. The approach to style is by way of plainness, simplicity, orderliness, sincerity.* (p. 69)

In other words, this and other books can teach you the mechanics of producing a document. You may have at hand the very latest software for word processing, grammar checking, outline making and a fine thesaurus, and all sophisticated formats and production values may be available to you, yet none of these can define or create your style. Style is an expression of the individual. Often, if you are familiar with the documents produced by different people in your office, you will be able to pick out which person wrote a particular paragraph because that individual "voice" is recognizable. Such an individual voice can and should be cultivated by planners.

UNDERLYING MESSAGES IN WORDS

Word choice is crucial when the reader's emotional reaction to the subject matter of an announcement or a statement of policy or intent is important. The most direct approach and simplest words may not be the most effective under these circumstances.

Certain words carry strong associations, which can have a more profound effect on the reader than the actual explicit meaning of the word. In addition, certain phrases or words serve as shorthand for larger concepts and implicit viewpoints; these need to be understood and used only when that is the intended message. Some of these are political "buzzwords." A planner needs to be sensitive to the vocabulary of the moment.

The Water Group's recommendation for a dam on the Pleasant River is likely to be controversial on environmental grounds. The executive summary of the report might contain the following sentences:

> The recommended dam on the Pleasant River will be a wise use of this important resource and will produce abundant energy for the development of economic prosperity in both Hiatonka and Victoria. While there

continued on page 279

While style may be a characteristic of the individual writer, it can be learned, refined and modified. Macris, in *Planning in Plain English* (2000), has an excellent discussion of the use of language, both for ease of reading and to convey information effectively. For most planning documents, it is important to use an individual style that does not distract from the substance of the material to be conveyed. A planner's use of language should not be a form of self-expression, but instead used to inform and communicate. Here are a few things to avoid:

- *Humor:* Individual tastes vary and a joke to one person may be an insult to another. Using humor in spoken presentations may be successful if care is used; in written communications that are intended to convey specific information, humor can be distracting at best and even misleading or offensive. For example, puns may confuse those looking for actual meaning in a clever construction or the humor may simply throw the reader out of their train of thought.

- *Colloquial or catchy phrases:* For some of the same reasons as humor, these should be avoided.

- *Overly "literary" style:* With complicated sentence construction, heavy allusions or a tendency for poetical expression, this style can be off-putting to those who are not familiar with Emerson or who consider Shakespeare's language a bit archaic.

- *Overuse of polysyllabic, scholarly words:* If a simpler word makes the point just as well, use it. A document laden with words unnecessary to the task at hand simply makes the text heavy and difficult, even if the audience understands the words perfectly well. If words are so obscure as to require consulting a dictionary, the text will be skipped by most readers.

- *Overly simplified vocabulary:* On the other hand, an overly simplified vocabulary may sound uneducated or appear as though you are talking down to the audience. Choose the level of vocabulary according to the audience and use words that carry precise meanings or just the needed nuance when appropriate.

- *Unfavorable word choices:* A word may very specifically denote and explicitly indicate a concept and have very strong connotations with associations and complex overtones. Use of a word that makes just the specific point needed is invaluable. As shown in the sidebar entitled "Underlying Messages in Words," nuances and connotations can modify the message in either favorable or unfavorable ways.

- *Incorrect use of words:* If you do use an unusual or polysyllabic word, be sure that you are using it correctly. A dictionary should be a frequently used tool for a writer. Nothing looks more foolish than to overreach on vocabulary and use words that do not have the intended meaning.

- *Bureaucratic style:* As noted by Macris and others (see the sidebar entitled "Writing Simply and Clearly"), use of jargon, passive sentences and nouns made from verbs (e.g., "utilization of a plan" rather than "use of a plan") are earmarks of a bureaucratic style, which should be avoided.

Usage

Another meaning of *style* is rules of usage, such as those that are explained in style manuals (see the "Bibliography"). Usage refers to the proper use of punctuation, capitalization, word placement, sentence structure, hyphenation of words and when to spell or not spell out a number.

It includes guidelines to such questions as: Do you capitalize the names of points of the compass when used as adjectives and not part of the proper name (e.g., "northwest Chicago" or Northwest Chicago")? (You do not.) Is it wrong to split an infinitive? (Modern usage allows you to judiciously split the infinitive.)

It is possible to write quite a lot and communicate reasonably well without a good feeling for these rules, but polished writers will take the time to look them up. Some readers will notice if these rules of usage are broken and it will detract from the effectiveness of the document.

Style is also used to mean format and usage standardization for certain publications. Professional journals often have style guidelines for authors, and there are several well-known sets of style guidelines, such as those maintained by the Modern Language Association. Citation of references is one of the major concerns. As mentioned, planning departments and consulting firms are likely to have a standard "style" for most documents, though it may be taught only through example. A planner needs to be aware of the style conventions that apply to the specific audience for their written communications.

Final Touches

Once the report is written, it is still only a draft until it is edited and proofread. Standard proofreading marks enable one to revise systematically and allow one to communicate to others who might be available to help in making the required changes to a document. The writer should:

- Read the text through word for word and check for spelling, grammar, spacing and punctuation.
- Check all calculations and numerical figures for accuracy, including consistency in references to data in tables and charts in the body and appendices.
- Make sure that it is in the proper document format and that style conventions have been followed.
- Check to see that all bibliographic references and references to charts, tables or graphic illustrations are correct and numbered properly.

Only after these self-correcting steps are completed should the draft be handed over to a co-worker, friend or supervisor for review. It is inconsiderate to ask another person to clean up a sloppy

continued from page 278

will be some erosion of the sandstone cliffs along the river, it will endanger only the eagles' nests above the dam. Engineering approaches may be able to lessen the damage.

Negative words ("endanger," "erosion" and "damage") imply that economic interests are more important than environmental concerns. The term "wise use" has been associated with the viewpoint that natural systems are a "resource" to be used and "development" implies an escalation of use. Instead, the report read:

> The recommended dam on the Pleasant River will be a clean source of the energy needed for the sustained economic prosperity of Hiatonka and Victoria. Eagle breeding habitats below the dam will not be affected; however, we recommend that active habitat restoration measures should be studied, as well as engineering approaches to maintain the integrity of the sandstone cliffs above the dam.

This version has positive words ("clean" and "integrity"), implies only a "sustained" economic benefit rather than an escalating one and uses the environmentally sensitive word "habitat" in two positive phrases.

EDITING AND PROOFREADING

Editing is made easier by the use of standard proofreading marks. Here are just a few of the most common:

Proofreading Marks	
delete	ℓ
capitalize	a̲
make lowercase	A̸
close up space	⌒
insert	∧
insert period	⊙
insert comma	⌄
new paragraph	¶
indent	⌐

document. It is essential for an important report that someone read it to tell you whether it presents the ideas clearly and logically, whether the conclusions and assertions you have made seem to be supported by the information presented and whether the tone and style are appropriate or not. They may also catch some embarrassing typographical errors.

If a friendly editor makes suggestions for rewriting a large section of the report, you may find it helpful. You are not obligated to follow every suggestion, however. Personal style differs and you are entitled to yours.

ORDINANCES

The planning process sometimes concludes with implementation steps that require the adoption of ordinances or other legislation, the drawing up of regulations or policy documents and the passage of resolutions to initiate one of these. These documents are legalistic in nature and require special care with the precision and clarity of the language.

Planners are often responsible for drafting ordinances to be passed by city councils, planning commissions or other elected or appointed boards. These may vary from single-issue short ordinances ("An Ordinance to Regulate the Height of Fences on Residential Parcels in Middlesville") to massive projects, such as a revision of the entire zoning ordinance for the city. Sometimes *model ordinances* are drafted to support a particular policy direction that is being promoted throughout the county or state. For example, the county planning commission may wish to encourage villages and cities throughout the county to use setback variances as a tool to encourage developers to preserve wetlands. The planning staff would draw up the model ordinance to be used in educational workshops throughout the county in order to promote the adoption of a similar ordinance by each municipality.

Formats for ordinances will generally be standardized within a unit of government. An ordinance usually has a title, which should be as descriptive as possible. The ordinance may then begin "The City of Middlesville decrees . . ." and the date on which it is adopted will be at the end of the document. Sometimes reference may be made to other authorities, such as to the city charter, the zoning code or a state law. Those references should be very complete, with the name, number and date of the state law or the section and paragraph of the city charter. If the ordinance amends or replaces a previous one, that should be clearly indicated as well.

The language of ordinances is very formal. There are a number of conventions and some of them use archaic language. A common example is that "shall" is used to indicate a requirement, while "will" or "may" indicate optional choices. For example, "Fences within the 40-foot front setback *shall* be no higher than 4 feet and *shall* not be constructed of wire or other impermanent fencing material. Fences beyond the front setback and at least 4 feet from the side and rear lot lines *may* be of any material. No fence constructed on residential parcels *shall* be greater than 10 feet in height." Consult recently passed ordinances for a sense of how the language is used in a particular location.

Ordinances are kept to the essentials of the law or code being expressed. There is no flowery language or explanation of the rationale behind the requirements and no introduction or conclusion. Some ordinances do have a brief statement of intent as a preface to the ordinance. Since this is a legal document, the language should be as precise as possible and the text carefully proofread.

Many ordinances have a list of definitions. Although the words used may be common words, their definitions will specifically include or exclude possible interpretations. For example, "Residential parcels: Those parcels defined as residential in sections IV.1.a. through VI.6.e. of this Code." (Note that this definition does exclude some types of residences. For example, Middlesville also has residences in downtown loft apartments, which do not fall under those sections, thus would not be covered by this ordinance.)

Where an ordinance is merely a technical issue or correction, planning staff may simply draft and present it to the body that is to pass it. Many ordinances, however, are either drafted in part by elected officials or by a committee that is appointed to study the issue. Often, the specific provisions can be a matter of debate and negotiation. If a planner is assigned to help with this process, they should be scrupulous in tracking proposed changes and draft versions. One convention is to use a strikeout font to show deletions and a bold font to show new text as changes are made to the draft document. The date of the draft should be indicated in the header or footer (e.g. "DRAFT 8/18/01").

The planner's expertise should be applied in anticipating and explaining the planning implications of the actions being taken, including the word choice used. Most governmental entities will have an appointed attorney or counsel who should review the ordinance for compliance with the law.

Resolutions

Ordinances are commonly adopted by resolution of the body that votes on them. The preparation of the resolution is often part of the work of preparing the ordinance. As with ordinances, resolutions may be drafted, modified through negotiation and discussion and then voted on in a final form. Resolutions are where the intent behind the ordinance is articulated as part of the general background of the policies behind it.

The common format is to have a series of *Whereas* statements of intent, followed by one or more *Resolved* lines that have the force of law. Where the purpose is to adopt an ordinance, this is stated in the Resolved line, while the Whereas statements are written in expansive language, citing larger goals than the issue specifically dealt with by the ordinance but also explaining the rationale for the ordinance.

Whereas, enhancement of the quality of life for residents is a primary goal of the City of Middlesville; and

Where an ordinance is merely a technical issue or correction, planning staff may simply draft and present it to the body that is to pass it.

Whereas, the City of Middlesville has many neighborhoods solely devoted to residential use; and

Whereas the Zoning Code calls for a front setback in all residential parcels; and

Whereas, the quality of life in the city's neighborhoods is affected by the visual impact of structures within the front setbacks; and

Whereas, temporary fencing is unsightly; and

Whereas, fencing that obscures residential structures from the street may be a threat to public safety;

Now be it resolved that the Middlesville City Council adopts An Ordinance to Regulate the Height of Fences on Residential Parcels in Middlesville as Ordinance #2806, and as amendment to the Zoning Code part VIII. 3.c.

SUPPORT FOR PLANNING GROUPS

Planners often serve as the facilitators or coordinators for small or large groups engaged in discussing a planning issue, including specially appointed or convened committees. See Chapter 5, "Working With Small Groups," for a discussion of small group dynamics and Chapter 6, "Public Participation," for public participation processes. There are several types of documents that planners are called upon to provide the staff support for such groups or for a planning commission or other appointed board. These documents are discussed in the following sections.

Agendas

The agenda often serves as a meeting notice, with the time, date and place at the top of the document. It also and principally serves to direct the course of the

Task forces and small groups assigned to study an issue need agendas that are carefully designed to move the process along.

meeting. Appointed bodies such as planning commissions will usually have a standing format for the agenda, with items such as "Approval of minutes," "Approval of agenda" or "Report of the planning director." In consultation with the chair of the group, the planner will include the items currently under consideration in the sequence in which they will be addressed.

Task forces and small groups assigned to study an issue need agendas that are carefully designed to move the process along. As part of "facilitation" of such a group, the planner should work with the chair to consider where the group has arrived in the deliberations thus far and what the hoped-for decisions or resolution of issues for the upcoming meeting should be. The agenda is then arranged in an order that will culminate in the discussion of these topics. It might include presentations by named individuals (be sure to include their affiliation when listing their name), review of some previous decisions or findings and then a final item naming the issue.

A skillful group facilitator or chair (or the two working together, if they are not the same person) can wield the agenda as a powerful tool in directing the course of action by the group. The inclusion or omission of items, the priority assigned to an item by the place on the agenda and the assignment of individuals to report (or their absence on the agenda) can all influence the outcome of the meeting and the group's action as a whole. Consider the effect of an agenda that consists of the following items:

I.   Call to order
II.   Approval of the minutes
III. Introduction of guests
IV.   Staff updates on the project
V.   Discussion and next steps
VI.   New business
VII. Next meeting time
VIII. Adjourn

It might be tempting for a busy person receiving this agenda to conclude that this could be a meeting to miss. No one is going to be put on the spot. Also, it appears that the discussion under Items V and VI could take almost any direction. There is no indication that specific decisions will be made. Here is the agenda for the neighborhood group opposing the Middlesville Central Renaissance Project (see "A Planning Case Study"):

I.   Roll call (6:00)
II.   Approval of the minutes
III. Treasurer's report (6:10)
IV.   Presentation: "Importance of Carpenter Gothic to the Domestic Architecture of the Midwest," James McInhofer, Middlesville Historic District Commission (6:15)
V.   Report: Housing availability subcommittee, Catherine Schmidt (6:45)
VI.   Report: Traffic subcommittee, Kim Onofre (7:00)
VII. The Middlesville Zoning Review process: Assistant Planner, City Planning Department (7:15)
VIII. ACTION ITEM: Assessment of individual households to pay legal and planning fees (7:30)
IX.   Items for future discussion

X.   Adjourn to next meeting, 6:00 PM, Monday, February 28, 2010, St. Luke's basement

Note that specific persons from the group will be called on to report. The presentation on historic architecture is near the beginning of the meeting, while the action item involving self-assessment of funding to fight the project is near the end, so that people won't be tempted to leave until the meeting is over. Certainly no one would want to miss a meeting where so much information and an important action were all on the agenda (or a meeting in which their absence will be recorded by a roll call).

The use of time limits for sections of the agenda is not common but is used by very firm chairs who are trying to keep meetings from going on for a long time. The Middlesville neighborhood group agreed at the beginning that they didn't want meetings to exceed two hours on school nights. The use of suggested time limits also helps speakers organize their material for efficient presentation.

A major purpose of the agenda is to allow the chair to cut short tangential discussion not relevant to the issue at hand. However, a too-carefully drawn agenda can channel the conduct of a group discussion so well that individuals are not allowed to raise issues related to the topic but not in the direct line of discussion.

While this makes discussion of business more efficient, it may serve to make members of the group feel stifled. Better overall participation can be fostered by adding an item, usually near the end of the agenda, named "Other items," "Items for future

A major purpose of the agenda is to allow the chair to cut short tangential discussion not relevant to the issue at hand.

Minutes are the official record of actions taken by the body and deserve careful attention. They . . . should be formatted for quick review, using bullets and short paragraphs.

discussion" or similar invitation, to speak on issues not named elsewhere.

Another way to do this is to have an opportunity for group members to add to the agenda at the beginning (this would usually be under "Approval of the agenda"). Since the agenda is such a powerful control mechanism for groups, the chair should use it wisely and well. (See Chapter 5, "Working With Small Groups," for a discussion of group dynamics.)

Public bodies subject to open meetings laws may be required to have an item called "Public comment" or "Public participation" under which members of the audience may speak.

Minutes

Minutes are the official record of actions taken by the body and deserve careful attention. They should record the names of the individuals present, the date of the meeting and the actions taken. Often, the agenda can be used as an outline for recording the items discussed and their outcome. The main conclusions and perhaps the main arguments for and against an action are summarized.

There is an art to accurately recording the outcome of group discussions without offending individuals who may feel that they have been misquoted or ignored. It is not usually helpful to record the back-and-forth details of discussions or to name individuals (unless they make a motion that should be recorded verbatim). Conclusions should be reported succinctly and in a neutral tone. Minutes should not be lengthy documents but instead should be formatted for quick review, using bullets and short paragraphs.

Recording the work of a task force whose charge is to address a specific problem or issue is more complex than standard minute-taking. The end product of such a task force is often in the form of a report, as in the work of the Water Group. In addition to minutes showing attendance and actions taken, interim reports and summaries may be needed.

Presentations

Written outlines and support material for presentations may be needed as part of the group process. (See Chapter 6, "Public Participation" and Chapter 8, "Speaking Skills for Presentations," for discussion of organizing verbal presentations.) Often a copy of the PowerPoint slides, with or without a supporting outline, is a part of the meeting packet.

Announcements

Meetings to which the public or a general population (such as all members of the chamber of commerce and not just members of a committee) is invited often require an announcement sheet that can be mailed or posted. A typical announcement should include the following elements, usually center-justified. (See also Chapter 6, "Public Participation," for a discussion of effective announcements for public meetings.)

- *Title:* The title should be as descriptive as possible, such as "A Public Meeting to Discuss the Middlesville Central Renaissance Project" or

"Middlesville's Downtown Littering Problem: Proposed Solutions."

- *Description:* Usually one paragraph is enough for a brief description of the purpose and agenda of the meeting.
- *Date, time and place:* The date, time and place should be clearly separated from the rest of the text so that they can be read easily and with a quick glance. The location should include not only the address but the room number and directions, if the location is not easily understood from the address (e.g., "Public meeting room, 1st Bank of Middlesville, 6 Applewood Way (on the north side of the Apple Orchard Shopping Center)"). Sometimes a sketch showing a map of the location is needed.
- *Contact number:* The telephone number of a person who can answer questions about the meeting should be included.
- *Public participation opportunities:* The public should be informed if there is an opportunity to speak. If written comments may be sent ahead of time, this should also be indicated, as well as the address to which they are to be sent.

Assembling Packets

Packets containing all necessary documents are useful for many committees, boards and commissions, as well as for some public meetings. A typical packet would include the agenda, minutes, background material for any actions to be taken, resolutions to be passed and outlines or printed copies of slides for presentations to be given during the meeting. For example, the BPW packet (for the day Assistant Planner appeared before them to ask for a change in the downtown refuse collection schedules) included their agenda, minutes and Assistant Planner's summary memo, technical report and draft resolution. All of these were sent to the BPW several days in advance of the meeting so that they had time to review the material.

A cover memo may be appropriate to include with the packet, especially if it is to a new committee that has just been appointed or, if for some reason more information about the contents is considered necessary. If so, the memo should include a list of the materials contained in the packet.

For task forces and committees studying a particular topic, a binder-style packet may be useful. The binder can be handed out at the first meeting and can include sections marked with tabs.

Sections might include one with the enabling legislation or other action that established the committee; a sheet showing the members of the committee, their affiliations, addresses, phone numbers and e-mail addresses; one with background information, such as previous studies, draft plans or data sheets; one with a schedule for several months' worth of meetings and their locations; and several empty sections intended for insertion of agendas and minutes of future meetings. Thick binders should have a table of contents at the front. Subsequent handouts to the committee should be three-hole punched for easy insertion into the binder.

Packets containing all necessary documents are useful for many committees, boards and commissions, as well as for some public meetings.

PROPOSALS

Planners in governmental or nonprofit agencies may submit grant proposals to foundations or other governmental agencies. This calls for persuasive writing, which differs from the expository writing used in most documents discussed thus far in this chapter. It requires a more fluid and eloquent style and the careful marshalling of arguments, especially in the portion that seeks to justify the award to your agency or group. This subject of writing proposals could and has easily occupied entire chapters and books and is outside the scope of this one. Some excellent and comprehensive sources about writing grant proposals are listed in the "Bibliography."

Here are a couple of points that planners need to keep in mind when approaching the task of writing a proposal. Remember: it is a document that is trying to persuade, "sell" and appeal for resources. It is therefore important to adhere to the rules the reader or evaluator has set and to meet their expectations and requirements.

- Carefully review the information from the funding source to be sure that your proposal is actually suitable and that they will fund proposals from the type of organization you represent.
- Scrupulously follow the guidelines for the format and information to be submitted. Proposals that do not follow these guidelines are usually discarded without being read.
- Meet the deadlines for submittal. They are usually nonnegotiable.

THREE PLANNERS, THREE VIEWS

In the case study, a developer proposes a high-density luxury housing project on the fringes of the Middlesville central business district (CBD). This will require a rezoning, which is scheduled to come before the city planning commission. The Middlesville Central Renaissance Project, as it is called by the developer, is controversial. It will displace 19 rental units in houses of some historical value and will bring much more traffic to the surrounding area. A group of citizen activists, Friends of Historic Middlesville, has formed and is actively campaigning against the project. Meanwhile, the chamber of commerce is enthusiastic about bringing more affluent shoppers to the CBD and about economic development in that slightly depressed corner of town. This puts pressure on the planning commission to approve the project.

Three planners have prepared reports on the project. Planner X works for a consulting firm hired by the developer. Planner Y has been hired by the citizen group. Finally, Assistant Planner has been assigned to review the project for the planning commission. All three planners are well-educated, skilled professional planners. All three reports are written using factual data and good planning principles; however, the conclusions of the reports are very different.

Planner X

The Middlesville Central Renaissance Project will increase the supply of available housing from 19 to 50 units. The project will improve the aesthetic qualities of the area by the demolition and cleanup of the abandoned industrial buildings, the high quality of the buildings' design and the extensive landscaping throughout the project. Surrounding neighborhoods will benefit from the pedestrian walkways, which will be constructed from the project to the nearby business area. It is expected that the project will bring more services to the commercial area as has been recommended by the city's Strategic Plan for Economic Development. Middlesville will also be benefited by the increase in the assessed value of the parcels involved and by the donation that the developer has agreed to make to the city's affordable housing fund. *This rezoning should be approved without delay.*

Planner Y

This upscale development will eliminate 19 affordable housing units and displace many families and individuals who have lived in the area for decades. This is contrary to the city's Affordable Housing Task Force report, which calls for maintaining as many rental units as possible. The surrounding neighborhood of quiet family homes will be disrupted by the additional traffic from the site and is likely to see increased parking along their streets since the developer has proposed only one parking spot per housing unit. The city's Historic Development District has rated the two buildings in the Carpenter Gothic style as "structures of significant architectural and historic merit." The nearby commercial area cited by the chamber of commerce as "underutilized" has recently become the location for many artists' studios and an alternative theater project. The emerging ambience of the area as a low-cost, diverse, culturally stimulating pocket of the city is threatened by construction of a high-density luxury development. *This rezoning should be denied.*

Assistant Planner

Some questions still need to be resolved. Recent federal regulations on storm water management and state standards for sewer service have implications for this project. The proposed increase in impervious surfaces would require reduction in them elsewhere in the storm water drainage area. City sewer mains serving these parcels are 50 years old and may need enlargement and upgrading to serve such an increased number of housing units. The city master plan for the affected area has not recently been revised. The issue of the number of housing units accessible to families at below-median income levels needs to be reviewed for that entire quadrant of the city. A traffic study has not been done but is required for increases in housing units of the magnitude proposed.

This rezoning should be tabled by the planning commission pending engineering and traffic studies and the developer should work with the housing staff on affordable housing concerns. He should also work with the Historic District Commission for a solution that might preserve, move or incorporate the historic structures.

- Find out whether your institution requires payment of indirect costs (an assessment for administration of the grant) and whether the granting agency is willing to pay them.
- Find out whether any matching funds are needed.

Planners working for private consulting firms may also need to prepare proposals to obtain work, either in response to a request for proposal (RFP) or to generate interest in the firm and make suggestions for areas of work that are needed and should be funded. The firm will probably have a standard format for such proposals. The guidelines stated in an RFP must be followed carefully as to format and information provided.

CONCLUSION

Once the formats and uses of the many types of documents discussed here have been mastered, there is still the question of how to write to achieve a specific purpose with a given audience. It should be understood that planners will be writing from many different perspectives, depending on their roles and responsibilities in a particular project (see the sidebar entitled "Three Planners, Three Views").

The ability to write a summary or analysis that supports the conclusions or recommendations that the planner wishes to make will partly be a function of selective use of information, partly rhetorical ability (the ability to make a persuasive argument through the use of language) and partly knowledge of the audience and what will move them. The writer will be supported in their purpose by becoming skilled at the mechanics of preparing a document; by creating all the necessary sections in the proper format; by including all appropriate information; and by correct usage of spelling, grammar and word choice.

The final test of good writing is the ability to connect with the intended reader and to speak through your words so that your thoughts are carried to their mind. That ability must be gained through effort, experience and a readiness to observe how others accomplish this feat with flair and style. The planner who succeeds in this direct and effective communication with the reader will possess one of the strongest tools among the many necessary to the successful conduct of the planning profession.

APPLICATIONS

The following exercises are all based on the case study of the city/county transportation plan (see "Issue #2 (City/County Scale): Transportation Plan for Middlesville" in the chapter entitled "A Planning Case Study"). The City of Middlesville is working with its county government on a highway extension project funded by the federal government. There is an alternative vision, which would instead use federal funds for increased public transit and pedestrian/bicycle access. The county is involved because its planning commission must approve the exit from the existing highway in accordance with its master plan. The Middlesville Planning Commission would also have to approve changes in the city master plan, but is otherwise not directly involved since no zoning issues are on the table.

Some players:

- *Local fed:* the head of the federal transportation department for this region
- *Congresswoman Exemplar:* represents the city and county in Congress
- *Ann Fine:* county commissioner for northern Middlesville, where the project is proposed
- *Eric Low:* city council representative for northern Middlesville
- *Barbara Casado:* spokesperson for the northern Middlesville neighborhood, which would be split by the highway
- *Richard Shure:* developer for the Middlesville Central Renaissance Project, 1½ miles from the proposed highway
- *Imogene Lincoln:* chair of the Middlesville Planning Commission
- *Busby Key:* chair of the chamber of commerce
- *Smithfield Jones:* head of the Middlesville transportation department
- *Terry Osaka:* head of the county planning department

- *Mike Anderson:* chair of Citizens for Alternative Transportation
- *Sam Treese:* chair of the local branch of the Sierra Club
- *Planning director of Middlesville*
- *Assistant Planner*
- *Mayor Lorch*

1. Write a memo or letter for each purpose and audience listed (showing appropriate CCs and BCCs):

   a. from Mike Anderson to Congresswoman Exemplar regarding the use of federal funds for mass transit and bikeways

   b. from the planning director to Mayor Lorch outlining the procedural steps in master plan change approval by the Middlesville Planning Commission

   c. from Busby Key to Mayor Lorch regarding the commercial advantages of a highway extension

   d. from Sam Treese to Ann Fine regarding the county policy on maintaining wetlands and its implication to the highway extension

   e. from Assistant Planner inviting participants to a discussion of the implications of the two competing proposals to the city master plan

   f. from Eric Low to Mike Anderson in reply to a letter asking for information on city transportation planning and funding

   g. from the character with whom you most identify to the best audience to make a persuasive case for the alternative you prefer

2. Plan an agenda for each group and purpose listed. Name presenters for items as appropriate.

   a. a meeting of the chamber of commerce to discuss the business impact of the proposed extension and a strategy to promote it if the group agrees

   b. a special meeting of the county planning commission called to discuss issues related to master plan review

   c. a meeting of Citizens for Alternative Transportation to review the funding proposals for the two plans and the procedure for approval of master plan revisions; and to discuss arguments, strategies and possible coalitions for pushing the alternative transportation plan

   d. a working session (without votes) of the Middlesville Planning Commission regarding the entire issue, including legal and procedural steps for resolving it

3. Outline a report from each meeting in the previous exercise. Write a conclusion based on your outline.

4. In an attempt to placate the alternative transportation crowd, the Middlesville City Council is putting together a package of new resolutions and ordinances that are intended to enhance the pedestrian and bicycling experi-

ence in Middlesville. Try writing one of each of these.

5. Review and edit some of your writing that has been in the file for a while. Note the title and the use of spacing, fonts and headings. How is the style? Are there any usage questions? Is it possible to make recommendations for changes in the way this piece of writing was done?

BIBLIOGRAPHY

Style and Usage

Baker, Sheridan. *The Complete Stylist.* New York: Thomas Y. Crowell Co., 1972.

This is a guide to writing expository and even literary works and is based on the classic fundamentals of logic, grammar and rhetoric. Much attention is paid to sentence and paragraph development for effective presentation of concepts. Grammar and usage are also included.

The Chicago Manual of Style. 14th ed. Chicago: University of Chicago Press, 1993.

Considered the comprehensive great-aunt of style manuals and a recognized authority, this manual needs practice to use easily but has an answer for nearly every question of usage. It includes everything from punctuation and capitalization to specialized terminology, proper use of geographical references, composition of tables, special foreign language characters and how to edit and index manuscripts.

Strunk, William, Jr. and E. B. White. *The Elements of Style.* 4th ed. Needham Heights, MA: Allyn & Bacon, 2000.

Considered a classic (over 80 years since the 1st ed.), this book is still easily read and a much used summary of important rules of usage, with a discussion of style and suggestions for composition.

Troyka, Lynn Quitman. *Simon & Schuster Handbook for Writers.* 6th ed. Upper Saddle River, NJ: Prentice Hall, 1990.

A substantial, heavily documented usage handbook with a strong emphasis on grammar and basic English usage, which includes style guidelines from professional societies such as the Modern Language Association, the American Psychological Society and the Council of Biological Editors. Likely to be especially useful for writing academic papers and reports. Includes access codes to a Web site for online help.

Writing to Communicate Effectively

Bates, Jefferson D. *Writing with Precision.* Herndon, VA: Acropolis Books, 1991.

A guide to "writing so that you cannot possibly be misunderstood," with precision and clarity. This book lists 10 principles and illustrates them, often humorously, and includes some comments on usage, practical comments on editing and pointers on writing as a discipline.

Macris, Natalie. *Planning in Plain English.* Chicago: APA Planners Press, 2000.

An eloquent, brief and elegantly spare plea for plain language in documents produced by planners. It is especially targeted to planners in the discussion of acronyms, how to explain technical processes and the consideration of different audiences. Other useful sections explain how to avoid the use of jargon and the effective use of bulleted points.

Proposals

Hall, Mary S. *Getting funded: a complete guide to proposal writing.* Portland, OR: Continuing Education Publications, Portland State University, 1988.

In addition to information on how to write a proposal, this contains especially thoughtful approaches on how to evaluate one's own program in terms of capability and a discussion of the evaluation components in the proposal.

Lauffer, Armand. *Grantsmanship.* Beverly Hills, CA: Sage Publications, 1983.

This is a methodical, step-by-step guide to proposal writing, which also includes a discussion of different types of sources of funds.

Internet Sources

www.plainlanguage.gov

This Web site is an Internet compendium of efforts to see that official documents are written in plain language.

www.kcitraining.com/styleguide

"The KCI Reader-based Style guide is designed to help you bullet-proof your writing. Use it to learn the elements of classic business writing style, to find answers to frequently asked questions about preferred usages, or to trouble-shoot a document before you send it out." KCI is a business communication training company.

www.io.com/~hcexres/tcm1603/acchtml/acctoc.htm

This is an online technical writing textbook by David A. McMurray, which is also available in expanded book version and intended both for individual use and as a text for courses.

Graphic Communication

Andrea Frank

Seventy percent of the body's sense receptors cluster in the eyes, and it is mainly through seeing the world that we appraise it and understand it.
— ACKERMAN, DIANE. *A NATURAL HISTORY OF THE SENSES.* NEW YORK: RANDOM HOUSE; LONDON: CHAPMAN, 1990, P. 230.

Graphics are a potent tool with which planners communicate their plans, ideas and information by visual means. People have long used symbols to convey concepts fundamental to their existence. Communicating directly with graphics opens up new ways of understanding spatial relationships for both the individual making the drawing and the observer. The contribution graphics can make to a planner's task, described some years ago, remains the same today.

This chapter discusses the various uses of graphics during the planning process, illustrating with examples the possibilities and judicious choices that must be made for effective communication in different planning situations. The most important types of graphics, the graphic tools and techniques—both traditional and digital—that are available to the planner are included. A discussion on integrating graphics into oral and written presentations follows, and concludes with a reference to applications, computer programs and readings—all designed to help planners hone professional graphic communication skills.

Visual aids do not merely act as illustrations or as eye-bait . . .; they are parts of the explanations themselves.

— NEURATH, OTTO. *MODERN MAN IN THE MAKING.* LONDON: SECKER & WARBUG PUBLISHERS, 1939.

LEARNING TO USE GRAPHICS WITH CONFIDENCE

Planners who are also architects, landscape architects or engineers tend to draw. They lavish affection on graphic presentations as a primary and almost exclusive communication medium. On the other hand, planners trained in the social sciences do not draw and often use graphics only when they cannot avoid them. Either position leaves considerable room for improvement in effective communication.

Although it is untrue that every picture is worth a thousand words, graphics of various kinds are often essential for clear communication in the planning profession. There are verbal ideas and nonverbal ideas, and each requires the right medium to convey the message. The right graphic in the right place, at the right time, can be instrumental in making a good decision, winning a project or clinching an argument.

The extent to which graphics are used in projects should and does vary greatly depending on the type of planning project at hand. Generally, physical planning projects necessitate more use of graphics and less written material than social, economic or policy planning projects. However, it appears that the use of graphics in planning is linked to an individual's ability and skills. Those planners who know how to draw easily and well will often have great difficulty writing a three-page memo but can "talk" (sketch) with pencil and tracing paper in hand; others, who do not draw, will omit using even the simplest maps in places where their inclusion would be very helpful. This state of affairs is unfortunate.

Advances in technology and computer applications are making the development and use of graphics easier. Most general office packages include graphic functions that can generate charts and tables, and enable the incorporation of graphics into text documents. Computer-aided drafting and Geographic Information Systems—with easy-to-use, pull-down

continued on page 296

continued from page 295

menus—are widely available and affordable. In addition, digital imagery and the Internet provide new avenues for graphic communication. Images can be downloaded from the Internet as well as broadcast to a large public audience.

With ever-evolving graphic techniques—often computerized—it is important for planners to become familiar with the range of graphics available for use and to learn to integrate them throughout the planning process. Practitioners who allow their lack of graphic skills to prevent them from using illustrations in their various professional communications are denying themselves the use of an evocative communication technique.

In conjunction with written descriptions and statistical information (often expressed graphically by charts, diagrams and graphs), graphics form the backbone of communication in planning. In fact, in the layperson's mind, maps, charts and diagrams are probably the major tools of the planning profession.

A good planning practitioner does not have to personally develop a desired graphic product. Learning the intricacies of a particular graphic form is a long-term endeavor involving highly specific, technical and professional skills. Creating complex graphics, such as animations and multimedia presentations, is best left to specialists. Rather, it is sufficient and more important to know where a particular kind of graphic or medium is needed and to be able to explain the ideas clearly to someone who can execute the work. The ability to conceptualize applications rather than know specific techniques is most important.

The ability to convey ideas with the most basic tools—a stick to draw images in the sand, chalk and chalkboard, pencil and tracing paper, relying not primarily on drafting skills but on the ability to conceptualize and communicate with universal graphic symbols—is a skill that will not be rendered obsolete by high technology. These simple techniques and tools will also be successful when one works—as planners do—in places where the supply of electric power is not dependable and means of transporting equipment are often incompatible with delicate machinery.

Thus, it is helpful for planners to be skilled in, and to use, the simplest and least expensive techniques that will do an effective job of communicating. Hand-drawn graphics and sketches exude an artistic flair and warmth and can stimulate the imagination of the observer. Moreover, for testing initial ideas, layouts, basic relationships and/or data flows, hand drawings are often produced more quickly and are more appropriate.

This chapter provides an overview and conceptual guide to where, how and why graphics can be used in various parts of the planning process. The objective is to stimulate planners to use graphics effectively. Ever-more sophisticated technology enables even the most untutored in drawing and drafting skills to use graphics. However, even the most advanced software and algorithms cannot prevent "bad" graphics; neither is the computer program capable of selecting the appropriate format for a particular purpose.

In this chapter, as in this chapter in the first edition of this book, the suggestion that future developments will make discussions of graphics anachronistic (i.e., that technology and computers will suffice) is rejected. A machine may perhaps execute symbols and graphics in a technically more finished form, but the imagination and sense of which ones to use, where and how to use them, effectively comes with discretion and the cultivation of professional judgment for which there is no substitute.

Common-sense organization and thinking through of the use of visuals in the planning process, as stressed here, do not become dated. To the contrary, with an increasing amount of data and information penetrating our daily life, the translation of ideas and concepts into easy-to-understand and meaningful images becomes more and more important.

Dandekar, Hemalata C., editor. *The Planner's Use of Information*. 1st ed. Chicago: American Planning Association, 1988, adapted from pp. 188-189.

WHAT GRAPHICS
CONTRIBUTE TO PLANNING

Graphics are an alternative language, which can complement written and oral communication. Graphics in planning are mostly used as a means to interpret and amplify a message. They do some things particularly well.

- Graphics, like no other form of communication, help planners synthesize, organize and condense complex situational information and relationships into a pictorial representation, which can be quickly grasped and communicated. For example, a chart depicting the changes in population demographics in a community over several census periods tells a complicated story in a simple, memorable and accessible form—one which no amount of text would convey. Research shows that graphics enable viewers to process information with fewer mistakes and greater speed than the same information presented in narrative form.

- Graphics are useful in overcoming barriers of language, class, education and interest. In a rapidly globalizing environment, where urban populations grow ever more diverse, graphics can help communicate across different population groups. Graphics reach people who cannot read or who cannot read well. Often, photographs and images need little or no explanation to convey a message. For example, most travelers can understand the signs, symbols and pictograms used in airports and on underground transportation maps. Looking at images is fun and intuitive and readers often look at pictures before they read the text. An interesting image may seduce the reluctant or disinterested audience to read on or to listen more closely for background and related information.

- Graphics can provide another perspective on a problem or an idea. In the example in Figure 10-1, navigation directions are conveyed either as a string of text with turning instructions and distances or graphically using a map with a highlighted route. The two representations are not entirely interchangeable in their information content and use. While the verbal instruction may allow a driver to get from one destination (A) to another (B), the map provides additional contextual information. For example, it enables the driver to find a detour if an accident or congestion blocks the delineated route. Given just the text table in Figure 10-1, it may be difficult for the traveler to decide which direction is south, especially if it is a cloudy or dark day.

Communication may best be served by a balanced approach, where both graphic and nongraphic means of communicating information complement each other in a creative way. In the example in Figure 10-1, the written instructions give exact distances and an indication of the time needed to cover the terrain, which would be difficult to read from the map. The user will get the most complete information from a combination of both forms of communication.

Graphics are an alternative language, which can complement written and oral communication.

Travel directions from A to B

1. Start out going South on BONISTEEL BLVD   0.3 miles
   towards MURFIN AVE by turning right

2. Turn RIGHT onto FULLER RD   0.3 miles

3. FULLER RD becomes FULLER ST   0.5 miles

4. Turn SLIGHT LEFT onto GLEN AVE   0.3 miles

5. Turn RIGHT onto E HURON ST/US-23 BR   0.7 miles

6. Stay straight to go onto W HURON ST   0.0 miles

ESTIMATED TRAVEL TIME: 5 minutes

TOTAL DISTANCE: 2.1 miles

10-1. Travel directions as text and as a map

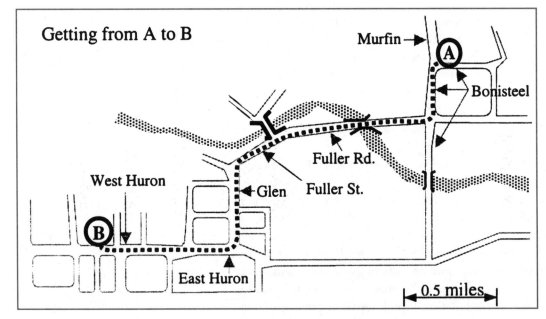

In the most successful examples, text and image together form more than the sum of the parts—a gestalt.

Graphic communication is sometimes considered an art. However, as used in planning, it is better viewed as a craft whose principles can be adapted and learned. The emerging disciplines of information graphics and information architecture, which aim to make the mounting flows of data accessible to the end user, support this view. Like any skill, using graphics needs to be polished and improves with practice.

Graphic communication in a professional planning context is not to be confused with "decorating" pages of reports. There is little planning value in incorporating graphics on only artistic or aesthetic grounds. Graphics in planning require thoughtful transformation of information—whether raw data, actions or a process—into a visual that an audience can grasp without misinterpretation. This is especially true in the use of color and symbols, as the meanings of these are sometimes ambiguous and inconsistent across cultures or even age groups. Inappropriate choices can cause confusion and even offend (e.g., consider the color red where, depending on the context, it is associated with danger or love).

Graphics use needs to be adapted to the type and stage of a project. Urban design and physical planning projects naturally make use of graphics. However, a social policy report might benefit from a logo, photo image or coloring—not only to enhance readability, but also to support identification and to communicate more effectively the human dimensions of the subject. More elaborate graphics, such as three-dimensional visualizations of new developments, can be instrumental to assist in decision making, win a project or support an argument. Flip charts, sketches and hand-drawn charts may be useful during an impromptu brainstorming session, while well-designed overheads or slides can effectively support an official presentation.

USES OF GRAPHICS IN PLANNING

For an overview of the uses of graphics in planning, the following five broad categories are discussed with examples:
1. illustration and documentation
2. analysis and visualization
3. communication of concepts and ideas
4. persuasion through emotional engagement
5. identity building

First, graphics are used to *illustrate, record* and *document* conditions at a place. Many different graphic media are used. For example, photographs or a video/camcorder recording may be used to document the dilapidated conditions at a local housing estate. The images of broken windows and doors, missing stair rails and evidence of water leakage used in a planning meeting will substantiate the need for repairs and investments. A second set of recordings could document the improvements made, as in a before-and-after documentation for the report to the housing authority.

Sketches, line drawings and annotations on maps can serve the same function. For example, in "Issue #1 (Neighborhood Scale): Urban Development in Middlesville" (see the chapter entitled "A Planning Case Study"), local residents—with the help of a student activist—could create an asset map of their neighborhood to highlight the resources that would be lost in case the developer is allowed to go ahead with his plans. The asset map might show the location of historic buildings, open spaces, mature trees, a historic plaque, services and existing retail. The asset map would serve to illustrate that the land site for the development is not a waste area or empty parcel, but contains valuable community resources whose destruction must be well considered.

Documentation, with the help of aerial photographs or land use maps from different years, is very effective to highlight urban growth and the extent of sprawl, or to compare development patterns among different cities. To ease comparison, each map should cover the same area at the same scale. For a public presentation, images, photographs and maps can be converted into overheads, slides or a PowerPoint presentation, depending on the size of the audience.

Second, and equally important, graphics are used for *data analysis and visualization*. Large amounts of data can often be better understood by rendering them in the form of graphs and diagrams. In graphical form, patterns and trends are much more easily detected than by pouring over hundreds or thousands of numbers. The scatter plot in Figure 10-2 indicates that, in the data set provided, there is a linear

More elaborate graphics, such as three-dimensional visualizations of new developments, can be instrumental to assist in decision making, win a project or support an argument.

relationship between axis *x* crime and axis *y* income. The outlier that is clearly denoted on the graph may be difficult to define when looking at a table. Pattern detection is a strength of human vision; despite much research, computers so far cannot match this human capability. (See also Chapter 4, "Analytical Methods in Planning.")

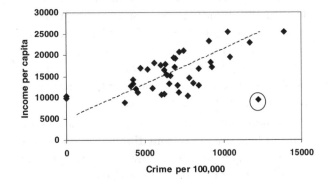

10-2. Relationship between income and crime

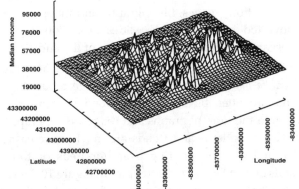

10-3. 3D presentation of Genesee County income data

Much of the data that planners use is spatial (i.e., it is linked to a geographic location). For example, mapping housing units by their construction dates helps trace urban growth and development. Traffic counts on city roads can be visualized using a road map. Heavy traffic streets can be shown with dark, heavy lines and less traffic with lighter, thinner lines. Areas of concern are visually highlighted and are much more comprehensible than numeric lists. Furthermore, the spatial display can reveal that a road parallel to the most congested one is not used, which poses the opportunity to create a one-way system of roads, distributing the traffic equally and saving on costly road-widening plans.

Visual thinking, or *visualization*, is sometimes helpful in making decisions. Exploratory data analysis is often used when there is a flood of data that, on first sight, does not seem to make sense. Simulation software is increasingly employed to provide different perspectives of data and help display multivariate data for exploratory analysis of relationships and trends (see Figure 10-3).

Third, graphics are used to communicate *ideas*—to the public, to investors or in order to share ideas with project team members. A drawing or perspective sketch of the landscaping of the new park is a great tool to communicate the ideas of the designer and architect to the planning board and to the public audience (Figure 10-4).

In essence, the graphic depiction allows the designer to present the future experience of a space with a perspective drawing. Different design schemes can be presented to the audience and comparisons and feedback can be solicited. A range of techniques can be used from quick sketches to collages and computer-aided renderings. For large projects with suitably large budgets, it may be useful to produce a model or virtual reality animation, which shows what the future development will look like. If mounted on a Web site, visitors may be able to "walk through" a simulation of a prospective development that allows them to experience such features as façades, lights and water features. Participative projects can provide visitors with the option to comment on features of the plan.

Fourth, planners may use images to convey a certain viewpoint and *persuade* the public of the importance of policy and action. Photographs and documentary films are especially powerful tools for evoking emotional reactions, which can be used to garner support. Photographs of wildlife strangled by barbed wire fences may induce feelings of compassion and convince the public to support a policy to ban such fencing. Related examples are the display of photographs of deformed fish and waterfowl to campaign for a costly water purification program.

As with much in the political arena, some care in selecting persuasive imagery needs to be exercised in order to avoid backfiring or negative reactions. For example, Assistant Planner's public education campaign supporting downtown beautification is helped more by a positive "cute" poster than by a dreary one. Consider how you would react to an image that

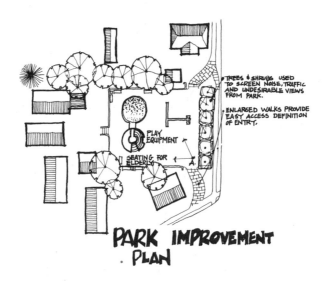

PARK IMPROVEMENT PLAN

View from Point A

10-4. Walk-through sketch

shows people behaving responsibly by depositing their waste in the available receptacles, underscored by an encouraging banner: "Come on! Pitch in and make downtown a destination!" Would you prefer one that shows a derelict and dirty Main street, with Uncle Sam pointing a finger and exclaiming "Pick up your trash, or else!"?

Fifth, planners use graphics for *marketing* and to *build identity*. Cities are increasingly marketing themselves as places with certain characteristics. They compete with each other for events, developments and the right mix of residents to maintain a healthy and livable environment. Sun City (the retirement community in Arizona) caters to the needs of older residents. Savannah, Georgia and Williamsburg, Virginia build on important historic characters. An ecological, sustainable identity is promoted by Portland, Oregon with growth boundary policies and a focus on alternative transportation, such as bicycling, and the city's Web site, which features numerous resources on the subject. Part of this marketing strategy is building identity, which often relies on unified street signage, color-coded district markers, logos to be found on Web sites, city plans, tourist brochures and other forms of publicity.

For effective graphic communication, the graphic content must fit the purpose, use and setting.

For effective graphic communication, the graphic content must fit the purpose, use and setting. Asking the following questions may help in selecting graphics for a particular project:

- *What is the objective of the particular task for which you are considering the graphic?* Are you trying to present and discuss ideas, report on a survey or facilitate decision making?

- *Who is the audience and who are the decision makers?* Some audiences are more receptive to graphic communications in the form of slides, maps or drawings than others. It may be essential to use certain types of graphics to reach some audiences, whereas others would find them too simplistic. Deciding on an appropriate graphic must be carefully considered in light of one's expected audience.

- *What is to be presented: data, ideas and/or visions?* If the graphics are to show facts based on numbers, then diagrams or charts may be most useful. If they are to show spatial distribution of a problem or policy, maps may be the graphic of choice.

- *What is the setting?* Is it a formal meeting or a presentation in a large room? Slides usually project better than overheads or liquid crystal display (LCD) projectors. If you have to cater to a large audience, perhaps slides or overheads will be best. If it is a small, less formal group, a few sketches and pinned-up diagrams on a wall may be sufficient.

To summarize, graphics have a wide variety of uses and methods of application. Different approaches are appropriate depending on the specific type of written information to be supported visually, as illustrated in Figure 10-5.

Text Narrative	▶ Information Type	▶▶ Graphic Type
10-liter trash containers cost either $300, $550 or $890. The cheap one is made of plastic; the other two are made of metal. 50-liter containers cost $150, $900 and $1,000. The cheap one is made of wood; the other two are made of metal.	▶ Exact, absolute numbers	▶▶ Table or ordered list 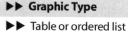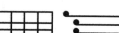
The population of Middlesville is 60% white, 29.3% black, 5% Native American, 2% Asian and 3.7% other races. In comparison, Opportune's population is made up of 76% white, 3.4% black and so on.	▶ Relative, proportional figures and comparison	▶▶ Bar or pie chart
Traffic passing through Middlesville has increased over the past years. Based on traffic counts in 1975, 1990 and 2000, there was an increase of 10% for motorcycles, 50% for lorries and 75% for passenger cars.	▶ Trends, change over time	▶▶ Scatter or line chart

Text Narrative	▶ Information Type	▶▶ Graphic Type
Ortonville city government consists of six different departments.	▶ Hierarchy and relationship	▶▶ Organization chart 
The development site in Middlesville is located between the central business district and the university district, between Main Street and High Street, and between 1st and 5th Avenues.	▶ Geographic location and spatial relationship	▶▶ Map
The building should be protected. It features invaluable historic, original details. Its placement in the well-maintained garden with many rare plants provides an educational setting unique to this city.	▶ Complex, three-dimensional, situational	▶▶ Documentary entry, fence and original feature/ photographs of rare plants 

10-5. Text narrative/information type/graphic type

GRAPHIC STYLES AND APPROACH

The same graphic type (e.g., a map) may be used for different purposes over the duration of a project. A map can be used to document, facilitate analysis, persuade or market. The style of the map will change according to the purpose, setting and audience.

In "Issue #1 (Neighborhood Scale): Urban Development in Middlesville" in the chapter entitled "A Planning Case Study," the initial proposal of the developer—a verbal description of the future development—is accompanied by a utilitarian and neutral-looking map of the development site. The map is nothing more than a redrawn parcel map with the site highlighted (see illustration accompanying this case study). For the public hearing, the developer focuses on the revenue and financial impact of the project.

Meanwhile, the neighborhood group has drawn a colorful neighborhood asset map of the same area. It shows

continued on page 305

GRAPHIC TYPES

Many different types of graphics are used in planning. Depending on the kind of data available, and the goals and objectives for the use of graphics, one graphic type might be preferable to another.

- Tables and charts are useful to present numeric data.
- Ideas, concepts and processes can be summarized in bubble diagrams, flow charts and schematics.
- Physical designs are often represented in drawings, sketches, models and three-dimensional renderings and animations.
- Maps help convey spatial relationships.
- Photographs and videos are useful to capture concrete conditions, document and record.

Here are some examples of applications, practical tips, benefits and drawbacks in the development of frequently used graphics.

Tables

The tabular format creates an orderly and organized display, which allows the reader to look at the numbers in more detail than when described in the text. Tables are an excellent way to present cross-tabs and frequency counts, which are commonly used in planning analysis. The side-by-side display of data facilitates comparisons and the exploration of relationships.

Tables substantiate what is said elsewhere in writing or verbally. It is possible to copy and paste tables directly from spreadsheets and statistics software such as Excel or SPSS. However, these tables are often not suitable for a report to the public without modification; truncated variable names need to be spelled out and legends and explanations added.

It is also useful to restrict the number of decimals. For example, there is no more information in stating a population density as 1050.434 persons/square mile rather than 1050 and it is more difficult to read. Whenever possible, tables should not be split; if they are, headings ought to be repeated on the following page to assist the reader. For large tables, important columns may be highlighted with shading or color to direct the viewer's eye. Tables may contain numbers, text or symbols.

Table 10-1 is a traditional table with text and numbers, whereas Option B of Figure 10-6 provides examples using symbols for the various categories.

TABLE 10-1
Table with Text and Numbers

	Container Specifications		
Size	**Material**	**Cost**	**Type**
10-liter bin	Plastic	300	A
	Metal	550	B
	Metal	890	C
50-liter bin	Wood	150	D
	Metal	900	E
	Metal	1,000	F

Option A

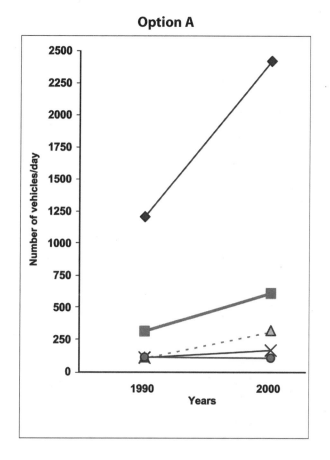

Option B

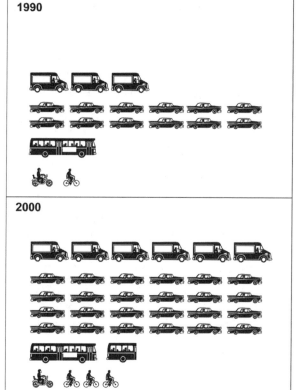

KEY

(Each figure represents 100 units)

Public Bus Traffic

Commercial Traffic

Car Traffic

Motorcycle Traffic

Bicycle Traffic

continued from page 304

the historic buildings, vegetation and community service buildings currently on the site. The images present the structures from their most pleasant sides. The intent is clearly to show the liveliness of the area and garner emotional support from others at the meeting.

In the subsequent weeks, the planning department does some analysis of the site with demographic and other data and finds that there is a lack of parkland and low-income housing in the area. They develop a map showing demographic and resource data. Meanwhile, the developer has made changes to his original plan. He now has a more detailed map showing the design and development phases and integration of existing assets.

The city mounts this on their interactive Web site to solicit public comments. The developer has also printed a glossy brochure with the plan, which is handed to the media and to decision makers wherever meetings are held to discuss the future of the project.

10-6. Different options for representing traffic count data

Bar Charts, Graphs and Diagrams

Another way to present numerical data and statistical information are bar charts and other types of graphs, such as histograms and pie charts. They provide a succinct means to visualize relationships and proportions. The display of demographic data in these formats has a long history. Early forms of graphic statistical diagrams date back to J. H. Lambert (1728–1777) in the United Kingdom. With a glance, one can follow the development of one or several variables over time, or compare parameters cross-sectionally at different locations.

Graphs of population figures over time form the basis for trend analyses and projections. Patterns may be discovered more easily through the visualization of data in graphic format rather than examining the numbers. Series of different scatter graphs are often used in exploratory data analysis. Graphs are best in presenting relationships or proportions, as in the following cases:

- linear or nonlinear
- equalities and inequalities
- relationships in time and space
- correlation and trends

Most spreadsheet and statistics programs have functions for the automated generation of tables and pie, bar or other types of charts, such as histograms. In designing diagrams, minimalist approaches are preferable. For example, color should only be used to improve readability. Simple black-and-white graph-

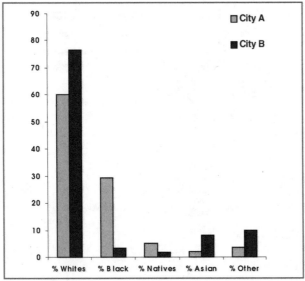

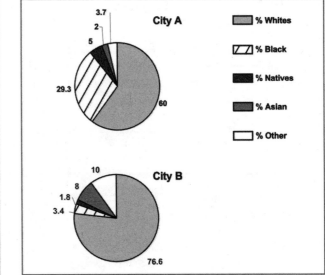

10-7. Two options to display racial composition data

ics are sufficient for small numbers of categories, while color is helpful when a greater number of categories need to be distinguished.

This can be achieved, for example, by using bright colors for the element(s) that are important or different and subdued or no color for background information. Further, three-dimensional display should be used with great care; it is not recommended for one- or two-dimensional data.

There is no absolute right or wrong method in selecting a graphic display for statistical data. Figure 10-7, like Figure 10-6, shows again two different ways to display the same data. The purpose of the chart is to facilitate the comparison of the racial composition of the cities of Middlesville and Opportune. Both the bar chart and the pie chart are appropriate—although the pie chart may be slightly easier to comprehend.

Bubble Diagrams

Bubble diagrams convey general ideas, interactions and relationships between individuals, groups or spaces in the system under observation. They are often used when relationships are vague or symbolic or not exactly defined. For example, a bubble diagram can be overlaid on an existing map defining the boundaries of ethnic neighborhoods, indicating flows and connections between them. Alternatively, a diagram may be used to define land use clusters in a master plan (at a macro scale) or functional spaces in a building or public park (at a micro scale).

A bubble diagram can also be used to show responsibilities for government agencies with over-

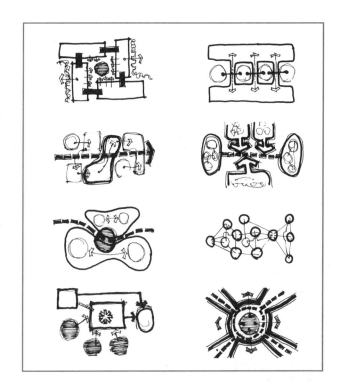

10-8. Bubble diagrams

lapping areas for shared functions. The connecting arrows and lines are used to define interactions and relationships, whether hierarchal, parallel, reciprocal or directional (as illustrated in Figure 10-8). As a rule, these types of diagrams use only approximate physical shape and dimensions. While bubble diagrams are often used to illustrate concepts in reports or presentations, they are also suitable for ad hoc use in discussions and focus groups where they can easily be sketched on a flip chart or chalkboard.

Flow and Organizational Charts

The use of flow charts and organizational charts are similar to bubble diagrams in that they convey relationships and interactions. Typically, however, the charts and diagrams are less sketchy and more precise than bubble diagrams. Gantt charts, a special type of flow chart, are often used to indicate long- and short-term scheduling and programming for

10-9. Flow or Gantt chart

projects. Parallel project activities, deadlines, milestones and the interdependencies of project deliverables can be viewed in their entirety (as illustrated in Figure 10-9). Thus, flow charts provide a tangible overview of the time period in which defined activities should take place.

It is also easy to trace consequences of delays and activities that will be impacted. While flow charts can be drawn manually or with a drafting program, the need to make changes repeatedly over the life of a project has led to the development of more flexible means to create flow charts. Office suppliers provide specific whiteboards with symbols for deadlines and intermittent deliverables. Alternatively, computer applications (like Project from the Microsoft Office suite) can also be used to produce project timetables.

Organizational charts are depictions of networks and hierarchical relationships between groups and individuals in an organization. They are useful in conveying the formal power structure and relationships. They can be used to analyze or explain important connections and bottlenecks in process design or to develop strategic interventions and reorganization.

Symbols and Logos

Symbols are pictorial or graphical elements that represent something else by association, resemblance or convention. Symbols are often used on maps or Web sites. Familiar map symbols include airplanes representing airports, a swimmer indicating a public beach and a tent for a campground. Symbols on the pages of a report can help emphasize its structure. Consider using symbols on divider tabs for a policy report on the future of community services in which the symbol for each section visually reinforces the section's theme (Figure 10-10).

If these symbols or logos are repeated on each page, they cue the reader to the section's content and purpose. Symbols can also be used in tables and diagrams. Consider Figure 10-6. Each transportation symbol is equivalent to 100 cars, trucks, buses and so on. For the representation, the actual figures must be rounded as the precise figures cannot be displayed on or read off the chart. However, in some cases, it may not be relevant whether the traffic increase is from 1,200 to 2,400 or 2,410 cars per day. The benefit of symbols is that they are highly evocative and therefore memorable. Looking at the graphic, one can literally see how the street space has become very crowded over time as each additional symbol fills the box. The equivalent line chart depicting the same data is much less dramatic.

Maps

An immense amount of information is condensed into a map. Maps of different contents, scales and types are widely used by planners. A map graphically expresses spatial patterns, relationships and forms, such as the relative location and association of roads, buildings, rivers and mountains. Historical maps are often very attractive but not necessarily accurate. Most modern maps, however, are very reliable in terms of measurement of area and distance,

which makes them very useful for planners. Planners in the U.S. have access to a wide variety of free or inexpensive digital spatial data from government sources, such as the USGS (see also Chapter 3, "Information from Secondary Sources"). From these data, planners can create and use maps quickly using GIS or mapping software, with relatively little effort and cost involved.

Maps can assist with three general tasks: illustration/explanation, navigation or way finding and analysis. The first two usage categories are straightforward. Land use and transportation maps illustrate context and pinpoint the location of a building site or development within the environment (see Figure 10-11). Site and neighborhood maps illustrate the extent of a new development or racial boundaries; maps of the transportation network, bus routes and subway system may serve to guide travelers and visitors.

The third application—analysis of map data—used to be the domain of geographers. However, within the emerging field of data visualization, maps are increasingly used in an interactive manner during the analysis process by many different disciplines, including planning practitioners. GISs support and help automate such analyses. At a very basic level, maps enable, for example, a visualization of aggregated census data, such as in Figure 10-12, which shows the population density at the state level in the U.S. in 1999. More advanced analyses rely on such tools as infrared and thermal satellite images, together with a reference map outlining the roads and other man-made features, to detect air pollution

10-10. Tab dividers with symbols

or the impact of vegetation on urban climate. Soil, vegetation and topographical maps provide base information for site suitability analyses. Together with subdivision maps, the results of the site analysis may be further developed into new map products, such as a zoning map or master plan.

Map design is an art as well as a science. It would be impossible to convey the results of centuries of cartographic developments here. When designing a map, it is useful to show only those elements that are important and relevant for the message the image conveys. Furthermore, following traditional map design conventions substantially enhances the level of readability and understanding, and only in rare cases are exceptions successful. For example, on elevation maps, higher elevations are typically colored brown and lowlands green. Water bodies (rivers, lakes and oceans) are typically colored in blue or shades of blue. Diverting from these traditions will likely confuse the observer. The map should include a title and a legend where symbols and color use is explained by text.

In addition, a map should have an indication of scale, either in the form of a numerical scale ratio, such as 1:10,000 or a scale bar (or both). The scale ratio (representative fraction scale) means that one measurement unit on the map equals 10,000 measurement units on the ground. Note that a scale bar remains valid when the map graphic is reduced or enlarged later on, while the numerical statement is rendered invalid. In the northern hemisphere, maps are often oriented so north is up, but it is safer to pro-

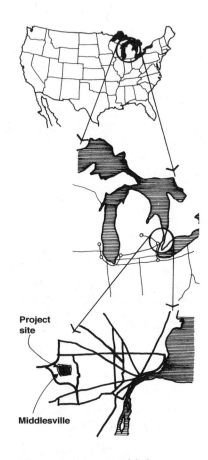

10-11. Maps to establish context

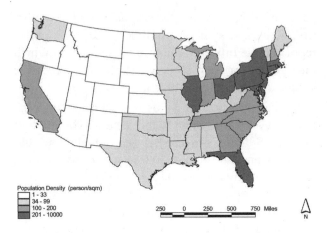

10-12. Map of population density by state (1999)

vide a north arrow to give confidence to the viewer as to the orientation of a map. Especially for digitally produced maps, metadata information (i.e., source data, producer and modifications made to the raw data) are invaluable information to judge the reliability of the map and actuality of the content.

There are many ways to arrange map elements (e.g., legend, title and north arrow) on a page. A typical layout may have the title at the center top or bottom of the sheet; the legend, scale and north arrow may be arranged to either side. Overall, there should be a visual balance in the layout of the page so that neither text nor drawing dominates and nothing is too dark, too light or too close to the edge. It is important to realize that each map has its particular design demands. The map maker needs to be aware of figure/ground distinctions and visual hierarchies that can be used to highlight the purpose of the map and key information. It may be useful to sketch out a few options before beginning with the actual design.

Color and textures, symbols, line thickness and typeface on maps need to be carefully selected as to not violate traditional conventions, good practice and the communicative effectiveness of the map. Geographic information software and computer mapping programs often randomly introduce color schemes; the map author needs to take care to amend these choices. It is useful to test color schemes early in the map development on the printers to be used,

as colors often appear different in print than they do on the computer screen. In general, pastel and subdued color schemes are preferable over highly saturated colors, especially when applied to larger areas. Tufte (1990) recommends choosing color differences only as strong as necessary to be visible.

Colors, symbols and textures should correspond to the type of data represented. For nominal data, symbols should vary by type; for ordinal data, symbol size or shade should vary as shown in Figure 10-13. For example, in a map showing average household income by census tract, the tract with the highest income should be dark and lower income areas

MAP PROJECTIONS

Depending on the purpose of the map, it is crucial to choose a suitable map projection in order not to distort the data depicted. Any attempt to display features from the curved surface of the earth onto a flat, two-dimensional sheet of paper distorts the proportions of the representation. This transformation is called *projection*. Modern projections can preserve

two of the three characteristics that define geographic space (i.e., distance, area and direction or angle). For most planning applications, we want area to be as accurate as possible and an appropriate projection needs to be chosen.

For example, the familiar Mercator projection of the world communicates a less precise understanding of land areas, particularly around the North and South poles, than is provided by other projections such as Peters.

Mercator's Projection of World Areas

Peter's Projection of World Areas

RASTER- AND VECTOR-BASED FORMATS

Computer-generated maps fall into one of two categories: *vector-based* or *raster-based*. In essence, vector and raster are different data structures (as discussed in Chapter 7, "Computers and Planning").

Most maps are vector-based: object-oriented projections of a three-dimensional surface onto a two-dimensional plane. Their graphical appearance is close to traditional paper maps. Points, lines and polygons are used to represent natural and human-made features. Depending on the scale, a town, village or city is represented by points or polygons. Rivers and roads are typically represented as lines and land parcels are depicted as polygons.

Raster maps use a field view to portray geographic space. Map images are divided into a regular grid; each grid cell has a value, which represents an average characteristic (temperature, color and radiation) for this area. Maps derived from digitally obtained satellite imagery are originally raster-based. Many modern Graphic Information Systems can integrate raster and vector formats.

should be gradually lighter. Good maps do not have to be colored. A black-and-white line map with some gray tone shadings can be aesthetically pleasing, equally informative and easier and cheaper to reproduce than a colored equivalent.

With the Internet, maps can now be disseminated via a Web site. This is very appealing for certain planning purposes, such as collaborative design project reviews, public announcements, tourist information and road or traffic updates. So-called Web maps can potentially be viewed by a large audience and can be easily updated. Web maps can be static or dynamic (i.e., display the change in traffic congestion or cloud cover every 10 minutes). In addition, some maps display change based on user interaction; that is, an individual can interact (click) on hot spots on the map to get to linked information or change the scale and area of the map through zooming and/or panning.

Design rules for paper maps also apply to Web maps; however, Web maps are limited in terms of (file) size and resolution. It is usually not effective to take a traditionally produced paper map and scan it, as the information density on a paper map is too high for the screen.

Drawings

The types of drawings used in planning can range from freehand sketches (made quickly on tracing paper, newsprint or a chalkboard during a discussion or presentation) to finished, drafted and accurate drawings that may become legal contractual documents (such as a zoning map). Perspectives, isometric and axonometric drawings that create a three-dimensional, simulated view (Figure 10-14) are popular devices for public presentations.

The development of these technical drawings used to require a great deal of skill and time. Increasingly, computer-generated maps and drawings are used in planning agencies. Plotters take over tedious, repetitive drawing jobs. Software programs automatically generate perspective and views from various angles once the building model has been developed.

Accuracy and precision of machine-produced drawings are high and cannot be matched by draftspeople. However, in many cases, hand-rendered drawings are still produced for presentations of projects because they appeal to the public and

10-13. Graphic map symbols (adapted from Robinson et al., 1995)

extract essential elements of place from the designer's perspective.

Cartoons and Caricatures

Cartoons and caricatures can be particularly powerful if developed with the right blend of professional insight and humor. Cartoons have often been used to communicate issues of social policy or power relationships in a proposed planning project. The graphics can be used to lighten up a presentation and get people to consider critical issues without directly being offensive.

Photographs and Slides

Photographs are widely used in planning documents and presentations. Good photographs that are well integrated into a report, or slides that are properly sequenced and thematically interjected into an oral presentation, are a relatively inexpensive and powerful means of communicating information. Today's cameras are easy to use and allow inexperienced users to produce reasonably good images and slides.

More importantly, the technology for developing and processing film and digital images has advanced tremendously over the past decade. With one film, a range of images and formats can be produced at relatively low cost. For example, it is fairly standard that digital images on a CD-ROM or disk can be obtained in addition to prints and negatives. These digital images are typically created so that an image is provided in various resolutions in a format that can be imported or manipulated by most software applica-

tions on the market. The low resolutions are about 72–100 dots per inch and are suitable for display on a Web site. High-resolution images are more than 300 dots per inch and are suitable for printed matter.

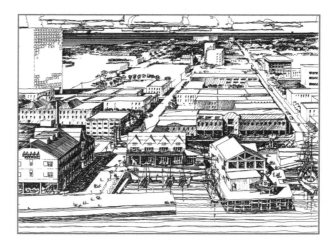

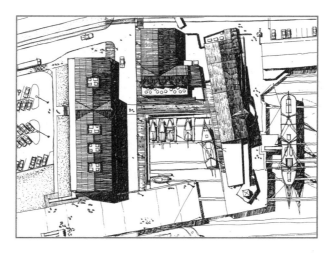

DIGITAL IMAGES AND FORMATS

Digital images are stored in various file formats. For raster images, the most common file formats are:

* *Graphic Interchange Format (GIF):* an older format and particularly good for line drawings, although continuous-tone images (photographs) are not very well reproduced

* *Tagged Image File Format (TIFF):* files with this format usually stem from scanning images; provides a lossless compression; is the best format to keep originals and master copies of scanned images; most universal file format; can be read and transferred across most platforms

* *Joint Photographic Experts Group (JPEG):* specifically developed for digital photographs; achieves a high level of compression to keep file sizes small while maintaining superior image quality

* *Portable Network Graphics (PNG):* increasingly replacing TIFF format

10-14. Hand-rendered sketches and drawings

The virtual model can be used to calculate views of the new building or development at different times of the day or year and to analyze shading of façades, sidewalks and places.

Digital images can be easily integrated into text documents, such as reports or media releases. They can also be uploaded on Web sites or used in digital presentations.

Crossing platforms is increasingly easy. Digitally prepared images can be converted into slides using specific slide makers, while slide scanners can digitize existing slides. Digital cameras provide images directly in electronic format. However, good digital cameras can be expensive and the transfer of images to a computer usually requires additional software and equipment.

Videotapes, Internet Animations and Films

Video and movies are excellent methods for documenting existing conditions or planning processes. For example, video recordings of a public space over a few days will demonstrate people's paths crossing the place and preferred seating arrangements. Video or digital taping can be used to both record and broadcast a public meeting to other venues or local television channels. Documentary films about the construction of infrastructure projects like dams, natural habitat regeneration or public services (such as health care or transportation services) can be used to record case studies or events, trigger discussion and educate various constituents. The cost of making a movie is relatively high; however, the impact of the product may be worth the investment. Low-cost alternatives are videotapes, digital tapes or interactive Web sites that include animations, sound and photographs.

Three-dimensional Models

Models of planned projects are widely used by physical planners. The scale of these models ranges from studies of infill developments to urban design and master plans. Lay people relate to models and understand them easier than sectional or abstract bird's-eye drawings. Models can be either physical miniatures of expected developments or virtual, three-dimensional simulations to be experienced on a computer screen. There are benefits to both; nowadays, the two are often related insofar as the physical model is developed via computer-aided manufacturing techniques. This means that the model is first built using a computer-aided drafting (CAD) software application, and then built from parts based on the virtual model and cut or carved out by a machine.

The virtual model can be used to calculate views of the new building or development at different times of the day or year and to analyze shading of façades, sidewalks and places. Since these images are digital, they can be loaded on a Web page and be accessible to a relatively wide audience, who can view and assess it without having to be physically present at a meeting or public showing.

In contrast, physical models are unique (often only one is built) as there are significant costs in terms of skill and time. While computer modeling of physical environments has become more sophisticated than 10 years ago, there is still a lot of skill and computing power involved to create realistic-looking renderings of buildings and street scenes. Thus, physical models are often used to simulate and analyze the impact of proposed projects within the existing urban fabric. They provide a three-dimensional experience. In particular, physical models of urban areas have been used to assess the impact of high rises on the shading of the streets and sidewalks and on the subsequent changes of wind flows.

Planners may choose to use models, boards and various artifacts to simulate processes of development. Games are sometimes used in community workshops and provide an opportunity for participants to see—modeled in three dimensions—what planning processes at work do to the physical environment. This type of interaction typically leads to a high level of personal involvement.

Virtual Reality

Immersive virtual reality (VR) simulations can be very powerful, but they are also very expensive to produce. Generally, special equipment (such as a binocular omni-oriented monitor (BOOM), or a head-mounted display that is used with a VR data glove that allows the user to grasp and manipulate virtual objects) is needed to experience VR.

The Cave Automatic Virtual Environment (CAVE) is the most sophisticated and advanced technology for immersive VR available to date. The CAVE may be best described as a surround-sound, surround-screen, multiprojection-based VR room. The illusion of immersion derives from projecting computer images so that corrective stereo glasses provide a correct perspective for a person linked to the computer via a tracker.

Despite much progress over the last decade, VR images are still crude and not very detailed. Furthermore, the immersive virtual environment cannot be easily shared. In a CAVE, the stereo images produced by a computer are correct only for the active viewer (the one who carries the tracker). While VR is used in medicine and engineering, planning applications so far are relatively rare but are likely to increase in the future as the technology becomes more accessible. Spin-off technology (i.e., low-key, three-dimensional environments displayed on a two-dimensional computer screen) replaces the immersive virtual environment described earlier. This technology is already used in various experiments for community planning and participation.

GRAPHIC TOOLS, MATERIALS AND PRODUCTION

Coming to grips with the different options for creating graphics is not always easy, especially as graphic production is always in a state of rapid technological transition. How has technology changed over the past two decades? Traditionally, pencils, black and colored felt-tip pens, ink pens, pastels and watercolors were used on various media ranging from newsprint and cheap yellow tracing paper to card stock and high-quality drafting paper. Straight edge, flexible rulers, stencils and erasing shields are still used but are complemented with drafting applications, geographic mapping software, plotters and laser printers.

Despite much progress over the last decade, VR images are still crude and not very detailed.

Computer technology and the Internet require a different set of skills, including the knowledge of how to import, export, transfer, manipulate and transform data and images, shifting them from analog to digital, in and out of computer applications. Instead of manually cutting and pasting drawings into a report, digital images are imported or inserted into a text document. Color printers and plotters produce most final drawings now, replacing manual drafting methods.

On the one hand, this technology has streamlined much of the production process. In the past, corrections of drawings involved careful erasing and sometimes time-consuming redrafting; mistakes on computer-generated diagrams and graphics may now be corrected with as little as a keystroke or two. On the other hand, time savings are often less than expected, especially when staff is not well trained or the system was recently changed or updated.

The computer revolution in the planning office comes with its own problems (see Chapter 7, "Computers and Planning"). Different but equally costly mishaps can happen: files are corrupted; colors print out differently than the screen image; or the plotter runs out of memory and aborts the production process. Furthermore, audiences raised on television, video and computers, who therefore expect slick and professional-looking graphics and presentations, are constantly pushing quality standards.

Regardless of the technique chosen, the process of designing and producing graphics needs considerable advance planning. The first step is to choose between the many different media. There are no hard-and-fast rules for this. The decision has to be made in the case of each project on the basis of suitability and appropriateness for purpose, time constraints, cost, future use and experience of available personnel.

In the case of urban design projects, it is common that initial ideas are drafted by hand and, once a final concept is chosen, the plans are entered in a CAD package. From that point, changes are made to a succession of digital files. In some cases, designers have moved away from this tradition and are experimenting with designing the project using various sketching programs. These allow initial drawings and sketches to be produced to convey the tentative nature of the design concept to the client or at public consultation meetings.

Medium choice will influence a graphic's future. Graphics that will be used often or require frequent changes, such as a regional zoning map, are best created and stored in digital format as the digital file is more easily changed than the physical one. The versatility with which a digital drawing can be reproduced, enlarged, altered and reprinted is a good reason to invest in quality digital production—although, initially, the time and cost to produce an image digitally may be greater than a quick, handcrafted drawing.

For projects with a limited budget, some expensive visualization techniques, such as animation, may not be considered at all, as the cost would exceed available funds. However, if time is not an issue, the planning director may invite their friend

For projects with a limited budget, some expensive visualization techniques, such as animation, may not be considered at all, as the cost would exceed available funds.

(the planning professor from Hiatonka State University) to make the project a final-year topic for his graduate urban planning class as a way to generate some alternatives to be considered.

Under time pressure, it is often worthwhile to stick to techniques with which one feels comfortable and where good products can be achieved within the given time frame. However, there is also merit in experimenting with new approaches and ideas. A new look, using a computer-animated video—rather than the traditional watercolor drawings for a new waterfront development project—will get fresh attention from the audience. If new techniques are used for the first time, additional time should be budgeted to compensate for delays due to inexperience.

Different graphic media and tools have benefits and drawbacks, some of which will be elaborated in the following text, which is divided into three parts:

1. traditional graphic media and tools
2. electronic media and tools
3. transformations between formats

Traditional Graphic Media and Tools

One of the simplest, but nonetheless most versatile, graphic tools is the *pencil* and its relatives, *charcoal* and *sketch pens*. The latter two produce thick lines and broad strokes and are typically used to create sketches of ideas or schematic diagrams, flow charts and the like. Pencils (see the sidebar entitled "Types of Pencils and Their Use") come in two general types: wood-encased or mechanical. Mechanical pencils are lead holders that allow adjustment of the lead length available for use. Modern micro leads for pencils come in sizes from 0.7 mm to 0.3 mm and need no sharpening. In addition, pencils come with different types of lead and can be used to produce renderings, sketches and technical construction drawings.

Technical ink pens are used for drafting crisp technical and presentation drawings. When used on white paper or vellum (semitransparent white paper), these drawings can be copied and reproduced easily. Technical pens come in different pen point sizes varying from 0.13 mm (0.005 inches) to the very wide 2 mm (0.079 inches). Using technical pens requires some practice, as the pens need to be held close to a vertical position to ensure equal line thickness and ink flow. Furthermore, when using a straight edge or ruler, one needs to take care that the ruler is elevated over the paper to avoid the ink bleeding along the ruler's edge.

Ink pens require careful handling and cleaning to prevent clogging. Very fine ink pens (0.18 mm or smaller) are especially fragile and their functioning can be hampered by dirt on the drawing surface or rough papers. They tend to fail easily (often in critical moments of time pressure); thus, it is advisable to have replacement tips handy for important projects. The availability of pens with ink cartridges, rather than those that must be refilled from ink bottles, has reduced the risk of clogging.

Markers and *felt-tip pens* come in color assortments with narrow, round or chiseled tips. Black felt-tip pens are an alternative to charcoal and thick pencil and are quite useful for making sketches, flow

TYPES OF PENCILS AND THEIR USE

Soft lead pencils are labeled B, 1B, 2B and up to 6B, indicating increasing softness; they produce a dark and heavy mark. Hard pencils are labeled H, 1H, 2H and up to 9H in increasing order of hardness; they produce lighter and well-defined lines. Pencils labeled #2, F or HB are general purpose and have a medium grade and softness that lies between H and B. Special pencils can be used to draw lines that will not show in a reproduction.

Line weights vary with the pressure applied to the pencil lead on the drawing surface. Regardless of pressure, softer pencils usually produce thicker and darker lines than hard pencils. Hard-lead pencils are employed when accurate technical drawings are required, whereas softer leads are typically employed for lettering, arrows and freehand work.

Line thickness and appearance also depend on the drawing surface. The smoother the surface, the harder the pencil needed. If uniform lines are required on a grainy, rough paper, one needs to select a hard pencil. Soft pencils on rough papers will produce thick and irregular lines that tend to smear. Humidity also impacts the quality of the pencil lines. High humidity tends to make the leads harder.

diagrams or stylized maps. Narrow, pointed markers are often used to redraw or trace pencil drawings to give the final image a freehand, informal look. High-end felt-tip pens with gauged sizes are often used instead of the more volatile and expensive ink pens. Yet, the micro-tip felt-tip pens do not create the same darkness and solid color as waterproof ink.

Colored felt-tip pens and magic markers are often used to produce sketches and color in line drawings. As colors and the effects achieved by felt pens and colored markers vary with the paper, testing is advised to avoid bleeding and muddy-looking results. In general, it is impossible to get uniformly consistent colors with felt pens, as strokes remain visible and overlaps of lines result in darker coloring. An image may look neatest with all strokes going in the same direction.

If these characteristics are taken into account, the effects can be regularized to give texture and patterns that enhance the overall effect. Felt tips and markers dry out easily and should always be capped when not in use. Even with good care, the color density of a marker fades with age and use, thus new pens of the same tone will give a different result than older ones.

Watercolors, *pastels* and *colored pencils* are other means of coloring drawings and diagrams. In contrast to felt-tip pens, these tools produce softer and more delicate colors. Pastels are easy to work with and can produce exquisite results on various types of papers—even tracing paper. Watercolor is also a wonderful medium that requires special rag paper for good results. It can create beautiful graphics once a reasonable skill level is attained.

For quicker results, a similar effect can be achieved using water-soluble colored pencils, where the drawing is initially colored with pencils and then wetted with a few brush strokes in strategic places. The advantage of this technique is that less water is used and the paper consistency is typically not a problem, although some sample tests are advised. Any decent quality drawing paper will work.

Airbrushing is a graphic technique that produces effects by spraying paint on a drawing or model. The skilled airbrush artist can create subtle colors and gradations. At one time, this made airbrushing the medium of choice for realistic-looking presentation drawings; today, it is often replaced by rendered computer drawings.

10-15. Drawing tools

A variety of different *papers* and *card stocks* are available to suit the medium and purpose of the graphic. There is a range of tracing papers, which are semitranslucent and useful for tracing drawings, photographs or other images. Tracing paper comes in different sizes and qualities. Flimsy, thin (often yellow or "canary") tracing paper is sometimes used as sketching paper.

An idea or design can be developed successively through multiple overlays in which details get changed slightly. Heavier weight tracing papers are sturdier and are used for ink drawings, which are to be reproduced through copying or diazo processing. Alternatively, ink drawings are made on vellum or polyester film. This is the most expensive option but, in the right situation, is well worth the cost.

Polyester drawing film is durable and dimensionally stable. It is therefore particularly suited for drawings that are reused and serve as base information for future work, such as boundary lines, street patterns or existing vegetation. All of these papers come in standard-size sheets or on rolls up to a width of 36 inches.

Colored papers, card stock, linen and rag papers and illustration boards are also commonly used. Specialty papers, like linen and rag papers, can be used for design sketches. If they are not too thick, a line drawing can be copied onto them with the help of a photocopier. The drawing can then be embellished with pastels or colored pencil. Nice effects can be achieved using pastel on colored and structured papers. Illustration boards are thick, opaque boards. This requires that drawings be made directly on them. Erasing on these boards is difficult as it almost always dampens the glossy finish. Rather than using illustration boards directly for drawings, planners may use them as a background and a mounting surface for illustrative materials and text.

Other equipment for graphic production includes a wide variety of *rulers, straight edges* and *guides*, vinyl rub-on lettering, stamps and templates. The straight edge or parallel rule is the basic tool that, together with triangles, allows drawing orthogonal horizontal and vertical lines without much effort. Triangles typically come in 30-, 45- and 60-degree angles; fancier ones are adjustable to any degree between 0–90 degrees.

Bendable rubber rulers or French curves facilitate the drawing of complex shaped lines. A compass or template is useful for drawing circles and

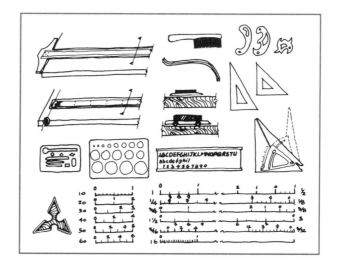

10-16. Drafting tools

other regular shapes. As everyone makes mistakes or adjustments to drawings, a range of erasers (suited to various media and paper) needs to be at hand. Rubber or gum is used to erase charcoal, pastels and soft pencil. Hard erasers, razor blades or electrical erasers are used to scrub off ink from drafting film. Thin steel erasing shields help limit the area on which the rubber is applied.

Text is applied by hand lettering for sketches or by using templates for more refined drawings. To streamline the production of drawings and maps, preprinted labels with the project name, north arrow, scales and agency name can be glued to drawing sheets. Typically, titles and the like are copied on self-adhesive film ("sticky back"), which is then transferred onto the vellum or polyester film. Rub-on lettering and self-adhesive tone papers for textures are also available.

Lettering and font choices should be made so that the typography matches the drawing. For example, the text for drawings with thin lines and light coloring should also be fine and airy, whereas bolder drawings can be complemented with darker, heavier fonts.

When embarking on manual drafting and drawing, it is important to configure your workspace appropriately. It helps to have an area in the office designated for graphic design, with a large table featuring a smooth, light surface. Having one with an adjustable height and a tilting mechanism is useful but not necessary.

More important is proper lighting, which is best achieved with a movable lamp so shadows can be minimized. A brush to dust away rubber and loose

More and more, design professionals rely on digital media to assist them in creating graphics. Images can be created digitally from scratch or by using a mixture of techniques.

graphite is also very useful in keeping your drawings clean and tidy.

Electronic Media and Tools

More and more, design professionals rely on digital media to assist them in creating graphics. Images can be created digitally from scratch or by using a mixture of techniques.

Input: The computer keyboard, mouse or trackball, stylus and digitizing tablets (the largest ones look similar to drafting machines) are input devices with which one creates form, builds digital models, chooses colors and manipulates graphic characteristics. Scanners are in a somewhat different category; they operate more like a photocopier. Rather than creating a physical color or black-and-white copy, scanners create a dot-by-dot digital copy of photographs, drawings, sketches and diagrams. Large-format scanners can accept up to 48-inch-wide drawings or maps.

The graphic is displayed on the computer screen and scanning software includes a variety of tools to control the capture of the image. In order to work efficiently with large-size graphics and maps, the computer monitor should be large (19–21 inches) with a relatively high resolution (see also Chapter 7, "Computers and Planning"). Although the resolution on the output will not match that on the screen, a high-resolution monitor supports image creation.

Software: Graphics files come in one of two types: *raster* or *vector*. These differ in the way the graphic information is stored in the computer. Raster images consist of an array of dots or pixels, which have various color or gray values associated with them. A low-resolution raster image has fewer pixels than a high-resolution image of the same physical size. When enlarged, raster images often become blurry and lack definition. The file size of a raster image is proportional to its resolution; file sizes for high-resolution images can be very large.

In contrast, vector-based images store information about the drawing via mathematical equations. Most graphics programs, except when they specialize in photographic image manipulation, work with the vector model. The vector model is also the choice for product and architectural modeling. File sizes are generally smaller for the same representation if the image is vector-based. However, the graphic image output is often raster-based.

File formats help to indicate the type of image format that is used. Raster file formats include:

- Joint Photographic Experts Group (JPEG)
- Graphic Interchange Format (GIF)
- Bitmap (BMP)
- Portable Network Graphics (PNG)
- Tagged Image File Format (TIFF)

Examples of vector-based file formats include:

- Windows Meta File (WMF)
- Initial Graphics Exchange Specification (IGES)
- Drawing eXchange Format (DXF)
- PostScript (PS), Encapsulated PostScript (EPS)

See also Chapter 7, "Computers and Planning."

Most graphics software is task- or profession-specific. Tailored applications exist for data visual-ization, drawing and painting, drafting and three-dimensional modeling and mapping.

Some of the more accessible *data visualization* programs are spreadsheet and statistics software, which provide standardized functions for graphing data. Histograms, scatter plots, bar charts and other chart types are produced from a selected data range. Appropriate legends can also be produced and manipulated to suit specific purposes. The output can be in black and white or color, and a range of background textures and letter fonts are available to refine the appearance of the graphic.

Many programs allow you to simply "copy and paste" graphs and charts into other programs to incorporate them into larger drawings, presentations or text documents. This is the easiest and fastest option but one that is not always available.

Another option is to export the image. Typical export formats include JPEG, GIF or WMF. In some cases, the output can be written into PostScript files. PostScript files can be imported into most word processing applications but are not always visible because they are dependent upon the setup and program used. However, as long as the printer and plotter are capable of Postscript output, the image will print correctly.

Drawing and *painting* programs usually focus on two-dimensional representations of graphics. They contain a set of functions to manipulate raster-type images (GIFs, JPEGs, BMPs), such as scanned photographs, and allow the creation of simple, vector-based line drawings. To facilitate drafting, they contain templates with basic shapes, such as triangles,

Most graphics software is task- or profession-specific.

squares, circles and arrows. Shapes can be resized, rotated and mirrored by the click of the mouse. Again, images can typically be transferred ("copied and pasted") into other programs.

In contrast, CAD software uses one of three different *three-dimensional modeling* approaches (solid modeling, extrusion and wire frame). It is the preferred software of architects, landscape architects and engineers. The applications are powerful enough to handle large datasets and generally focus on vector-type drawings. The software facilitates the creation of three-dimensional digital models of cityscapes or buildings, which can then be represented as sections or perspective drawings. Volume and materials used can be calculated from the model, as well as structural dimensions. Such three-dimensional digital models are the basis for virtual walk-throughs and animations.

For map design and spatial analysis, GIS specialist software packages are used. In addition to map representations, most programs provide spatial analysis functions such as buffering and overlays.

Two other types of software used in planning, which are not primarily graphics applications but make use of graphics, are word processing programs (essential for reports) and presentation software, such as PowerPoint. Both of these permit insertion of graphic images into text and have some graphics creation capability.

Output (printers, plotters, video and film): Although digital graphics can be embedded as files directly into a presentation, e-mailed to a project team member or linked to a Web site, most files are (still) printed on traditional surfaces (paper or drawing film) using black-and-white and color printers with a capability of up to 10 × 17-inch formats.

Various types of plotters—pen plotters, electrostatic color plotters or ink-jet plotters—are available to print larger images and maps to opaque white or colored paper, vellum, polyester film on precut sheets or print media available in rolls up to 36 inches wide. When working on large projects, it is prudent to check on ink supplies so that specific colors do not run out during a project. (See also Chapter 7, "Computers and Planning.")

Transformations Between Formats

These days, graphic production is seldom constrained to one technique. Computer graphics are colored by hand, hand-drawn images are transformed into digital formats and other transformations make possible the effective use of graphics in planning practice. Technology facilitates the transfer of graphics from one medium to another. This creates great flexibility in terms of presentation techniques, data acquisition and image transfer.

For example, in the past, slide presentations required using a camera and slide film. Any drawing material or text to be incorporated into the presentation needed to be photographed on a copy stand. Computer applications can help avoid this step. Text, images and graphics are put together and either printed out on overheads or directly presented.

As the resolution of digital projectors is not always satisfactory, especially when addressing large

Technology facilitates the transfer of graphics from one medium to another.

audiences, analog slides can be produced directly from the presentation software by high-end photo services with a slide maker. The reverse conversion (from analog to digital) is also common. Old documents, photographs in journals and from archives, title sheets of legal documents, diagrams or excerpts from newspapers can be reproduced in various ways by photographing or copying them. They also can be converted to digital objects through scanning. A specialized slide scanner will convert old slides into a digital graphics format such as JPEG or GIF, which can then be used in reports or digital presentations.

Traditional film can be digitized when it is developed, while originals can be scanned and digitized for use in text documents, Web pages and presentations. Movies can be converted into videotapes. Large drum scanners are used to scan maps for later use in different drawing or GIS programs.

Scanning typically results in a raster format, which then needs to be vectorized for use in a typical object-oriented drafting or GIS program. Most software for processing scanned images can do this; however, dirty or damaged maps and drawings may result in scans that contain too much noise to be vectorized. Therefore, it may be necessary to digitize or trace the map before it can be used in a GIS.

It needs to be noted that, for some images, the analog-to-digital conversion will lead to considerable loss in quality. For example, maps that are scanned and then presented on a Web site are usually not very readable. The resolution on a Web site is typi-

cally 72 dots per inch, whereas the resolution of a paper map is 600 or 1,200 dots per inch.

Using the computer to produce graphs, diagrams and drawings makes it easy to combine color, text and graphics and to transform images. In professional drawing packages, functions such as pastels, charcoal or watercolor exist as an option for rendering and transformation.

Figure 10-17 shows how a scanned photo has been transformed using different "filter" functions of a

10-17. Digital photo transformation

Original photograph

Line conversion

Color explorations

Artistic representation

computer application. Shading and texturing, which was difficult and time-consuming to do with sticky-back labels, can now be easily achieved with digital graphics. Banners, background colors and clip art are also readily available.

FORM AND STYLE

Whilst part of what we perceive comes through our senses from the object before us, another part (and it may be the larger part) always comes out of our head.
—JAMES, WILLIAM.
THE PRINCIPLES OF PSYCHOLOGY,
NEW YORK: H. HOLT AND COMPANY, 1980.

Selecting a medium and presentation format appropriate for the purpose at hand is a key component to successful graphic communication. Each medium has its own limitations and characteristics. The nonverbal message intrinsic in graphic formats, styles or media should also be considered. A report may contain many detailed graphics with explanations that a reader can browse, study and digest at their own pace, while the information provided during a presentation with overheads or slides must focus on key issues, as the amount and resolution of graphics and text that can be presented is limited.

Further, it is important to remember that prior experience and associations influence the perceptions of individuals. Often people see (only) what they know or want to see. Aside from explaining graphics during a presentation or in the text, it is useful to adhere to established conventions. One such tradition is the color scheme for zoning maps and

master plans (e.g., depicting vegetation, parks and recreation areas in green; water in blue; residential areas in yellow; and commercial ones in red). Solid lines are often used to show existing roads and features, whereas dotted or dashed lines may show planned extensions, nonpaved footpaths or tentative features.

Graphics depicting plans for multistage development projects often rely on color coding to distinguish between the various development phases. Coloring the most current stage in bold colors and future ones in successively lighter shades is intuitively understood. The scheme reflects a common experience, as features in the far distance become hazy and appear lighter in color.

Style, materials and media contribute substantially to the nonverbal message of a graphic. It is important to get the audience into the intended mode of thinking and perception early to avoid wrong impressions, which are frequently hard to overcome. The use of graphics for preliminary works, for example, should reflect the formative stage of a project. Merely labeling a graphic or presentation as preliminary is not sufficient. The format and layout of a draft document should be simple. Likewise, graphics developed for presenting initial ideas need to give the client or community group the impression that the ideas are amenable to change.

Citizen groups can become nervous and even hostile if they are presented with what appears to be an accomplished fact when they are expecting a dialogue and discussion of ideas. Soft colors, pastel or

Style, materials and media contribute substantially to the nonverbal message of a graphic.

pencil sketches, hand lettering and alternative versions can help underscore the message that a project is in a conceptual stage. The use of cheap rather than glossy paper further supports the message that the project is not yet finished. A model with removable parts is another option to highlight the preliminary nature of the design. Working models or games can be used effectively in community workshops to incorporate residents' own ideas into development plans.

Mechanically printed CAD or GIS drawings, with their uniform coloring and precise lines, indicate that the design is complete and finished, undermining any tentative notion. For this reason, many offices avoid using computer graphics for preliminary design presentations. Several techniques can be employed to soften the appearance of computer drawings. Sometimes software provides the functionality to modify lines and images so they appear uneven and hand drawn. This may or may not work in convincing the audience of the formative level of the design.

A better option is to trace the computer drawings, hand color and then embellish them with a few additional lines. Another effective strategy to highlight the tentativeness of a design is to integrate computer drawings into a collage of clippings, sketches and brainstorm lists. By contrast, final presentations should be polished, organized, proofread and printed on high-quality paper or card stock. A highly organized display or skillful presentation instills authority, pride and confidence. The final report may be lavish and even use color plates and foldouts.

Graphics in Presentation

The importance of learning to make a convincing and organized presentation cannot be overstated. Particularly as planners increasingly assume more than a technical adviser role, they are in the business of selling ideas and solutions or facilitating negotiations. Graphics, such as drawings and photographs of places and people, as well as charts, can effectively support all kinds of presentations and arguments.

In oral presentations, graphics and visuals conventionally consist of slides, overheads or projected digital images. Alternatively, videotape can be shown, or original drawings mounted on boards, to illustrate the points a presenter makes. For urban design projects, three-dimensional scale models of the project make impressive exhibits. The presenter may draw on one or several of the above options; however, for the sake of coherence and consistency, not too many types of media should be mixed.

Presentation medium and setting: A presentation needs careful planning in terms of the amount of information, level of detail and order of images presented. Many presentations today make use of LCD projectors, which transmit digital images or text directly from a computer onto a screen rather than using traditional slide projectors and overheads. Some LCD projector models have the high light capacity and refresh rate to project video as well.

The use of this technology can be very effective as the presentation software (e.g., PowerPoint) facilitates animations and hotlinks, which allow the presenter to phase in and out of images or "jump" to

In oral presentations, graphics and visuals conventionally consist of slides, overheads or projected digital images.

The choice of presentation medium also depends on the size of the room and the audience.

different parts of the presentation in nonsequential order. As a result, the focus of the presentation can be adapted to the needs of different audiences. Images that have been shown during a presentation can be quickly brought up again for the question-and-answer session without having to run tediously through half the slide show. However, digitally projected images often lack the contrast and resolution needed to clearly display complex graphics and maps; therefore, maps or detailed drawings are better presented as slides, overheads or originals, which are mounted on boards.

The choice of presentation medium also depends on the size of the room and the audience. Larger audiences are better served using slides, as it may be difficult for people seated in the back to view original drawings; for small audiences, display boards may work well. Graphics that can be mounted and hung on walls have an advantage over projected images, because they can be left in place and the audience can examine them before and after the presentation. This is effective, especially when alternative design schemes from a competition are presented.

Prolonged and repeated opportunities for the audience to review the designs allow them to identify and familiarize themselves with the options to a greater extent than possible in a one-time presentation. In evening sessions, the activity of walking from drawing to drawing keeps the audiences alert and engaged. On the other hand, a well-designed slide or PowerPoint presentation gives the planner the advantage to focus and stress those aspects of a

project or policy that they deem important. Showing slides and commenting on them gives the presenter more control over the audience's attention than when the audience reviews graphics on its own.

Graphics need to be designed as much as possible for a specific purpose. The size of the drawing and lettering, and major symbols, should be large enough to be recognizable at the back of the room. A good rule of thumb in deciding on letter size is to remember that a 1-inch cap height type can be read by an audience at 50 feet with proper lighting, and a 2-inch cap height type can be read at 100 feet.

High contrast between text and background increases readability. Coloring can help emphasize important elements; however, color choices and contrasts need to be carefully considered. Dark blue text on a dark green background is difficult to decipher. Color contrast works best with light colors on dark backgrounds (e.g., yellow text on dark blue background). White type on a black background (reverse type) looks 10% larger than the normal black type on a white background. Light/dark contrast also helps insure legibility for color-blind observers. If you are presenting to adults, avoid the overuse of primary colors when more subtle hues are available.

For slide presentations, only the most necessary text, good color contrast and strong baselines should be employed to enhance readability at a distance. Bullet-point lists should be short, single spaced and preferably left justified. If at all possible, the format should be uniform with some overarching connecting design features, such as a project logo, similar color schemes and graphic techniques.

If display boards or a wall mounting is used, displays should correspond in sequence to the presentation itself. Typically, they are arranged in the order to which they are referred in the presentation, so the presenter can go down the line and summarize what has been said. Alternatively, the boards can be first presented by a speaker in front of the audience and then subsequently mounted on the walls by an assistant.

Prepare and test, practice and rehearse: Before a presentation, equipment such as overhead, slide or LCD projectors and videotape recorders should be checked to make sure that they are positioned correctly and are in good working order. This is particularly critical if more than one projector or technology is to be used. It is disconcerting to both the audience and the speakers if mechanical difficulties disrupt the flow of the presentation.

When presenting at a location away from the home office, checking the availability of technology in the remote location is wise. Phoning the local technician for details on software versions, Internet access speed (if necessary) and hardware requirements a few days ahead of the event is useful to fine tune the presentation and to be sure that the files are in appropriate formats. The most impressive digital slide presentation is no good if the software, computer and projector are incompatible.

It is also a good idea, when working in an unfamiliar setting, to take files on several different media (e.g., a Zip disk and a CD-ROM or e-mail the file ahead of time to the local technician). Always bring a low-tech backup, such as overhead slides, just in case. In technology-poor environments, formats requiring less technology are often more reliable unless you can afford to bring your own equipment. When slides or films are used, the room should be sufficiently dark to allow for glare-free viewing of the images. At the same time, completely darkened rooms prevent the audience from taking notes. It is helpful to have some spotlight on the speaker (from above, not below). Display materials and models should also be sufficiently lighted.

Timing is crucial. The presentation should be kept within the limits of the time allocated. If you overrun, you may not be allowed to finish your conclusion and recommendations—or worse, people may leave before you can make your most important points. The number of slides and images needs to be kept to a manageable amount. There is nothing to be gained by overtaxing the patience and attention span of an audience. If you are unsure about the timing of your presentation, make a trial run with a friendly audience, such as your colleagues. This is a good way to obtain feedback and reactions. (See also Chapter 8, "Speaking Skills for Presentations.")

Useful hints and tricks: One way to keep an audience's attention is to have a good mix of both the subject material you present and of media used. For instance, graphics can be of physical spaces in the form of photographs and drawings; of data in the form of charts, diagrams and graphs; of people, to lend some

When presenting at a location away from the home office, checking the availability of technology in the remote location is wise.

human interest and dynamics; and of historical pieces that establish continuity with past traditions.

A good mix of graphic types (e.g., charts, slides, photographs, diagrams and handouts) coupled with perhaps more than one person to make the presentation can liven the proceedings. Avoid reading out the text or bullet points of slides, which the audience can read themselves. Memorable presentations can consist of presenters role-playing a city planning commission hearing or a formal advisory panel, to the delight and amusement of the audience, as well as convincingly communicating their point of view. Techniques need to be carefully adjusted to the situation. The medium must fit the message and the audience.

It is obvious that planners using graphic illustrations in presentations before groups should stand beside the chart or diagram (to avoid obscuring the graphic) and the speaker should talk to the audience. It is very disconcerting to listen to a speaker who talks to the image on the wall. It may be useful to have a laser pointer or baton to point to key items such as locations on a map or highlight important outliers on a chart.

A summary handout sheet for the audience, using the same graphics in reduced form, will remind them of the main points of the presentation. Software such as PowerPoint lets you print out entire presentations in a format where four to six images are reduced so they fit on one standard, letter-size page. This handout can serve as a guide or a program to the presentation. The audience's attention should be drawn to it so they understand what it contains. The presenter should refer to it throughout the talk and remind the audience of it; otherwise, an audience will generally not read it, especially if the presentation is lively and informative. However, repeating key words and figures in the handout can reinforce the verbal and visual message.

In most cases, the planner is interested in assuring that handout material is read, taken home and referenced. Handouts and materials for dissemination are particularly necessary if local television, radio and newspaper reporters are present. Providing them with well-organized material enhances one's chances to get good and accurate coverage.

Explaining graphics: Although graphics are often self-explanatory, they should be referred to and explained in presentations. Those who routinely use maps, plans and elevations in their work tend to forget that many people are not as well trained to visualize objects from two-dimensional abstract drawings.

It is important to remember that the audience may not necessarily interpret the graphs and diagrams in the intended way. Sometimes, they may not be able to read the text but can see the colored trend lines; explaining the chart helps them better understand what is presented.

If you are using a map juxtaposed with slides to walk people through an area, point out on the map the vantage point from which the slide is taken, and move back and forth between the map and the slide so the audience understands the connections between the two graphics being shown.

> *It is important to remember that the audience may not necessarily interpret the graphs and diagrams in the intended way.*

Document Design and Planning

Document design is important because it helps readers find and understand information more quickly. Page layout, typography and sequence of content all need to be considered in designing a report, a set of drawings or a Web site. In compiling a final report, the planner can draw on the graphic material produced for the project up to that time and plan to integrate as much of it as possible.

Using some of the material that has had a favorable response during the intermediate stages of the project will, when used in the final report, give a sense of continuity to the reader who has been previously involved with the project. Modifying some of the work slightly (e.g., reducing it in size and adding labels or explanatory notes and legends to existing graphics) may make them appropriate for the final report, publicity releases or the Web site. As many of the graphics may exist in digital form, it should be easy to format them with the same fonts and color scheme to achieve a coherent appearance throughout the report.

Page layout: The layout of a page, a poster or a report defines the spatial arrangement of text, images, symbols and "white space" on a sheet. The way information is presented on the page impacts the way it is perceived. For example, centrally formatted text in a narrow column is generally assumed to be poetry; dense, multicolumn texts are associated with newspaper print.

The thoughtful spatial organization of graphics and text on a page—either a traditional paper document, an interactive Web page or a display board—helps to prioritize information, furthers the communication with the observer, conveys implicit meaning and directs a reader's attention. Clarity and order on a page convey the presenter's control over the subject and inspire the audience's trust. A badly organized presentation or report is likely to be much more critically assessed. In the worst case, the reader focuses on spellings and alignment instead of content, or gives up reading the document entirely.

A good mixture of visuals, text information and white space will help to capture the attention of readers and observers, whereas a dense text document without much contrast or structure is difficult to read. Visual balance, hierarchy, contrast and consistency are important elements of good page layout. The concept of visual balance and stability is derived from our physical sense of balance and refers to a visual sense of equilibrium on the page(s). (Note that you need to consider left and right pages as a unit when you are working with double-sided print.)

While the physical equilibrium experienced in reality is easy to comprehend, visual balance on a two-dimensional sheet is a trickier concept. Symmetry or approximate symmetry may be achievable with a map or drawing but difficult with text, unless one opts for right- and left-justified text and centered images. Large, unusually shaped page elements (e.g., an image or a headline) attract a reader's attention first. Headings and indentations, font size and types or color can help create a visual hierarchy that structures the page into relatively easy-to-comprehend elements.

A good mixture of visuals, text information and white space will help to capture the attention of readers and observers, whereas a dense text document without much contrast or structure is difficult to read.

Another issue is visual consistency, which applies equally to a report or a set of drawings that will be on display. One way to achieve consistency is to apply a grid, which divides the page into more or less regular sectors for the placement of text blocks, headings, images and captions. The grid pattern shown in Figure 10-18 is designed for a letter-size page with a three-column option. Different possibilities of how this framework might be divided are presented.

The choice of the number of columns is largely a matter of aesthetics. Single-column documents are easier to produce and are preferred by some readers. Multiple columns give more flexibility in terms of placing figures and captions. A shorter line length improves legibility of the text. A compromise may be a narrower, single-column text area with sidebars for thumbnail images, citations, symbols and headings.

Consistent headings and footers, page borders and font choice also help create a unified look. Font sizes and graphic reductions should be planned so that, in the final publication, text sizes are consistent. Templates and stylesheets insure the consistency throughout a document. Although they may be tedious to initially develop, these preparations will save much valued time later on in formatting and fine tuning the appearance of text documents.

Typography: Another important visual cue in reports, presentations and charts is the choice of font. The three major classes of fonts are serif (strokes or little cross lines), sans serif (no strokes or cross lines) and specialty fonts. Other classifications distinguish

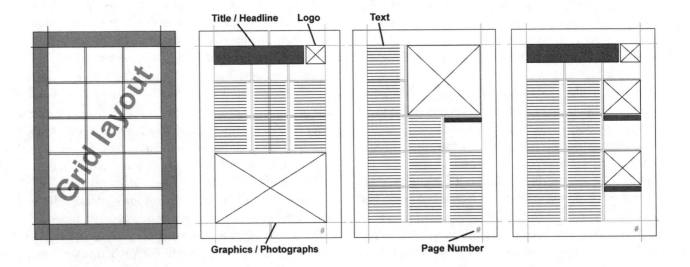

10-18. Page layout based on grid

between classic fonts, which show little distinction between thin and thick lines; and modern fonts, which have strong variance between thin and thick lines, monospaced and proportional typefaces.

Serif fonts, such as Times New Roman, have serifs at the end of the letters. These fonts exude an aura of seriousness, dignity and class. Sans serif fonts lack the serifs. They often appear more geometric and simple. As western cultures are not accustomed to reading sans serif fonts, large text portions should be done using serif typefaces to facilitate reading speed. Sans serif fonts, such as Arial or Futura, are perceived as unusual and thus read more slowly. They are often selected to emphasize document elements like headings and titles.

Specialty fonts are expressive and are generally reserved for graphics such as drawings or advertisements. They can be very useful for enhancing the message of posters. Fonts that mimic handwriting signal an informal, conversational tone. Script and specialty fonts are typically not used for professional reports or documents. In making font selections, readability as well as appropriateness for the purpose need to be considered. Table 10-2 shows a range of font types and associated characteristics.

When choosing fonts for a document, report or drawing, the type of font should be appropriate to the purpose. For publications in which text dominates, the font types should not vary to a great extent, as this makes the text look too busy. Rather, visual hierarchy can be established by using different font sizes and weights (light, bold or extra bold).

TABLE 10-2
Font Types

Font Class	Name	Character
Serif	Bodoni	Formal, aristocratic, modern
	Baskerville BE Regular	Beautiful, has quality, urban
	Times New Roman	Traditional, efficient
	Century Schoolbook	Clear, elegant
	Garamond	Graceful, fragile
Sans Serif	Franklin Gothic	Urgent, blunt
	Futura	Severe, utilitarian
	Helvetica	Simple, contemporary
	Arial	Modern
	Berlin Sans FB	Contemporary, ultra modern
Specialty	Helvetica Neue Bold Outline	Outline: classic, dignified
	HELVETICA	Italics: speedy, emphatic
	Zapf Chancery	Graceful, handwriting, personality
	Westminster	Computer-like, sci-fi
	Bauhaus 93	Architectural, designy
	Old English Text MT	Irish, Celtic
	SHOWCARD GOTHIC	Playful

TABLE 10-3

Font Sizes

Element	Type Size (in points)
Chapter titles	18–36
1st order headings	14–24
2nd order headings	10–18
Body text	8–12
Figure captions	6–10
Figure labels, notes	6–10
Page headers and footers	6–10
Annotations in graphics	5–8

TABLE 10-4

Monospaced vs. Proportional Fonts

Opportune City	ML00	789,040
Middlesville	JI18	579,000
Hiatonka	XX76	1,400,356
Opportune City	ML00	789,040
Middlesville	JI18	579,000
Hiatonka	XX76	1,400,356

There are no hard-and-fast rules on the use of font size, but the listing in Table 10-3 provides a starting point for the design of reports. It is also a good practice to examine other documents for guidance. Other means to provide structure and emphasis on text pages are underlining, italics, outlining, shadows, color, line spacing or indentations of text blocks. However, if used without consideration, these modifications can seriously impede readability and overall appearance. Long passages in UPPERCASE or *italics* are more difficult to read than lower-case text. Thus, it is wise to limit upper-case use, except perhaps for high-level headings.

Typographical choices for graphs, drawings and maps are particularly difficult. Tables and lists may look neater with monospaced fonts where each character takes up exactly the same space; for proportional fonts, the character space is adjusted to the width of the letter or number. Table 10-4 shows the differences between the monospaced Courier (top) and the proportional Palatino (bottom). A somewhat irritating effect arises where the four-digit proportional font code for Middlesville is much narrower than the ones for Hiatonka and Opportune City.

Font use on Web pages is an entirely different and complex issue. The designer cannot exactly control the appearance of a Web page as with a printed document. Screen resolution, browsers and monitor sizes vary significantly—all of which influence how a viewer will see the Web page. Personal settings of individuals can change typefaces and font sizes. Legibility should be of greatest concern. A simple ordering and clear hierarchy is even more important here than on paper. The use of complex graphics or specialty fonts that require the use of images should be avoided where possible to reduce the upload time. For a detailed discussion, see the resources in the "Bibliography."

Organization: Effective communication is facilitated by a well-structured report or presentation. Storyboards or a dummy are useful tools to help organize and plan a presentation or report. A storyboard consists of a series of panels or sections that narrate a story in which the text may only be outlines of the points to be made, accompanied by rough sketches of any illustrations that may be needed. (The emphasis is on the narrative.) A dummy focuses on the layout, organization and look of a printed document or presentation. (The emphasis is on the graphics and production of the final product.) Both are needed to ensure an uninterrupted logical flow of the narrative and the accompanying illustrations.

A dummy for a report involves attention to the page layout, and helps plan how blocks of space can be used for various bits of information, artwork, maps and diagrams and to insure visual consistency. A dummy (Figure 10-19) also gives a sense of how long the report might become, what additional work must be completed and/or an assessment of production costs.

Sideways graphics should be avoided if possible and large graphics may usefully be divided or reduced in size. The dummy can be used to schedule a team's work, decide on the quality and cost of reproduction techniques, use of colors and sizing of graph-

ics. Furthermore, the overview achieved through the dummy layout can help prevent duplication or omissions. A report should not be padded with repetitions of maps and graphics that are not enlightening or useful in further clarifications. To the reader who is paying attention, such padding is annoying; to the one who is skimming, it is confusing.

Planners must leave enough time when completing a final report to proofread it. All pages should be

10-19. Preparing a dummy for a report

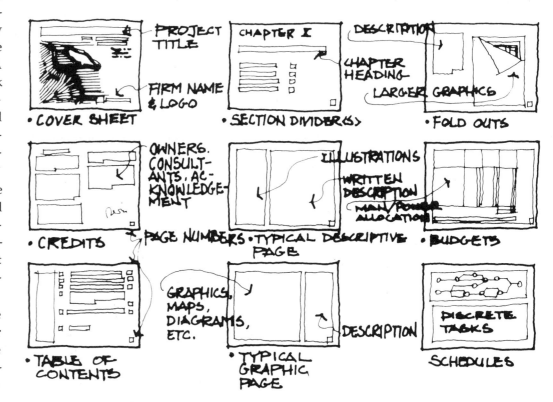

numbered, including those containing figures, illustrations and diagrams. Cross-references, tables of contents, figure numbers and references need to be checked. Much of this work is aided by word processing software, especially spelling- and grammar-checking functions, and the automated creation of tables of contents.

However, technology is just an aid and is no replacement for manual proofing. There are mistakes that spell-checking software does not flag (e.g., when words with the wrong meaning are used but are spelled correctly). For example, if "errant" is misspelled as "errand," the spell-checking software will not detect this error. Also, if the style template is not consistently used or a heading is mislabeled, the table of contents will be incorrect.

Regular backups during work in a word processing program are a must. Incorporation of diagrams and images increases file sizes and handling may become slow. It is a good practice to insert figures toward the end of the report production and merely refer to them during most of the document preparation.

In the atmosphere of crisis that prevails when a project is being completed, leaving aside the final half-day for such checking is difficult. Conversely, a well-integrated, complete manuscript evokes confidence in the author and the work. It is generally worthwhile to have a thoroughly completed and cross-checked document rather than one more illustration or one more paragraph. There is nothing more dismaying than to find, after one has produced hundreds of copies of a manuscript, that a client's name is missing or, worse yet, misspelled; that pages are out of order; and tables that are mentioned in the text are not included or show something different than what was intended.

APPLICATIONS

1. Review a planning report from a local or regional planning agency. Examine the categories of graphics used and evaluate how well they are integrated into and augment the text. Are there instances where additional graphics would have been more effective? Compare this report with others from different agencies for their use of fonts, color and layout. Trace the underlying grid structure of the pages and evaluate the organization of the layout. How many different heading types and fonts are used? Are contrasts between colors and font sizes, for example, sufficient or too weak? Which layouts do you find attractive (or not attractive) and why? It may be a good idea to keep a scrapbook or folder with particularly effective graphics and layouts for your personal reference.

2. Put together a storyboard for a report or presentation on which you are currently working. This may include the design of a master layout of a presentation (using multimedia, overheads and/or PowerPoint).

   a. Judge the color and readability of your projection. Are there any details that you would change?

b. Break down the work into categories. Estimate time and skills required for the production of graphics and text.

c. Estimate the cost of reproduction. It would be wise to keep accounts of actual time and materials used in completing the report and compare it with your estimations. Identify the items that you under- or overestimated.

3. Attend a public presentation of a planning project and assess the graphics presented with respect to:

a. quality and readability of graphics from your vantage point

b. appropriateness of graphic means for purpose of presentation

c. balance of verbal and graphic components of the presentation

d. integration of graphics with oral presentation

e. efficiency of presentation (did audiovisual equipment function? did the presenter have mastery over it?)

4. Review the Web site of a city and/or county government agency.

a. How slow or fast is the page loading? What is the image-to-text ratio?

b. How relevant and interesting is the site to citizens?

c. Is the layout clear or rather busy and confusing? How easy or difficult is the navigation? What kinds of information are provided? What would you change on the site?

RESOURCES

The Microsoft Office suite includes a range of software modules that aid in the production of simple Web pages, graphics, tables and charts (e.g., Excel and the graphing and HTML functions within Microsoft Word). Graphic tools are also included in most statistical software packages such as SPSS and SAS. In addition, a range of specialist software packages exists for three-dimensional design and rendering, layout and desktop publishing, mapping and GIS, as well as Web page design. While some of these software packages are easy to use, others do require training for effective use. Popular specialized graphic software applications include:

- *Three-dimensional design, modeling and rendering:* AutoCAD, FormZ, Intergraph
- *Drawing/drafting:* Adobe Illustrator, Adobe Photoshop, Corel Draw, Corel Paint, MacDraw
- *Layout and desktop publishing:* Adobe Page-Maker, QuarkXPress
- *Mapping and GIS:* MapInfo, ArcInfo, ArcView, Idrisi, ERDASS
- *Presentation/multimedia:* Microsoft PowerPoint
- *Web page design:* Macromedia Dreamweaver, Adobe PageMill, NetObjects Fusion, Claris Home Page, Microsoft FrontPage

BIBLIOGRAPHY

Books covering graphic communication, drafting, rendering and layout skills are generally aimed at professions such as architecture, landscape architecture and graphic design, but not specifically for planners. Instead, planners must read selectively about techniques and applications aimed at these other audiences.

Architectural and Landscape Graphics (Drafting, Rendering, Presentation)

Ching, Francis D. K. *Architectural Drawing*. 3rd ed. New York: Van Nostrand Reinhold, 1996.

> Ching offers a basic primer on traditional drafting equipment and materials, the site plan, landscape and ground textures, graphic presentation symbols, hand lettering and presentation.

____. *Design Drawing*. New York: Van Nostrand Reinhold, 1998.

> Similar to Ching's other book, *Architectural Drawing*, this innovative package of book and CD-ROM offers insights on how to share plans and visions with colleagues and the public. The volume covers hand-rendered illustrations and digital techniques.

Cohen, Jonathan. *Communication and Design with the Internet*. London and New York: W. W. Norton & Company, 2000.

> This book explains the concepts of how professionals in the built environment make use of the Internet for effective multimedia communication with clients, collaborators and the public. See particularly Chapter 4, "Creating Effective Websites"; Chapter 5, "Graphics and Multimedia"; and Chapter 9, "City Planning on the Internet."

Davis, David A. and Theodore D. Walker. *Plan Graphics*. 5th ed. New York: Wiley & Sons, 2000.

> This is an extensive source book with a compilation of examples and ideas to create persuasive graphics ranging from pencil sketches to elaborate computer-assisted renderings. Topics include site analysis, conceptual design and construction documents. Illustrations cover large- and small-scale plans.

Goldman, Glenn. *Architectural Graphics: traditional and digital communication*. Upper Saddle River, NJ: Prentice Hall, 1997.

> Goldman presents a comprehensive review of traditional and computerized drawing techniques and tools.

Laseau, Paul. *Graphic Thinking for Architects & Designers*. 3rd ed. New York: John Wiley & Sons, 2001.

> The text provides an introduction to basic and applied graphic skills, including drawing, conventions, expression, analysis and public design.

Uddin, Saleh M. *Digital Architecture*. New York: McGraw Hill, 1999.

> The focus of this publication is on digitally produced images, virtual models and renderings. Examples are accompanied by information on how they were produced, including software and hardware requirements.

Maps and Cartography

Kraak, Menno-Jan and Allan Brown. *Web Cartography: Developments and Prospects*. London and New York: Taylor and Francis, 2001.

> This book investigates the possibilities and problems of Web cartography for a wide spectrum of topics. Very useful are Chapters 5, "Basic cartographic principles"; Chapter 6, "Publishing maps on the Web" (e.g., hints for Web-safe color choices); and Chapter 7, "Web map design in practice."

Laurini, Robert. *Information Systems for Urban Planning: A Hypermedia Co-operative Approach*. London and New York: Taylor & Francis, 2001.

> This book has a scope far beyond maps and cartography. Especially useful are Chapter 5, "Hypermaps and

Websites for Urban Planning" and Chapter 7, "Visualisation for displaying and accessing urban information," which contain highly relevant information on graphic communication with many excellent examples.

Madej, Ed. *Cartographic Design using ArcView GIS.* Albany, NY: OnWord Press, 2001.

This book shows how to effectively apply cartographic design principles to produce high-quality maps for various purposes, including the Web, using ArcView GIS software.

Monmonier, Mark S. *How to Lie with Maps.* Chicago: University of Chicago Press, 1991, 1996 (2nd ed.).

This book is fun to read. It exposes blunders and distortions in maps, and is about do's and don'ts in map design.

____. *Mapping It Out: Expository Cartography for Health and Social Sciences.* Chicago: University of Chicago Press, 1993.

Extremely useful and very readable, this nontechnical volume describes basic principles of map design and use of maps in a social science context. Scale, projections, cartographic generalization and graphic logic are lucidly explained with illustrative examples.

Muehrcke, Philip C., Juliana O. Muehrcke and A. Jon Kimerling. *Map Use.* 4th ed. Madison, WI: JP Publications, 1998.

This is a revised version of a very useful book on how maps can be used to intelligently augment and illustrate the difficulties and conflicts of intervening in the physical dimensions of regions. This 4th ed. has been updated to include computer applications to the task.

Robinson, Arthur H., Joel Morrison, P. Muehrcke, A. J. Kimerling and Stephen C. Guptill (editors). *Elements of Cartography.* 6th ed. New York: John Wiley & Sons, 1995.

This book includes many useful hints and tips on cartographic design, layout and color use in maps.

Charts and Schematic Design

Henry, Gary T. *Graphing Data: Techniques for Display and Analysis.* Applied Social Research Methods Series, Vol. 36. Thousand Oaks, CA: Sage Publications, 1995.

This volume is a well-organized and comprehensive treatise on effectively graphing statistical and other data. Graph design principles and advantages and disadvantages of various graph types (e.g., pie charts, bar charts, scatter plots and histograms) are discussed.

Horton, William. *Illustrating Computer Documentation: The Art of Presenting Information Graphically on Paper and Online.* New York: John Wiley & Sons, 1991.

This volume is oriented toward the practitioner; it is succinctly written with checklists and snippy references to theory and psychology of perception. The focus is on clearly communicating complex (technical) information with the use of graphics. Particularly applicable to planning are Chapter 1, "The Need to Show"; Chapter 12, "Global Graphics"; Chapter 13, "Color"; Chapter 14, "Enriching Graphics"; and Chapter 15, "Page as Picture."

Tufte, Edward R. *The Visual Display of Quantitative Information.* Cheshire, CT: Graphics Press, 1983.

First of a series of three classics, this edition contains a range of examples for the idea of visual communication and thinking and is mostly concerned with the design of statistical graphics. Particularly notable is Chapter 2 on "Graphic Integrity."

____. *Envisioning Information: Narratives of Space and Time.* Cheshire, CT: Graphics Press, 1990.

This second volume of the visual communication series is particularly useful. It provides examples and information in Chapter 2, "Micro/Macro Readings" and Chapter 5, "Color and Information."

____. *Visual Explanations: Images and Quantities, Evidence and Narrative.* Cheshire, CT: Graphics Press, 1997.

This is the third volume of the beautifully crafted book series. Useful ideas for planners are found in Chapter 2, "Visual and Statistical Thinking" and Chapter 4, "The Smallest Effective Difference."

Wildbur, Peter and Michael Burke. *Information Graphics: Innovative Solutions in Contemporary Design.* London: Thames and Hudson Ltd., 1998.

A great source of novel ideas for visual communication, this book includes exquisite examples of different types of graphics (such as maps, flow diagrams, statistical diagrams and signing systems) for different uses.

Wurman, R. S. *Information Architects.* Zürich: Graphis Press Corporation, 1996.

Over 100 superb examples are presented on how to creatively organize information and data from transportation networks, including schedules to statistical data visualization and exploration. Each example is annotated with the designer's thought process.

Web Site Design

Lynch, J. Patrick and Sarah Horton. *Web Style Guide: Basic Design Principles for Creating Web Sites.* 2nd ed. New Haven, CT: Yale University Press, 2002.

Siegel, David. *Creating Killer Web Sites: The Art of Third Generation Site Design.* 2nd ed. Indianapolis: Hayden Books, 1997.

This book covers everything from page layout tips, to preparing graphics for the Web, to how to best update Web pages and transition an agency/office Web site to an improved structure.

Web Style Guide
(www.webstyleguide.com/index.html?/contents.htm)

This handy, online style manual reflects an adaptation of lessons learned from multimedia software design, graphic interface design and book design to the new medium of Web pages and site design. It contains useful information for people new to Web design. It is also available in book form.

Text and Page Layout

Bringhurst, R. *The Elements of Typographic Style.* 2d ed. Point Roberts, WA: Hartley and Marks Publishers, 1996.

All there is to know about fonts and typesetting is presented in this book. Most useful are hints about page layout and the selection of fonts for character and resonance with the text.

Gray, Bill. *Tips on Type.* New York: Van Nostrand Reinhold, 1983.

This was written before the widespread use of computers and word processors. It provides characteristics of various typefaces and how to design with them.

Hurlburt, Allen. *Layout: The Design of the Printed Page.* New York: Watson-Guptill, 1977.

____. *The Grid—A Modular System of the Design and Production of Newspapers, Magazines and Books.* New York: Van Nostrand Reinhold, 1978.

Both volumes by Hurlburt contain excellent examples of different grid layouts, including rules for proportional design.

Meggs, P. B. *Type and Image: The Language of Graphic Design.* 2d ed. New York: Van Nostrand Reinhold, 1992.

The author discusses graphic design elements and the process of developing holistic resonating configurations from words, pictures and images into powerful visual communication. Comparative examples are masterfully used to explain and illustrate principles like visual hierarchy or graphic resonance.

Nelson, Roy P. *Publication Design.* 4th ed. Dubuque, IA: WCB Publishers, 1987.

This is a comprehensive volume on publication design, including books, reports, folders and newsletters. Three chapters contain especially valuable practical advice: Chapter 3 covers production issues, such as color and layout; Chapter 4 focuses on typography; and Chapter 5 discusses the selection and incorporation of art and image.

Planning in the
Political Context

Kristina Ford

This chapter invites the reader to consider practical experience and demonstrates how being successful requires assimilating the points made in the preceding chapters.

INTRODUCTION

The preceding chapters of this book have provided methods by which planners can gather, analyze and present information. These constitute the array of skills that planners bring to the job as a result of their professional education. However, the point of this chapter is to reveal how using information in a political context is different from the rational process often described in books on planning methods, wherein it would appear that using information successfully in professional practice depends upon the *quality* of the information.

Methods texts instruct their readers on issues of quality: ensuring that questions on a survey do not lead to the "correct" answer, or that a sample reliably represents a population, or that hypotheses are articulated *a priori*. Surely, these are all things planners need to know to ensure that their recommendations are based on reliable information, but getting to use information at all can be a large (and largely unexpected) obstacle to successful practice—an obstacle that arises from the *political realities* of place and context.

This chapter is about effectively introducing information into political decisions. It will discuss strategies appropriate to the political context in which planning—and the use of information—must operate. Some strategies are appropriate when a decision maker has an analytic mind; others are persuasive when, for example, a political leader is most comfortable with intuitive methods of reaching a decision. In some contexts, it is acceptable to the citizenry that an elected official explain that rationality has informed their decision; in others, such an explanation would seem elitist, or worse, condescending. A professionally competent planner knows how to gather information and how to interpret it; a successful, practicing planner has these skills and also knows how to use them persuasively.

This chapter invites the reader to consider practical experience and demonstrates how being successful requires assimilating the points made in the preceding chapters. There is an intuitively rational process that a planner uses to determine how to bring information together and to communicate effectively in a context that is structured on political reality. In a sense, planning in a public agency is a performance before an audience of decision makers and all other citizens in a community—many of whom are critics. Much of the performance is improvisational—responding to some unexpected event or to some new actor on the city's stage. As with any performance, success requires preparation, study and effective communication skills.

A Welcome, of Sorts

Late in 1992, development proposals were scarce in New Orleans as the economy was stilled by the decline in oil prices that occurred in the mid-'80s. The oil bust—as it is locally known—put an end to the overconfident days of prosperity when even building doubtful tourist attractions for the 1984 World's Fair had promised extravagant returns on investment.

The collapse of oil prices caused several large oil corporations to "downsize" operations in New Orleans, moving white-collar workers elsewhere and taking away a crucial underpinning of the local economy. In the succeeding several years, the city sought vainly for workable ideas to replace the oil industry with another, equally lucrative and attractive to investors. The State of Louisiana, in the storied person of Governor Edwin Edwards, ultimately stepped in with its solution: legalized gambling in New Orleans. The city's mayor embraced the idea with little skepticism, buoyed by advisors who looked at annual reports from Mississippi's casinos and concluded, oddly, that "there is no end to the demand for gambling." Governor Edwards had in mind that the state would take a huge share of profits first, allowing New Orleans to take whatever was left over. The mayor went along with this scheme, believing the returns would be so huge—and so unending—that the city would prosper no matter how much the state extracted.

The proposal for the casino—the first such venture in an American city outside Las Vegas—was to be submitted in the first month of my tenure as planning director in New Orleans. I asked my staff to suggest what information would be necessary to ensure that this new business could harmoniously fit into New Orleans. The staff prepared a list of 125 pieces of information they would need including:

- projected number of casino customers
- building elevations, traffic studies
- parking requirements
- construction period traffic plans, even the number of hours pile driving would be necessary in the construction process (significant to hoteliers in the city's tourist-driven economy)
- security measures

I questioned the utility of each item (i.e., how the information would be used in formulating suggestions that would ensure the casino's fitting into the city without disruption) and, in the process, learned something about the individual enthusiasms of my staff. For example, one planner wanted the developer to provide particulars of the casino's interior design, hoping, in his words, to determine whether the casino would in fact be the "must-see" destination various casino operators promised.

The question—and indeed its answer—was beyond a planner's expertise; even more importantly, to require its answer would corroborate a commonplace perception that city planning delays projects by requiring preparation of unnecessary documents. Finally, on a mid-December afternoon, we recommended to the city's planning commission that it require any application for developing the casino to include more than 100 pieces of information. The planning commission agreed.

I went home that afternoon, proud of the thoroughness of the staff's requirements, satisfied that I could justify the necessity of each piece of required information and happy with the commission's decision. I was writing Christmas cards when the phone rang at 7:30 PM, two hours after the commission had adjourned. It was the mayor and his economic

The State of Louisiana, in the storied person of Governor Edwin Edwards, ultimately stepped in with its solution: legalized gambling in New Orleans.

The mayor and his advisor hung up, clearly annoyed with my job performance after three short weeks.

development advisor on the speakerphone. The mayor said, "I've heard that the planning commission is going to require an enormous amount of information from the casino developer. What do you think you're doing?"

An easy question to answer, I thought. Speaking almost offhandedly, I said, "Mr. Mayor, we're just suggesting what information is necessary to make sure the casino fits . . ." I was cut short with a testy observation about how planners were always anti-business, always getting in the way of obviously needed jobs and tax revenues and always oblivious to the needs of the city. The mayor and his advisor hung up, clearly annoyed with my job performance after three short weeks.

This call was somewhat alarming. Certainly, I perceived an imminent danger that the mayor would see to it that the casino developer was not required to answer the questions the planning commission had authorized. New Orleans has a strong mayor form of government, and this mayor—having recently been president of the city council—had effective allies there, where the ultimate decision about what was required would be made. I called the chairman of the city's planning commission—a woman who, a short month earlier, had introduced me to the mayor as the planning commission's unanimous choice for director and had glowingly described my credentials. She said the mayor had called her before calling me.

To him, she'd said, "Oh, Kristina can explain; it's just some things that planners think are important." She perceived that he was unconvinced and reminded me that, because the casino was very unpopular with some powerful factions in the city, the mayor was sensitive to anything that might seem to be criticism of the idea or that might signal a movement to derail its progress.

In discussions with the governor, it seemed he hadn't been working on the level of factual, operational questions, but rather on the level of hopeful visions: assuming the casino is built, the conversation went, what is the proper way to split profits? The mayor's sensitivity to criticism, combined with the fact that he didn't know me personally—and therefore might have worried that I was allied with the opponents to the casino—meant that what I saw as neutral questions in search of useful information were seen by him as potentially laying groundwork for opposition.

My next phone call was to the mayor's political advisor, a former professor of political science at Xavier University. Because of his academic background, I thought he might be sympathetic to the possibility that the planning commission's quest for information about the casino's operations was only that, and had no political overtones. More importantly, because of his close relationship to the mayor, he could reassure him at a personal level. The phone call went well and he offered to help. He also gave me some advice: in the future, clear your ideas with the mayor in advance.

The wisdom of asking for information about any proposed casino—and how one might come into this old city without disrupting its traditions and ordinary functions—persuaded the city council just as it had the planning commission, and applicants were required to provide answers to the staff's requests. Based on these answers, many changes were made to the proposal that was advocated by the mayor; in fact, the building was completely redesigned based on the staff's analysis. Eventually, the mayor's sole interest—that the casino be built—came to pass, and whatever had been his pre-Christmas dislike of the planning staff's role and the qualities of its director were washed away by his enthusiasm for the casino's opening.

The Political Context of Planning Practice

There is much to be learned from this anecdote. Begin by considering the professional staff work that had created the list of information to be gathered from the casino operator. It's exhilarating for planners to work together trying to solve a problem—here, how to make sure that the huge, modern land use would fit into this small-scale, historic city—but the political world doesn't often share such professional enthusiasm and can easily be convinced it is biased against business.

The basis of planning has to be explained and made to seem important in terms that elected decision makers understand—most typically what will satisfy their constituents that some shared sense of congenial community life will continue undisturbed. Commonplace, commonsense examples of planning principles work best here:

- Providing adequate parking, for example, prevents problems of traffic tie-ups occurring in the future.
- Requiring landscaping contributes to an aesthetically pleasing streetscape, which in turn assures strong property values.
- Requiring awnings over sidewalks provides protection from rain and sun in this hot, humid, thunderstorm-prone climate.

A successful planner must be able to explain any planning precept in ordinary terms. The scenario also emphasizes the necessity for strict adherence to explainable planning principles. Planners' personal biases or preferences are inappropriate without professional justification. Asking for details of interior design in order to assess the validity of a casino developer's marketing strategy is beyond the training of professional planners.

A second lesson is the importance of understanding how the mayor—or any other authority—perceives the search for information. In a locale where information is not usually used—or where only commonly accepted information is usual (every developer recites projections of jobs to be produced and property tax revenue to be created)—an analytic question, and the information necessary to answer it, seem threatening. Here again, a commonsense explanation is the only practicable justification. Appeals to academic literature or methods textbooks are not persuasive in this environment; only rationales completely and clearly demonstrated by examples commonly known in the jurisdiction are convincing.

A third lesson is the importance of having an ally close to decision makers who is willing to speak up for the value of information. In the example, it was fortuitous that a former academic was so close to the mayor; in other jurisdictions, it will be necessary to discover such an ally.

Finally, memory and reflection are important in seasoning planners about the world in which they operate. In this example, the chairman of the planning commission framed the context of the mayor's unease and his assistant reminded me of the importance of not surprising a decision maker. A receptive planner will always have the opportunity to learn from experience—even from displeasing experience.

This chapter describes real situations that occurred while I was planning director in New Orleans between 1992 and 2000, and in Missoula, Montana between 1983 and 1985. A reader might wonder if this experience with the political context of planning is sufficiently various to bring forth widely applicable insights—a question readily answered by reading the similarities of planners' experience in such books as *What Planners Do: Power, Politics, and Persuasion* (Hoch 1994) and *Planners on Planning* (McClendon and Catanese 1996) (see the "Bibliography"). While names of actors change from city to city, as do their favored strategies for persuasion, the political environments within which planning operates—and the types of information appropriate to these environments—are the same in any American municipality. In fact, opponents of planning in Missoula, Montana, who in 1983 accused the staff of being antibusiness,

A third lesson is the importance of having an ally close to decision makers who is willing to speak up for the value of information.

were using the same arguments as opponents in New Orleans in 2000.

The New Orleans City Council has seven members (five represent individual districts and two are "at-large," representing the entire city). Term limits mean that an individual can only be in office for eight years. In seven years, I served 17 different council members—each represented different sectors of the city's diverse population and each had very different attitudes toward the function of city planning. Prior to that, in Montana, I served for two mayors, nine different city council members and three county commissioners.

Planning, whose tenets rely on a long-term view of a community, is not a particularly welcome concern of elected officials, who often perceive their chances of being re-elected as relying on tax rates and revenues, police protection and the responses to the usual complaints about any city's system of public works (potholes, broken sewerage lines and streetlights with burned-out bulbs). However, the council agenda in any city is primarily devoted to land use matters: zoning changes, subdivision requests, appeals from the decisions of officials in charge of issuing building permits and requests for waivers from the requirements of commissions, such as those constituted for purposes like wetlands conservation or historic preservation.

The business of local government is real estate, one quickly sees, and this explains the prominence of city planning in political decisions. Because land use matters are so much a part of their business, council members have to listen to planning principles and the information on which it relies. With the communication skills this book describes, both for discovering information and for conveying it, a dedicated planner can subtly interject the profession's concerns into the decision-making processes of elected officials.

In New Orleans and Missoula, I performed my duties for elected officials whose conception of planning was its utility in keeping unwanted activities—and people—out of "favored neighborhoods"; for council members who had concluded that any suggestion from city planning was antibusiness; for a populist mayor who thought legitimate planning required citizens from all sections of town be involved in land use decisions; and for single-issue council members who cared only about preservation, or only about tax revenues, or only about the environment, or only about a small group of constituents.

I served elected officials who made decisions based upon the most popular choice of action, for elected officials who made decisions based upon whose land was involved, for county commissioners who thought property rights were sacrosanct, and for other county officials who wanted to reduce the capital costs associated with unlimited sprawl.

I've worked for elected officials who have said publicly that they "have no vision of what the future should be." I've worked for mayors who had comprehensive and generous visions of their city's developed future. Although I haven't worked in a homogeneously rich town—where leaders and citizens both seem united in a vision of the best future and the best

way to bring it about—I have worked for individual, elected representatives from such neighborhoods. Even here, I've found that the apparent unity of a constituency crumbles when some new idea for land development is introduced, when neighbors find disagreement where harmony had reigned before and when the guidance this book provides is demonstrably needed.

The rough-and-tumble, messy worlds of political decision making I've known provide actual scenarios of using information in a variety of contexts. There are common lessons to be drawn from these scenarios that are representative of planning practice in most American cities.

THE DAILY LIFE OF A PLANNING DIRECTOR

The dramatic pre-Christmas phone call from the mayor was very unusual—in fact, he never called me at home again—and my job as planning director settled into a routine of daily activities and decisions that finally accumulate into public policy. In this, the effective use of information is central. A review of a typical day in a planning director's life reveals the many obvious and subtle political ways that information is used in professional practice.

7:30 AM: The day begins with a speech to the chamber of commerce about how the planning commission's new land use plan will enhance economic development. This is a touchy subject, since the economy in New Orleans has only just begun to recover from the ravages of the decline in the oil industry,

The rough-and-tumble, messy worlds of political decision making I've known provide actual scenarios of using information in a variety of contexts.

and many developers are wary of regulatory documents such as the zoning ordinance, subdivision ordinance and even the land use plan.

I've decided to frame my remarks with facts of interest to the group by summarizing the projections made by the dean of the business school—a well-known authority to most of the chamber's membership. I remark that his research indicates the best projection for New Orleans' economy is slow but steady growth. We will not suffer (or enjoy) the results of explosive growth; however, as long as we wisely guide such entrepreneurial aspirations as arise, our city will continue to prosper. The point of the land use plan, then, is to offer guidance.

A fellow planner would recognize this hopeful view as an explanation of city planning's purpose in layman's terms. However, a hand is raised and the speaker says, "Slow but steady growth! We don't want to hear that!" Indeed, I think to myself—you *don't* want to hear that! I reconsider where I am: speaking to one of the most traditional boosters' clubs, whose members want to start their day with "Good News From The Chamber!" Quickly, I get to the substance of the talk, which is a list of probusiness measures that will be included in the new land use plan. These remarks are better received.

On the way back to the office, I think of the audience and how my speech had only summarized information to which they were all in fact accustomed; indeed, the chamber's newsletter always includes the business forecasts of the dean. It was my version of his data that had clearly been too bracing for the customary upbeat ambience of this audience, although it might have been appropriate for a group of analytic bankers or realty investors. I should have simply displayed economic projections without drawing a conclusion, and started the speech with the probusiness measures that would keep the upward trend going.

8:30 AM: Back at the planning office, I review with the assistant director the staff's recommendations to the planning commission regarding various zoning applications. Much of the analysis is strong and the planners have diligently visited the areas surrounding the site of each location, but I find that many conclusions rely too much on the slippery criterion of "appropriateness." The assistant director and I discuss the use of this imprecise term, which had become commonplace in the staff's reports in the years preceding my arrival. I suggest that she work with the planners to find phrasing more closely tied to professional standards rather than to an individual's sense of taste. I also suggest that while we encourage the staff to continue their use of field visits to gather information about applications, we will also insist that they analyze what they find with a more objective set of criteria. (See Chapter 1, "Field Methods for Collecting Information.")

9:30 AM: A developer wants to see me. He assures me he enjoyed my speech this morning and was pleased that I was so sensible about spurring economic development through provisions in the land use plan. He continues, "I have five votes on the council, but I thought I'd show you the hotel we're thinking of doing that requires a map change."

I should have simply displayed economic projections without drawing a conclusion, and started the speech with the probusiness measures that would keep the upward trend going.

This sentence needs decoding. "Requires a map change" means he wants to change the zoning district that is currently assigned to his property. A spot zone (i.e., a request to be treated differently from every other property on the block) is being requested. The staff, as well as the planning commission, usually recommends that the city council deny such requests. The fact that the council usually doesn't follow the commission's advice when it applies to constituents they know (or have confidence in) explains the significance of the developer's opening clause, "I have five votes." This is meant to remind me that if five of the seven city council members disagree with the city planning commission's recommendation, it will be overruled. In short, what we recommend is irrelevant!

The developer's single sentence of introduction might seem to undercut the planning commission's discretion regarding this project. I have no doubt about the information he has used to persuade five council members to support his hotel project prior to the city planning commission's review. He has promised jobs and increased tax revenues.

These words are used to justify proposals to elected officials and have become such regimental rationales that further analysis is rarely contemplated. No official asks about infrastructure costs the project might cause, for example. The developer also assures me that the commission "has no problem" with this project—a remark that is intended to warn me that to oppose (or even suggest alterations to) his project will run me afoul of the commission. The

remark also reveals that phone calls to commissioners are swirling around items on their agenda.

He stays in my office with my staff for 15 minutes, showing elevations from several aspects, floor plans and an artist's rendering of the lobby area of his proposed hotel. My staff asks for some particulars, such as where the parking and loading docks will be—all necessary for the developer's application for a map change—but the essence of the conversation seemed implicit: this is a done deal and city planning is a bump in the road.

Confident about the questions the staff is asking, my attention turns to the fact that I'm facing two problems here:

1. How do I suggest alterations to this particular application?
2. How do I change what I now see as the usual way of thinking about planning? One might call it the operative paradigm in this community: planning decisions are binary. The city council will either approve or deny a developer's application. In this winner-take-all formulation, planners and developers are cast as adversaries; other outcomes, such as the staff's suggesting modifications to the application, aren't contemplated.

Planning is best understood as mutual accommodation by developers and planners. Planning should evaluate a proposal in terms of the full range of a community's priorities, which includes economic development (and, yes, jobs and tax revenues), and make recommendations based on those

How do I change what I now see as the usual way of thinking about planning?

Reporters cover every commission meeting and their rendition of the commission's actions is what most people rely on for a sense of planning.

terms. Getting to this understanding will require several strategies for communicating with the public, the city council, the mayor, the development community and even the planning commission.

Some of these communications can be direct (e.g., speaking specifically to the subject of city planning's value). Most of them will have to be subtle and will have to accumulate over time. For example, the staff must explain to individual developers, in common-sense terms, the reasons they think modifications to a site plan are beneficial; the planning commission must explain why it is making its recommendation (especially if the recommendation is for denial of a project) in terms the public can understand.

Reporters cover every commission meeting and their rendition of the commission's actions is what most people rely on for a sense of planning. This last thought leads me to wonder how recently the community has reviewed its land use plan—an activity that can revitalize citizens' engagement with planning in its most hopeful terms. Clearly, changing an encrusted paradigm will require perseverance and patience because it will take a long time. In thinking about the appropriate set of strategies, I first need to figure out how we've gotten to this point and what previous directors (or staff) have done that either contributed to this formulation or failed to change it.

Some of it I can discern for myself. I consider how the developer's opening remarks assured me of the irrelevance of what my staff might suggest. It's certainly possible that the planning staff has not offered the kind of common-sense supporting rationale for

their analysis necessary in a political environment. Perhaps planners have not pointed out how their modifications actually can improve projects, nor have they convincingly argued that their goal is not to stop development, as some council members might believe.

I remember my first meeting with one county commissioner in Missoula, who started our conversation by asking "Are you against development?"

I answered, "I'm against bad development."

She laughed. "Well, I can agree with that!"

My direct language surprised her and opened a small window for planning to come through, as long as the arguments we made seemed to her good common sense. For example, a cul-de-sac in a proposed subdivision was too small for a fire truck to turn around in. She voted with our recommendation that the radius be increased, despite the developer's assurance that the cost of extra paving would "kill" the project. (It didn't.) This memory corroborates what I'm beginning to sense in New Orleans: some failures of planners to persuade are at least partly traceable to reliance on such evasive terms as "appropriateness" rather than a clearly demonstrable shortcoming of a project.

Back to the developer in my office. Perhaps his being able to convince city council members to approve his project in advance of the planning commission's recommendation is traceable to our not having been effective in communicating the fact that economic development (and the resultant jobs and tax revenues) are only some of the important items on the community's agenda. I also realize this particular conversation will most probably result only in small changes to this developer's plans.

Like many who present their plans to us, he has already made a considerable investment in the site plan and prettily drawn elevations (and perhaps an option on the land itself), and quite understandably is reluctant to be sent back to the drawing board. Bearing this in mind, toward the end of the conversation I ask him to consider whether the staff's questions and suggestions weren't sensible. I suggest that he come see us earlier when he plans future projects. Perhaps our suggestions could be incorporated before he has paid consultants to design the buildings, I remark, trying in this small way to insinuate the value of planning.

10:30 AM: It is time to return phone calls accumulated during the morning, write some press releases about future public meetings and plan for a retreat with the planning commission to discuss the reasons for prohibitions against their receiving ex parte information. This refers to information given without the other side present (in this case, private conversations with developers without hearing another side).

The developer's assurance that the commission "has no problem" with his project could be wishful thinking or bullying, or it could be based upon his having already argued his case and privately solicited individual commissioner's opinions—ex parte. The latter possibility can be addressed, although delicately, since members of citizens' boards typically have confidence in their judgment about others and,

without some compelling explanation of the different standards they must achieve in their public role, will not act in a way that might seem, in their private life, to be impolite!

In any town, many developers or their supporters know several commissioners personally, and it would be awkward for the commissioner not to listen to a friend's point of view regarding an item on an upcoming agenda. Oddly, my job is to interpose a new standard for conversation and, of course, to explain the reason it is important to individuals who might not have questioned their own behavior or judgment about other people in years. I must exercise diplomacy in explaining the reasons that ex parte information is inappropriate (i.e., its potential to bias a result by not exposing the information to an opposing point of view nor to analyze its basis) and then to suggest phrases the commissioners can use to politely exit such a conversation.

I'm thinking of this metaphor: Developers invite us to look at the world from within their property. From this vantage, most of what any developer imagines makes internal sense. City planning must at least walk across the street, metaphorically, and see how well the proposal fits in to the rest of the scene. Will it cause traffic congestion? Will it be out of scale with the surrounding properties?

One reason for prohibition of one-sided conversations is that the information presented is not analyzed. Developers are, of course, partisans of their own projects and they might have ignored or misinterpreted important information. Without hearing

the staff's analysis of what has been presented, or without hearing the other side, it's very easy not to *walk across the street from the project* and determine objectively how it might fit into the rest of the city.

Also at the retreat, I will begin my paradigm-shift strategy by discussing the nature of the recommendations the commission makes: I'm trying to change the notion that theirs is a binary choice, with one side "winning" and the other "losing." Here, too, examples based on familiar situations will be most persuasive, although I'll avoid using actual cases that have come before the commission because individual members might feel embarrassed or affronted at being criticized.

11:45 AM: A citizen calls and, in a noticeably shy manner, says that he lives in the part of town next to the locally famous firm that manufactures Mardi Gras floats. Worried that the firm intends to expand its operations by buying adjacent houses, he and his neighbors have formed a neighborhood association and would like me to come speak at their next meeting.

"We want to know what you have planned for us," he says. It's a very poignant moment and, even as I agree to come early the next week, I can't help compare this conversation—with a citizen who has practically no knowledge of city planning and how it operates—to the conversation with the developer who assured me he "had five votes." I plan for both of them and largely based upon the same type of information; however, the persuasive task is quite different for each.

LUNCH: I've arranged for a GIS consultant to make a presentation on this new technology and to describe its possibilities to city department heads who regularly use geographically based information (e.g., municipal address, block and lot, and city streets).

New Orleans lies below sea level and suffers from flooding whenever there is a severe storm. The city has received a generous federal grant to create a GIS that will model alternative flood prevention measures, and that the Federal Emergency Management Agency (FEMA) trusts will reduce future disaster claims. The grant provides funds to set up a system for the city's 350,000 individual parcels, which means that with a little creativity, the descriptive and analytic needs of many agencies—not just those that deal with flooding—could be enhanced.

Locations of street reconstructions, complaints reported and responded to, and where new capital facilities will be located are all useful maps the GIS could produce and that departments could use to analyze their own performance, deploy their staff more efficiently and convey to the public the breadth of city services.

Using information from California (where the consultant's firm has installed a prototype GIS), the speaker's first example shows how the common requirement for sending legal notices for public hearings can be automatically generated by the system, how the best route for an ambulance responding to a 911 call can be determined and how patterns of assessment can be analyzed.

> *I'm trying to change the notion that theirs is a binary choice, with one side "winning" and the other "losing."*

The consultant even shows that if a public building such as an elementary school is on fire, the GIS can show fire fighters the locations of the most volatile areas (e.g., oil-burning furnaces and electrical fuse boxes) while they are driving to the blazing building.

The consultant is very well spoken and has dazzling visual displays. There are no questions; I'd even say that many eyes had glazed over—and not just from the aftereffects of the lunch we served! I realize that the audience of department heads—dedicated and smart as they are about what they do—are very poor at generalizing. If the demonstration is not particularized to New Orleans, if the analyses GIS can perform do not precisely respond to questions they've been asked before and if the system isn't already available, they can't see its application.

Although this example may seem prosaic or dated to a planner who works where GIS has been embraced, the scenario is really about new technology—whatever it is. In Missoula, the new technology in 1983 was word processing; many city agencies were unconvinced that it could possibly improve the performance of a particularly talented secretary or that professionals could overcome the notion that their status was threatened if they started doing "clerical" work.

Chapter 7, "Computers and Planning," talks about how computerization varies greatly from city to city and remarks how some areas are still poorly equipped. One might think that such locales would be eager to receive new technology and put it to use.

However, though the abstract principles may seem persuasive to the well-informed planner or consultant, department heads think more on the here-and-now level of practicality. Taking the time to use actual examples from actual departments helps, as does making references to questions asked by citizens and elected officials in the city.

In short, thoughtful preparation for a particular audience is crucial to success. It is also helpful to enlist support from the mayor or governing authority. In New Orleans, when the financial officer set about installing a new computerized financial management system, he initiated a series of lessons to teach employees how to use it, but overcame the grousing at these classes by announcing at the outset that, after a certain date, no checks (including paychecks) would be issued from the old system. It was this last preparatory action that "convinced" the bureaucracy—much as the threat of a failing grade "convinces" a reluctant student. Finally, competition is a confederate of persuasion. If one department head gives a successful GIS presentation at a budget hearing, other department heads will want to seem equally professional when they make their case to budget decision makers.

Reflecting on the flat response to the lunchtime presentation, I consider a different strategy from today's, when I tried to galvanize interest from "below." Although I am sympathetic to overworked department heads who see implementing this technology as an additional chore, I can see that ultimately GIS would make any of our jobs more

. . . thoughtful preparation for a particular audience is crucial to success.

AN ELECTED LEADER'S RESISTANCE TO ANALYSIS

I once appeared before the Sewerage and Water Board (the agency responsible for the storm water and sewerage system, for operating the pumps that remove the water from New Orleans streets and, in this low-lying city, for making it possible for people to continue to live here). I came to ask that the Board consider matching some money allocated by the city to develop the Geographic Information System (GIS). This didn't seem like an outlandish request, particularly at this time, which was the week after a tropical storm had passed over New Orleans, flooding many neighborhoods. The reason the federal government was assisting in the system's development was to help the Board create a mathematical model of rising storm water under different conditions of wind and rain duration; based on that data, they were to determine where to increase pumping capacity to prevent flooding.

At the end of my presentation, one Board member (a woman who was also a member of the city council) asked, "How would this system have helped the lady who stood at her front door last week, watching the floodwaters rise up over her front porch?" Her question could be answered, of

continued on page 355

effective in terms of simply and vividly explaining our value to a skeptical public.

Why is this important? I consider the people whose very job depends on being able to convince citizens of their value: the elected leaders. If they could be convinced of the utility of this technology, elected officials could insist that departments prepare reports using it.

I think back to recent city council meetings and the types of questions the members ask. I will ask the consultant to prepare a GIS presentation for the city council at which there will be maps of each councilmanic district. We will show where streets are under repair; to indicate growth, we'll show where building permits have been issued; we'll prepare city-wide maps of public recreational facilities open after school, or where there is the greatest incidence of broken sewer or water lines.

By choosing the type of information most consequential to the elected leaders, and by choosing to demonstrate a visual way of presenting information they often request, I'm trying to enhance the probability that GIS will be embraced by the people who can require its implementation.

1:30 PM: It is time for the semimonthly city planning commission's public hearing—always interesting because it's where planners hear information from citizens. Today's first case involves authorizing a snowball stand (which sells crushed ice flavored with syrup) in a poorer part of town. The stand would be a small building erected in the middle of what is now a vacant lot. The staff recommended

approval, noting that the entrepreneur was "going to put this vacant parcel back into commerce"—a planner's version of regimental information, equivalent to developers' "Jobs!" or "Tax revenue!"

However, in one of the unexpected turns of human society that can occur at public hearings, the proposal turns out to be controversial to neighbors near the site. An elderly man comes to the podium with his wife and identifies himself as a retired police officer. He tells us that he'd learned, in his years on the New Orleans Police Department, that snowball stands sell products other than snowball cones—an observation loudly applauded by his neighbors in the audience. ("Drugs" were the implied "other product.")

He concludes by presenting to the commission a petition signed by 100 residents in the area who opposed the snowball stand. His wife speaks next, holding up a hand-drawn map that depicts her sense of the stand's market area: a circle with a 10-block radius, which includes in its northern quadrant a notoriously dangerous housing project. On the map, she had drawn the paths she expected teenagers from that housing project would follow to the stand, bringing with them the potential for the violence that accompanies drug sales. She ends her presentation in an even voice, saying, "We know where we live and we're willing to put up with our fair share of murders—but we don't want to put up with more than our fair share."

The man who proposed the snowball stand reassures the planning commission that he intended to sell nothing more than snowballs and observes that, in his opinion, the petition had not been signed by a representative group of the neighborhood, but only by the retired police officer's family and friends.

After asking a few questions of both the neighbors and the applicant, the planning commission recommends denial of the zoning change.

This is an interesting case in almost every way, partly because it reinforced my sense of the power of maps as visual aids to decisions and partly because it reaffirmed my belief that everyone who lives in an urban setting is a city planner by circumstance. Perhaps it demonstrates most of all that what might seem objectively a small matter can actually be very large in the ordinary workings of a neighborhood. It also provides an unusually vivid rationale for the traditional requirement of holding a public hearing on land use requests—a tradition that seems tedious and outdated to many citizens and an unnecessary delay to many developers, but which, as in this case, can elicit a point of view previously unknown or unconsidered.

The opponents in this case (the retired policeman and his eloquent wife) were unusually compelling, but wouldn't the concerns they described have been equally valid if articulated less vividly? Today's meeting was dramatic, but it was also lucky that these people came ready to speak so directly. Rather than relying on such luck, planners must find ways to be in touch with all constituencies in a city, perhaps by seeking out informal "informants."

Where the planning staff is larger than in New Orleans, planners can be assigned to specific parts of town precisely to stay in touch with localized concerns. With or without informants, however, it is helpful for planners to walk the streets of an area—much as Assistant Planner did in the Middlesville trash receptacle scenario (see the sidebar "Two Scenarios" from the chapter entitled "Introduction")—to learn more about neighborhood dynamics, how community life can be kept healthy and what threatens to disrupt harmony. The various communication skills described in several chapters in this book are used by planners to discern a neighborhood's feelings.

Responsive planning commissions rely on the staff's informal contacts throughout the city; they do not simply take testimony over some development proposal, awaiting a chance remark that resolves an issue unambiguously. Such reliance is analogous to expecting courtroom trials to reach Perry Mason denouements when the guilty party confesses!

4:30 PM: The last meeting of the day is with the city council president—a civil rights hero in New Orleans and the former principal of an elementary school. Today, she wants to hear about the commission's decision on the snowball stand because she has had many constituents call her, alarmed that the staff had recommended approval. We talk about how the meeting went and how the neighborhood had convinced the commission that the proposal was about more than bringing a vacant lot "back into commerce."

In fact, I say, the incident is actually an excellent example of why there are planning commissions, which function in part to temper rationally logical

continued from page 354

course, but not on its implicit terms of immediate fixes.

I said, "The purpose of the GIS is to model storms and to devise mechanisms to prevent flooding. At the point a drainage ditch has overflowed its banks, GIS cannot help."

The Board member said, "I thought so," and surely thought she had undercut my request. To continue in this discussion would be pointless and would lose the sympathy of the other board members who could see the wisdom of modeling flooding to prevent its recurrence.

A staff member later said to me, "You should have said that we could make sandbags out of the discarded computer paper generated when the model was being tested. She cannot conceptualize what a mathematical model can do!" His response was funny and relieved the tension caused by the meeting. However, it's very useful to remember that planners are sometimes most persuasive by not having the last word, but by relying on the strength of the whole argument to carry a vote. Insisting on having the last word can make a planner seem to be a "know it all" at best, and argumentative and confrontational at worst.

professional advice with a more intuitive sense, grounded on qualitative information about what a neighborhood requires to keep it healthy. Because she will have to pass on the planning commission's budget in the future, it seems like a good time to mention the utility of having a staff large enough that we can assign planners to particular parts of town to learn the complex dynamics of different areas.

As I leave this conversation, I wonder whether we would have recommended denial of the developer's request even if we had had the model of planning in place that I described, in which the staff had discerned how the neighborhood would respond to the snowball stand. Aren't the reasons offered by the staff for approval—bringing an abandoned piece of land back into commerce, for example—valid? Would we have recommended denial because the operation *might* become a locus of illegal activity? Probably not, because such a recommendation would have been based more upon the inadequacy of enforcement and policing in this neighborhood than upon professional planning principles.

Had planners known more about this neighborhood, we could have recommended approval subject to conditions that responded to the neighbors' concerns.

Had planners known more about this neighborhood, we could have recommended approval subject to conditions that responded to the neighbors' concerns. We could have assured proper operation by requiring the operator to provide a private security patrol or we could have limited hours of operation to times of the day when there was ample foot traffic. With the appropriate information, the "right" decision could have been reached and perhaps this use could in fact have been a welcome addition to the local economy. This is an example I can use at the planning commissioner's retreat, as a way of explaining the type of change in perception about city planning I hope we can achieve by demonstrating our responsiveness to real concerns of every type of neighborhood. *We are not gatekeepers; we are problem solvers.*

This day is typical for the way information has been used and imparted. It is also instructive about work in a political context. Planners in government use information, analyze problems—sometimes before they exist—and develop solutions that they then try to persuade an authorized authority to adopt. For example, planners ask a developer who wants to build a casino to estimate the number of customers who might gamble on ordinary days, as well as on "peak" days, in order to anticipate and provide for parking needs. Failing to do this would mean traffic tie-ups and discouraged customers who might even decide that it is too difficult to go gambling at the casino again.

Planners try to anticipate common urban problems (as well as unforeseen problems) and forestall these problems in ways I just suggested about the snowball stand. Working with the community, they try to articulate a common "community good" and bring it about. They try to understand a citizenry's aspirations for the future. In all these activities, planners need information, but they also must explain why they need it.

The example of the casino parking, which explains why asking for the predicted number of customers is related to the adequate provision of parking, uses ordinary urban events and can be a model for planners trying to explain why they need any piece of information. Indeed, both the developer who assured me that he had five votes and the mayor who worried about hidden reasons for asking the casino operator questions were arguably unaware of the rationale behind the planning staff's request for information. Citizens, too, can be uninformed about what planners do and the basis upon which they make recommendations.

There are several reasons for this. One is professional laziness on the part of planning staff that tire of providing explanations for what seems obvious to them. For example, when a citizen asks why planners ask about the dimensions of a sign, the planner who replies "Because the zoning ordinance requires it" has lost an opportunity to make planning rationales clear; worse, the planner has made planning seem obscure, rigid or arcane. This perception, of course, loses the citizen as an ally—or even as a sympathetic observer—in the future.

Another reason that people don't understand planners' needing information is more willful, as in the instance of developers who hope to stonewall any revisions to their site plan by arguing that there is no need to provide particular pieces of information that might raise questions. Yet another reason is a tendency to portray anything that government requires as "antibusiness"—a slogan that is particularly powerful when a local economy is weak and

when the planners have not been diligent in explaining what they do.

As students become urban planners, they assimilate the planning rationale that lies behind their quest for information, and concentrate on ways of gathering information reliably and presenting it clearly. In the political realm, what is equally important—and rarely taught in a graduate-school seminar—is how to be persuasive on the political stage. Put most crudely, it isn't enough to be "right"—an observation that junior planners are most usually, and most unhappily, surprised to discover. To be successful, planners must persuade a skeptical audience.

How, then, does a planner persuade? As a day in the life of a planning director demonstrates, the answer to this question depends in large part upon *who* is being persuaded. In other words, in order to develop strategies for using information, an effective planner must understand the actors before whom a case must be made. The practice of local government planning is a very public task, executed on a stage with many other actors.

THE COMMUNITY AS A STAGE

Communities are an assemblage of individuals who have different reasons for living there, different reasons for staying there and different notions about what constitutes the best future for their community. Despite obvious differences, citizens accommodate one another's point of view because of some shared sense of their community that allows events to be understood within that context. Discovering that

The practice of local government planning is a very public task, executed on a stage with many other actors.

shared sense is an intellectual quest for all planners—even those who practice where they've always lived. In addition, there are subareas of town where citizens feel a part of the larger area but, on a day-to-day basis, more typically identify with their immediate neighborhood.

When I came to live in New Orleans, I received much friendly guidance about how to "understand" the city. This town is really two towns, I was usually told, though the character of those two towns in these descriptions varied across narrators. It was the French Quarter and everything else; it was the West Bank of the Mississippi River and the East Bank; it was Protestant and Catholic. Mostly, it was Above or Below Canal Street—uptown and downtown. I listened to these pairings, tried them out as organizing principles and eventually discarded them as unnatural reductions of what I know cities contain.

Place

A planner's ongoing task is to comprehend and reconcile both the tangible fact of a city—New Orleans, in this first example—and the less easily calculable attitudes of its inhabitants. City maps are a good beginning because they display geographic relationships. They also record the evolution of municipal and private action taken upon how land is used (e.g., naming streets, installation of public works, building housing developments and dedicating parks). In Chapter 1, "Field Methods for Collecting Information," it is noted that in preparing even rudimentary maps to represent factual data, planners "... might

City maps are a good beginning because they display geographic relationships.

learn of greater complexity in social relations, which are embedded in the spatial layout, than had been imagined in the original community model."

In New Orleans, I saw a town that developed by accommodating to a difficult terrain and to diverse and changing forces of nature. At first encounter, it was probably unimaginable to create a lasting city here—in a swampy bog below sea level and alongside a river that could flood every year. The map underscores that our forebears chose not to trust the power of human rationality in developing the town.

Consider how New Orleans might have developed. The city was started as the French Quarter: a neat, 66-square grid, laid out with the precision to be expected of a French military engineer designing a fortified town. If this orderly arrangement had been insisted on, subsequent streets would have paralleled the original grid, resulting in a town as predictable as Chicago, built on a postulate that man's order can dominate natural uncertainty.

The map of New Orleans, however, displays a different principle at work: a provisional relationship with the Mississippi River. There are levees and canals, as well as the solution to a perplexing problem in geometry: how to provide a useful, reasonably predictable matrix of streets parallel to the sweeping 180-degree arc of the Mississippi (the source of the descriptive phrase, "The Crescent City"). Evidently, there was no imperious city engineer insisting that streets be straight in order to provide an efficient traffic flow; as a consequence, the major avenues through town generally curve along with the river.

A planner surmises that what the map shows as an accommodation to natural forces must vividly or at least implicitly reflect the town's civic humors. Having accepted the incommodious nature of the city's placement, citizens live with awareness that life is provisional, hence New Orleans' seeming willingness to indulge all manner of human enterprise and behavior.

How better to explain the woman opposed to the snowball stand, saying she is willing to "put up with her fair share of murders"? "Seize life while it lasts" is one understanding of the town's unofficial motto "Laissez les bon temps rouler." I've come to believe that New Orleanians share a tolerance for the superior natural force of the Mississippi River, and that unusual tolerance implies the possibility of accommodation for the differences among the people who live here now.

This perception describes the stage upon which civic events in New Orleans occur and upon which planning takes its place. It is imperative that a planner understands the stage or else recommendations will not be grounded in a reality that citizens can grasp. In Montana's Missoula County, a topographic map of the Bitterroot River valley shows tens of thousands of acres gradually rising to the Bitterroot Mountains on the west side of the river, and tens of thousands more acres on the eastern side rising to the front of the Garnet Range—lots of land and an

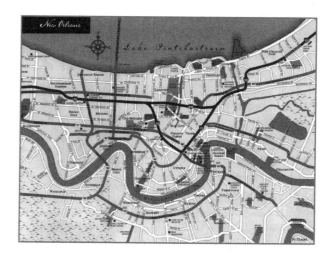

11-1. Map of New Orleans

almost unimaginable expanse, even when you are standing there looking at it!

In large part, this geographic fact explains the area's fierce devotion to the rallying cry, "It's my land and I'll do what I want with it!" There is so much land there, so close to water, that individuals can't imagine what they do on their 20-acre parcel will affect anyone else, which leads them to accept the antiplanning sentiment shared by so many rural citizens.

Planners who come here have to work within the political confines that the map suggests, and must find pertinent information (such as the high cost of providing fire protection to a spread-out development pattern) as they explain the value of curbing some individual property rights on behalf of a pleasing community.

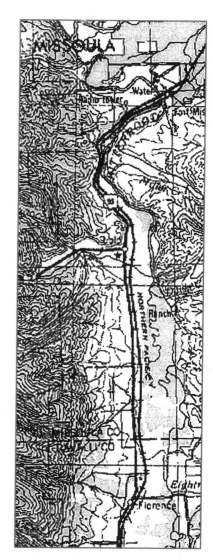

11-2. Map of Missoula County

ELECTED OFFICIALS AND THEIR CONSTITUENTS

Voters in New Orleans passed a bond issue that included money for repairing minor streets in each council member's district. The council members were all new to the job—a result of recent term-limit legislation.

They thought one of the happy duties of their public office would be choosing which streets would be repaired, not realizing that the money the voters had agreed to borrow would pay for only 1/20th of the total needing repair. To choose one street over another without a rational basis for that choice would make the residents of that particular street happy, but deeply annoy residents living elsewhere.

Together with the deputy chief administrative officer responsible for capital improvements, we presented a "best practices" method of evaluating streets, and suggested that the council members use the results to explain to unhappy constituents why certain streets had not been selected. Most council members readily agreed to this advice.

The maps that accompanied the evaluation sheets for minor streets included the phrase "Prepared by the City Planning Commission" as a subtle reminder of the variety of services the office could provide to elected officials.

Maps, of course, are not the only source of information about social relationships and shared civic values. A planner should seek out explanations of community attitudes and try to elicit the sort of cultural understanding that explains, in nonplanning terms, what the attitude toward planning will be. This holds true even for planners who work where they grew up.

There are perceptions in every part of town, and in every constituency group, that will surprise you and offer the view of a city that a good planner tries to widen. As the sidebar entitled "Observation from a Novelist" shows, historical or even fictional sources can be useful in learning to understand these intangible aspects of a community.

People

Circumstances of place can influence the attitudes of a town's citizens. One city's residents may seem very individualistic; another city may seem characterized by mutual accommodation. With regard to who affects planning decisions, there are often identifiable groups of actors whose roles are useful to understand and whose attitudes are similarly motivated in any city. Here, too, individual differences are important (e.g., a city council member who is a lawyer by training will be different from one who is a former realtor) and those differences influence the type of information each finds persuasive.

Elected officials: Elected officials are the individuals who ultimately decide whether or not a planner's advice will result in governmental action. Although

it is commonplace among planners to assume that an elected official is driven more by short-term issues than by the long-term future that planning is usually trying to influence, it is a mistake to dismiss the aspirations of leaders so blithely.

In fact, this point of view not only diminishes the elected official, it just as surely diminishes a planner's potential by suggesting that no imaginative way of persuasion will be effective. What follows this oversimplified perception is even more insidious, which is to cast decision makers as adversaries and then to stop trying to find ways to convince them. Even with term limitations, an elected official is in office a long time in terms of the number of planning issues that will arise.

A better strategy is to think that you may not have convinced them with whatever information you have used before and try to find a new method. One useful strategy is to perceive that most elected officials are students of what their constituents need and desire, and to frame planning advice in terms that underscore that connection, as the sidebar entitled "Elected Officials and Their Constituents" illustrates.

Another approach to persuading elected officials is to convince their constituents of the value of planning in the community—a strategy that will affect elected officials even when planners aren't present. This is the utility of a land use plan with strong citizen support, as will be described later in this chapter.

Citizens/neighborhood organizations/interest groups: Various types of citizens' groups are the very people who will largely determine the interests of an elected

OBSERVATION FROM A NOVELIST

"When he had worked in the switch yards at Helena, the old heads used to say that once the river had been where the town was now, and that the town was set up on the Kudzu bluff that overlooked the present town, and where the town of West Helena is now. They said one night the river simply changed its course, removing itself five miles to the east, leaving a thick muddy plain for the residents of the bluff to stare at and get nervous about. They said little by little the people on the bluff ventured down and started establishing themselves where the river had been, and building stores and houses. And after a while everyone moved down and they changed the name of the town to West Helena and called the new one in the bottom Helena. The men in the yard called this movement The Great Comedown, and swore that the town, by coming off the bluff, had exercised bad judgment and would have to suffer misfortune because, and it seemed to make good sense, the town now existed at the pleasure of the river, and they believed anything that owed to the river would have to pay, and when it paid, the price would be steep."

—Ford, Richard. *A Piece of My Heart.*
New York: Harper and Row, 1976, p. 54-55.

Reading this would probably help a planner in Helena understand what had been perceived as a dogged determination to make the town permanent—the city's capital budget unusually devoted to streets, curbs and gutters, or the number of statues honoring heroes from the low-lying new city. Speculations like these might lead to cultural insights of use to a planner.

official. Most people appreciate government that works invisibly and well. They want the garbage collected on time, streets swept clean and development to gradually accumulate around them in pleasing ways. They can be galvanized, of course, by something that threatens their sense of civic harmony but, for the most part, they expect the city—and its governing entities—to provide a pleasing backdrop for their day-to-day lives.

Citizens' groups have the greatest potential for changing how elected officials view the work of planners. They can insist that, once a land use plan has been adopted, land use decisions be made consistent with planning documents. They can also hold elected officials accountable for their land use decisions. Keeping this constituency interested in planning is the challenge for planners—a challenge best approached by providing ready access to planning documents, such as the land use plan.

Certainly, the Internet makes such access easier, but only for citizens able to use computers. A vigilant planner finds and keeps up with new methods of disseminating information to all citizens. Visual information—maps, drawings and photographs—that highlight individual parts of town are crucial to maintaining interest among citizens and their organizations.

It's very unusual that citizens think in terms of a city-wide development future, and more usual to think about the areas surrounding where they live. The user-friendly capabilities of a GIS make individual preparation much easier than in previous years. It can be exploited to convey an explicit message

Citizens' groups have the greatest potential for changing how elected officials view the work of planners.

that, while city planning must have a comprehensive perspective of a city, its operations are at the fine scale of recognizable neighborhoods with specific issues and potentials.

Although the interests of neighborhood or citizen groups can often be very parochial (i.e., up in arms about what is happening in their single neighborhood or something that threatens their single interest group), a skillful planner can forge alliances among groups by finding common points of view. See Chapter 5, "Working With Small Groups," and Chapter 6, "Public Participation," for discussion of the many skills and approaches necessary to build consensus among (or within) groups that may not realize they have anything in common.

Listening is the key method of information gathering here. It sounds easy enough, but it involves more than not interrupting, as many people I've observed seem to think. Using such phrases as "I'm with you" or "I hear you" implies that the planner is thinking, "I already know that, but I'll wait until you finish before I tell you what I already thought when I walked in the room."

Real listening requires the capacity to expect to be surprised, as we all were with the remark about the "fair share of murders." Effective planners realize that all good ideas don't originate in city planning (and its textbooks). By their every action, planners convey the fact that their professional training and expertise has trained them to hear a good idea from a citizen and figure out how to make it happen, or hear a remark and understand what it means in the terms

that a person or a neighborhood sees their position in the larger world. From that, they are drawn into a community consensus.

For example, when the New Orleans Planning Commission was conducting public workshops to develop a new land use plan, we heard at the first neighborhood meeting that the citizens there felt orphaned from the city and that their neighborhood was ignored in policy decisions. We noticed the remark and listened to the evidence the speakers used as verification. After 10 of these meetings, we realized that every neighborhood had articulated the same perception! This is surprising information and can be very useful to developing a feeling of common concern. We asked what could explain why each neighborhood felt this way and then used the various answers as a basis for developing a consensus land use plan that left no one feeling left out. In a sense, searching for common ground is a planner's chief political skill.

Developers: Developers have an interest in the economic use of property, and their sophistication with regard to planning and political decision making varies widely. My earlier metaphor suggests that developers invite you to stand within their property lines; from this vantage, all they have in mind makes a kind of sense, even a parking pattern that would cause cars to back out into the public thoroughfare. "Don't worry about that," the developer will assure you. "All the customers will arrive by taxi during rush hours." A city planner has to at least walk across the street (even if figuratively) and look at the

Developers have an interest in the economic use of property, and their sophistication with regard to planning and political decision making varies widely.

property in the context of the neighborhood within which it lies—gauging, for example, the capacity of the street leading to it.

In a sense, making headway with contemporary developers is analogous to how planning made a place for itself in the earliest days of its professional existence, when advocates made the case that a well-planned community would enjoy increased property values while a poorly planned community would lose value. A contemporary planner will invite the developer to take a mental drive past thriving, well-planned commercial areas and past those that are not. Every town has examples of each and the planner can draw persuasive conclusions for the developer. An effective planning staff is able to make suggestions for how the site plan might be redrawn, to give the developer a sense that other solutions are possible. A staff able to rough out an alternative plan, literally on the back of an envelope, is invaluable in this discussion and supports the implicit message that city planners are useful.

In dealing with developers, a willingness to be direct is important. I've been able to say, "You're proposing something that this neighborhood has effectively stopped the last five times that something similar was imagined," listing the particular reasons for the prior opposition and the neighborhood organizations that have a particular interest in the issue.

In my experience, planning commissions (and city councils) are very uncomfortable with having to choose between warring constituents, and often defer their decision by suggesting the developer "work with" the community. Planners are usually much more aware of the dynamics of decision-making bodies than developers, simply because planning staff appears at every council meeting while an individual developer goes only on occasion. Planner who are confident of their observational skills will be able to convey such useful guidance; in this way, they can corroborate the value of planners' experience with both the public and their elected officials.

Business community: The business community is a loose arrangement of people who, because they comprise the most obvious part of a city's tax base, can be powerful (individually or when joined together) to put a stop to a policy or decision they understand to be "antibusiness." They are skeptical of planners, particularly of their reliance on citizen participation to develop plans for the future and their use of phrases such as "common community goals." They are more comfortable with planning that is based upon bankers' reports about investment trends in various segments of the market or economists analyzing long-term business projections.

For example, when a community engages in drafting the goals of an economic development plan, planners have a difficult time drawing actors from the business sector into a public discussion simply because their training and experience hasn't given them confidence that anything valuable can come out of it.

Rather than expecting businessmen to appear at a public meeting, it is better to solicit their views using a small group. Just as dealing with neighborhood

An effective planning staff is able to make suggestions for how the site plan might be redrawn, to give the developer a sense that other solutions are possible.

organizations is simplified by tailoring information to the specific area and citizens, working with the business community is eased by using information that is as precise as what they are used to seeing in, for example, *The Wall Street Journal*. Projections of economic activity in the city, employment rates, property valuations and housing starts get their attention, particularly when presented in the factually professional manner of a board room. "Your concerns are ours" is the message an effective city planner has to convey and to reaffirm explicitly that the planner knows a town's economy is the underpinning of its future.

Latent allies of city planning: When planners feel beleaguered, they tend to close ranks, to stay within the office and to talk to those already on their side. However, there are many latent allies that can be rallied, although they shouldn't be called upon in the heat of a controversy because few people have the stomach for public discord. Rather, the support these allies can provide is by making phone calls to elected officials or the editorial board of the paper; these are the sorts of communications the planning office never hears about directly.

These allies, of course, need to be cultivated—long before their support is necessary for anything in particular—by referring to the goals they share with city planning. Such allies include the local chapter of the APA, the local chapter of American Institute of Architects, the League of Women Voters, professors of urban planning and land use law, as well as journalists and editors of newspapers. In every community, the relative power of each group—and their

Planners typically enter professional practice prepared with an altruistic ardor and academic training and can energize city hall with their energy and creative ideas.

willingness to engage in planning issues—is different. Of course, this changes over time and over particular issues, but the dialogue with these allies should be continuous.

Not all arguments in behalf of planning occur in a public forum. The method of communication will vary. A planner can offer to come to annual meetings and make a presentation whose contents—and visual components—will be tailored to each group's particular expertise or interest. This will build confidence over time in the professionalism and competence of the planning staff.

Planners: Planners typically enter professional practice prepared with an altruistic ardor and academic training and can energize city hall with their energy and creative ideas. However, they need pragmatic guidance through the intersection of abstract planning principles and the gritty reality of political decision making that constitutes professional practice. Without careful management, they can become content with seeing themselves as modern Cassandras whose "pure" principles are not believed by their opponents, whom they cast as community luddites. This attitude diminishes creative urges to find new ways of persuasion.

Young planners can be guided to see that although citizens may agree about the end they have in mind—developing a community where college graduates can find well-paying jobs, for example—different individuals can have very different ideas for how to achieve that end. A planner's job is to join different visions; it is not to impose an individual sense of the best course, nor to choose which citizen's idea has the most merit in terms of abstract planning principles.

At their least persuasive, planners use jargon (always meant to imply that the listener does not know as much or is not as smart as the speaker) and abstract examples to explain their points, which forestalls the give-and-take discussion that would result from an example close to home. Planners become essentially useless as public servants if they cast people with different points of view as adversaries, because they have then implicitly removed themselves from a public discussion that might reveal worthy points from the presentation of another side.

At their best, planners are able to listen responsively to different points of view and help form a consensus; they are able to figure out solutions to conflicts between different land uses; and they can translate citizens' unorganized sentiments and inarticulately expressed aspirations for the future into a coherent plan.

In any town, there are many other groups with common interests than have been described here. In New Orleans, there are preservationists; in Missoula, there were environmentalists and members of the Posse Comitatus (dogmatists of individuality); in each town, there are elected officials from other levels of government or people temporarily out of office but who are planning to undertake another campaign. Any of these groups can seize upon a planning issue. Planners should be aware of the latent political power of such groups and keep in contact with them, just as they keep in contact with the other groups discussed.

THE NATURE OF PUBLIC DISCOURSE

Planning issues in most cities are of two types. The first (and most common) arises because a proposed development requires a change to the zoning text, a change to the zoning map or a subdivision approval. Because this planning issue is so common, the actors described in the preceding section can seem to be reading from a well-rehearsed script, with no regard to the particulars of the case. While developers typically present handsomely drawn elevations of their proposed projects, they think the most persuasive argument is the simplest: that their project will bring tax revenue and jobs. Sometimes this position is backed up by a description of the secondary and tertiary economic benefits of the proposed development, but the promise of tax revenues and jobs is never questioned!

Opponents to particular projects are typically defenders of particular neighborhoods and are as set in their remarks as developers. In New Orleans, when a development proposal is offered for the French Quarter—the old, historic district that tourists keep coming to see—we hear that the proposal is an example of "creeping commercialism" and that we must remember that the "French Quarter is the crown jewel of New Orleans."

Listening to both sides of an argument made in these terms, one can think that there isn't a dialogue

Opponents to particular projects are typically defenders of particular neighborhoods and are as set in their remarks as developers.

here—it is as if the parties are holding different conversations. Consider the setup: the planning commission sits at a table in the front of the hearing chamber, staff sits facing them, and the audience (the public) sits behind the staff in some sort of auditorium arrangement. The developer presents a proposal, the staff makes its recommendation and the public hearing is opened. Serially, individuals come to the podium to express support or opposition, but there is no dialogue among speakers. It's as if the commission were being handed a platter of bits of information, opinion and metaphorical description, including individual perceptions, bits of conventional wisdom and pat slogans.

In this scenario, a commission will rely heavily on the staff's report to create a context, to integrate the competing arguments and to present information sufficient to allow a responsible decision. However, citizens often feel badly served in this situation, feeling that their comments have not been heard properly, and that the commission is too reliant on the professional staff rather than on "real" people.

Much is lost in this scenario. No doubt the opposing sides would like to answer criticisms made by all speakers but, within the time constraints and rules of a public hearing, they are not given that opportunity. The commission (and the staff) are criticized for what in fact are the constraints of public hearings.

Robert's Rules of Order requires that speakers address the commission rather than one another. Even the order of discussion, in which proponents present their proposal after which opponents speak,

NEW ORLEANS' LAND USE PLAN PROCESS

Earlier in this chapter, two instances of citizens' perceptions of planning and their understanding of their community were described. One perspective was, "What do you have planned for us?" The other was the remarkable instance of the woman willing to put up with her "fair share" of murders. In a very important sense, most urban citizens are planners by the simple fact of where they live and what they notice, but they often don't realize that the city's plan benefits from and needs to reflect precisely these perceptions.

In New Orleans, there had not been a new land use plan developed since 1970—and much had changed, including the demographics of the town. The long-term results of the oil bust meant that a large portion of the city's middle class left the city, and the devastated economy meant that young people left for good jobs elsewhere after they graduated from any of the five universities located in New Orleans.

By 1990, the city was two-thirds African American. Its governing bodies had become similarly constituted, and most Caucasian children went to private or parochial schools. As the new planning director, this information meant that the population was very unevenly prepared to discuss a land use plan, and the primary goal in achieving consensus would have to be inclusion of people who perhaps hadn't ever understood the nature of a plan or what it meant. Their posture was well represented by the question, "What do you have planned for us?"

The *first task was to get the public interested.* The mayor helped by naming a planning advisory committee that equally represented every part of town—meaning that the diversity that makes New Orleans seem exotic to a visitor was replicated in the group of citizens charged with taking an interest in the land use plan. Commissioners and staff members made speeches at meetings of neighborhood organizations explaining the usefulness of a land use plan and showing how it would be based on what citizens themselves wanted for the future.

The mayor wrote letters to the large population of religious leaders asking that they talk about this matter with their congregations. Meetings were held with various business organizations and the media were briefed. All these activities established a popular view of the need for a new land use plan, which was formally recognized by the city council's allocating money for it out of a very tight municipal budget.

The *second task was to try to make people equally willing to talk* about the topics that comprise a land use plan. Some years earlier, the commission was criticized by the more sophisticated neighborhood groups for the fact that people in less sophisticated areas didn't stick to the subject of planning issues, but had started talking about potholes and unmown median strips, as though these were not planning concerns.

We used a survey that first explained what the phrase "land use" meant, then asked commonplace questions about which land uses the respondent would like to see more of, which ones caused problems and why. The survey was placed in neighborhood stores throughout the city, in all public buildings and given out in schools with the direction that children give them to their parents. We asked people to bring the survey with them when they came to the charettes that were going to take place all over town to discuss the new land use plan.

The surveys could be completed and put in the mail, or dropped off at libraries and community centers, and the commission received several hundred of them. Although we "analyzed" the results and displayed them at various venues, the purpose of the survey was not the results themselves; it was to provide a common vocabulary for citizens who were interested in participating in the creation of the plan.

The *third task was to bring people together to talk* about guiding future development. We divided the city into 10 planning areas and held a charette in each. Our method was to break the citizens into subgroups of about 12 people, and give them markers and a base map of the planning area that had street names and some well-known landmarks. With the use of a facilitator, we asked each group to designate the future land uses they would like to see.

After about an hour, the whole citizen group came together and listened to the results of each subgroup. With a facilitator, we were able to arrive at a consensus and to identify items for which there was no consensus yet and that required further discussion. The groups discussed setting priorities about items that needed further discussion and arranged subgroup meetings to further develop points of disagreement. Once this step was complete, the consultants chosen to oversee this project created a single map that combined the findings for each planning district. We had another round of meetings so that people could correct, or rethink, what was shown on the map and resolve any of the points of disagreement. On some issues, the groups agreed that further study was needed but that overall land use plan development did not have to be delayed.

We provided evaluations for participants and were gratified with the positive reception we received to this approach for soliciting public comment. The plan was adopted. We had developed consensus, largely because of the information we provided, the information we gathered, the method of displaying it and the fact that we engaged the community at large.

Ultimately, citizens came up with an idea that could completely change the context of planning in New Orleans—from the "I have five votes" model of planning (in which decisions are made out of sight of the public) to a model in which elected officials are accountable for land use decisions. Following adoption of the land use plan, the mayor's planning advisory committee suggested that a "score sheet" be used to keep track of land use decisions made by the city council.

The score sheet would tally the decisions that a neighborhood organization found to be consistent or inconsistent with the plan, and use this score sheet when the district council member stood for re-election. Information, long ignored and misunderstood in New Orleans, has reasserted itself in the public policy agenda. Said another way, information has changed the political context of planning decisions, making them more democratic and making the decision makers more accountable.

frames the discussion as adversarial. This means that, irrespective of the outcome, the experience weakens the good will among fellow citizens that makes successful public policy possible.

If such a situation were defined as a battle (as it often is) and if people with a differing point of view are identified as opponents, this common scenario makes future encounters adversarial even before citizens hear one another's pont of view. Instead, citizens listen only for flaws in the other side's logic and get used to this as a valid analytic process. By framing public policy as a battle, any issue is reduced to being about who wins, often losing sight of the large and important goal of community harmony.

Sympathy for one another, patience with another's point of view and recognition of our common aspirations all suffer. In fact, when the "victors" acknowledge some lesson learned in the course of the battle, they seem condescending. When the "loser" compliments some change made by the "victor," it seems grudging or insincere. Few developers are "bad guys" from anyone's point of view; often, they simply have an idea of how to improve the city's economy that they've talked about with friends and investors and simply haven't considered that some people might have a different view of their approach.

Community groups are not necessarily selfish and narrow, but often have a genuine interest in contributing to the integrity of the community. The larger point here is the importance of communication and of working with small groups; failure to do so can bring

The larger point here is the importance of communication and of working with small groups; failure to do so can bring about hugely divisive, unnecessary and dysfunctional rifts among otherwise peaceful fellow citizens.

about hugely divisive, unnecessary and dysfunctional rifts among otherwise peaceful fellow citizens.

Commissions often try to avoid these confrontations by deferring action, suggesting that the developer meet with the neighbors and develop a consensus. This strategy is usually successful because a neighborhood's concern can be resolved. Often, all that might have been lacking is a developer's realization of what the neighbors thought was important to a proposal's success. However, if the community has a land use plan that articulates what the community desires, if the zoning ordinance has been specifically written to bring about the future articulated in the plan's objectives and if these documents enjoy consensus acceptance in the community, then the commission's job is easier, and the developer can then be more certain about the outcome of a request and make it compatible with what the neighborhood wants.

A second type of planning issue that arises in cities is the process of articulating the community's desired future—most typically in a land use plan—and developing consensus about the plan. The standard public hearing format is not useful in this task because consensus can only occur if citizens talk to one another, rather than to a group of planning commissioners sitting in the front of a room. See Chapter 6, "Public Participation," for a description of the ways that planners can structure meetings and opportunities for conversation and exchange to build consensus. The sidebar entitled "New Orleans' Land

Use Plan Process" describes our experience in New Orleans with a successful land use plan process.

CONCLUSION: A MATTER OF STYLE AND ENGAGEMENT

For a planner, putting all this together—the underlying civic humors of a city, its actors and its manner of public discussion—is an ongoing quest for understanding and for framing persuasive arguments, precisely because any component can change. A sweetening economy can cause a council member to change from thinking the city needs development so badly that few, if any, changes to a developer's proposal should be considered, to a person with a more hopefully skeptical eye who thinks, "We need more development, to be sure, but we also need to ensure that it doesn't disrupt our community with traffic jams, unsightly exteriors or lack of landscaping."

A successful planner is attuned to such changes and alters arguments, information or methods of presentation accordingly. This chapter was designed as a guide in figuring out the political environment of a city and, from that, in figuring out how to gather, analyze and use information on behalf of good planning principles within that environment. Political decisions are not made formulaically (i.e., even if planners could know all the variables brought to bear on a land use matter, they could not definitively predict its outcome). Effective planners increase the probability that decisions are made based upon professional advice.

An intellectual style most compatible with practicing planning in a governmental setting is one that combines curiosity with sympathy for what human beings do in a society. A successful planner is not someone who wants the future nailed down, but who is engaged by the ever-shifting, ever-changeable world of professional practice in a political environment.

While the role of the planning director may be to see to it that information is used, and the role of the staff may be to gather information and ready its presentation, the two roles are inseparably intertwined on one point: the information itself must be excellent so that its substance is not impugnable. Only when information is accurate and unbiased, and developed according to the standards implicit in this book, can planners engage in the steps necessary to see that their advice becomes a part of the decision-making process.

Every piece of information, method of analysis or style of presentation—no matter how clever, popular or effective—becomes routine with repeated use. Whatever is routine becomes predictable and is therefore either easily countered or dismissed. Using an array of methods is necessary for continued professional effectiveness.

Another reason for choosing different methods of gathering or conveying information is that each method carries with it implicit intellectual or technological constraints. Certainly, using a Web page to convey information limits the potential audience to people able to access and use computers. However, technology can constrain full discussion and even imagination—a point demonstrable with PowerPoint

slide presentations, which have become a widely popular way to convey information. The software forces speakers to format slides for presentations according to a logical progression from one point to the next, with information presented in a bullet-point format.

While it is true that the regimented format this technology imposes puts an end to rambling, disjointed, unthought-through lectures, and has helped nervous speakers get through their lectures successfully, PowerPoint also puts an end to spontaneity, which some lecturers can achieve by using, for example, hand-drawn charts, to move audiences in ways that bullet points on a slide cannot. The point is that relying on any one way of collecting, analyzing or presenting information is doomed to becoming unpersuasive. See Chapter 6 ("Public Participation"), Chapter 8 ("Speaking Skills for Presentations") and Chapter 10 ("Graphic Communication") for a variety of suggestions on effective presentations.

Developing an aptitude for using an array of methods is also necessary at a more personal level, as individuals evaluate whether engaging in professional planning practice continues to be satisfying. Over time, excellent planners will develop and exhaust several methods of gathering and communicating information. Not only does this pattern of continual change in methods refresh their contributions to a community, it is also how their minds remain engaged despite the routines of professional planning practice.

This book is clearly a source for finding different methods of gathering, analyzing and conveying information.

This book is clearly a source for finding different methods of gathering, analyzing and conveying information. Because it so clearly describes the attributes of using information effectively, it also provides a protocol for evaluating methods not known at the time of this writing. Having read this book, a planner can figure out the appropriate questions to ask in determining the efficacy of a new method or technology. The book will be underutilized if its reader seizes upon one very clever way of using information and thinks no more about it. Planners, in my experience, need many arrows in their quivers—and this book offers many.

One implicit message of this chapter on political context is the importance of ordinary language. A planner in practice is a translator of planning principles into common-sense language; I think the translation is most successful if examples are employed. Examples turn academic jargon into something demonstrable and particularize a conversation to an audience (e.g., when talking to neighborhood groups, an example of what you are trying to demonstrate close by will be more effective than an abstraction; speaking to city councilmembers is most profitable if the examples are from their individual districts). Surely this implies the importance of remembering cases, perhaps with the use of a notebook, that you think will later be useful to demonstrate a certain point you might want to make.

There is little doubt that practicing planning in a political environment can be frustrating; the most carefully gathered information, presented with clarity and precision, can fail to succeed. However, the actual work—the daily life of a planner—can be sufficiently exhilarating to make up for the frustrations. Battles well fought, explanations well made and well received, better planned development projects and plans for the future that enjoy consensus within the community are all satisfying results of professional planning. Take pleasure from each of these results (even as you file them away for later use as practical examples) as they happen.

Emphasize to yourself when you've been successful or when you've been valiant, and you will continue to be engaged by the gritty world in which you find yourself. You can even take heart from politically inspired criticism if you can remember what the mayor once said to me: "Don't let them get you down. Sometimes you can be proud of who your enemies are!"

APPLICATIONS

1. Look back on a recent effort you made to persuade a group about your point of view and choose one in which you felt you were unsuccessful. After reading this chapter, can you suggest an explanation for your lack of success? Can you imagine how you might have been more effective?

2. Most people notice the lack of planning (e.g., strip commercial parking spaces that require customers to back directly into the right of way, or the lack of landscaping, or particularly badly designed intersections). The counterpoint is odd: rather than thinking a community is "well planned," people are more likely to observe that a town is prosperous, "pretty" or "inviting." In the spirit of trying to find examples to prove the value of professional planning advice, drive around your town and find examples of "bad" or "negligent" site design. Then try to find a counterexample of each. Can you explain the difference in layperson's language?

3. Consider this scenario: A building permit has been issued, legally, for increasing the size of a sign advertising a bar that has annoyed its surrounding neighborhood for years. The council member who represents the area has been criticized because he hadn't known the permit was being issued, and therefore had been unable to either forewarn his constituents or to take some extraordinary action to have the permit delayed. Stung by this criticism, he has asked that the planning department's budget, which is now being used to develop the city's GIS, be redirected. He wants to be provided with a computerized listing of all building permits about to be issued each week, arranged according to the city council district where construction would occur. How would you assess the consequences of this request in terms of the actors in a community (e.g., developers and business community)? What arguments would you advance to the council member if you think it's not a good idea? If he persists, or if you think the idea has some merit, how would

you suggest he modify his request? What arguments would you use to bolster your case?

4. Think back on a practical planning project of which you were particularly proud or for which you received praise. Remember the information you used and the arguments you made in behalf of your position. Assume that you were your own adversary and that you want to disagree with your former conclusion. What were the informational weaknesses or vulnerabilities in your presentation of your point of view? In other words, in this exercise, consider how you would counter yourself.

BIBLIOGRAPHY

Planning Books
These books principally offer solace to planners surprised by the political realm within which they practice. The titles listed below are especially wise, in large part because of the sympathy they display toward the communities—and the elected decision makers—where they work.

Cullingworth, Barry. *Planning in the USA: Policies, Issues and Processes*. London and New York: Routledge, 1997.

This is a comprehensive analysis of what many planners find to be the troublesome nature of policy making. Rather than the purposive world they might have expected from reading planning textbooks, they confront a world in which very different political agendas affect land use decisions. The first chapter, "The Nature of Planning," provides a sophisticated discussion of how to reconcile the very different political aims of people and groups that affect land use decisions.

Hoch, Charles. *What Planners Do: Power, Politics, and Persuasion*. Chicago: American Planning Association, 1994.

This excellent text describes the bracing differences between professional training—with its theoretical and specialized knowledge—and the kinds of practical problems that practicing planners face. The book has many insights for planners, either those about to undertake professional practice or those needing some fortification after a few years of encountering practical politics. I especially recommend Chapter 3, "The Rational Protocol and Political Conflict."

McClendon, Bruce W. and Anthony James Catanese. *Planners on Planning*. San Francisco: Jossey-Bass Inc., 1996.

This is a compendium of excellently written descriptions of actual experiences by more than 20 practitioners at various levels of responsibility. Part II of the book is entitled "Lessons on Politics" and focuses clearly on the realities of persuasion in a wide variety of political contexts.

Other Sources
Planners must know more than what they learn in textbooks, which often take the rational view of proper planning decisions. Surely planners must be accomplished in what these textbooks teach, but they can only be effective if they are also able to see the world—and the political decisions made there—from the perspective of different disciplines as well as people's variable points of view. A healthy sense of curiosity about human society and perceptions is valuable. Reading widely in contemporary fiction and nonfiction will add breadth. Here are two resource books as a start.

Monmonier, Mark. *How to Lie with Maps*. Chicago and London: The University of Chicago Press, 1991.

This winning little book is an excellent primer for planners who want to know how (with the phrase used in this chapter) "to walk across the street" from a developer's project. An early point made in "How to Lie with Maps" is about how a single map depicts reality. This point is apt for any of the methods of communication that this book has discussed: ". . . a single map is but one of an infinitely large number of maps that might be produced for the same situation or from the same data." An entire chapter especially important for a city planner who must deal with developers and their site plans is entitled "Development Maps (or, How to Seduce the Town Board)."

Reps, John W. *Bird's Eye Views: Historic Lithographs of North American Cities.* New York: Princeton Architecture Press, 1998.

This is an excellent starting point for the reader interested in trying to discern community attitudes by looking at maps. One approach is to start by reading the short descriptions that accompany each city map in this book and speculate about what the map suggests regarding the public sentiments of people living there. What are the essential geographic features of where the city lies? Does it seem that the city has tried to overcome some of these features (e.g., bridging rivers and blasting tunnels)? What might that suggest in terms of local land use policies? In the flat plains of middle America, where towns grew up around railroad stations, can you find evidence that local leaders laid out development in an orderly arrangement that enhanced rail commerce? Is there evidence of efforts to overcome the ugly effects of manufacturing? Where do you suppose the richest part of town is? The poorest? Does anything about their spatial relationship suggest how they accommodate one another?

Acronyms

AML	Arc Macro Language	EDVAC	Electronic Discrete Variable Automatic Computer
APA	American Planning Association	EIS	environmental impact statement
ARPANET	Advanced Research Projects Agency Network	ENIAC	Electronic Numerical Integrator and Computer
BCIS	Bureau of Citizenship and Immigration Services	EPA	[U.S.] Environmental Protection Agency
BEA	Bureau of Economic Analysis	EPS	Encapsulated PostScript
BEARFACTS	Bureau of Economic Analysis Regional Facts	ESRI	Environmental Systems Research Institute
BIOS	Basic Input Output System	FBI	Federal Bureau of Investigation
BMP	Bitmap	FEMA	Federal Emergency Management Agency
BOOM	binocular omni-oriented monitor	FHA	Federal Highway Administration
BPW	Board of Public Works	FIPS	Federal Information Processing Standard
CAD	computer-aided drafting	FIRE	finance, insurance and real estate
CAT	Citizens Against Towers	GIF	Graphic Interchange Format
CATI	computer-assisted telephone interviewing	GIS	Geographic Information System
CAVE	Cave Automatic Virtual Environment	GPO	Government Printing Office
CBD	central business district	GUI	graphical user interface (or "gooey")
CDC	Centers for Disease Control	HCFA	Health Care Financing Administration
CD-ROM	Compact Disk–Read-Only Memory	HIV	Human Immunodeficiency Virus
CD-RW	Compact Disk–Read-Write	HTML	Hypertext Markup Language
CHIRLA	Coalition for Humane Immigrant Rights in Los Angeles	http	Hypertext Transfer Protocol
CPI	Consumer Price Index	HUD	[U. S. Department of] Housing and Urban Development
CPU	central processing unit	ICMA	International City/County Management Association
CV	coefficient of determination	IGES	Initial Graphics Exchange Specification
DEMs	Digital Elevation Models	INTERPOL	International Criminal Police Organization
DHTML	Dynamic HTML	IP	Internet protocol
DOS	Disk Operating System	IQR	interquartile range
DVD	digital video disc	ISPs	Internet Service Providers
DXF	Drawing eXchange Format	JCCI	Jacksonville Community Council Inc.

JOIN-N	Jefferson County (Missouri) Online Information Network
JPEG	Joint Photographic Experts Group
LAN	Local-area Network
LANDSAT	land satellite data
LCD	liquid crystal display
MSAs	Metropolitan Statistical Areas
NAIC	North American Industrial Classification
NASS	National Agriculture Statistical Services
NCES	National Center for Education Statistics
NCJRS	National Crime Justice Reference Service
NESDIS	National Environmental Satellite, Data and Information Service
NIMA	National Imagery and Mapping Agency
NKLA	Neighborhood Knowledge Los Angeles
NOAA	National Oceanic and Atmospheric Administration
NODC	National Oceanic Data Center
NOS	National Ocean Service
NWI	national wetlands inventory
OCR	Optical Character Recognition
OLS	Ordinary Least Squares
PCs	personal computers
PDF	Portable Document Format
PNG	Portable Network Graphics
PS	PostScript
PUMA	Public Use Microdata Area
PUMS	Public Use Microdata Samples
RAM	Random Access Memory
RDBMS	relational database management systems
REIS	Regional Economic Information System
RFP	request for proposal
RHNAs	Regional Housing Needs Assessments
ROM	Read-Only Memory
RTDs	Regional Transit Districts
SDC	State Data Center
SIC	Standard Industrial Classification
TCU	transportation, communications and utilities
TIFF	Tagged Image File Format
TIGER	Topologically Integrated Geographic Encoding and Referencing
UN ODCCP	United Nations Office of Drug Control and Crime Prevention
UN-HABITAT	United Nations Human Settlements Programme
UNICS	Uniplexed Information and Computing Service (UNIX)
UNIVAC	Universal Variable Computer
URL	Uniform Resource Locator
USGS	United States Geological Survey
UTMS	Urban Transportation Model System
VBA	Visual Basic for Applications
VR	virtual reality
WAN	Wide-area Network
WDRT	Woodberry Down Regeneration Team
WHO	World Health Organization
WMF	Windows Meta File
WYSIWYG	"What You See Is What You Get"
XML	Extensible Markup Language

About the Authors

HEMALATA C. DANDEKAR is Director and Professor, School of Planning and Landscape Architecture, Arizona State University. Formerly, as Professor of Urban Planning at the University of Michigan, she taught courses on planning techniques, urban and regional theory and international planning. Dr. Dandekar's professional experience as architect-planner spans diverse regions and cultures and includes work in India, Japan, South Africa and the United States. She is the author of several scholarly books and articles on topics that include effective communications, qualitative methods, globalization and city space, urbanization, and women and housing.

VIVIENNE N. ARMENTROUT is a county commissioner in Washtenaw County, Michigan, where she also serves on the Planning Advisory Board and the Board of Public Works. She holds a Ph.D. in botany and plant pathology from the University of Wisconsin–Madison and is a freelance editor and small publisher (Oakleaf Press).

PETER ASH is an Associate Professor of Psychiatry and Behavioral Sciences and Director of the Psychiatry and Law Service at Emory University in Atlanta, Georgia. He is a forensic child psychiatrist with a continuing interest in psychiatric aspects of conflict resolution at different levels, including the intrapsychic, interpersonal, group and legal system. His recent research focuses on adolescent motivations for carrying and using guns to settle conflicts.

ELAINE COGAN is Principal Cogan Owens Cogan, LLC. Nationally recognized as a designer and facilitator of public participation processes, she conducts workshops and seminars at national, state and local planners' conferences. Her work includes the Future Focus strategic plan for Portland, Oregon, which received an Outstanding Achievement Award from the U.S. Conference of Mayors; and planning for Clackamas County in the Portland metropolitan region, which received the Public Education Award from the APA. She is author of *Successful Public Meetings, a Practical Guide* (APA), and co-author of *You Can Talk to (Almost) Anybody about (Almost) Anything, a Speaking Guide for Business and Professional People.*

RICHARD CREPEAU is an Assistant Professor of Geography and Planning at Appalachian State University in Boone, North Carolina. Dr. Crepeau's interests are in transportation planning, metropolitan evolution and applying methods of landscape ecology to issues of transportation, land use and urbanization. Aside from his research interests, Dr. Crepeau has also been involved in drafting the plan for North Carolina's statewide greenhouse gas mitigation strategies and North Carolina's State Energy Plan. He is also a member of the Town of Boone's Zoning Board of Adjustment.

KRISTINA FORD was most recently the Executive Director of the New Orleans Building Corporation, a public benefit corporation created to develop city-owned properties. Immediately prior to that, she was the Executive Director of the New Orleans City Planning Commission for seven years and received the Outstanding Leadership Award from the APA, Louisiana Chapter. Dr. Ford has taught at New York University and Williams College, as a Research Professor at Rutgers University and founded the Public Policy Research Institute at the University of Montana. Her book, *Planning Small Town America* (APA) recounts her experience as planning director in Missoula, Montana. She is now writing a book about the history of public service.

ANDREA I. FRANK is a research fellow in the Department of City and Regional Planning at Cardiff University in Wales (United Kingdom) with degrees in Architecture and Urban and Regional Planning. Dr. Frank is a member of the Centre for Education in the Built Environment (www.cebe.ltsn.ac.uk), which supports quality learning and teaching in the fields of architecture, landscape architecture, building and surveying and planning in the UK. Her interest and research include urban design, graphic communication and presentation, GIS, spatial analysis and mapping.

NANCY NISHIKAWA is a planning consultant in Honolulu, Hawaii with more than 15 years of professional experience. As a graduate student at the University of Michigan, she concentrated in "generalist planning" and continues to practice in a wide range of planning subfields from environmental to economic development. She has taught planning courses at California State University at Northridge, San Francisco State University and the University of Wisconsin–Milwaukee.

ALFRED W. STOREY retired from the University of Michigan as Director Emeritus University Extension Service (a state-wide adult and continuing education program) and Associate Professor Emeritus of Speech Communication (public speaking, group discussion and radio and television). Currently, he conducts workshops for business and industry on public speaking skills and/or leadership skills in small group discussion.

MARIA YEN is an assistant professor at California State University, Northridge in the Departments of Urban Studies and Planning and Sociology. She received her Ph.D. in city and regional planning from the University of California, Berkeley. Maria has a master's degree in urban planning from the University of Michigan. She has taught courses on planning and politics, planning methods, demographics and citizen participation. Her research and practice interests include understanding ethnic conflict in demographically changing neighborhoods and finding ways to resolve these conflicts.

GRACE YORK has been a government documents librarian at the University of Michigan for over 30 years. She has taught numerous classes in urban planning on the use of government information. Her department was one of the first to distribute government data on the internet (1991-92), and her Documents Center Web site (http://lib.umich.edu/govedocs) has been recognized worldwide. She is the recipient of the American Library Association's "Documents to the People Award" for improving public access.

ILLUSTRATIONS

LISA K. LANGLOIS (formerly Lisa Stout) is a doctoral candidate in Japanese Art History at the University of Michigan. Her dissertation involves gender and national identity in Japan's exhibits at the World's Columbian Exposition of 1893. Cartooning provides a creative and playful distraction from academic writing.

YU-LONG YANG, AIA, is Director of Productions with the firm of Ford, Powell and Carson, Architects and Planners Inc., in San Antonio, Texas.

Index